From the Past to the Fu
The History of
Leamington & District
Referees Association

From 1921 to 2006

Published by Arnold W Rouse

December 2006 Warwick

Leamington & District Referees Association

Published in 2006 by

A W Rouse
130 Stratford Road, Warwick, Warwickshire. CV34-6BQ.

Obtainable from the address above

Printed and bound by
T W Printing Associates Ltd
Leamington Spa
08712 260 222

Copyright © Arnold Rouse

All rights reserved

ISBN 095550040-0

9 780955 500404

Leamington & District Sunday Football League

Founded 1966

(Affiliated to Birmingham County Football Association)

Foreword

It was indeed an honour to be asked to write a forward to this booklet, so patiently compiled by Arnold Rouse for the benefit of local football Refereeing history.

It covers the period from the inauguration of the Leamington & District Referees Association in 1921 to the present 2006

Arnold has relied on his memory as well as contacting others, to record not a total history of the Association, that has not been possible, but facts and the recording of personal achievements will give reader an enjoyable insight of what has been achieved.

These Referees have given unselfish service to the Refereeing fraternity and of course local football. Some have gone on to higher planes, even to International level, so you can now read of how they progressed and for the younger reader it will be a target for you to emulate,

Finally I would take this opportunity to mention the pleasure it gave me when I as elected a Vice- President of Leamington Referees Association for my assistance in fund raising to help the Association stage the 1976 National Conference.

Tracey Thomas.

Introduction

The History of Leamington and District Referees Association which dates from 1921 to 1939 and from 1948 to the present 2006

Whilst an attempt is being made to put together the History of the Association difficulties will arise due to loss of minutes of certain periods. What will be written will be as near and as accurate as possible.

This book is not about one person but will involve all referees from the turn of the Century and 1921 up to 2006. Each and every one has contributed in some small way to the benefit of the Association, we have had and still have members very much involved with local Football and County bodies and they too have benefited the Association

The first period of 1921 to 1931 is devoid of minutes, and from records that may have been recorded, we know that the Association started around 1921. We were fortunate in meeting up with the first Secretary, who was over 80 years of age. He told us who the Chairman was and the involvement with the Leagues in the area and the changes that were made in 1926

The period 1931 to 1939 was a well ordered Association with a very strict and strong position in local refereeing and football. The Association appointed referees to the various Leagues in the district and. a few referees obtained promotion to officiate in the senior Leagues. A different view came about in 1936 when a new Secretary was elected to the local Saturday Football League; this caused problems with members of the Leamington Referees Association over match appointments.

In 1939 the Association closed down due to the War and a few referees joined Coventry Referees Association; they remained with Coventry but refereed at Leamington when the League reformed after the War, senior members eventually meeting and reforming the Association in 1948. The Association was gradually re-built with support from the members.

New members were joining, finances were improving slowly. "Promotion to the members from the County FA" was slow and continued until the beginning of the 1960 period .When referees began to receive promotion they soon moved into the Senior Leagues..

Minutes were kept from 1948 up to 1952; once again the records between 1952 and 1960 were lost. We had five Secretaries between 1948 and 1960. Two new Leagues were formed in 1953 and 1955, by George Dutton and it became difficult to be placed on the League unless you were a Class 1 with refereeing experience on a Senior League.

In 1960-1970, a gradual change took place in the Association, meetings were made interesting and an excellent management was formed, majority being professional people Discussions took place concerning staging of seminars for Class 2 and 3 referees; we also designed our own neck tie.

We succeeded in obtaining permission to stage the "1976 Conference," the committee set out to raise money by various means, such as rummage sales, stop watch competition and a sponsored walks. A joint effort with a named charity over £1,000 was raised and then split on a 50/50 basis with the charity.

The first Car to be raffled for the 1976 Conference was obtained by Leamington. The Colleague's from Coventry who came and formed the Committee to help raise the money was successful and it helped the Conference Committee. Eventually they organised the Car raffle on a yearly basis to help fund the National Referees Association.

We competed on level terms with other Associations on the sports field, in football and Cricket, winning the Cricket competition three times in four years. We also won the Benevolent Cup twice and were runners up three times (more about the Cup in Charity Cups) we also had success in Quiz Competitions. Social events were always well attended; dinner dances became a social enjoyment. We had referees on junior leagues, and officiating in various Leagues up to the Football League through the feeder and contributory system.

We have two excellent Charity Cup competitions, started by the Association in memory of George Dutton and Andy Campbell, the committee who were all referees organised the competitions. The Leamington & District Sunday Football League participated in both, quite a lot of money is being raised for charity.

New members were joining the Association and different views were forthcoming; we had successful six-a-side Football Competitions, with side-stalls, following on from 1976 Conference and the money raised each year was donated to the Benevolent Fund.

In the 1990s, we had excellent speakers, certain items and issues were coming to a head with changes in management and Secretaries; we also had changes in the structure of the Football League with the Premier League being formed, new Headquarters for the National Referees' Association were bought in Coventry. These were eventually opened by the Lord Mayor of Coventry. VAT caused a problem and the National President Peter Willis was involved and eventually settled the issue. The Association was beginning to settle down as we moved towards the 21st Century with changes in the structure of the Referees Association, also changes in the way referees are appointed to the various contributory and supply leagues, and a new classification for referees was being talked about. All the changes during this period will be part of the future of Leamington Referees.

Writing about the Leamington & District Referees Association, various articles recorded from the minutes or local newspapers will appear as they have been written. If changes are made it may not suit everyone, all articles from the Minutes will be basically the highlights of that particular period, loss of certain records making accurate statements almost impossible. Great care has been taken in compiling these details, so the story will have a meaning as we travel through the years Whilst we are not a large Association, in comparison to other organisations, what will be written it is hoped will make it interesting to read.

Arnold W Rouse. President

Acknowledgements

In acknowledging the people who have given me advice and support in compiling this book on the Leamington &District Referees Association, the first person who I feel should be mentioned he even sent me photographs of Football Teams from 1904 onwards. That is the late Arthur Gibbons my chats with him over the phone were of great interest

Members from my own Association have been very helpful such as Andy Semple, John Sollis and David Clarke. Ken Eastbury was another member who found articles that could be used concerning the Leamington Saturday League. Pat Gwynne has also sent me a fair amount of information especially on Ladies Football.
In moving to members who have given me articles to reproduce we have Tracey Thomas, John Austin, John Mander and John Sharp. We also have the organisers of Charity competitions who have been very helpful and they are Brian Knibb, Bobby Hancocks, Brian Skidmore and Guy Reeves. Thanks must also go to the ordinary members of the Association for the general information given.
My thanks must go to Mrs Jackson wife of Charlie Jackson, Mrs Margaret Chapman, daughter of John Wildsmith and Roy Joyner, the information they gave to me was very valuable.

There have been items that needed to be placed in this article otherwise a gap would have been left and it is thanks to these Gentlemen that approval has been given and they are. Geoffrey Thompson Chairman of the Football Association and Vice-President UEFA, Peter Willis Life Vice- President Referees Association, Arthur Smith General Secretary Referees Association and John Baker Head of Refereeing Football Association also Alan Poulain the Chairman of the Referees Association of England.

My thanks must also go to FIFA and Heinz Tannler Director Legal Division. For allowing me to use and print part of the "Laws of Association Football"
The Courier Press for allowing me to use articles from the earlier editions of the "Warwick and Warwickshire Advertiser," the "Leamington Courier Newspaper." Also Mr Brown from Kineton for his information on the First President. My grateful thanks to Andrew Meanley and Alan Sturley also Tracey Thomas for the advice given.

Many thanks to the Guardian Newspaper and the Hereford Times for permission to use articles previously used in the Assoociation Newsletter.
To my sponsors my greatful thanks for your support and to approve donating the money to Charity. To Jos for his help in producung the cover of the book , to Ted Ring, Brian Hackleton, Tony Engel and Jeff Brockwell your help is greatly appreciated.

Finally to my wife Sheila for her patience and help and my two sons Paul and Peter also Bob Johnson for their help.

Graphics by Jos Harrison.

Preface

Having compiled the information in the book, it will I hope be interesting to every referee in the district whether they are members of the Association or not. It will also mention referees who were refereeing before 1921 when Leamington was formed.

The first part covers the History from 1921 to 1939 with as much information that could be found. After the War and on the resumption of the Association we gradually move through the decades giving an insight to the problems referees become involved with and the changes that was for everyones benefit. The inclusion of Leagues, Charity Cup Competitions, Assessors, and Licensed Instructors are all part of what a referee encounters if they are members of an Association and wish to progress in the refereeing world.

Also mentioned is the service a referee has given as well as Cup finals he may have received. The future of referees and the new Referee Association of England is well documented.

In compiling facts and figures has not been easy with so many sections missing. What has been written has been done in good faith.

SPONSORSHIP

To assist me in compiling this book the following people and organisations have offered sponsorship to enable the finished book to be printed.
I am extremely grateful to everyone mentioned for the support they have given me :-

Leamington &District Sunday Football League
Leamington &District Referees Association
Norman Stephens Unlimited Leamington
Coventry Turned Parts Ltd Warwick
League Managers Association
Simon Rouse Esq
Anthony Engel Esq
The Rouse Family
Gordon Nicholls A C Lloyd (Builders) Ltd
Sheila Perry & Family
Michael Brady Leamington F C
Jeff Brockwell (Business Link Coventry &Warwickshire)
Ian Oliver Wolsey UK
Patrick Murphy (Murphy & Salisbury) Accountants.
Terry Arnold (T W Associates)
Paul Rouse (KAPA Training & Evaluation Services Ltd.)
Matthew Rouse Esq.

Contents

Chapter 1

Leamington & District Referees Association
1921 to 1931

The Beginning

It was by a stroke of luck that Andy Semple and myself found the first Secretary of the Association, both of us decided to find as much information as we could, and in 1970, an approach was made to the Leamington Spa Courier, who printed our request.

The result was a phone call from Harolds Daughter who said that her Father was the first Secretary in forming the Association in, August 1921, by calling a meeting of all Referees who were officiating in the area. This was held at the, 'Trades Hall Leamington.' His name was Harold Elkington and he was living with his Daughter at Budbroke, Warwick.

Andy Semple and myself made an appointment to see Mr Elkington, and were very surprised to meet a gentleman who was over 80 years old, very active and well informed. We asked him about the Association, although he said it was called the Society when they started, Pepper Talbot and Harold Elkington contacted the Referees who were refereeing on the Leamington & District Football League as well as the Warwick & District Football League. About twelve referees attended a meeting at the 'Trades Hall Leamington.' The Society was formed after a lengthy discussion with Pepper Talbot as the Chairman and Harold Elkington became the Secretary.

During the talk he informed us about the Referees and the Leagues they officiated on and the standard of football played. He talked to us about the Referees who had joined the Society and said quite a few refereed every week-end. This depended on the type of job they had, the fee they received supplemented their income. We had members who just refereed once or twice a month. Referees in those days were just used by Clubs and not treated very well. The Fee from the Leagues and Cup Competitions was miserly, varying between 2/6(two & sixpence) and the maximum 5/- (five shillings), which in some Leagues included expenses. In most cases when a game was local or just outside the Town the referees walked. If it was to places like Southam or Kineton most referees would use the local tram service or cycle to the ground, not many referees had Motor Cycles or Cars.

Another reason why Harold, as he liked to be called, decided with Pepper Talbot to form the Society because of lack of support from the Birmingham County Football Association. Most of the referees were registered with the County Football Association and until we started the Society the referees had no one to support them. Promotion was never mentioned and no one seemed to move from Class 3(three), although we did have members who received a County appointment which was usually in Coventry. He also told us that the 'Title' was changed from Society to Association.

In our talk to 'Harold' we never actually found out how the finances were organised, whether members paid a subscription to the Association or just gave a donation and we assumed they were not Affiliated to the National Referees Association

Harold and Pepper Talbot held those positions until 1926 when they retired, both through pressure of work. Harold was living in Bishops Tachbrook and employed as a Jobbing Gardener and free time was getting difficult. Pepper Talbot wanted to put more time in to the Warwick & District Football League.

Browsing through the Warwick & Warwickshire Advertiser, and the Leamington Gazette, I found an article written by the Secretary of the Leamington & District Referees Association concerning the fees that Southam & District League was discussing. Having read the letter, I realised that the information confirmed the talk Andy and I had with Harold Elkington that the Association was going strong in 1924.

This is the letter:-

Southam & District Football League Annual General Meeting August 30th 1924

The League Secretary Mr Amore, read the letter he had received from the Secretary of the Leamington &District Referees Association, Mr Harold Elkington.

It said that he took upon himself to agree to the terms to which the Southam League suggested as referees fees, which should be 3/6(three & sixpence) per match plus mileage.

The Secretary had observed that the only Club where the mileage system would be used, would be Priors Marston.

There were, he understood, only 2(two) Southam Referees available that season, adding that if they engaged a referee through the Leamington Referee's Association, they would not be able to cancel their matches at a minutes notice, as was done in some cases the previous year.

The Chairman Mr W Sturley remarked that as the mileage system would affect one club more than another, he thought it was the Clubs' duty to help one another and he suggested that they adopt an all round Fee of 5/-(five shillings).

The Secretary remarked that the letter from the Secretary of Leamington Referees contained the advice that Clubs should, "pay the referee what he was entitled to and not what he asks"

Mr Willoughby of Cubbington FC thought that the Fee of 5/-(five shillings) was fair for everyone.

Mr Sturley, Chairman, moved that the Secretary, Mr Amore, inform the Leamington Referees Secretary Mr Harold Elkington, the Fee would be fixed at 5/-(five shillings) inclusive per match The Motion was carried.

When reading the letter as it was printed in the paper it was definite proof that the Association was in existence in those early years and well organised

In 1926 a complete change occurred within the Association .when the previous Secretary and Chairman retired, the next Chairman to take over being George Dutton and the Secretary was John Wildsmith. Both holding these offices until the 1930's when they retired, and eventually holding other positions in the Association

We assumed George Dutton had joined the Association in the early 1920s and it seems that John Wildsmith started refereeing about the same time, because their service and promotion were almost parallel. (More about these two Gentlemen in the Referee's section)

Whilst reading the Warwick &Warwickshire Advertiser and the Leamington Gazette from 1920 up to 1929/1930 as I have mentioned earlier on, it seems that the information changed as well, for up to 1926 there always seemed to be a report about a match or the list of referee's appointments, or whether the referee had a good game, but from that year up to the 1930 era very little was mentioned about referees, although it was mentioned that George Dutton had been appointed to the Amateur Cup Game at Malvern against Hallam.

It seems the two gentlemen mentioned kept the Association moving along by appointing referees to matches with, (Walter Hemming and Tommy Tasker), distributing them as they had done for Harold Elkington. Again there did not seem to be any record of how funds were raised.

In 1933 Arthur Montgomery and John Wildsmith were presented with a gifts for their service as Secretary and Treasurer, we can only presume that Arthur Montgomery was Treasurer from either 1926 or served the previous Committee in 1921 when it was formed.

Herewith the Leagues that some of the Referees officiated on during that period:-

> **Henley-in-Arden & District Football League**
> **Kineton & District Football League**
> **Leamington & District Football League**
> **Southam & District Football League**
> **Stratford & District Football League**
> **Warwick & District Football League**

Referees also officiated on the Coventry & North Warwickshire Football League, and the Birmingham & District League as well as the Birmingham Combination. The Henley & District League is mentioned in the minutes, it seems to have been a thriving League, although not a great deal of information can be found about it.

Moving on from 1926 to the 1931 period with George Dutton and John Wildsmith as Chairman and Secretary and Arthur Montgomery as Treasurer, It is fortunate that minutes from 1931 to 1939 have been recorded. They show that Leamington Referees were in good hands, especially when appointments to referees were made by the Association so they could operate on the various Leagues.

Andy Semple who was Chairman of the Association 1972 tried to get Harold to our Meeting but of no avail. We did eventually manage to get Harold and his Daughter to our Annual Dinner in 1972 at the Charlecote, where we introduced Harold to Jim Finney who was the Guest Speaker. They enjoyed each others' company talking about football and referees between 1920 and 1939.

At one of our Council Meetings we decide to make Harold a, 'Vice-President' of the Association, and it was moved that he become a, 'Life Member' as well, This was Proposed by Arnold Rouse and Seconded by Pat Gwynne. We called an Extra Ordinary General Meeting to take place before the next Council Meeting
At the E. O. G. M. both items concerning Harold Elkington was put to the members, who voted in favour of the proposals.
The information was sent to Harold who replied with a very nice letter thanking everyone and wished us well for the future. It was unfortunate that Harold passed away a few years later

Chapter 2

PRE-WAR - 1931 TO 1939

The Association minute book from 1931 up to 1939 is the only recorded section giving you an insight as to how the Association was organised. It also shows how strong the Officers were in their control of Referees and how they appointed them to the various Leagues that were operating in the area during those years. They also made sure future Referees were members of the Association and paid all their subscriptions up to date. Problems were always discussed by the members and any serious or social issue was discussed at a special Management Meeting called for the purpose. It was my intention if possible to leave the Annual General Minutes and possibly the Monthly Minutes as they were written, this has turned out to be difficult The Headquarters during 1931 to 1939 was the, "Guards Inn" Public House High Street Leamington. The Landlady was Mrs Alderman

The first Annual General Meeting in 1931 was held in August and 12 members were in attendance, they were:- Chairman G Dutton, Messrs Baguley, Eynstone, Frost, Hawtin, Hulbert, Hunt, Hutching, Montgomery, Mumford. Thornton, Secretary J Wildsmith.
Apologies were accepted and they were:-Messrs Hemmings, W Hunt, Lines and Soden.

The Chairman welcomed everyone to the meeting and asked the Secretary John Wildsmith to read the minutes of the previous 1930 Annual General Meeting.
These were read and accepted, the Secretary then presented the Accounts to the meeting, after a general discussion the Accounts were accepted.
The Chairman remarkcd on the presentation of the Accounts and the Auditors said that they were well kept and informative. A remark was made as to the subsidizing of the Annual Dinner & Dance, the Chairman told the members that they should try and encourage members to attend because it was an excellent evening.

The rules were looked at and the members were concerned about Rule 11(eleven) which covers absent members who fail to send a written apology into the Secretary when they cannot attend a meeting. It was moved that the rule is strictly adhered to and absent members should pay the fine, (which is between three pence or sixpence per meeting.)
Another issue which was discussed was the subscription, it was moved that it remain the same as previous years i.e.: (six shillings and sixpence)

Election of Officers for 1931/1932 Season

President	**G Orme- Tiley Esq**
Chairman	**Mr G Dutton**
Vice-Chairman	**Mr W Enstone**
Hon Secretary	**Mr J E Wildsmith**
Hon Treasurer	**Mr A Montgomery**
Hon Auditors	**Mr G Baguley, Mr R Frost.**

The Election of Officers for the 1931-1932 season are printed in full so that members can see who was Chairman, Secretary and Treasurer at that tome. The three main Officers have been holding those positions since 1926.

September 1931

The Chairman George Dutton in opening the Meeting expressed his delight at the attendance; he said it must be a record, with eighteen members present and two apologies. There was also a new member to be accepted into the Association whilst three were waiting to take the Referees Examination.

The Secretary was appointed to represent the Association at the National Referees Association Meeting in Birmingham. The Secretary gave a talk on the Aims and Objects of the National Association, it was decided to invite Mr Richard Jackson Secretary of the National Referees, to attend a future meeting and give an Address on the National Referees.

N B (The statement seemed strange when the committee was talking about inviting the National Secretary to a meeting, in the 1928 Rule book the Association supposed to be in membership. It has been difficult to find out anything about the issue, as you read through you will come across a section where members were discussing the Rules of the National Association and the amount of Affiliation Fee to be paid. Further on we find that another meeting was held with Mr Jackson and a Special Meeting was convened by eight members to move that the Association join the National Referees Association.) .

Special Meeting

A newspaper cutting, plus other items concerning a move to set up a Society at Stratford were brought to the meeting by Mr Gardener of the Stratford Football League. The articles were read to the members and the Secretary was advised to request the attendance of the member who had set up the move, to attend a special Management Meeting

It was proposed that the Secretary and Chairman attend a meeting of the Stratford League, in order to explain the position of our Association, in regards to the suggested Society at Stratford.

Management December1931

Chairman George Dutton
Committee: Messrs W Enstone, F Mumford A Montgomery and J Wildsmith.
This was a special Meeting arranged in which the Referee concerned, was requested to attend and give an explanation of a newspaper cutting sent to the Association by Mr Gardener(Chairman of Stratford League)

Before opening the meeting the Chairman George Dutton read out the newspaper cutting to the members and told them he was concerned that this referee should attempt to split the Association, by trying to set up another Society or Association upsetting the distribution of Referees to the various Leagues.

He said he was at the meeting at Stratford when the information was presented. After a general discussion the members felt that the referee, who had failed to attend the meeting when requested too, should be invited to the next Management meeting in January to put his case and to ask the member why he is trying to cause trouble.

The Secretary told the Committee that the referee concerned has not paid his subscriptions yet, but he would write to the referee and invite him to the next meeting.

It was moved the member to attend a **Management Meeting in January 1932**. The member concerned did not attend the meeting but was present at the February meeting where his case was discussed. After a hearing the member was asked to leave the room.

The members expressed the unanimous opinion that his efforts were directed against the interests of the Leamington Referees Association and the following resolution was made.

"The member stands suspended from membership of the Leamington Referees Association, until such times as he ceases activities in areas at present served by this Association".

The member was recalled and **not informed** of the resolution, but was asked as to his future intentions, also could he give any reason for his action. His reply was that it was not

Association business as he had not paid his subscription for the year yet. He was informed very politely by the Chairman it was Association business where member referees are concerned.

After a lengthy discussion the referee was asked if he would cease his activities and hand over all news paper cuttings and letters to the Secretary He gave the assurance that he had decided to give up the idea and would hand to the Secretary correspondence received from prospective referees.

The Members accepted, and so his suspension was removed.

When asked to pay his subscriptions, he replied that he was unable to do so at the moment.

Monthly Meetings

A satisfactory report was given by the Chairman to Mr Hemmings concerning the unregistered referees at Stratford.. The Chairman told the members, he had received a letter from Whitnash Charity Cup Competition, stating that they were going to use Leamington Referees for their Matches.

The Secretary reported on the unfortunate circumstances of an unemployed member, who needed help. It was decided to grant the sum of £1 (one pound) in weekly instalments of 4/-(four shillings)

In February it was decided to send a donation of 10/-(ten shillings) to the Leamington Town F C.(The minutes do not say what the donation was for, unless it was to help the finances of the Club now they are in the Birmingham Combination. which is a very high standard of football and we do have referees who officiate in the Combination)..

In April a complaint was made against a Referee overcharging on certain Matches. The referee concerned was not at the Meeting and an explanation would be required from him the amounts over charged being 1/6(one & sixpence) to St Nicholas, and 1/-(one shilling) to Kenilworth W M Club the member would be informed that no appointments would be made until the money had been repaid.

June 1932

Annual General Meeting

Chairman Mr George Dutton

Minutes of the 1931 AGM were read and confirmed
Apologies were accepted.
The Secretary gave his report, and the Treasurer presented the Balance Sheet.
Satisfaction was expressed as to the financial position.

The Auditors, Mr G Baguley and Mr R Frost, testified as to the correctness of the Accounts, and Mr Frost drew attention to the fact that the Bank book was not shown at the Audit.

The circumstances were explained and the Bank book would be produced at the next Monthly Meeting.

Election of Officers

There were only two changes when the Election of Officers had taken place; the only change concerned Mr Sidney Soden who was elected to the Management. Mr George Dutton remained as Chairman.

The Rules of the Association were then read and revised as follows:-

- Rule (4) Subscriptions reduced from (6/6) Six and sixpence, to (5/-) Five shillings, including the National Association fee.
- It was proposed that the Secretary write to a suggested number of Gentlemen inviting them to become Vice- Presidents of the Association. The Secretary was instructed to convey the Thanks of the Association to Mrs Alderman for use of the Meeting Room.

Monthly Meeting

August was the start of a new season and Mr Partridge was elected to the Association as a new Member

The proposed alterations in the Rules of the National Association were then discussed and it was decided to accept the rules, with the exception of the proposal to increase the Fee from 1/-(one shilling) to 1s3d (one shilling & three pence).

Warwick & District Football League had been pleased to make a grant to our own Association of 10/6 (ten shillings & sixpence), also the same amount from the Stratford League. The Members appreciated their support

A general discussion took place at the meeting with the usual appeal for referees. It seems that we are managing to obtain referees but only one at a time. With regards to the shortage of referees, it was resolved that any referee, (not a member of this Association) desirous of taking matches in the area, should in the first place apply to the Secretary.(Mr J Wildsmith) in all probability they would be able to referee a match.

Members whose fees were unpaid would not receive appointments until their membership subscriptions were paid.

NB "The last sentence doesn't seem to make sense, we know the Association was very strict with members having paid their subscriptions, before they would receive appointments, surely it would have been logical to have them refereeing and get them to pay part of their fee towards the subscriptions. It obviously did not work like that until about 1936 when the system changes".

January 1933

Assault on a Referee

The Chairman gave his report of the Police Court proceedings to enquire into the assault on Richard West who was the Referee at Claverdon. The Chairman also told the members that the case, the first on record in the Leamington Area, had the sanction of the "Football Association " who made a grant of £5 (five pounds) towards the expenses

The player F Moody accused of the assault was proved guilty and fined £1(one pound) and £3 (three pounds) costs.

The case was brought up at 'Henley in Arden'

The Association was concerned about the Assault and members hoped it was not a start of unruly behaviour from players.

In researching for information on the above assault, which caused quite a stir in the Association as it was the first time a referee had been assaulted and Richard West was a very strong referee. We could not find any information from the County Library neither could we find any information from Stratford

Monthly Meetings

Management Meeting March 1933

Chairman Mr G Dutton

Members present:- Messrs Montgomery, Soden, Eynstone, and Secretary John Wildsmith.

An incident was brought to the notice of the Secretary concerning the attitude of two members, where unnecessary remarks had been made by one member about the other and the case had been brought before the Management. All this was denied when the two members were brought before the Management Committee, and the member concerned denied that he ever made such comments

The member who made the complaint had no witnesses to support his allegation, & the Committee had no option but to deem the case unproven.

The Chairman appealed to both members to avoid any such scandal in the future.

A letter was read from the Birmingham County. Football .Association relating to the Warwick & District Football League, in which a member was mentioned, as having given information relating to players under suspension.

The Chairman was not very pleased about this episode, discussing it at Management he said he was going to talk to the referee concerned and inform him.The person who has been suspended was not his business and in view of the fact that he had taken exception to his correspondence, the Chairman advised him to leave other people's affairs alone.

A further letter was also received from the County FA asking for an explanation, as to why the Leamington Referees Association had been appointing a member to referee matches when he had not paid the current season's subscriptions & referees examination fee for the previous year. The management members thoroughly discussed the problem and the Chairman decided to have words with the referee.

In view of this correspondence, all appointments were cancelled, and the member who was at the meeting was asked by the Chairman, if he could explain the reason why the County had written. The member went on to explain to the Chairman and members. He said he was quite convinced he had paid to the B.C.F.A., both the 2/6(two &sixpence) examination fee and the current seasons fee, but was unable to show the receipts, having apparently lost or destroyed them. The Chairman stressed the point of the harm that could be done, both to himself and his fellow members, the BCFA had announced no Appointments would be made, until confirmation had been received that all dues and demands had been met,

June 1933

Annual General Meeting

Chairman   Mr G Dutton

The Secretary gave his report and the Treasurer presented the balance sheet

It was Proposed by the Chairman, that the report and the adoption of the Balance sheet be accepted. This was carried.

Election of Officers

At this Annual General Meeting one or two changes were made. The President was elected again. A new Chairman Mr W Eynstone replaced George Dutton with Richard West becoming Vice-Chairman. George Dutton then moved on to the new Management Committee. In the previous year there was no mention of Auditors one would presume that the previous years Auditors were available to do the job. This year Mr G Smith and Mr J Lakin were accepted to that position. The Hon Secretary and Treasurer were both elected again to continue the good work they have done for a number of years

The Rules of the Association were then read and conformed. The new Chairman thanked members for attending the Meeting.

Life Membership

Proposed by the Secretary-- Mr J Wildsmith

Seconded by------------------ Mr W Eynstone

That Mr George Dutton is elected the First Life Member of the Leamington Referees Association, in recognition of his efforts on behalf of the Association during the past number of years as Chairman.

This is an Honour which is usually given to Members for Outstanding Service to the Association, by the wording above, the Award is well deserved, having seen the Award that Mr Dutton received, it was really appreciated.

Mr George Dutton expressed his appreciation for the honour the Society accorded him Mr Dutton having left the meeting, it was unanimously decided to make a presentation in early November at the Annual Dinner and the suggestion was 2/6 (two & six) per member. The gift the Association decided to purchase was a Chiming Mantle Clock at a value of no more then £4 (pounds)

September

Mr Orme-Tiley accepted the Presidency of the Association and was again generous with his donation and a grant was received from the Stratford & District Football League, Mr Poole from Stratford was elected a member after passing the Examination.

The Committee unanimously decided to loan the cost of the County F.A Subscriptions to all members who are unemployed.

Concern was expressed by the Secretary about the Assault case-- it seems that money from the Football Association has not been sent to the Treasurer. George Dutton said he would raise the issue with the Birmingham County F A

October 1933

Monthly Meetings

The Secretary attended a meeting of the Warwick &District Football League to resolve the claims outstanding from the previous year. He gave members a report on the meeting with the officers of the Warwick League and welcomed the Secretary Mr Hunt to the meeting.

Mr W Hunt, Hon Secretary of the Warwick League, talked to the members about the outstanding claims the members had made against the Warwick League. He accepted what they had said and the claims would be met tonight. Mr Hunt also said that it would help if referees notified the clubs, if they would not be able to accept the appointments and to arrive in good time to referee the match. The members thanked Mr Hunt who was a Referee as well for his talk and the following members received settlement; Messrs G Smith, R West, H Heath, E Smith, T Hawtin, S Soden. Each member received between 2/6(two & sixpence) and 5/-(five shillings)

April 1934

Resignations

The Secretary gave notice that owing to pressure of business, he regretted that he would have to tender his resignation at the next Annual Meeting. This was a blow to the members for every one regarded John Wildsmith as a regular pillar of solidarity, as well as being a very good Secretary.

The Treasurer Arthur Montgomery intimated that he would be resigning due to other interests at the Annual Meeting.

July 1934

Annual General Meeting

The Election of Officers at the Annual General Meeting was slightly different with the members voting to elect a new Secretary and a new Treasurer. Both these positions were soon filled with Richard West moving from being Vice- Chairman to Secretary and Arthur Montgomery resigning from being the Treasurer. This position went to Mr W T Hawtin.The only other changes made were with the Auditors and W Enefer and John Wildsmith accepted the position.

With new Oficers which includes a new Treasurer it was suggested that all Bank signatures be changed form Mr Dutton and Mr Wildsmith to Mr Eynstone and Mr West.

TheBirmingham County Football Association would accept the responsibility for the Balance of the cost in the prosecution case.

National Referees Association

Mr John Wildsmith was delegated to Birmingham to listen to Speakers from the National Referees Association. He went with George Dutton.

The Secretary gave a report of the two National Referees Association Meetings held in Birmingham He was able to inform the members after meeting with the Representatives.

They had obviously spoken to Mr Jackson the National Secretary, with reference Leamington joining the National Association, not every member of the Association was in favour of joining, this was shown by the voting that took place.

George Dutton had made a suggestion and talked to the members, giving the reason why we should join the National Referees Association. John Wildsmith explained the way the National Association works and how members would be affiliated, also the benefits that would be available to them, it is a big step for members to think about as well as all the benefits, what would be the cost to each member and would the Association fees go up.

After a lengthy discussion between the members, questions were asked and a few were answered, the awkward ones being left on the table. The Chairman then asked the members to vote and the result was as follows:-

It was proposed that we did not join the National Referees Association, this was seconded. An Amendment was put forward, that the Association did join the National Referees, this also was seconded

The Chairman Mr Eynstone put the Amendment to the meeting and the voting was in favour of the amendment, it was decided not to join, this was carried by six votes to four, with three abstentions, although they are not mentioned in the written minutes

Further talks will be made when the Officers meet the Secretary of the National Referees Association and most proberly invite him to a meeting with the members at a later date.

September

Monthly Meeting

It was moved by the Members a Gift should be made to Mr Wildsmith and to Mr Montgomery for the excellent work both Members have done for the Association over the Years, one as the Secretary and the other as Treasurer. Both Members are to choose their gifts to a certain amount, and the Association to pay for the Gifts.

An Amendment was made by the Secretary Mr West

Seconded by Mr Harris

That each member shall be asked to pay 2/6 (two & sixpence) The Amendment was carried

October

A Member was suspended by the Warwick & District Football League with no apparent reason given, at the same time the fixtures for the weekly matches were arriving late to the Secretary, who was having a job to allocate them to various referees, It was suggested the Secretary write to the Warwick League asking for an explanation why they suspended Mr Hawtin and the Warwick League send their fixtures to the Secretary of the Association on the Saturday prior to the match taking place.

It was suggested a letter be sent to all local Leagues and Cup committees, asking for help and support to raise the funds for Mr Wildsmith and Mr Montgomery for the service they have given to the Leagues and Cup Competitions in the area

It was proposed to hold a Dinner and Smoking concert and present Mr Wildsmith and Mr Montgomery with their Gifts. The date the concert would be held would be the 7th December at 7.30pm at the Crown Hotel. The Secretary is to ask Mrs Alderman to cater for the Dinner, failing Mrs Alderman, the Cadena Café Ltd.

November

National Referees Association

Mr Jackson the Secretary of the National Referees Association, attended the meeting, and gave members a very good talk on the Benefits of being an Associate Member of the National Referees. After talking to the members he had a lengthy discussion with Mr George Dutton with the members listening to what was being said, which was quite satisfying to the members present.

A vote of thanks to Mr Jackson for attending the Meeting

Proposed by Mr Wildsmith

Seconded by Mr Enefer

Those Eight members to sign a paper as per Rule (7) to convene a special Meeting.

The meeting was closed, so that the E G M could take place

The members who called the Extra- Ordinary General Meeting did so after listening to Mr Jackson and the discussion that took place between him and Mr Dutton, they felt that the previous meeting and the meetings the two members had been to in Birmingham, had given them enough information to become members of the National Referees Association.

November 1934   Extra-Ordinary General Meeting

Chairman Mr W Eynstone

"We the undersigned convene a special meeting of this Association, according to Rule 7 (seven) in order to deal with the question of re-joining the National Referees Association"

Signatures as follows: Mr R Hunt, Mr T Thornton, Mr F Poole, Mr F Hawtin, Mr G Hemmings, Mr Enefer, Mr J Wildsmith, Mr Eynstone, Mr R West, Mr F Mumford, Mr J Partridge, Mr S Castle,

It was Proposed by Mr Wildsmith, and Seconded by Mr Hemmings

That the Association rejoin the National Referees Association This was carried unanimously with no abstentions. (The Minutes of that time do not say if there were any other members attending who had not signed as per Rule 7).

March 1935

Monthly Meeting

Mr.B (Pepper) Talbot collapsed and after a short illness passed away, the Secretary was asked to arrange for a wreath to be sent to the family.

Mr Talbot was the Chairman of the Association from 1921 to 1926 and he supported the Association. His other involvement was the Warwick &District Football League where he had been the Secretary many years ago..

The members were asked to stand in respect for Mr Talbot and the member from Bishops Itchington. .

Mr Dutton presented to Mr Wildsmith a plate fully inscribed for his Bureau, which had recently been presented to Mr Wildsmith, and Mr Dutton made some very pleasing remarks about John Wildsmith during his eight years in office.

The Secretary, on behalf of the Association, Congratulated Mr Dutton on his appointment to Referee the Junior International match between Birmingham County Football Association and the Scottish Football Association.

Moving into the 1935 period we came across an episode of irate officers and lackadaisical members at an Annual General Meeting. There is nothing more worrying for any officers when it happens and in the case below another Annual General Meeting was called.

The first four years from 1931 have seen a gradual change in the Association with a few new members joining. The Management were very strict in dealing with wayward members. The President was very generous in his donation to the Association. Talks were always on –going with the members concerning joining the "National Referees Association".

Having a change of Officers in 1935 with the problems of a poor attendance, we will have to see what 1936 and the rest of the decade brings to the Association.

July 1935   Annual General Meeting

Chairman Mr G Dutton

The Secretary gave his Annual report and presented the statement of Accounts

It was proposed that the report and Balance sheet be adopted. 'This was carried'

Proposed by Mr Dutton   Seconded by Mr Poole

Owing to such a poor attendance at this meeting, the only officers that could be elected were the President and the Secretary and it was agreed to adjourn this meeting until Tuesday August 21st 1935

From the chair Mr Dutton proposed Mr Orme-Tiley as President for the season 1935-36. This was supported by every member present.

That Richard West remains as Secretary.

A vote of thanks was given to Mr Dutton for taking the Chair at the Annual General Meeting.

Mr Dutton, Chairman, made some striking remarks. He said it was disgusting to see such a small attendance at an Annual Meeting after all the work that had been put in to make the

Association what it was today and for its members to show little interest, but he hoped, what appeared to be a sinking ship, the members would rally round and would carry on the good work, where he and others had left it and keep the Association up to the standard to which it belongs.

August 1935   Adjourned Annual General Meeting

Chairman Mr J E Wildsmith

Arising out of the Minutes of the Annual General Meeting held on the 21st July 1935. Mr Dutton asked why his remarks were not registered. The Secretary made an apology that it was an oversight on his part

The correspondence was accepted.

Mr Orme –Tiley again accepted the Presidency of the Association and generously enclosed a cheque for £2.2s (Two pounds- two shillings)

The Secretary was instructed to convey the Association's thanks and appreciation

Stratford &District Football League made a donation of 10/6 (Ten shillings & six pence), and expressed great satisfaction in every way the Association had supported Stratford..

Election of Officers for Season 1935-36

President	**G Orme-Tiley Esq**
Chairman	**Mr J Wildsmith**
Vice- Chairman	**Mr S Soden**
Hon Treasurer	**Mr W T Hawtin**
Management Committee	**Mr G Dutton**
Hon Secretary	**Mr R M West**
Auditors	**Mr C Webb, Mr Enefer.**

The Chairman told the members that the Association owed a great deal to Mr Dutton for all the work and help he had given in trying to keep the Association to the front. The reason for the lack of attendance would be looked into and the Secretary was asked to find out as much as he could by talking to members.

September 1935

Mr George Dutton was elected as the new Secretary to the Leamington & District Saturday Football League.

This was a surprise to many of the Referees in the area; although he had been involved with the League His obvious task now would be to make sure all his League fixtures have Referees. Having been involved with the system the referees have been using for a number of years it seems it is about to change. As we read through the minutes strong words are used,

The new Secretary of the Leamington Saturday Football League sent a letter to the Secretary of the Association regarding the appointment of referees to Football matches in his League. The Secretary of the Leamington Referees Association sent a reply saying the Letter and request would be discussed at the next Monthly meeting

October 1935

Monthly Meeting

The Chairman, John Wildsmith welcomed the members to the meeting.

Apologies were accepted,

Correspondence was read to the members. The Secretary read out the Letter he had received from Mr Dutton concerning the appointment of referees.

The Members present had a lengthy discussion on the system of appointments and were very concerned about the request from the new Secretary. Exception was being taken to the proposed change in the system regarding the selection of referees

It was proposed and seconded: - If the Leamington League desires to appoint the referees for their matches, they should be requested to notify the referees concerned direct

Exception would be taken to the appointment of referees who were not members of their Association or Society. This was carried unanimously and further discussion took place on a similar issue with the appointments of referees to the Warwick League At that point the Secretary asked the members if they had outstanding claims for the previous season, they should forward same to him

The Chairman gave a report of the meeting of the Leamington League, to which the Management Committee of the Association was invited. In his report he stated that the Secretary of the League desired to have some control over the appointment of referees and considered that referees' from Coventry should be included.

The Association did not agree and the Secretary was requested to inform the Secretary of the Saturday League. The resolution passed at the meeting would be carried to effect.

The Secretary was asked to inform the Secretary of the Warwick League. The Association would be pleased to appoint referees from our list of members, to cover the matches in the League, but it was deemed impossible to submit a list of referees for their approval. It was proposed by the members. "That the Chairman and Secretary" seek permission from the Warwick & District Football League to attend their next Management Meeting to discuss the issue concerning referees."

November

"First of its kind" said the Chairman John Wildsmith after the members had listened to a talk given by Mr Tommy Gallant Chairman Coventry Referees and Mr Vic Edmunds Assistant Secretary. These two gentlemen were welcomed and introduced to the members after the business part of the meeting had finished. Both Gentlemen gave the members a very interesting talk on Football Refereeing and the Administrative side of having a large Association, the whole session being enjoyed by the members present.

On proposing a vote of thanks to Mr Gallant our Chairman Mr Wildsmith said it was the first of its kind at our monthly meetings for a long time but he hoped we should have more in the future. This was seconded by Mr Roberts

July 1936   Annual General Meeting

Chairman Mr J E Wildsmith

Chairman's remarks

He said how pleased he was to see such a good number at this Annual Meeting, he had heard remarks that people only took up refereeing for what they could get out of it, but to see such a large number on such a nice summer night showed those remarks were not true.

He was rather surprised to hear the Association had made no fewer than 600 appointments during the 1935-36 Season.

It shows how much this Association helped in the work of Football and he thanked all officials, members, and a special one for the Secretary for the work that had been done during last season and hoped, we should have another successful one this coming year.

Election of Officers 1936-1937

The President and Chairman were elected again. Mr G Lewis became the new Treasurer and Mr Eynstone became the Management member. The Auditors were Messrs Mumford and Thornton.

All the Association Rules were accepted, and Rule 11 is to be strictly enforced at meetings..

Mr George Dutton reported he had recommended 5 (five) members to Mr Walter Hunt for Appointments in the Football Association Cup Ties.

The meeting then closed at 9.50pm.

September

Arising from correspondence

The Chairman said it was very gratifying to know that Mr Orme-Tiley had again accepted the Presidency of the Association.

It was very pleasing to hear Mr Spiers had already placed his faith in this Association asking the Secretary to make several Line appointments for the Birmingham Combination.

It was proposed and seconded the Secretary write in answer to a letter he had received from Mr Dutton, Secretary of the Leamington & District Saturday Football League, asking the Secretary to place all the members on the list of Referees for the Leamington Saturday League and to mention a small donation would be appreciated, for work done by this Association during the past season.

Question of appointments in this area was brought up by the Secretary, he said he was sorry Mr Dutton was not present at this meeting. Mr Dutton would know all the business that was done but he did not want him to get it wrong. The Secretary said appointments in this area were beginning to get a very mixed up affair which was far from satisfactory to all concerned, it is a great pity this has come about, everything with regards to appointments was running very smoothly, until our little difficulty with the Leamington League arose,

He pointed out that two or three people sending out appointments to the same referees, was impossible to work successfully. It was a great pity that this has come about but no one can blame this Association for this. We did this work for years and were successful until this new Leamington League Management started 12 months ago. It was very disappointing to think that our old Chairman who had helped to get this scheme working nicely, should be in a position to take it away but he hoped we should soon come to some arrangement where by this overlapping of appointments would stop.

All members present discussed this and it was generally agreed that things were not running at all smoothly or satisfactorily. It was pointed out that this Association did not wish to dictate to Leagues, it was just a matter of all working together and not so much a one man show about it. After this long debate, it was proposed, the members should keep appointments from this Association in preference to any other local appointment if such appointments were received first.

October

Hospital Cup Committee Meeting

The Chairman opened the meeting and said he was pleased to have with us tonight members of **"Leamington Hospital Cup Committee"** to discuss a complaint regarding members failing to take appointments allocated to them by this committee.

Mr Dutton spoke on behalf of the Cup Committee, saying four members turned appointments down, but in two of the cases the refusals were justified. Mr Dutton said the other two turned their matches down and then took other appointments which were allocated by their own Association. Mr West, Secretary, spoke on behalf of one referee who was unable to be present and the other member spoke for himself saying he did not want a match at all, but his Association were short he took this small match to help the Secretary out.

The Chairman Mr J E Wildsmith said it was perfectly obvious from what had been said that the Leamington Hospital Cup had no case to answer. The members of the Association had decided at a previous meeting to give priority to appointments, they received through their own organisation and they intended to stand by that decision. He said we do not interfere with your affairs and we are not going to allow anyone to interfere with us.

The Secretary Mr West said that he and Mr Wildsmith were treated very discourteously at the last Hospital Cup Meeting and the Chairman Mr Wildsmith said he would not have this sort of thing. He respected everyone and in turn expected the same treatment but this was denied by other members of the Hospital Committee.

Mr Wildsmith said he would have this out at a further meeting of the Hospital Cup Members. The Hospital Committee then left and the meeting carried on as usual closing at 9.55pm

January 1937

A Referee was severely criticised by the Secretary of a Cup Competition for his action in turning down a Cup-tie, also for not turning up to a League match. It was proposed that a letter from this meeting be sent to a member for an explanation of his action in turning down a Cup-tie at the last minute and taking a Line appointment, also for not turning up in a Warwick League match on November28th with out letting anyone know.

The Secretary was instructed to inform the member that no more matches would be allocated to him until the issue in hand had been dealt with and he was requested to attend the next monthly meeting. The other members were reported for not appearing at the matches, the Secretary had heard from one member with his explanation, but not from the other referee..

April & May

Arising from the Correspondence, the meeting unanimously agreed to support Mr Brown of Bristol as the new Hon Secretary of the National Referees Association, the Secretary gave his report on the meeting of the this Association, which he attended last month and was a little surprised at the change of Secrtary.

Once again we come to a slow down at the "Annual General Meetings" This time it is the fact that the Secretary did not wish to be re-elected even though he had done a very good job in running the Association. In this case we have two Adjourned meetings mainly to elect a Secretary. All these meetings were held at the Guards Inn Leamington and to settle the issue a new member was brought into the Association with the intention of becoming Secretary providing he passes the Referees Examination.

. July 1937
Annual General Meeting
Chairman Mr JE Wildsmith

The Secretary gave his Annual report and Statement of Accounts, which gave great satisfaction and the Chairman congratulated the Secretary and Treasurer on there splendid work during the Season.

Mr Mumford gave his report as Auditor, saying everything was very satisfactory and he remarked how straight forward the Secretary kept his books, which gave him great credit and very little work, was left for him and Mr Thornton to do

Mr Mumford on behalf of the Warwick Cinderella Cup of which he is Secretary, Thanked all members who had helped to make his Competition a success.

The Chairman remarked that it was very pleasing to him to hear the Secretary's report and to find what great work this Association had done during the present Season. He paid special remarks to the Secretary for the capable manner in which he had carried out his work and said he was rather surprised to hear that the Secretary did not wish to seek re-election, but he hoped before the meeting ended they would be able to persuade Mr West to carry on. He also congratulated the Treasurer for producing an excellent set of Accounts and for the work he has done during the season.

He congratulated Mr Mumford on being promoted to Class1 (one), and said it was not out of turn, and Mr Mumford was still a young man but an old referee.

The Chairman also congratulated Mr Roberts on receiving his Class 2(two).

Election of Officers

A lengthy discussion followed in trying to elect a new Secretary, but no one would take on the secretary's job. So the Chairman had no alternative but to adjourn the meeting for a fortnight.

August 1937   Adjourned Annual General Meeting

Chairman Mr J E Wildsmith.

Members present as per Register   Apologies were accepted as read.

Continuation of the Adjourned Annual Meeting was continued, the election of Officers was again brought to a standstill, due to the fact the Association was unable to persuade the present Secretary to carry on and not being able to find a new Secretary.

This was discussed at length, and finding no one interested in becoming Secretary, it was decided to make no further appointments. Mr West was asked if he would inform all Leagues and Cup Competitions this decision with regret. It was decided to hold over other offices until the next

meeting, when Mr A Lewis said he might be able to find a successor to Mr West. He would then let him know so he could call a further Annual General Meeting.

It was proposed and seconded: the Subscription to the Association should be 2/6 (two & sixpence) annually including 1/-(one shilling) National Association Fees.

The Secretary was instructed to write to Mr F Partridge, thanking him for his service as one of our members. Mr Partridge was unable to carry on refereeing, due the change in his Employment.

November 1937   Second Adjourned Annual General Meeting

Chairman Mr J E Wildsmith.

Two new referees were introduced to the members, namely Mr R W Rowson and Mr D W Townsend, both these were elected members of the Association. The Chairman welcomed these two new members and said he wished both every success. The main item on the agenda was the Election of Officers, including a new Secretary.

Proposed by Mr Castle

Seconded by Mr Lewis

That Mr R W Rowson is appointed as the new Secretary. This was carried by the members who congratulated Mr Rowson in stepping into the breach at his first meeting and everyone hoped he would enjoy being Secretary.

It was suggested that the Society should pay 1d (one penny) per member annually to the National Referees Area Committee, for the purpose of carrying on its work, this money together with the National Referees Association Fee of 1/-(one shilling) to be paid out of members' 2/6 (two & sixpence) subscription each year.

The Association finally got its man through the efforts of Mr Lewis. Mr Rowson was elected Secretary and he continued until the 1939 period when the Association closed down. It seems that Mr Rowson did a good job whilst he was Secretary.

It was a special meeting for a special purpose it was fortunate the other positions in the Association were reasonably sound, so the only worry was the Secretary. It does happen sometimes when a newcomer joins the Association and immediately os elected on to a committee.

December

Monthly Meeting

So that consideration could be given to the Warwick and Stratford Leagues re-emergency appointments. Mr Rowson was asked to write to the two League Secretaries concerned, asking them to inform him not later than Friday in each week, of any match or matches for which they were unable to find a Referee Therefore the Secretary of the Leamington Referees would do whatever possible among members who were available on the day in Question, any expenses arising to be borne by the Leagues.

January 1938

Monthly Meeting

It was proposed and seconded that 10/6 (ten shillings & sixpence) be sent to the Testimonial fund for Mr Richard Jackson.

The Secretary was instructed to write to Mr Charles Jackson of Leek Wootton, asking if he had been placed on the official list of the County Football Association, if so, inviting him to become a member of the Leamington Referees' Association.

It was proposed and seconded, that this Association pass a resolution of extreme pleasure at the reinstatement of Mr J Tonkiss (Birmingham Referees Association) Further information was needed.

A letter was read out from the Referees Association (Midland Division) for the re-election of County Representatives. After a discussion on the issue, it was decided to let this letter lie on the table until further information was available.

September 1938.   Annual General Meeting (Guards Inn)

Chairman Mr J E Wildsmith

Members present Messrs, R West, S Soden, Holliday, C Jackson, Horley, Poole, Castle, and Secretary   Mr R Rowson.

Minutes of the previous Annual General Meeting were read and accepted.

The Balance sheet was read out, and slight discrepancies were found Money still owed from Evesham Society. It was decided to have the same Audited and passed at the next meeting.

It was decided to excuse Mr Holliday of Stratford from paying his subscription for season 1937-1938, this was because of an operation to Mr Holliday, and he had been unable to take an active part during the season.

Mr J E Wildsmith was nominated for the position as Chairman to the Area Committee.

Mr R West was nominated as a representative from the Association to attend an address by Mr S F Rous.

Congratulations were extended to Mr R West, on being promoted to a Class 1(one) Referee and being placed on the London Combination as a Linesman.

The Chairman extended a welcome to Mr Charles Jackson as a new member of the Association.

Election of Officers for season 1938-1939

President	**G Orme-Tiley Esq**
Chairman	**Mr J E Wildsmith**
Vice- Chairman	**Mr S Soden**
Secretary	**Mr R Rowson**
Treasurer	**Mr G H Lewis**
Management Committee	**Mr C Jackson**
Auditors	**Messrs Horley and West**

The election of officers has been left in full, as it is written in the minutes. It is the last Annual General Meeting of the Association that has been recorded in the period to 1939

The only changes that were made concerned the Management Member. Mr Charles Jackson was elected at his first meeting of the Association and the election of two new Auditors namely Messrs Horley and West.

Arising from the correspondence was a very sad letter from members of this Association, expressing sympathy to Mr Richard Jackson, who, owing to a prolonged illness had been compelled to relinquish his position as Hon Divisional Secretary National Referees Association.

It was proposed and seconded that. The Association send a Donation of 10/6 (Ten shillings & sixpence) to Mr Jackson, from the funds, to assist him in buying a few additional comforts during his stay in Hospital.

October 1938

Chairman Mr J E Wildsmith

Members present Messrs Holliday, Coie, Jackson, Castle, Poole, Horley, West, and Secretary.

Apologies received from Mr Roberts, Mr Soden and Mr Lewis,(Treasurer)

Prior to the normal council meeting an **Extra –Ordinary Meeting** was held to accept the Income and Expenditure Accounts and the Balance Sheet which was referred to at the last A.G.M, also to accept the Auditors report. The Amended Balance sheet, after Audit, was passed as a correct financial statement, this included an adjustment of 3/-(three shillings) received for photographs, from the Evesham Society.

It was decided to place on record appreciation to Mr G Orme-Tiley for his continued support as president of the Association, also for his generous donation of £2-2 (Two pounds two shillings). The Secretary's action of sending a letter of thanks was endorsed.

A letter was read out from Barnsley R regarding disablement insurance. It was decided to leave this on the table.

November

Monthly Meeting

The Chairman extended a welcome to Mr Bragg and Mr Adams, who were attending their first meeting of the Leamington Referees Association.

The Chairman made a sympathetic reference to the late Divisional Secretary Mr Richard Jackson, who passed away on October 31st 1938 after much suffering. The members stood in silence for one minute in reverence of his memory.

Mr Lewis the Treasurer thanked the Secretary Mr R Rowson for carrying out so efficiently his duties, also for providing members with appointments. This was supported by Mr Wildsmith, and Mr Soden.

The Secretary explained an idea he had in giving the Association publicity, by using the pump rooms and advertising our case, with an advert and printed cards giving details of the meetings, and refereeing. This was unanimously carried

The December meeting would be held as a social evening and it was hoped that the President would give a short address.

The date would be the 14th December 1938.

December Meeting and Social Evening

President   Mr G Orme-Tiley

Chairman   Mr J E Wildsmith

Members present Messrs Holliday, Poole, Castle, Soden, Jackson, E Adams, Horley, Joyner, Mann, Rogers, and Secretary Mr R Rowson.

Guests:

Mr W Gardener. Vice-President Stratford League

Mr   E Lesley.& Mr Hastings   Warwick & District League.

The Chairman extended a warm welcome to the President Mr Orme-Tiley..

The Social evening was enjoyed by everyone, and the President gave a very interesting address, that was entirely suitable to the occasion. Mr Orme –Tiley presented on behalf of the members a silver tankard to Mr Sidney Soden, who was retiring after 10 years from active Refereeing.

Mr Soden thanked everyone for whom he described as a most pleasant surprise, the tankard is inscribed to" S H Soden, from his fellow Referees Christmas 1938."

The entertainment was provided by Mr S Williams and Mr C Wimbrush, with additional items from the Guests and members.

Mr Lewis thanked Mr Orme-Tiley for attending the Evening and a vote of thanks was also given to the Entertainment.

The evening closed at 10.30 pm.

January 1939

The matter of the Referees Disablement Insurance was discussed and six members stated that it was their intention to participate in the scheme.

The Secretary reported this number was sufficient to have a policy issued and additional members could be added to the list when necessary. The Secretary informed members that he would contact the Insurance Company and try to have it completed by April.

A suggestion was raised, regarding having a debate between referees and players, after a discussion it was decided to ascertain if clubs would welcome this idea, before proceeding any further.

In reply to the question on the debate between referees and player,. the Secretary said that owing to the lateness of the season, he had decided to temporarily abandon it until next season.

The Secretary reported there had been an isolated case of two referees being sent to the same match and to avoid a recurrence, it was suggested that members acknowledge their appointments.

A discussion took place on the present financial position of the Association. The Secretary wasinstructed when sending out notices for the monthly meetings, to apply for subscriptions from the members who had not paid.

April 1939

This is the last Monthly Meeting of the season

Owing to the unavoidable absence of the Chairman, the Vice-Chairman Mr S Soden took the chair.

Members present:- Messrs Holliday, Castle, Bragg, Joyner, Poole, Rogers, Jackson, and the Secretary.

Apologies from Mr G Coie

It was confirmed that we hold the Annual General Meeting on September 6th 1939

A vote of appreciation was passed to the Warwick & District Football League for the sum of (21/-) Twenty one shillings received.

The following players were selected to play in the six-a-side contest at the Birmingham Polly on May 13th. As follows: - Rowson, Castle, Joyner, Rogers, Jackson, Roberts, reserve Holliday.

It was pointed out to the meeting that one of the Auditors Mr West had not attended since the beginning of the season and in the event of him not being agreeable to audit the Balance sheet, it was decided that Mr J Bragg be appointed temporarily as his successor.

The Secretary informed the following members, that the policy for Referees Disablement Insurance had been completed, and they were now covered by the scheme:

Mr J E Wildsmith, Mr R G Mann, Mr C W Jackson, Mr J C Bragg, Mr E Poole , Mr R W Rowson.

This is the last of the Minutes from the 1931 to 1939 Period, the," Annual General Meeting" was arranged for the 6th September 1939, and War was declared on Sunday 3rd September.

The minutes for that month have never been signed and no reference to the closing down of the Association can be found.

1939—1946 The War Years

In 1939 Leamington &District Referees Association decided to close down when the War started on Sunday 3rd of September. Gradually the smaller leagues and football in general was brought to a halt, although in certain areas football was being allowed to be played.

In Coventry the essential services were working at full blast, a certain amount of relaxation was allowed and football was one game that benefited with referees needed for the games. We had three members join Coventry Referees Association. They were George Dutton, Charlie Jackson, and Jack Joyner, George Dutton may have been a member of Coventry before the War due to the fact, his Employment was in Coventry and he was involved with referee candidates making sure they had been coached, and taking them through the examination at the BTH Club. Coventry.

George Pankhurst took up refereeing and passed the examination in 1941 at Coventry, and refereed in the local leagues that were operating at the time in the Coventry area. In 1942 Professional Football gradually started up again on a regional basis with permission from the Football Association the Secretary Stanley Rous, appointed George Dutton to arrange Referees and Linesmen for the matches, and with mid week matches being played. Finding officials could be difficult. John Wildsmith who stayed at Leamington was also placed on the list and George Pankhurst was placed on the list as a linesman.

The other two members from Leamington received appointments in the local Leagues and they could well have received appointments in the Birmingham Combination.

The members, who joined Coventry RA, stayed with the Coventry Referees Association until 1948 although there were referees who belonged to both Associations.

George Pankhurst was a member of Coventry RA and eventually served on the Management Committee. When Leamington was reformed in 1948, he became Secretary and transferred his membership to Leamington Referees...

Charlie Jackson continued his refereeing whilst serving in the Army, and Jack Joyner who was on essential services during the War, also did his fair share of refereeing around the Midlands After the War had finished and life began to get back to normal, it was noticed that a number of referees who had officiated before the war, did not take up refereeing again. There was no mention in any of the minutes as to whether they survived the war or whether the years were too large a gap to overcome, although quite a few began to get involved with the Leamington Saturday Football League and the Leagues from the Coventry area.

Chapter 3

1948 To 1952
An Association Reformed

From 1939 the Leamington &District Referee's Association was quietly put to sleep until the end of hostilities. The members responsible for looking after the Accounts and the minute book kept them safe and in good order so that when the opportunity to reform the Association was possible they were able to do so with ease.

John Wildsmith who was the Chairman in 1939 and George Lewis with Sidney Soden were the referees who stayed in Leamington. Quite a few of the members were eventually called up to the colours and members like George Dutton, Jack Joyner and Charlie Jackson joined Coventry Referees and refereed in that area. All these changes took place mostly due to the involvement of the War.

The Majority of the Leagues and competitions were closed down during the War although a few were allowed to carry on which was for everyone's benefit and to help the War effort. It meant that Football was being played in Coventry this enabled a few referees to carry on refereeing. It was obvious that referees were being coached and passing the referees examination in Coventry. This is where George Pankhurst started his career when he became a referee in 1941 and joined Coventry Referees; he also refereed in that area and eventually went on the Senior League as a Linesman. This was a good move and when Stanley Rous who was the Secretary of the Football Association at the time decided to allow certain Clubs to play League Football, it was called the Midland Football League. This was evidently a booster to the general public, that Football was on its way again. It was a wonderful opportunity for the referees who were officiating at that time to take part in a higher standard of Football.

After the war years, permission was given for Junior Leagues to begin playing Football again, and Leamington & District Football League was re-formed in 1946. It was obvious that there would be a shortage of referees and to alleviate this problem, the Coventry Referees formed an Allocation system to distribute referees to Leagues in an even manner so that no league would have all the referees. To help the Leamington & District Football League, Referees came over from Rugby to officiate. The fact that there wasn't a Referees Association in Leamington caused some difficulties in obtaining referees.

An article appeared in the Leamington Courier, informing referees and ex-referees that a meeting was called for the **19th June 1948, commencing at 8pm, at the 'Guards Inn' Leamington Spa**

This meeting was duly held under Chairman John Wildsmith, who informed the referees who were at the meeting, what had been done and how the Accounts had been looked after since 1939. At this meeting were the following Referees:- Messrs J Wildsmith, G Dutton, G Lewis, S Soden, G Pankhurst, C Jackson, J Joyner, G Perks, H Owen, L Cecil, A Walters, T Story, H Shuttleworth, J White, H Hall, B Calahane.

The Association was active again and referees began to join. Coaching was a mixture, you were either coached by a referee on a one to one basis, or you taught yourself. The other alternative was to go to Coventry where coaching classes were held. All examinations were held in Coventry at the BTH Club, although eventually coaching classes were held at the Leamington Boys Club. This depended on the referee who was doing the coaching. Every effort was being made to obtain referees and, clubs were asked to nominate ex-players.

George Dutton who was elected Chairman in 1948 decided to retire in 1950 so that he could concentrate on being Secretary of the Leamington & District Saturday Football League.

The new Chairman was Tom Story. By the time we had reached the 1952/53 season the Association had Referees on a variety of Leagues. The majority started on the Leamington League, a few went on the Stratford-on-Avon District Football League, or joined the Allocation system and officiated in Coventry. We had senior members on the Birmingham Combination, the Football Combination and Linesmen on the Football League. We also had John Wildsmith and George Dutton both refereeing on the Football League.

After the first meeting at the Home Guard Club, the Association held their second meeting at the Bedford Inn. This was the Headquarters for two years and difficulties began to arise over meeting nights. At this time Ken Cox joined the Association and his Father was the Landlord of the Willoughby Arms, which gave the Association the opportunity to eventually move.. Mr Cox was a Professional Footballer in his early days with Northampton Town FC he was a very good landlord and we knew we would be well looked after.

The Management Committee was increased from one member to two and eventually a Social Committee was set up. This was a suggestion from Don Tyson, who considered it would help the Association raise funds which were badly needed. It would also be ideal in organising events for the benefit of the Association.

The following extracts are taken from the minutes 1948 to September 1952 with a full description of the first meeting which was to select the Officers for the Association

Annual General Meeting 19th July 1948

Held at the Guard's Inn Leamington

This was the first Annual General Meeting of the Association since 1939. One would presume preliminary talks had taken place over the last 12 months, with the previous Chairman Treasurer and other interested bodies.
The Chairman John Wildsmith opened the meeting at 8pm.
In his opening remarks, he gave a brief resume of what had been done in keeping the Association accounts and cash book up to date The Minutes of the last Annual General Meeting were read and signed. A statement of accounts was presented, moved and adopted.

Various members commented on the very sparse attendance and it was suggested by more than one that not enough publicity had been given to interested parties about the meeting being held..
The Chairman insisted that although the attendance is small, the election of Officers, should now take place, he also said that the Association should be in the hands of active members and therefore he did not wish to be nominated for any Office. This also applied to Mr George Lewis the present Treasurer and to Mr Sidney Soden
The following were elected;
.

President	**Mr G Orme-tiley**
Chairman	**Mr G D utton**
Vice-Chairman	**Mr H Owen**
Secretary	**Mr G Pankhurst**
Treasurer	**Mr G Pankhurst.**
Management	**Mr J Joyner**
Auditors	**Messrs L Cecil, Mr Lewi**

The Question of Rules was left to a further meeting.

Very sincere votes of thanks were recorded to Mr John Wildsmith, to Mr George Lewis and Mr Sidney Soden for their efforts over the period of years that the Association was inactive. This was reference to the War years from 1939 to 1946

Minutes were kept from 1948 until 1952 and only interesting highlights will be printed, although this may be sometimes impossible.

After the Annual General Meeting, the next meeting was held at 8pm on Friday 20th August 1948 at the. Bedford Inn, Bedford Street, Leamington Spa

Mr G Dutton Chairman

Members present were - Messrs H Owen, L Cecil, J Wright, J Joyner, C Jackson, H Shuttleworth, J White, T Story and B Calahane.
The Chairman George Dutton pointed out to members the object of reviving the Association and hoped members would support the same and make it a flourishing Association

Rules were discussed and alterations were to be made.
Secretary to purchase 50 Copies and members were to pay for same on receipt.

Mr Charlie Jackson was elected to serve on the Management; the Monthly meeting was changed to the Third Monday in the Month. It was Proposed, Subscriptions should be 6s.6d (six shillings & sixpence) including the National Referees Affiliation

The Secretary pointed out that care should be taken with the accounts and it was felt that the financial position should not deteriorate. We should try to maintain a similar balance to what the last Treasurer handed over.

Tom Story raised the point of highlighting the Referees Association and the Benefits gained by being full members.
The position of Peter Watson becoming a member was raised and in view of the fact he was only 17, it was proposed and seconded, that he be granted Honorary Membership for the Season.
A letter from Mr W Rogers inviting the Association to becoming members of the County Referees Association was deferred for further details re-expenses, etc.

A Financial statement was given by the Secretary showing that there were 13 members' subscriptions, with the Donation giving a credit balance of
(Three pounds twelve shillings, five pence) £3.12.5p
Members were asked to reply as promptly as they could with correspondence from Clubs, and League Secretaries.

1949

Once the 1948 season had finished, an approach was made to the referees who were officiating before 1939, to find out if they would be interested in taking up active refereeing or become an Associate Member of the Association..
The Chairman remarked on the younger members we have and quoted Peter Watson nearly 18 years old and doing quite well as a Referee. These were the sort of members the Association was looking for.

When George Dutton addressed the meeting every one enjoyed his talk. He suggested the Association obtain speakers to cover other subjects. The County Referees Secretary Wilf Rogers who was invited along with Mr John Tonkiss gave members plenty of information on the Benefits of membership to the County Referees Committee, the aims of the Committee and the financial commitment. He also told members that problems in the refereeing world
were gradually being discussed at County Level through the insistence of the County Committee. The Association members after listening to Mr Rogers decided to join the County Referees Committee. This was voted on and carried; the cost per member was 6d (sixpence)

The Chairman then invited Mr Tonkiss who had been Secretary of the National Referees Association as well as holding a very important position in the Birmingham County Football Association, to give members a broad view of County Matters, which was to everyone's benefit. He talked of promotion and the movement of referees, also appointments in County games such as the Senior and the Junior Cup Competitions

He went on to give an excellent talk on all the aspects of Football and the County F.A's view and the way they approach the various problems that do happen.

Mr Rogers reminded every one of the County Rally and explained what the Rally was about and how all the Referees Associations or Societies in the Warwickshire and the Birmingham area sent teams to compete against each other, whether it be Cricket, Athletics, or Football. The idea is for a different Association or Society to organise it every year and invite all the Associations or Societies in the Birmingham and Warwickshire area. All the profits go to the organising Association or Society.

Both gentlemen were thanked for giving every one a pleasant evening this was proposed by the Chairman and seconded by H Owen.

A complaint was raised by a member Leslie Cecil concerning the press report in the local paper reference criticism of referees. This was left in the hands of the Chairman and Secretary who would investigate.

It was moved that we continue with Rule 11 (non-attendance). This is a fine of either 3d or 6d (three pence or sixpence) it seems to vary.

The Annual General Meeting would be held in May

Proposed and seconded that election of officers be by ballot at the open meeting, it was also brought to the notice of the members that the rules need looking at.

Promotion to Class1 (one) was extended to Jack Joyner and Charlie Jackson also Alex Walters, and Steve Barnett obtaining his Class 2 (two).

May 1949   Annual General Meeting

Held at the Bedford Inn Leamington

Chairman Mr George Dutton

The Chairman welcomed everyone to the meeting and remarked that it was nice to see our President in attendance, he also suggested that although it is the first Annual General Meeting since the Association was reformed, it is an opportunity to take a look at the Association Rules and set up a Committee to scrutinise and report back to the Council Meeting.

Previous Annual General Minutes were read and confirmed.

Election of Officers

President	Mr G Orme-Tiley
Chairman	Mr G Dutton
Vice –Chairman	Mr H Owen
Secretary	Mr G Pankhurst
Treasurer	Mr G Pankhurst
Management	Mr J Joyner & Mr C Jackson
Auditors	Messrs L Cecil & G Lewis

The Chairman did suggest a change of Meeting night as the Landlord is finding Monday Evening difficult and has asked if a change could be made. We could either change the evening or find another meeting place.

After a discussion the members proposed and seconded that we change the evening from a Monday to the Second Thursday in the month, this was carried by all the members present, the Landlord would be informed.

The Chairman closed the Annual General Meeting after that discussion and an ordinary Council meeting took place.

Promotion was the first item for discussion and the Chairman told members not to expect promotion too quickly and assured the members that he would further their aims.

A lengthy discussion took place on the position of local referees and the Coventry Allocation Committee, arising out of the letter from George Dutton, concerning the shortage of Referees for the Leamington Saturday League. The majority of members considered that it is up to the individual referee to officiate on what league he wishes to be on, although if you are tied to the Allocation system you do move from one League to another. Other referees said we should support the Leamington League and after the discussion the Chairman closed the meeting

A letter was received on Insurance for Referees. This was read to the members and it was agreed that if anyone wished to avail themselves of same, members were to contact the Secretary.

Alec Walters spoke about referees who officiate on the Memorial Park Coventry. If an Accident took place during the game requiring the services of the," St Johns First Aid", the Referee should give 3 (three) Blasts on his Whistle.

Alex Walters stated that at the Coventry Meeting the1951 Conference was discussed and Leamington was suggested as a likely venue. A lengthy discussion took place and the Secretary said we should wait until we get more information from the Midland Division.

Alex Walters suggested the Association have its own Referees Badge. Various members aired their views and it was agreed, that certain quotations be obtained for two or three dozen and members informed of the cost..

A letter was received from the Leamington League re a complaint from Radford St Nicholas FC, stating that a Warwick Referee had charged 4/- (four shillings) expenses, which was considered rather high. It was agreed that the letter lay on the table until the referee's explanation was forthcoming.

County Report by Jack Joyner. Football Magazine was now in Publication again. The Burton RA delegate reported that trouble still existed with the local FA. A member wanted support from the County RA, if a slander action was brought, he was told of the correct procedure to adopt.

Don Tyson asked, what would his position be if he did not receive a match from the Leamington League by Thursday? Could he take a match in the Stratford League? The Answer was "yes."

The Association has now been reformed since 1948 and the members have settled down reasonably well. Quite a few have obtained Promotion to the Senior Leagues after obtaining their Class1) or Class 2. The Secretary /Treasurer was responsible in keeping a watchful eye on the Accounts. By doing so it has allowed the Association to obtain good quality speakers.

The relationship between the Association and the various Leagues in the District has been beneficial to the members, who have benefited from the type of games they have been given by the Secretaries of the Leagues concerned. There was a little trouble with the Coventry Allocation system that was eventually sorted out. This pleased the Secretary of the Leamington & District Saturday Football League so that he could appoint referees to all his matches. Concern was expressed over some Leagues gradually building up the number of referees and one League has been generally selecting referees of a reasonable standard to officiate on their League. The Allocation Committee was in discussion with these Leagues and was hoping to settle the problem to everyone's benefit.

1950

George Dutton gave an excellent talk to the members on the attendance at meetings and the reason why every member should attend. It is for your benefit he said, if you want to progress in the Refereeing world. He urged referees to keep up the good standard, and told those who had received promotion in the latter year to keep working as there could be changes on the way. He said there was always room for improvement

He also invited all the Members to the next monthly meeting of the League, as a presentation would be made to Mr Harry Webster, the League Chairman who was retiring after a number of years in office. After his retirement he will be moving away from Leamington,

George Dutton told the members to keep up their subscriptions and it was proposed and seconded that members who had not paid their Subscriptions be written to and failing to reply their membership be discontinued.

County Report

Redditch Referees Association delegate at the County Referees meeting, suggested that a knock-out Quiz, be arranged between all the Associations, each Association having 6 members per team, and Questions be set on the Laws of the Game, Rules would have to be set up, most delegates welcomed the Competition, one suggestion was that the competition have three rounds of hard questions on a minute basis and one round of quick fire questions. This idea was sent to all the Associations in Birmingham &Warwickshire so the delegates could discus the Competition amongst their own members. Recommendation was moved at Leamington and the suggested Competition was considered a good idea, Secretary to inform the County Committee of the Associations approval. It was proposed that we enter a team in the competition, providing travelling was local

Secretary brought to the notice of members the cost of Blazer Badges at a cost of 76/-(seventy six shillings)per dozen. After a discussion it was suggested that a strip shall be worn under the National Badge, emblazoned, 'Leamington Association,' a strip designed by Brian Morfitt was accepted and to proceed, but we should have it altered to fit above the Badge. Most referees wore the badge on a Blazer and quite a number fitted them on to the Referees shirt.

It was agreed to enforce Rule 11 (this Rule is a fine of either 3 pence or 6 pence for failing to send apologies to the meeting.)..
It was proposed, the Leamington & District Saturday Football League Secretary be notified that Messrs Handy, Alcock and Neal, by virtue of unpaid subscriptions, are not now members of this Association.

May 1950   Annual General Meeting

Chairman George Dutton

The Chairman proceeded with the Election of Officers for the 1950/51 season.

George Orme-Tiley Esq was elected President again with the approval of the members and Mr George Dutton remained as Chairman for the next twelve months. The Vice- Chairman, Secretary, Treasurer and Management members were also elected to serve another twelve months. The two Auditors were quite happy to carry on auditing the Accounts.

The Chairman in his remarks thanked the members for the manner in which they had carried out their duties in connection with the Saturday League and considered that the standard of ability was very high in this area. He also spoke about the members who had been promoted to the Senior Leagues. He told them to work hard and enjoy the higher standard of Football.

Don Tyson spoke on the advisability of having a Social Committee, in view of the need to augment the Association Funds. This was set up and the elected members were co-opted on to the Management. This was the beginning and it proved very valuable to the Association eventually being incorporated into the Association Management Committee

The strictness of the Association in this period was very similar to the Pre-War era when members were fined and not given matches. I am still amazed every time I read those minutes, of how strict the Association was and the fines that were incurred when there was so much trouble in the Industrial World that you wondered how they survived, because money was very, very, hard to earn.

We move on now to the latter stages of the1950 and into the 1951 era.

Congratulations were given to Mr McTavish, on winning the Veterans' Race at the Tamworth Rally.

1951 Another lengthy discussion took place concerning the Conference it seems that members of other Associations talking about staging a Conference are guessing on the actual amount with figures of £25 or £50 (pounds) each Association has to give. The Secretary stated that some Associations had guaranteed a definite amount, but it was left to each Association or Society.

It was decided to get the final answer at the next County RA Meeting.

The Secretary spoke on the subject of having a Minute Secretary. If the situation arose that he could not attend a meeting, he would be able to take over and. have the Minutes up to date Henry Hall was elected as Minute Secretary

1951 Conference

This Association contributed £10 (Ten pounds) to the Conference Fund, and concern was still being expressed that the Conference may be staged in Leamington. This was dispelled when at the next County Meeting, it was moved the Conference be staged at Stratford, by Stratford Referees Association. This allowed Leamington to move on to other things such as a Sports Forum plus other events to raise funds and for the benefit of the members

Jack Joyner stated that Sir Stanley Rous was addressing the Birmingham Referees in November, and all Association had been invited and given the opportunity to listen to him It was felt that if possible some of our members might care to attend. Secretary to apply for 10 Tickets

Leamington Referees had been invited to enter the Coventry Referees Benevolent Cup unfortunately they were at home to Birmingham Referees who have a very strong team. It was suggested we try to get permission to stage the match at the Lockheed ground on Easter Tuesday. The Secretary said he had made a provisional request to stage the match there but was met with a firm no.

An autographed Ball will be used as a prize for the raffle, at the match on Easter Tuesday afternoon against Birmingham R.A.

Bernard Lowe suggested he could probably arrange for the match to be played on Henry Griffiths ground. The offer was accepted and the match took place on Easter Tuesday with Birmingham winning comfortably. The gate money raised 24/-(twenty four shillings) which went to the Benevolent Fund and the Expenses of 25/-(twenty five shillings) was paid for out of Association funds. .

Leslie Barnett enquired about the Ingersoll Referee's 45 minutes watch, could it be obtained..
The Secretary said that you could get one from Mr Jarvis Nuneaton @ 27/- (Twenty seven shillings) or in Leamington @ 30/- (Thirty shillings)

It was proposed the next speaker would be Harry Barratt, Coventry City Captain. He would be invited to address the meeting which could be held at either the Avenue Hotel, or the Willougby Arms, with all local Clubs and Officials invited to be present In the absence of Harry Barratt, Mr N D Evans be invited.
Congratulations to Jack Joyner on his F A Cup Appointment.

1951

An invitation by Coventry Referees Association, to members, on the occasion of the visit of Mr Walter Winterbottom England Team Manager, this was accepted with thanks.

Derek Clark raised the question of very late notification by the home clubs and stated a case where he received some post dated the Saturday on which the match was played. Another point was brought to the notice of the meeting that some clubs were not providing Linesmen as laid down in the League Rules. It should be brought to the notice of the Secretary of the Leamington League.
Congratulations of this Association were extended to Harry Owen and George Pankhurst, in being selected to officiate at the Amateur International England v Ireland, on February 3rd 1951.
It was proposed and seconded that a vote of thanks be accorded to Henry Hall and Alcc Walters for the effort they have put in coaching candidates for the Referees Examination, having a 100% pass rate.

Harry Barratt Coventry City FC

The Chairman on behalf of the Members welcomed Harry Barratt Coventry City F.C, also Doug Paget Warwickshire RA representative and Vic Edmunds (Coventry Referees.).
Harry Barratt gave members a talk of Professional Football but no report on his talk was recorded and nothing from the other two guest in the minutes of the meeting.

The provisional date for the R A Quiz 2nd round Leamington v Birmingham. was Tuesday 20th March, at 8pm.
It was proposed and seconded that refreshments be provided for the Evening, the Team to be selected from the following members; Messrs, Jack Joyner, Alex Walters, Jack Wright, Henry Hall, Ken Cox, Don Tyson.
.
The Secretary informed the members that he had received a letter from a member who was asking for help and explaining that he was in very distressful circumstances, the Secretary refused to name the member and after a lengthy discussion it was:-proposed that this Association grant the member 10/-(Ten Shillings) per week for one Month, when various circumstances had been looked into, also that the information be passed on to the National Referees Association for their observation.

The Chairman stated that a Referee had cancelled a game as the ground was unfit for play and he understood the League Secretary sought a second opinion on the matter, which he Alex Walters did not consider justified.   .
Congratulations were extended to Jack Wright on obtaining his Class One, and to Messrs Bernard Lowe, Cyril Aldred, William Aldred, and Peter Watson to Class Two..
Mr Jack Joyner was proposed as the Delegate to the Conference at Stratford in June.

June 1951 Annual General Meeting

Held at The Willoughby Arms

The Chairman

George Dutton welcomed members at the beginning of the Annual General Meeting also everyone to the Willoughby Arms, at the same time he introduced Mr and Mrs Cox who were the new Landlords. He told every one that all meetings would be held at the Willoughby from tonight. In welcoming Mr Ben Cox, the Chairman allowed him to say a few words and Mr Cox began by welcoming the Association to the Willoughby and hoped
that our stay would be a happy one. He told every one he was a Professional player and finished his playing days at Northampton Town, who were a good Club to play for.
The Chairman opened the A G M when Mr Cox had finished, by telling every one that he would be relinquishing the Office of Chairman due to pressure of business.
The Chairman was thanked for his service to the Association and the help he had always given.

The Accounts were presented and accepted the only changes made at the A G M was a new Chairman in Tom Story who was elected after a four way vote. Alex Walters was elected Vice-Chairman and George Pankhurst became Secretary / Treasurer for the fourth year running and he was pleased that Henry Hall had become the Assistant Secretary. Ken Cox and Peter Watson became Auditors for the next twelve months. The Management Committee members Jack Joyner and Charlie Jackson were again elected as well.

The President George Orme-Tiley gave a very pleasant address to the members and said how pleased he was to be involved. He wished every one well and hoped they enjoyed their football
The Social Committee was proposed by Alex Walters and seconded by Charlie Jackson, who both remarked on how beneficial this new committee is to the Association and hoped they continued to be so. The members elected were Jack Wright and Don Tyson.

Rules:- The rules were passed as they stand, except that in future all Meetings will be at **the Willoughby Arms, on the 2nd Tuesday every Month commencing at 7.30pm.**
The meeting closed with the, 'Health of the President'.

Council Business

Arising from the Council Business it was proposed that we stick strictly to Rule 11.
The following new members were welcomed into the Association, they were, Messrs, J Mortimer, Bert Gwynne, G Elstone and F Millerchip, after passing the Examination.
The County R.A, report was presented by the Secretary and was duly adopted.
A donation of 10/-(Ten shillings) be sent for the Rally Prize Fund
A lengthy discussion took place reference a complaint against a member regarding his control at one of their matches, the complainant being Stratford MSC. It was proposed and seconded that the Club be written to for a more detailed explanation, and a copy sent to the Referee for his comments. The matter is to be discussed at a future meeting.
It was proposed by Harry Owen and seconded by Alex Walters that the Leamington Saturday League is asked to allow a delegate from the Association to attend their
Council Meetings Alex Walters was nominated and elected. League Secretary is to be informed.
Arising out of the complaint by Stratford MSC Concerning the referee, the Club had been asked to send a fuller explanation. The Secretary reported that no correspondence had been received from the football Club, and information had been received by the Treasurer that the referee concerned was not a member of this Association

The Chairman decided that the issue should remain on file and inform Stratford MSC that the matter is closed.

The question of late starts on the local league was again brought up and after various members had made further complaints it was agreed that the representative of the League
should report it to the meeting. Another point was discussed, concerning Clubs with similar colours this could also be raised at the League Meeting.
The issues had been brought to the notice of the League by the delegate and it was left in the hands of the clubs.

A letter was received from Coventry Referees Association, re the question of members participating in the Allocation System. This caused a lengthy discussion, the members feeling it should be left to individual members, It was proposed by Peter Watson and
seconded by Don Tyson, that no action be taken for the remainder of the Season and that the matter be raised again at the April meeting 1952.

A letter was received from Captain George Allen, Chairman London Army FA and it was agreed that the date and arrangements be left in the hands of the Secretary
Bernard Lowe complained about the Leamington League's method of appointments, stating that he had refereed the last four games of E.M.E.B., Secretary asked for the information in writing, so that he could look into it
Leamington South End complained at the lack of co-operation by referees with club linesman.

1952

A Special Meeting was arranged for the 18th January 1952, commencing at 8pm. The Speaker for the Evening was Captain George Allen of the London Army Football Association; Captain Allen was Treasurer of the National Referees Association.
Captain Allen gave an extremely interesting address to about 25 referees and players. At the conclusion a vote of thanks was moved by George Dutton and seconded by Henry Hall. Captain Allen suitably responded.

Alex Walters raised the question of Election of Officers at the Annual Meeting. After a discussion, it was proposed by Jack Wright and seconded by Stan Brown that nominations to be handed in by the April Meeting. Voting papers to be sent to each member, containing nominations for respective officers and to be returned for the Annual General Meeting.

A letter from Whitnash Charity Cup inviting the Association to provide Linesmen for their Competition this year was read. It was proposed and seconded that appointments shall be made by Ballot, but Class One Referees should not be included. This was defeated and all members are to be included.

Correspondence from the Divisional Secretary was read regarding Notice of Motions, which was put forward by the various Societies for alteration of Rules at the Annual Conference. They were discussed at length and the following recommendations were made
Election of Divisional Vice President It was proposed Leamington Referees Association to nominate Mr Tom Owen of Coventry Referees, for the position of Vice-President Midland Division.

Coventry Referees' Benevolent Cup Football Match, Leamington v Coventry, played on April 22nd at Coventry Amateurs ground. Kick-off 7pm.

Leamington's Team as follows: Fred Mortimer, Leslie Barnett and Alex Walters, George Elstone Ken Cox, Jack Wright, A (Bert) Gwynne, David Clark, Ron Pemberton Brian Lowe, and Reg Woodward.

Ballot papers were sent out to the Members, with notice of A.G.M.

The Association had been successful in obtaining 2 (two) Cup final Tickets, draw to take place at the Social Evening.

Congratulations were offered to Charlie Jackson on his election to the Parish Council at LeekWootton.

Coventry Allocation Committee

This matter had been deferred until this meeting, the previous correspondence from Coventry Referees Association was read and after a lengthy discussion it was proposed by John Millerchip, seconded by Brian Lowe, that each member should be at liberty to officiate on either the Leamington League, or the Allocation Committee, providing their intention was made known to the Secretary of the Leamington Referees' Association. A circular is to be sent to all members, for that purpose . .

A presentation was made to Mr & Mrs Cox at the Social Evening, in appreciation of the service we had received whilst using the Willoughby as our Headquarters.

Mr A Carr Secretary of the Coventry Benevolent Cup, informed Leamington that we play Stratford Referees on August 31st

A report on the 1952 Conference was given; this was held at Southport in June.

Congratulations were accorded to George Dutton on his recent Appointment as Chairman of the Birmingham County Referees Committee.

Appointments to the Birmingham Senior Cup Competition either as Referee or Linesmen are as follows: - Harry Owen, Jack Wright, Jack Joyner and Henry Hall.

Mr Arthur Ellis the Football Referee, who is on the List of International Referees, would be coming to Leamington in November

Suggested venues were discussed so that interested people and members would be able to listen to Mr Ellis.

It was proposed that it is left to the Social Committee and that Ken Cox and Arnold Rouse be co-opted on to the Committee. The Committee to make the necessary arrangements

It was suggested that we enter the Quiz competition again this season.

Social activities were discussed and the possibility of a Christmas Party being organised.

The team to play Stratford Referees at Football was selected from the following.

Charlie Jackson, or Fred Mortimer, Leslie Barnett, Alex Walters, George Elstone, Ken Cox, Jack Wright, A(Bert) Gwynne, Arnold Rouse, Jack Wilson, David Clarke, Reg Woodward, or Cyril Aldred. Linesman Henry Hall

30th September 1952

Extra Ordinary Meeting was called at the Willoughby Arms

Chairman presiding supported by other members.
The meeting was called at the express wish of George Dutton Secretary of the Leamington Saturday League Since the request was made George Dutton was taken ill, and George Pankhurst briefly outlined the object of the Meeting.

The Leamington Saturday League were greatly concerned at the small number of referees being Allocated to the League, by the Coventry Allocation Committee, this together with the Leamington members who had left the district and members who had not registered for the season was causing the League to be about 8(eight) referees short every month.
George Dutton asked members to consider temporarily withdrawing from the Allocation System, and when they have open dates to give first consideration to the Leamington Saturday League.

The September Minutes were the last ones to be taken by the Secretary, another minute book was started and minutes recorded until the December of 1959. These Minutes were evidently misplaced and information concerning member's promotion and service to the Association was lost,

A written article has been produced from the 1952/53 to the 1960's giving facts and figures covering the improvements the Association has made where possible, with general information given by the few ex-Referees who were members at the time.

Referees who were members of the Association from 1948 up to 1952/3 season

Messrs G Dutton, G Pankhurst, C Jackson, J Joyner, H Owen, L Cecil, J Wright, G Perks, M Clarke, P White, Morfitt, T Story, V Hunt, J McTavish, A Walters, H Hall, S Barnett, W Aldred, C Aldred, E Teale, K Cox, P Watson, C Ayton, R Woodward, D Tyson, D Clarke, R Pemberton, J Wyatt, F Mortimer, A Rouse, D Tayler, B Lowe, A Gwynne J Brown, B Millerchip, A Elstone, E Alcock.

Allocation System

After the War when Leagues and Clubs were re-forming, it became obvious there would be a desperate shortage of Referees and it was felt some kind of allocation system was needed. The referees would then be evenly distributed amongst the Leagues. Coventry was the only area where football was played during the war. Leagues were beginning to organise fixture lists for Clubs taking part, and referees were soon officiating on the leagues they had been allocated to.

The first Allocation Secretary was Albert Carr from Coventry Referees Association and a committee was then set up. George Robinson and Cyril Gould were elected and other senior referees joined the committee. This enabled referees to be placed on the various leagues in Coventry and the surrounding District. In 1952 the system was going strong and you were allocated to a league by the committee, you were unable to pick and choose. The system was a good thing for referees, it gave you very valuable experience and once you received promotion you were given better games to referee.

Although it was Coventry who set up the allocation system, the involvement of George Dutton in the scheme was apparent. He was the Secretary of the Leamington Saturday Football League and with the serious shortage of Referees the League should have benefited. This was not the case and the Secretary was always seeking referees to cover his matches The problem gradually got worse when one league in Coventry decided to form their own list of Referees,

This was in 1953. The Management Committee of the League were not happy with the standard of referees they were allocated. They considered they needed good quality referees to benefit the clubs in the league and they eventually obtained sufficient number of referees to complete the fixtures. This opened the door for others to follow. It wasn't a good thing to ave happened. Nearly all the Leagues eventually had their own list of referees.

The allocation system disbanded shortly afterwards and in its place the clearing house was set up. Again it was the same Committee that organised the matches; George Robinson and Cyril Gould were the Coventry members.

If any referees from Coventry, Leamington, or other Associations wanted a game. They could ring the phone number and possibly get one. It did not matter what sort of match you were given, you had a game. The clearing house as it was known carried on until the late 1970's.

Chapter 4

1953 to1960
Headquarters – Willoughby Arms   Leamington Spa

The minutes of this period have been misplaced which is rather unfortunate. It means to record the events that took place, as accurately as possible help was needed from colleagues like John Sollis, Frank and Bill Wall, Ken Eastbury who were members at the time. It was also handy having the League Handbook of 1957, all these little things helped. The Association was quite healthy as far as members were concerned and we had referees on the various Leagues in the area and making full use of the allocation system.

The members we had on the Football League kept an interest in the Association and so did the referees on the Birmingham Combination. The local Referees were very fortunate in the choice of Leagues they could officiate on, the standard was very high and the experience gained was valuable especially when they were trying to get their promotion so they would be able to referee higher grade football

Whilst we are trying to put together a picture of the Association it is essential that all referees obtain the experience by refereeing on junior leagues. As the experience grows so does the confidence, which is what a referee requires reaching the standard needed for the County Referees Committee to promote them, either to a Class 2 or a Class 1. Since 1948 a gradual change has taken place, we have referees in a position to reach the Football League with new members joining Leamington who were already on the Football League.

We had changes amongst the Officers in 1954, a new Secretary /Treasurer in Ken Cox was elected, also we had a new Chairman in George Pankhurst who took over from Tom Story. Others who have been with the Association since 1948 were still holding various offices, people like Harry Owen, Alex Walters and Henry Hall and of course George Dutton who kept an eye on the way the Association was moving.

We had the allocation system, promoted by Coventry RA. This allocated referees to the various Leagues, suitable to the Referees qualifications, which again was very good experience. It was unfortunate a League wanted to set up their own list of referees. The League eventually succeeded, it was the finish of the system.

It has always been the aim of the Association to keep the referees moving and having two members like Alex and Henry on the coaching side, it helped the new members who had taken up refereeing. The period between 1954 and 1959 was difficult for the members of the Association although there was plenty of refereeing available for the referees who have only just joined, but the more experienced referees that had gained experience were itching to move forward. This was not easy especially with the change of Secretary and committee and the new Leagues did not really benefit the members straight away. Time would be on their side, it depends on the County Football Association.

With the Monthly meetings at the Willoughby Arms and being well looked after by Mr & Mrs Cox the meetings were always a pleasant affair and we had members from other Associations come and talk to us.

Every one enjoyed listening to them it didn't matter whether the subject was important or not they made it interesting. We even enjoyed the banter that went on at the meetings, a lot of positive thoughts came out of these discussions and most of them were on the 'Laws of Association Football'

Meeting nights at the time were held on a Friday Evening, this seemed to be the best night and it helped referee members who worked at the local factories where shift work and nights were a regular feature.

There were occasions when it was difficult to make the meeting, so your apology was always recorded and if any information was important you would be told by members who would be at the meeting.

Promotion was a bone of contention. And from 1954 we seemed to miss out, it was disappointing to some members when they were getting good results from the matches they refereed and the Clubs were also giving them good marks. It was noted that referees from Coventry were getting promoted, questions were asked at the monthly meetings, and we were told that League Secretaries were not sending the marks referees were getting from clubs to the County Referees Committee. This was a disappointment to the members and we all felt that if promotion relied on the Secretary of the League sending the marks to the County FA, another type of system of promoting referees should be looked at, also if members do not get promoted, their chances of refereeing in senior football would not be available.

Rumours occasionally rebound when they are talked about, the rumours that were being mentioned consisted of new Leagues being formed by George Dutton and the changes would benefit referees especially the younger members. We were told referees and linesmen would be needed, and everyone was asked to make an effort to obtain candidates to become referees, there would not be a shortage when the new Leagues started.

Tom Story and George Pankhurst, along with Alex Walters and Henry Hall, made every effort to obtain referees, so they could eliminate the shortage. All candidates were assessed by Alex and Henry and coached on the 'Laws of the Game.' They did not have any fancy equipment, just the 'Referees Chart' which was a little green covered booklet with the 17 Laws inside and a few pictures describing the Offside Law.

After being coached and ready for the Examination, the nearest place to go was the B T H Social Club, Coventry, to be examined by George Dutton, Tom Cook, and Cyril Stafford. You had to answer 20 Questions on the 'Laws of Association Football' and you also had a colour test just to see if you were colour blind or not. If you had a problem you sat down and had a talk to George Dutton, if he was satisfied with your answers he would pass you. The next job was to register with the Birmingham County Football Association, This would cost you a small amount, and you were given a number, and told that you were a Class 3 referee. After being registered with the County FA you had a choice and the opportunity to join your local Referees Association and placed on the League as a Referee

A big change came about in 1954 when Ken Cox became the Secretary /Treasurer in place of George Pankhurst and Tom Story lost his position as Chairman to George Pankhurst
Most of the other officers were the same including the Social Committee which was formed a few years ago by Don Tyson and the two elected were Peter Watson and Arnold Rouse. Another change was being considered and that was a new Football League set up by George Dutton, with teams of good standing from the Leamington Saturday League and other Leagues in the area.

This League would benefit the referees in the Association and those who were Class 1(one) would definitely benefit, which is why promotion to the referees was essential.

Most of the members were pleased about the changes and for once it seemed the rumours that were talked about a few months ago were coming to fruition. Instead of one new League it finished up with two new Leagues, one in 1953 and the other in 1955. Both being set up by George Dutton and they were comprised of good quality teams. In fact one of the Leagues was the stepping stone to the Football League. Mr Dutton did have a very good idea for referees although it was never used due to the changes. In fact quite a few referees lost out for no reason at all, because promotion was not available. It made you wonder whether certain people in local Football were pulling strings More information on the Leagues in (Football Leagues)

George Pankhurst became the Chairman of the Leamington Saturday League with Frank Bambrook as Secretary. It seemed George Pankhurst would be leading a very busy life and concern was expressed that we as referees may suffer, although it did not seem a problem at first but George did say that Friday evening was not a good night for him to attend meetings. He always tried to attend even if it was late. One such problem that happened was when a Dinner/Dance was being organised in 1955 /1956 season.

This had to be cancelled through lack of support, a meeting was held and strong words were expressed. One member resigned through the arguments and the Chairman told another member to shut up and stop waffling, just make your point. The trouble was members were not interested in going, they preferred the Spa Hotel where we were the previous year. We were made very welcome, we also had a good meal and the drinks were not expensive, the only problem was we were restricted to numbers.
Within a couple of years the Association had another problem when Ken Cox retired as Secretary/Treasurer due to his Company moving down to Portsmouth to set up business. We lost a good Secretary and a good friend.

The next member to take on the Secretary's job was Wilf Blount. He was ex-RAF and lived in Wellesbourne. He was voted into both jobs at the next Annual General Meeting. With George Pankhurst still the Chairman. The Social Committee was not disbanded as some members thought it would be but became involved with the Committee that formed the Management, so Peter Watson and Arnold Rouse carried on as Management and Social Members although they were only used when the Chairman thought it necessary.

A surprise was on the cards at the Annual General Meeting when Tom Story became the second member to be made a Life –Member of the Association for the service he had given to the Association since 1948. This was a surprise, all Tom had been was as Chairman and Vice-Chairman of the Association, still the members elected him. Although Tom had done quite a lot of work on behalf of the Association and he was very well liked by the members
The Association's first member was George Dutton who was made a Life-Member in 1936 this again was for the amount of work he did outside the Association as well as being involved with internal matters.

In August we were very surprised to hear of the illness that overtook the President Mr Orme-Tiley. It seems that he was taken ill and passed away the same month. Having met the President at our Meetings it was a shock. When you met George Orme-Tiley, you found him very pleasant and he was always interested in what you were doing and how far you were hoping to get as a referee.

He passed away in August 1955. At the A G M in May he seemed full of life and gave every one an excellent talk and all he had was a Football and a piece of Leather After the meeting we all had a drink and drank to his health. Quite a few of the members who were able to go to his funeral and at the Council Meeting in September a minutes silence was held.

After Tom Story was made a Life-Member in 1955 a move was on the cards for George Pankhurst who had worked hard since the Association was reformed in 1948. It was moved that he should be made a Life-Member at the next Annual General Meeting, this made George the third Life-Member. The work that George did for the Association as Secretary /Treasurer was important and made the Association stronger as the members moved on. With George on the Football League as well the name of Leamington would be mentioned quite a number of times, his involvement with the new Combination was a big help. .

One of our referees Henry Hall suffered a serious accident whilst refereeing. It seems that he slipped on a tuft of grass and snapped the Tendons in both feet. He was taken to Hospital and had quite a few operations to repair the damage done to his ankles. None were successful so Henry finished up on crutches and never walked properly again.
This was a blow to the Association because Henry was a very active man and helped Alex Walters do the Coaching. He would be missed by the members although he always said he would instruct any one who wanted to be a referee.

The period of time between 1956 and 1960 is very difficult to put together, the movement of referees was gradual with Alex Walters and Peter Watson on the Southern League and West Midland Regional League. Both finished up on the Football League we also had George Pankhurst as a referee although he retired from the Football League during this period. We still had Geoff Perks and the newcomer to the Association, John Jays who was a referee on the Football Combination. He was also on the Football League, as a Linesman.

The Referees that were Class 2(two) or Class 3(three) were impatiently waiting to see if promotion was coming their way. Unfortunately for them it was not possible and promotion for any Classification was becoming scarce. A number of referees who joined the Association in the 1956 period were the ones that were being frustrated, it did not matter who the referee was, and you would be hoping to get some encouragement from the County Football Association.
We have complained before about the problem of Promotion and we were still getting the stock answer from the County blaming the Leagues. We found this was not quite correct in the Leamington area, because the League had sent them through to the County Football Association. It was a very disappointing period for some of the referees who had been refereeing since 1953.
A question was asked why we are having these problems when we have two members of our Association as members of the Birmingham County Football Association and one was the Delegate to the Birmingham Referees County Committee.

Disappointment was affecting some of the referees because there were plenty of opportunities for the up and coming referees to ply their trade in the Warwickshire Combination with most of the referees below Class 1 (one) operating as linesmen and if you received your Class 1 (one) you still had to do 12 (twelve) months as a linesman and you may get the occasional chance to referee, so it was up to you to have a good game, the same thing happened to referees who moved into the area. They still had to do 12 (months) as a linesman.   .
What upset a few of the referees was the fact that some of the referees who were on the Warwickshire Combination List were Ex-Football League Referees and well pass their sell by date.

George Pankhurst, told the members when he was questioned, that they were only doing a few matches to help the League get more stability His reasoning was correct because by the 1960s all the Referees on the list were the ones that had moved on through the system when the Combination had started..

Even with all the problems the Association was having we were still getting candidates joining and taking the examination to become referees. We had plenty of activities taking place with Quiz competitions against other Associations a Buffet would be laid on which was enjoyed by everyone. We played Coventry and Stratford at football, they were enjoyable matches.. The meetings were always interesting and majority of the subjects concerned problems that members were having when they went out refereeing.

In 1957 we had another Secretary leave the Association. Wilf Blount had been offered a position in an Arab Airline Company so he resigned from the Association and with his wife moved out to the Arab States. This meant the Association would have to find another Secretary. The member who took on this position was Peter Watson, but he became Secretary only and Jack Wright became the Treasurer.

The Association carried on as normal with the monthly meetings still being held on a Friday Evening. Speakers were occasionally invited to come and speak to the members and we always seemed to have Ron Warnke (Football League) and David Scholfield coming along to Leamington to talk to us.

They were always interesting especially when they talked about refereeing on the Football League and the problems you may have and how you quickly learned to deal with them.

The National Press reporters were a little bit different and you had to be careful what you said and how you said it.

We had Alf Bond from London who gave us a talk about his experiences whilst refereeing on the Football League. Alf Bond had been on the Football League for a number of years. He was different to other referees in that he had only one arm. This did not stop him becoming a very good referee and his talk to the packed meeting room was full of stories and interesting situations that he came across whilst he was refereeing. The reason we were able to have Alf Bond at our meeting was that he was the referee at Coventry City FC home game and he stayed over for the week-end with Mr and Mrs Pankhurst. A similar situation happened when we had Arthur Ellis come to Leamington to give the members a talk. He was another Referee who had reached the top and the advice he gave members was very informative and those who took it on board found it instructional. One thing he told the members was when he was 16 (sixteen) he was told by a member from his County FA who was watching him to put his refereeing kit away and forget refereeing. That annoyed me he told his audience, so I worked very hard, kept myself fit and proved him wrong.

As far as the Association was concerned the latter years of the 50s were beginning to benefit the Association. Membership was on a high and referees were having good reports whilst the Willoughby Arms was still catering for the members. It was a sad loss to the Association when Mrs Cox passed away after a short illness. Mr Cox ran the Pub on his own until he brought in a manageress who took over organising everything. Then we started to have trouble with bookings. Quite often we found the room was double booked, it did not make any difference to the manageress; we told her we had booked the rooms on a twelve monthly basis. We often had to use another Public house just up the road and they were very helpful allowing us to use the smoke room. With all this happening, although no blame could be placed on the Committee, the problem was the manageress who was making a mess of the bookings, which were not recorded properly.

Pressure of work did not help the Secretary and the Chairman who was Secretary of the Warwickshire Combination, told members that Friday Evening was becoming very difficult for him to attend. His priorities at the moment was the Combination with matches being cancelled and referees cancelling appointments   George always apologised for his absence and would attend when he was able to.

The Leamington Saturday Football League which had been established since 1909 was in the process of organising a celebration for the League's 50 (fifty) years. All sorts of plans were being looked at, with a special match against the Amateur Club Pegasus. Fund raising was essential (a section has been written about the event in Leagues).

Problems arose at the beginning of the 1960 season, this was over another Annual Dinner having to be cancelled, which had been arranged yet there was very little support for it. This episode seemed to upset the officers and the members were told they would hold a special meeting to find out the reason why nobody was interested. The members preferred to go to another Hotel where prices were reasonable. It was a difficult time and a number of referees were very disappointed at the lack of promotion again. Concern about promotion which is essential to referees, so they can move up the promotion ladder was more important than the Annual Dinner. A few members were talking about having a change of Management at the next Annual General Meeting.
One of the senior member said that events for the last few years had been very frustrating for every one and the problems with the Willoughby had been settled so the Association should be able to move forward and express their views at the meetings instead of talking outside .That would be the correct thing to do. With all the problems, no one can blame the Secretary or the Chairman they had done everything they could to keep the Association on an even keel. We have to look forward to the 1960s.

The extracts from the minutes between 1960 and 1970 will give you an insight into the workings of the Association, the changes that were made, and how the young referees and newcomers to the Association started to put Leamington on the map. It was a move in the right direction

Chapter 5

Leamington &District Referees' Association

President's -1921 to 2006

The Association has had three long serving Presidents from 1931 until the present date.

The first President was a gentleman named," George Orme-Tiley," who was invited to stand by the Association in 1931 and continued in office until 1939, when the Referees Association closed down.

After the war and the Association were reformed, "George Orme-Tiley," was invited once again to become the President of Leamington Referees, which office he accepted and served until 1955 when he died in the August of that year.

Between 1955 and 1961, the Presidents of the Association were the Mayor's of Leamington. And again in 1964 to1965

In 1960, Councillor Edwin H Fryer was made President of the Association and hc held that office until 1964

In 1965 the members decided to bring about a change and George Dutton was invited to become the Association's President. George Dutton, who was already a "Life Member "of the Association, accepted the position and was President until 1976, when he passed away after a short illness in February that year.

At the 1976 Annual General Meeting the Members proposed Arnold W Rouse to become the President of the Association, a position that was accepted and he has remained in office up to the present.

A brief history of the Presidents follows on from here.

George Orme- Tiley

President from 1931 to1938, and 1947 to 1955

Mr George Orme-Tiley was born in 1883 at Bath.
He was Educated in Bath and became a Chartered Accountant.
He was a private Secretary to a Somerset Member of Parliament, and was recommended for similar service to the Honourable R.G Verney, who later became the 10th Lord Willoughby –de-Broke.

During his service to Lord Willoughby–de-Broke, George Orme-Tiley became Joint Secretary to the Warwickshire Hunt Horse School and the Warwickshire Brood Mare Society.
His interest in Sport involved, Boxing, Football and Cricket, although he was well known in Kineton for his generosity and a great supporter of Village life. He organised fetes, athletic events and boxing Tournaments.

He was a promoter of Tiley's sparring Eight-Boxing Team and a Donor of Tiley's Perpetual Challenge Cup; this was for teams from the South Warwickshire Football Clubs.

He was also a President of Stratford-on-Avon Boxing Club and in 1952 he became President of Kineton Wasps Football Club.

In 1922 he became a Scout Master in Kineton, taking Scouts on Camping Holidays to the Seaside. George Orme-Tiley was the Clerk of the Parish of Kineton retiring in 1952 after 33 years' service.

Despite all this activity over the years he still found time to become President of the Leamington &District Referees Association. He was invited to become President by George Dutton, accepting this position which he retained until 1939, when the War caused Leamington Referees to close down.
On the Resumption of the Association, George Dutton and George Pankhurst wrote to George Orme-Tiley inviting him to become President again. This he did and his generosity showed when he sent a donation to the Association funds. He continued as President until 1955.

During his time as President he usually attended the Annual General Meetings and always gave a very interesting address, although in 1953 he gave a talk to the members concerning Leather it was absolutely brilliant. All the time he held the office of President whilst in the Association. George Orme-Tiley was held in affection by the members for the generous way he treated and respected people.

George Orme-Tiley was married to Alice
Alice died on the 22nd August 1950 aged 66.
George died on the 25th August 1955 aged 73.

It seems that George Orme-Tiley spread his support in a very wide area and his generosity knew no bounds.
At his Funeral, the Rev Wilson- Horswill, referred to him as "This Great Man" who spent so much of his life giving service to others. .

Presidents
The period from 1955 to 1965

During this period and after the previous President (Mr George Orme-Tiley) had passed away in the August of 1955.
It was decided at the Annual General Meeting of the Association to invite the Mayors of Leamington to become the Association's Presidents whilst they held the office of Mayor.

This was carried out until 1960 when the nominated Mayor declined the opportunity, and it was offered to Councillor Robert Fryer, who had been Mayor of Leamington in 1953 to 1955.

Councillor Fryer accepted the Honour.

Herewith the Presidents from:

1956 to 1958   The Mayor of Leamington - Councillor Eric Lucas

1958 to 1959   The Mayor of Leamington - Councillor Frank Grundy

1959 to 1960   The Mayor of Leamington - Councillor Thomas H Saunders

1960 to 1964   The Mayor of Leamington - Councillor Edwin, H Fryer

1964 to 1965   The Mayor of Leamington - Councillor Norman Slater

The Mayors of Leamington that were elected from 1956 to 1960 were not really interested in the Association and they did not seem very interested in Football.

Although we did have one who was very keen to talk about the Sport and that was Councillor Thomas Saunders.

We retained Teddy Fryer as our President until 1964, he was a little more affable than the majority of the previous Mayors and he attended all the functions he was invited to

Alderman Fryer was very interesting to listen to when he attended our Annual General Meetings and he enjoyed the banter between the members

One of the reasons he was elected to be President was that the members enjoyed his company and Leamington had a succession of Lady Mayors who were not interested in Football in general, so the Members voted for him to carry on We considered that he was a good servant to town as a Councillor and eventually an Alderman.

George Dutton

President 1965 to 1976

George was elected to the position of President of the Association in 1965. This was a position he thoroughly enjoyed and as long as you kept him informed of events in the Association he was quite happy.

George took up Refereeing in the 1920's, Joining the Leamington &District Referees Association as well as being a member of Coventry Referee's Association.
Chairman of Leamington Referees in 1926, he retained that position until 1934 and served on the Management of the Association.
George was made a 'Life Member' of the Leamington & District Referees Association in 1936 and was presented with an inscribed Mantle Clock.
During the War years he was involved with Coventry Referees, yet still retained his links with referees from Leamington
He helped reform the Association in 1948 and was Chairman until 1951 when he retired from holding office to concentrate on the Leamington & District Saturday Football League
In 1953, George Dutton started the, "South Warwickshire Football League" and then became Secretary to the South Birmingham & District Football League with the Birmingham Combination eventually becoming the "West Midland Regional Football League" taking on the Secretary's Job until the early 1960's when he retired.

As the delegate to the Birmingham County Football Association, George eventually became more involved with County matters and became Chairman of various Committees as well as becoming Chairman of the County Football Association from 1955 till 1970 and finally he became a Councillor to the Football Association. Until 1976

During the War George Dutton was co-opted on to the Town Council as a Conservative Members for the East Ward of Warwick, successfully retaining that seat until 1947 when he was defeated at the polls. He was a regular member, of 'All Saints Church' Emscote and involved in Church activities

George received many Cup games and was on the Football League as a Linesman in the earlier part of the 1930s

His service to the Football League will be in the Chapter 'Football Referees'

George Dutton was a dour man, very stern and strict and discipline was his Forte. He passed away in Warwick Hospital after a short illness on February 25th 1976

Arnold William Rouse
Life Member National Referees Association 2003
President 1976

Arnold Rouse was 28 years old when he took up refereeing and was coached by Henry Hall. He then passed the Examination at the B.T.H Club Coventry in 1952 and joined the Referees Association in August of that year. He was elected to the Social Committee at the 1952 September meeting, since that date he has held the following positions in the Association such as Auditor and Social & Management member.

Became Treasurer in 1960

Secretary & Treasurer in 1966 retiring from being treasurer in 1968

Secretary until he resigned in 1972/73 season.

Became the Meetings Organiser in 1973 till 1975

He then became Chairman in 1975. In 1976 he was asked if he would like to become the Association President since George Dutton had passed away

This was accepted and he is still the President now (2006)

Since 1976 he has supported the functions and sporting events that have been organised and attended as many management and Council meetings as he could.

Arnold became an Assessor in 1969 for the Birmingham County FA and has enjoyed assessing the young referees being particularly pleased when they received promotion to Senior Football Leagues.

The newsletter was his next objective and in 1995 he became the Editor and produced the monthly newsletter with help from two members until 2004

He Received his Meritorious Service Award in 1979 from the Divisional Vice-President Eric Adams Esq

He was made a Life Member of Leamington Referees Association in 1981.

50th Year Service Award from the National Referees Association 2002

50th Year Service Award from the Football Association 2002

He became a Life Member of the National Referees Association at the Cheltenham Conference 2003 the Award being presented to him by Peter Willis Esq Immediate Past President and the Life Members Trophy and the 50th year award were finally presented by the President John Bunn Esq at the Annual General Meeting in Leamington, February 2004.

The Football Association award was presented to Arnold by Jim Horrocks Vice-Chairman Birmingham County FA

Delegate to the Leamington & District Football Leagues (Saturdays), Coventry and North Warwickshire League and the Birmingham &Warwickshire Joint Referees County Committee.

Has been a member of the Management Committee of the Leamington & District Sunday Football League, since the 1970's, becoming, Vice –Chairman, Chairman and eventually President in 1994 Promoted with Andy Semple, the George Dutton Challenge Cup, and a Charity Competition in 1976, he then started the, 'Andy –Campbell Charity Cup' in 1984.
Secretary for both Cups until, 1990 and then Chairman
Vice-President of the Cancer Cup
Arnold's motto is 'Service before self'-- it always has been and still is.

Presidents Photographs

George Dutton Esq President 1965 – 1976   George Orme-Tiley Esq President 1931 –
1955

Arnold Rouse Esq
President 1976
Association Life Member 1981
Meritorious Service Award 1979
National Referees Association Life Member
Conference 2003

LIFE MEMBERSHIP

Life- Membership in the Leamington District & Referees Association is awarded to members who in the opinion of the of Management Committee have given valuable service to the Association over a number of years, the first one given was in 1936 and only seven have been awarded since then.

The first one was
GEORGE DUTTON ESQ 1936:- FOR SERVICE to the ASSOCIATION from 1926 to 1939 During the War years to 1945. Supported the Association from 1948. Eventually made President 1965.

The second one was
TOM STORY ESQ 1955:- FOR SERVICE to the ASSOCIATION from 1948. As Chairman of the Association and guiding the members through a difficult time as Leagues and Referees were finding it difficult to settle and adjust.

The third one was
GEORGE PANKHURST ESQ 1956 :- FOR SERVICE to the ASSOCIATION from 1948, being the Secretary and Treasurer and keeping the members informed of changes also as treasurer making sure the Finances are sound and in good order.

The fourth one was
JACK JOYNER ESQ 1964:- FOR SERVICE to the ASSOCIATION 1936 to 1939 During the War years and acted in various offices during the re-forming of the Association from 1948. A Delegate to the County Referees.

The fifth one was
HAROLD ELKINGTON ESQ 1972:- The ASSOCIATION FIRST SECRETARY IN 1921
The Members considered that the formation of the Association the effort produced by Harold deserved him being made a LIFE-MEMBER of the Association.

The sixth one was
ARNOLD ROUSE ESQ 1981:- FOR SERVICE to the ASSOCIATION since 1952 and the effort and support he has given the Members over the years, also as Accommodation Secretary of the 1976 Conference.

The seventh one was
DAVID CLARKE ESQ 1991:- FOR SERVICE to the ASSOCIATION from 1964 and his involement as Secretary of the Conference1976 and the amount of praise the Association received after the Conference.

The eighth one was
PATRICK GWYNNE ESQ 2002:- FOR SERVICE to the ASSOCIATION his assistance in raising funds for the Association has helped.

ROLL OF HONOUR 1921 to 2006

CHAIRMAN	SECRETARY	TREASURER
1921-1926 H TALBOT	1921-1926 H ELKINGTON	1921-1926 H ELKINGTON
1926-1932 G DUTTON	1926-1933 J WILDSMITH	1926-1933 A MONTGOMERY
1193-1934 W EYNSTONE	1933-1936 R WEST	1933-1935 T HAWTIN
1934-1939 J WILDSMITH	1936-1939 R ROWSON	1935-1939 G LEWIS
1939-1948 J WILDSMITH	1939-1948 G LEWIS	1939-1948 G LEWIS
1948-1954 T STORY	1948-1954 G PANKHURST	1948-1954 G PANKHURST
1954-1959G PANKHURST	1954-1955 K COX	1954-1955 K COX
1959-1967 T STORY	1955-1957 W BLOUNT	1955-1957 W BLOUNT
1967-1970 F WALL	1957-1959 P WATSON	1957-1959 J WRIGHT
1970-1974 A SEMPLE	1959-1964 J JAYS	1959-1968 A W ROUSE
1974-1976 A W ROUSE	1964-1966 A D CLARKE	1968-1970 D LOCK
1976-1978 A SEMPLE	1966-1972 A W ROUSE	1970- 1981 D SILK
1978-1981 D MACAULAY	1972 (pro tem) A SEMPLE	1981-1985 C ACKROYDE
1981-1982 T MACHIN	1973-1978 D REYNOLDS	1985-1987 A DALZIEL
1982-1985 D SILK	1978-1989 J AUSTIN	1987-1994 S ROGERS
1985-1989 D MACAULAY	1989-1985 B HACKLETON	1994-2000 S PORTCH
1989-1992 J MANDER	1985-1998 R MORGAN	2000-2005 R MORGAN.
1992-1993 D MACAULAY	1998-2001 J SHARP	2005-2006 G SHANLEY
1993-1997 J MANDER	2001-2006 D MACAULAY	
1997-2001 D ASTON		
2001-2006 J SHARP		

Vice -Presidents

The privilege of being proposed and seconded at the Annual General Meeting to become a Vice-President of the Association is in recognition for the support the Gentleman concerned have given to the Association.

Since 1948 the following gentleman have been elected as a Vice-President, the year they were elected and the year they either passed away or retired.

S Soden	1948 to 1967	1971 to 1994	G Pankhurst
R West	1948 to 1967	1972 to 1973	H Elkington
E Jarvis	1948 to 1969	1973 to 1974	J Bott
E R Bartlett	1962 to 196	1974 to 1994	T Story
J Rawlings	1962 to 1964	1975 to 1988	S Sharp
H Hall	1962 to 1965	1979 to 1988	H Boardman
E Curtis	1962 to 1967	1979 to present	A D Clarke
F B ambrook	1962 to 1968	1981 to 1984	F Wall
S Shuff	1962 to 1968	1983-to 1990	G Hyam
P Horsley	1966 to 1985	1987 to present	J Brockwell
J Jays	1967 to 1968	1988 to present	D Silk
GCH King OBE	1967 to 1970	1990 to 1997	D Reynolds
E Vollemaere	1968 to 1971	1990 to present	A J Engel
E Brooks	1968 to 1978	1990 to present	B Field
D Schofield	1968 to 198	1990 to present	A Semple
T Thomas	1968 to present	1996 to present	W Alderson
P Watson	1971 to 1972	1996 to present	J Austin
E Hapgood	1971 to 1972	1996 to present	M Smith
R Warnke	1971 to 1974	1997 to present	P Gwynne
Sir J Scamp	1971 to 1975	2002 to present	P Wright
J Joyner	1971 to 1975		

Tracey Thomas is the longest serving Vice-President.
G C H King is Group Captain H King OBE

Chapter 6

1961—1970
Moving Forward

When the Association moved into the 1960's the members should have been full of optimism, the referees who wished to progress would benefit from the positive attitude by the County Football Association in recognising the need for higher standards of Football and promotion for Referees in certain age groups, This became possible when a new League was formed with the amalgamation of the Birmingham Combination and the South Birmingham League creating a Senior League. It gave the referee the opportunity to progress. It was entirely up to the referees who wanted to move up the ladder to take up the challenge.

Unfortunately, plans however well laid, did not materialise and quite a few referees were struggling to obtain promotion, the reason for that was documented in a previous article.

At the first Annual General Meeting in 1960 it was obvious that changes would be made. The younger members were not happy with the Association. They were showing keenness in getting elected to the Management Committee. Once the changes had taken place a certain amount of discipline was brought into the Association, with John Jays the new Secretary requesting support from the members as well as attendance at Management and Council Meetings.

New format was discussed, speakers were listed and invited to the Association Meetings, Social events were planned and finally through the County Referees Committee referees promotion was openly discussed and appointments from the County Football Association were being evenly distributed. Everything depended on the members supporting the elected officers and at the same time applying for promotion. Judging by the support the Secretary received everything was possible The Association was moving forward in the right direction and the highlighted situation will be recorded up to December 1970.

The minutes in my possession from the meeting on Friday 19th February 1960, were the first, recorded minutes since 1952.

Items discussed, in the absence of the Officers. John Jays, (Temporary Secretary) outlined the situation with the Annual Dinner and lack of support. Only 12 tickets had been taken up and the 12 people responsible were at the meeting. Dismay was apparent when two of the invited guests were unable to attend. It was moved that the Annual Dinner be postponed indefinitely. This was seconded, a further discussion to take place at the March meeting. Although the above may seem trivia, to the members it was a problem, lack of support from the top and lack of finances were the main reason. If the Annual Dinner arrangements were allowed to carry on, it would have been too late to cancel. This would have left the Association with an unnecessary expense.

The Leamington League delegate reported to the meeting, of a shortage of referees. This could affect the number of Clubs on the League and a request was made for the Association if possible to get more candidates to take the referees coaching course. If we can get a group of candidates we could coach in an organised group.

The Association Rules needed upgrading and produced in book form for the members, we also had referees join the Association from R.A.F Gaydon, which helped the League.

Complaints about vandalism, mostly, in the changing rooms on the parks pitches. Referees and players were advised not to leave valuables in the dressing rooms.

A question was asked if any Leamington League games were played without a registered referee, the answer was "Not recently".

Special Meeting March 1960

The Chairman, George Pankhurst on hearing about the cancellation of the Annual Dinner, was not very happy and called a special meeting. All association members were notified and present at the meeting were the Chairman and eight other members, which included the temporary Secretary and Treasurer.

The Chairman spoke on the additional efforts both he and other officers had made to make alternative arrangements. He also commented on the deplorable lack of interest among members and a general discussion took place. It was generally felt the meetings were not interesting. The Chairman replied the meetings and arrangements were in the hands of the members. We have organised speakers and the result was a poorly attended meeting. Twenty eight circulars were sent out with reference to this particular meeting, only thirteen replies were received of which four were apologies, further discussion was to be made at the March meeting

Whilst it was only a minor issue, the officers seemed loathed to let it go and at the March meeting the lack of interest was discussed again The Chairman, addressed the meeting and made reference to the poor response to the Annual dinner.

A pro-forma would be sent out to all members to be returned by the April meeting, to find out if members preferred a Social event or an Annual Dinner/Dance.

Annual General Meeting May 1960

President	**Councillor E Fryer (Mayor of Leamington Spa)**
Chairman	**Mr Tom Story**
Vice Chairman	**Mr Jack Joyner**
Secretary	**Mr. John Jays**
Treasurer	**Mr Jack Wright**

1960

George Dutton, Chairman of the Birmingham County RefereesCommittee gave a talk to the members, he told everyone he was interested in all referees and was prepared to help a referee, but they should bear in mind that they should help themselves.

Talking of Junior Football, he said Referees should show good control and ensure that games were conducted in a proper manner. The whole game revolves around the referee's ability, his knowledge of the "Laws", and the ability to apply them correctly.

He said he would be prepared to attend meetings when possible and would have a chat or answer questions to any referee who was interested. A vote of thanks was proposed by Ron Pemberton, who congratulated George Dutton on the added interest we have when he talks to members, this was duly seconded by Jack Joyner

A letter was read out by the Chairman regarding derogatory remarks made against a member when he was officiating as a Linesman. These remarks were made during the match and directed at the member concerned. The gentleman responsible for the remarks was on the Football League and from another Association. It was moved that a letter be sent to the Association concerned, requesting an apology and informing him it is not the "done thing" to castigate a junior referee but in his position, he should have offered to help or give advice.

Jack Wright had resigned as Treasurer due to health problems.
Ted Warwick proposed, seconded by Jack Joyner that a letter of thanks should be sent to the Treasurer thanking him for his service to the Association. This was carried.

Arnold Rouse had previously intimated his willingness to take on the position of Treasurer. The Secretary, proposed and it was seconded by Ron Pemberton that we accept his offer and Secretary to write to Arnold, carried unanimously.

Management members of the League were visiting grounds, reference accommodation and the standard of pitches.

A request was made to the Secretary of the Leamington & District Saturday Football League for more information on the new Club Linesmen marking system.

Speaker Mr Frank Bambrook. Secretary, Leamington and District League.

Members were treated to a lively address on local affairs. He urged all referees to be strong and exercise the maximum control at all times.

The League would not condone any kind of conduct liable to bring the game into disrepute. He conceded a point put by the members concerning the Club Linesmen marking and would make some amendments. All questions, some pertinent, were very well answered by Frank Bambrook. A hearty vote of thanks was proposed, seconded and carried unanimously.

1961

Mr W Collins Secretary of the Birmingham County Football Association,.

He was introduced to the members by George Dutton. Mr Collins opened his address by saying how very pleased he was to come to Leamington and meet referees. He had been a referee himself, but concentrated on League /Club Management.

He said that in many instances the County F.A. was considered to be an –"Ogre". All they expected referees to do was pay their "subs". Not true! He said; the County were out to do all in their power to assist referees. He stressed that too much attention was given to those who criticise referees, only the referee knows what sort of a game he has had. If things go wrong, he should heed his own conscience and endeavour to sort out in his mind what had gone wrong.

Mr Collins paid tribute to George Dutton, for the valuable assistance he had been given we were fortunate to have his support. He then went on to give a resume of procedure at the County Football Association. He explained to members the registration forms and record sheets were kept for each individual referee over a 30 year period, giving details of County appointments, the Classification of referees and the Leagues they officiate on. County Junior Cup games from round one to round three were given to newly promoted Class 2(two) referees.

We get good reports and it was a good way to blood referees, so they could get experience. He said promotion was always a "bone of contention" among referees, we cannot please every referee neither can we enter into correspondence about whether you should not have received the promotion you wanted. Mr Collins said his office had a grievance against referees. He quoted officials who sent in misconduct reports on all sorts of bits of paper, unable to read the written article making it difficult to make a decision on the player. He said that referees should always use the correct form and send it to the County on time.

Before the war, the Midlands had quite a few Referees and Linesmen on the Football League. We do not have the same number now

Questions were put to Mr Collins and answered to everyone's satisfaction. A vote of thanks was proposed to Mr Collins for coming to Leamington, this was appreciated by all the members.

League Reports

Clubs were giving excellent reports on the referees who handled their games. Whitnash reported very favourably on referees and a colleague from Rugby was mentioned, the information being passed on to Rugby Referees.

A.O.B. In the matter of Hughie Eyton's illness, and subsequent stroke, which has left him very ill, and having to leave work, the Secretary was instructed to forward letters to the County and National Referee's Associations also the Leamington League and the Warwickshire Combination, enlisting their help for this colleague. It was proposed and seconded; we send a donation of £3.3s (Three guineas) also a letter of sympathy.

Chairman read a passage from the R.A. Review, wherein it was stated it was becoming a practice for referees to allocate to club linesmen other duties than laid down in the referees chart. Too much reliance was being placed on club linesmen and the wrong use was affecting junior referees' promotion. They were not neutral linesmen and referees were not justified in asking them to act as such.

Coventry Referees Benevolent Cup Final. The Secretary John Jays was asked to Referee the Final. He was unable to accept and Arnold Rouse was offered the appointment and accepted.

Chairman reported on County Referees meeting, finances were mentioned and Leamington had paid all dues. The Chairman congratulated the Treasurer for his promptness in paying subs etc. 1961 Conference at Coventry, cash was still needed (Leamington had not yet donated)

Management Meeting April 1961

Item discussed with a full attendance of Management members. The agenda concerned the Annual Dinner in the absence of the President, Alderman Fryer, Alderman Bartlett was invited, this was accepted, flowers only for the wives of the Guests, Chairman and Secretary, a small gift was to be presented to two members and their wives who had recently got married, Mrs Sollis and Mrs Greenway. The event was being staged at the Globe Hotel, Warwick.

League Reports

A member was commended for his firm handling and the action in cautioning and sending off incidents, concerning two players. One of the players had been suspended sine-die, for playing whilst under suspension.

Cup Appointments- A discussion took place on the lack of representation among the local men on the local Cup ties. It was suggested that more "plums" should be given to the men who referee and devote all the season to the League, yet they seemed to be left out in favour of the referees from Coventry and Stratford. Several members supported the views, and suggested a letter be sent to the League Secretary. A member spoke against the line of action and said without figures we are out on a limb. We have three local referees who received Cup appointments; this was not a bad representation. We are in the hands of the League we officiate on

Annual General Meeting – May 1961

The Election of a Chairman, Secretary and Treasurer, from 1961 were entered into a special book for Annual General Meetings up to 1990

Chairman- Tom.Story.

The Chairman congratulated the officers for their hard work for the Association, he also mentioned the successful Annual Dinner.

The Secretary spoke of his sincere appreciation of the way the majority of members had given assistance during the year, the increase in membership as well as attendance at meetings.

Dennis.Hodson complimented the Treasurer on an outstanding job of work and had great pleasure in moving the adoption of the Balance sheet for the 1960-61 season.

Ken Eastbury made a point regarding promotion. He said he was instructed to apply to Senior Leagues by the end of April if he achieved promotion. He could not do that because he was not told of his promotion until the end of May, this rather precluded his chances

Because most Leagues would have completed their list; making it impossible for any referee who had just been promoted the opportunity to move onto a Senior League. I am fully aware that it is up to the referee to apply, but how can he when the County do not let the referee know in good time. The local Leagues should send a list of all the referees, applying for promotion to the Birmingham County Football Association. Would the Delegate take the issue to the Birmingham & Warwickshire County Referees Committee

September 1961   Management Committee

The Committee discussed at some length the organisation and staffing of a coaching course It was suggested we use the Willoughby Arms and contact the Landlord to arrange booking for seven weekly sessions of two hours each.

Management members are to have a copy of the FA Coaching syllabus, and do one session each working in pairs. Secretary to be in attendance to cover each session subject to League appointments

Birmingham County Football Association to be informed, also arrange examination dates and cost.

Council Business

The complaint against the Leamington Saturday League from a member –(insufficient games this season, several idle Saturdays when he alleges probationers have been taking games and he has been unable to get appointments). This was debated at some length and several points were put by different members of the committee.

It was pointed out that we were servants of the Leagues and therefore had no control over the way they made appointments, this was apparent even as far as Football League etc. It was, however, agreed that we, as an Association had a certain duty to all members and it was up to us to get some satisfactory answer to this problem. The Vice Chairman was deputised to investigate this affair in the first instance, as we did not want to go into lengthy correspondence or try to "wield the big stick" Relations with local Leagues should be kept as friendly and sincere as possible and it was agreed to await the Vice- Chairman's report.

Mr, David Schofield, Coventry R.A. Delegate to the Midland Division.

Having been elected as the Warwickshire Delegate to the Midland Division, we were the first Association to invite him to talk to the members. He thanked everyone for the invitation. David spoke of the need for all referees to join a Referees Association and he went on to explain the work a local Association does both on and off the field also the benefits you get by being a member He also spoke on the fraternity and brotherhood of referees. Experienced referees should endeavour to help their junior colleagues when they have the opportunity, Importance of looking the part and thus gaining respect.

David spoke on the recent directive to leagues to use neutral linesmen, he felt it would be to the detriment of junior leagues when the larger leagues take the offer up, it could easily cause a shortage of referees in the smaller leagues.

This was a matter for Senior Leagues to work out on their own we can only wait to see what develops. David Schofield was thanked for his excellent talk to the members. Questions were asked which were answered in a clear concise manner by the speaker. A vote of thanks to David was proposed and carried unanimously.

George Dutton said he was delighted at the tremendous interest shown and his support to the Association would continue. Referee John Burrell (RAF) was congratulated by the Secretary of the Leamington Saturday League. Frank Bambrook, on his action in connection with a serious injury during a game he refereed (a player had a serious broken leg).

League Reports

A Club had objected to the League on the appointment of a Referee. The League had replied to the Club that they alone held the responsibility of sending referees to local matches and reserved the right to appoint whosoever they felt fit.

The member, who has complained about appointments, was allowed to speak briefly regarding his lack of appointments from the league this season. He felt he was receiving unjust treatment. The Chairman pointed out that the matter was still being discussed by the League Management Committee. It was not in order to discuss it fully at this stage. It was factual. All Leagues had the power to appoint or not appoint whoever they felt fit providing the referee was on their list of officials. Other senior members offered advice, which the member accepted, but was still aggrieved by the League's attitude.

George Dutton was reported to have been impressed with the high standard of the Leamington League Football Team at a recent Cancer Research match.

At the talk given by George Dutton, he said the Referees Examination would be held on Thursday 21st December. The County were disturbed with regard to the conduct of club officials. Referees were being shabbily treated.

Concern was also expressed about the number of disciplinary cases due to bad behaviour of players. Questions were put to George Dutton; replies were given about promotion, application to Senior Leagues etc.

Referees Forum was held; the panel consisted of Tom.Story, Ron.Pemberton, Arnold Rouse, Reg Curwen. Several issues on the "Laws of the game" were discussed and quite a few disagreements came to the fore.

The Conference of the Football League Referees and Linesmen would be held in Leamington, in 1963. Assistance at the Conference would be needed.

1962

The Speaker was Mr G Pankhurst Secretary Warwickshire Combination.

He thanked members for inviting him and said he was anxious to follow up the talk given by George Dutton, with regard to the increase in disciplinary cases in certain areas. He was more concerned with reports sent in by officials to the County F.A. wording of some reports were very vague and misleading, only the relevant facts should be given and the incident clearly and fully reported.

George mentioned the County F.A. handbook in which details of procedure with regard to disciplinary matters for the edification of referees. In his talk he stressed how important it was to get uniformity of decisions among referees; one salient point was that 22 players were expected to interpret the mind of one referee. It is essential that a state should be reached where players should not or have no need to ask, "what was that for ref"? Instead of officiousness, assistance should be given to players and spectators in the interpretation of his decisions.

A letter was received from Cyril Arch concerning his illness and collapse which happened at the Quiz. Secretary instructed to write to Cyril and convey our best wishes and hope he makes a speedy recovery.

Referees Examination – A referee candidate wrote, saying he was disappointed at failing the examination and thought his age was against him. Secretary was instructed to write to the gentleman and advise him to re-take the exam. His age was not an issue.

The Association sent congratulations to David Schofield Coventry R.A. on receiving the Birmingham Senior Cup Final.

Arnold Rouse asked the Management to consider arrangements for speakers for next season and suggested it be fixed well in advance so that a full programme could be arranged in time to give all members sufficient notice.

A serviceman referee had reported a Committee member of the Football Club for bad behaviour to the League concerned. This was noted and the referee was commended for his action. The League would be dealing with the Club Official at their Management Meetings. The referee considered the information should be brought before the meeting the Chairman replied the names would only be given if they were our members.

Several situations had been mentioned these did not concern the Association; the people concerned were either from another Association or not affiliated. Corner flags,- players and officials were too idle to put them out It was up to the referee to make sure the flags were either available and used or report the Club to the League.

May 1962   Annual General Meeting

Chairman, Secretary and Treasurer submitted their Annual reports and general census was that costs are rising regarding to postage and telephone use, also a request from the Treasurer for more assistance in raising funds. Proposed by E. Warwick, subscriptions to be raised from 10/- to 12s.6d with the increase in membership it would help finances. Seconded by D Hodson, this was carried and the finances were improved, although the Treasurer asked again for ideas or support to raise funds.

Speakers at the meeting: Mr Frank Bambrook and Mr George Pankhurst.

Frank Bambrook_thanked members for their past services and looked forward to another successful season. To new referees he said that he was there to help and difficulties should be brought to his notice. All Clubs had been circularised, re the wearing of all black strip and referees were asked to report any Club caught wearing the black strip..

George Pankhurst congratulated members who had received promotion. He said he was pleased with the 'Warwickshire Combination' instructional course, the many referees who had attended would be satisfied with the outcome and felt it will be good for uniformity.
Football was changing, competitions were becoming more severe, only the best referees would be wanted, .fitness and the right attitude towards the game were important. Interpretation of laws and uniformity of action virtually affects everyone, clubs and referees alike, members should be given the opportunity each month to discuss "points of law" and duties of a referee, refresher courses are important, both speakers were thanked for giving an excellent talk.

1963

The Treasurer said we had only thirty paid up members. There were about fifteen new referees in the area who have not joined the Association. Was Friday the most suitable evening for meetings, it was suggested we try and alternate the evenings to be included in monthly circular
Everyone was pleased to see Hughie Eyton at the meeting and the Chairman wished him well.
The Secretary was congratulated on his Football Association appointment in the European Champion Clubs, in Prague 13th March

League Reports

Leamington League – a discussion was taking place on the formation of a Premier Division and clubs with ground facilities had been contacted, members of the Association were a little concerned at the move and felt that it could mean a select band of Referees officiating in the Premier League only. The Secretary said that he would be looking into the situation and would have a word with the League Secretary.

Ted Warwick had been informed that he had an appointment on the line in the "Featherstone Cup". This appointment was received with good humour by the members because Ted was always complaining that he was always the one referee who was left out. This is a County Appointment and Ted received the congratulations of the members.

Association Business

The business of the meeting was delayed so that the film show could be presented. This would give the projectionist Mr Nelson a reasonable time to travel back to Sutton Coldfield. The film show was enjoyable giving members an insight into the capabilities of the older generation's football ability during the showing of the 1952 and 53 Cup Finals. The other films that were shown were of great interest from an unusual point of view. Mr Nelson was thanked by the Chairman and the films were appreciated by the members present.

Treasurer spoke of the changing room accommodation on the Eagle sports ground, Leamington, in relation to petty pilfering. He told referees to see the Clubs do not leave valuables in the changing rooms.

A member spoke on behalf of a Junior Referee, who was punched after attempting to send off two players during a local game. The young referee was complimented on his courage in finishing the game and it was suggested the Secretary write to the referee on those lines. Members were appalled at this treatment of a junior referee and many members spoke on the subject. A senior member, said because the clubs pay us 12s.6d, they consider we are there to be abused in any way they think fit and if this state of affairs continues, we shall find it extremely difficult to invite referees to join us..

Members were advised to wait until Leamington League meeting was held, to see what action they were going to take. One referee said the idea was good because he himself had been abused and had received all assistance, possible from the Association. Other members then said that we should, if nothing further is done, instruct Secretary to inform the Football League Secretary. The members will not participate in any games where this club are concerned either away or at home. The Treasurer said although they were strong words, the fee paid to members was not sufficient to allow members to be abused by any team or club.

The Chairman, who wound this debate up by saying it's unfortunate because this Club had a very good Secretary and no blame should be attached to him, let us wait and see what the league would do, through the Leagues Management Committee and would inform members accordingly. He also stressed the importance of notifying your .R.A. Secretary and reporting any incident to the meeting where senior members could and would give advice. .

The Chairman referred to the death of the Landlord of the Willoughby Arms, Mr Ben Cox. Together with the Treasurer he had sent a wreath on behalf of the Association members,

Tom Story said he would write to Mr Cox's son Ken and send the Associations condolences, Mr Cox was a good friend to the Association.

As Semi-Finals and Finals of local Cups competitions were now imminent, Chairman asked Frank Wall, Dennis Hodson, and John Sollis, to address members on the duties of Official Linesmen. A very interesting and informative discussion ensued and several points of agreement and disagreement were brought up.

With regard to the forthcoming A.G.M. the Secretary said that in the past this meeting had been very poorly attended, and if members continued to show so little interest in what was perhaps the most important meeting of the year, he would seriously consider not putting up for office for next season. A member said in his opinion the meetings were not interesting enough and the programme should be more varied, less time devoted to business and more to discussion and speakers etc. Members were in sympathy with this view, the Chairman pointed out we had tried with speakers on several occasions, but it was not good enough to ask people to come to address a meeting about 12 to 15 members on some occasions we had even less.

Even with the recent excellent film show which had been arranged by Arnold Rouse, we had only 16 people present. However he was prepared to support the member in any improvement that could be brought about.

May 1963

A change of meeting night was again placed under discussion regarding the best evening   for meetings to be held. This point had been under discussion for some time, a recent poll amongst members had shown it would appear either Tuesday or Thursday would be suitable. After a long and animated discussion, it was agreed for trial period of Tuesday or Thursday evenings giving members a bi-monthly opportunity to attend either evening it was moved that August circular be sent to all local referees, leagues and the press. A separate committee would be set up to deal solely with social and educational interests of the Association. Time wasting needs to be cut out at meetings, giving more time for essential discussions, on vital matters, Business restricted to 30 minutes only.

A question was put to the Chairman concerning the young referee who was assaulted last month. Has the County Football Association or the Leamington League made a decision on the incident? At the moment, nothing. The County R.A. Delegate Proposed to bring this up at the County meeting.
Dennis Hodson was nominated the delegate to the Leamington League.
Ted Warwick is a member of the Leamington League Management Committee.
George Dutton has been elected to the Football Association's Referees Committee. Congratulations from the Association were sent to Mr Dutton.

A controversial letter was received from one of the top Clubs in the League concerning a referee's ability and requesting the league not to appoint him again to their matches. The referee in question is fully supported by the league. It was mentioned they had made their position quite clear to the Club and had informed them the League are the only ones who can appoint a referee to officiate at fixtures set out by the League. In replying to the letter received from the Club the Association Secretary John Jays, informed them the league only deal with referee's appointments.

Quiz and Social Competition

Members were informed that Kineton Albion Football Club would like to entertain a Quiz team from the Association. The offer had been accepted, to take place at the Red Lion Kineton in October i.e., 10th or 15th.

The team was selected from the Association, and when we met the players from Kineton Albion we realised they had been swotting up on the Laws of the Game. This made the evening a great success, everyone enjoyed the event and an excellent buffet was laid on.

Referees Instructors Course at Rednal

A report was given by Frank.Wall and David.Clarke who attended the course. The main object was to show better methods of instruction, practical demonstrations, and visual aids and field exercises were all part of the course. Frank Wall remarked "it was a very instructional course and David Clarke and I were quite. Prepared to set up sessions at monthly meetings," If Football Clubs are interested, we are prepared to visit and explain the Laws of the game.

Correspondence was received from Frank Bambrook, Secretary Leamington & District Saturday Football League, the letter concerned Sunday Football and Referees, and it seems that referees are to make sure that clubs who want to play football are registered with the County Football Association.

Speaker for the October 1963 Meeting was Inspector Scarth of Warwickshire Constabulary.

He gave a very interesting and enlightening address to the members on the formation of the Police Force, its make up, duties etc., and question time produced some amusing replies.

This item, a break from the usual activities of the Association, suggested by our newly re-formed social committee was a great success and a warm welcome was extended to the Inspector.

Before he left, he was kind enough to extend, an invitation to visit Leek Wootton Police Headquarters. A vote of thanks was recorded by all. He was escorted to the bar where he drank our health before departing, a letter of thanks was sent to the Chief Constable for his interest in our activities.

County R.A. Chairman Mr Jim Griffiths

The Chairman of the County Referees Association spoke to the members on County matters. More coaching courses were being arranged and spread over a wider area. The poor quality of reports sent in by referees concerning players' misconduct was discussed at some length. It was really surprising the haphazard way referees made out reports. It was obvious that a majority of referees had no idea how to put a report together. Junior referees were asked to contact senior members when making out County reports. It was suggested that each Association have a session on misconduct writing, and may be the forms need changing The Management Committee would look into the idea of holding a meeting on that issue..

Congratulations were given to John Jays, Secretary, on his F.A.Cup line appointment, Burnley v Huddersfield Town, Also to John Sollis on his 5th Round Charity Cup appointment and D.Hodson, Stratford League v West Midland Alliance. W.Wall congratulated on line appointment Birmingham Senior Cup.

1964

Leamington League delegate spoke briefly on the resignation of the League Secretary Frank Bambrook According to the delegate no reason seemed to be given, every one was concerned by the statement, and most of the referees who officiated on the League liked Frank Bambrook and considered he was a gentleman. He was fair in his distribution of League and Cup appointments The Secretary was instructed to write to Frank on behalf of the Association.

Ron Byles Oxford County Coach

The business of the meeting was suspended and David Clarke introduced **Mr Ron Byles**, the **Oxford County Coach**. Ron Byles then proceeded to address the meeting on the subject of Laws 5 and 11, using diagrams and visual aids to assist his lectures. A very interesting session followed, and the "Laws of the Game" were looked at and examined objectively. Examples and incidents were quoted and discussed at length with great care and it was interesting on everyone's part. Frank Wall proposed a hearty vote of thanks to Ron Byles who had travelled a considerable distance to be with us. Reg Curran seconded the proposal; refreshments were available which ensured a very interesting evening.

Annual General Meeting May 1964

Jack Joyner was nominated and accepted as a Life Member of the Association. the nomination was for the amount of work Jack had done in the Association before the War and since the Association was reformed. He had always kept the members well informed when he attended the County Referees Committee Meetings. Jack was well liked and respected by the Members. His Nomination was approved by everyone.

A change of Secretary took place at this AGM, the previous Secretary John Jays having retired and David Clark became the Secretary, no other position was changed.

The meeting night was held on the third Friday every month. This was carried after a discussion. The Treasurer in his report said he was concerned about the finances, we need to make some attempt to raise funds, it is better for the Association to have extra money in the accounts rather than to keep struggling on a shoe string. The reason for the loss of revenue was the cost of hiring the room which has increased, whilst no-one was selling the football tickets and donations were our only income at the moment.

The membership fee is at a reasonable level and he did not wish to see it increased, he intend to introduce a new type of draw, support from the members would be appreciated, we did make a small profit from the Annual Dinner. The Treasurer was complimented on the excellent condition of the books and the amount of work he had done for the Association by Dennis Hodson on behalf of the auditors.

Chairman in his report spoke of the Coventry Benevolent Cup and said that at the meeting with Doug Paget, it was proposed to alter Rule 2 of the competition and future donations and monies raised would not be divided by competing Associations. The amount raised would go to Charity, the Charity to be nominated. Members approved of the change. The Chairman said he was pleased with the success of Leamington in reaching the Final against Wolverhampton Referees Association, unfortunately we lost by the odd goal.

Rules – Proposed amendments – A proposition by David.Clarke, seconded by Frank.Wall
There was also a new office of Meetings Organiser in place of the re-formed Social Committee and a change in the members of the Management Committee, which was though to be over-populated with 9 members.
A discussion took place on eleven points as the Rules proposals were read through to members, with the exception of an amendment to Rule 5 which was that the Chairman and Secretary is empowered to act for members in an emergency. It was proposed Arnold Rouse seconded John.Sollis, that the proposals be accepted. This was carried with three abstentions. The new Meeting Organiser was Frank.Wall   (Rules in a separate Chapter).

Mr Ron Locke, the new Secretary Leamington &District Saturday League

Mr Locke was introduced to the members. In his address, he emphasised that he is new to the District and will no doubt make mistakes, but is trying hard to be as fair as possible. Any difficulties or queries about appointments should be discussed on the phone with Mr Locke.

He appealed for referees to send in their open dates as soon as they are known and to answer correspondence promptly.

1964-1966

David Clarke was elected Secretary at the Annual General Meeting taking over from John Jays who was retiring; this resulted in changes with Management who began to meet on a monthly basis.

Majority of the business was conducted at Management and only the important business was placed before the Council members who had the last say in the way they voted.

The 30 minute Rule recently passed was used at the meetings, although some members were doubtful of its benefit to the Association in general.

The new Meetings Organiser passed at the last Annual General Meeting. Frank Wall told members that a twelve monthly programme had been arranged.

Mr.Walter Brooks, Vice Chairman Birmingham County Football Association Referee's committee, was the speaker as follows:-

1. Method of recruiting Referees – no recruiting by the County F.A.
2. Training – County arrange courses for Referees. They also pay for Referees to be trained by F.A. Coaches at such places as Lilleshall and Crystal Palace. Difficulties stem mainly from apathy.
3. Promotion- Normally two seasons as a Class 3(three) before being considered for Class 2(two) and two seasons as a Class 2(two) before being considered for Class1 (one). Promotions on ability as a referee and reports are sent on by clubs and assessors. League Secretaries are asked for their opinion and ability of the candidate and number of matches he has refereed. All candidates must be on the lists of two Leagues to stand a chance of promotion. The County is divided into areas and members of Referees Committee allocated to each. They report to County Committee who decide whether to promote or not
    Lining – this is not taken into account for promotion, once a month considered ample. Promotion to higher Leagues. Application for this to be in hands of County by March backdoor entry to Senior Leagues has now been closed. English League – Referee for two years on a Senior League and promotion to the list as a .Linesman is automatic
4. Appointments – Cup Ties, Referees Committee study the draw, geographically for the Six-Area. County members propose referees for matches, also linesmen. Class 2 men will get County Appointment
5. Discipline- each member of County F.A. is eligible to sit on the Disciplinary Committees, this is split into areas and a Chairman elected. Every player is given a chance to answer the charge in writing and ask for personal hearing. Committee must ask for both Clubs' view on the incident. Guilty or not guilty decisions are made and then recorded before deciding sentence. Decision notified by post. An appeal can be lodged. Mr W.Brooks was thanked for his address and appreciation was shown by the members.

August 1964

The first item for discussion concerned the Life Members of the Association. We have three. Reading the Minute book of 1931 to 1939 it was noted that the Life Member had received a gift from the Association. The Members felt that some form of recognition should be made to the present three. This was left for further discussion.

To advertise the Association a little bit more so that we can encourage referees a Press Officer was elected and his job was to advertise in the local newspaper and to have a talk with the Sports Editor

The Association congratulated George Dutton on his Election as President of the Birmingham County FA.

November 1964

Recruiting and Training of Referees

It was admitted in a recent talk by Mr Walter Brookes Deputy Chairman of the Birmingham County FA. Referees Committee, that there is no organised method of recruiting or of training candidates to pass their initial examination. This item was thoroughly discussed by the Associations Management, they felt that it was an important part of a Referees training and was vital to his future success.

Would the County Football Association co-operate with the Referees Association. To ensure the Training Officer is fully competent to train candidates in the correct way to apply and interpret the Law.

These were the following points the management sent to the County FA

1. The Training officer of each Referee's Association was recognised by the County FA, as the competent person in that area to teach the Laws.
2. The County FA, to arrange for the correct teaching instruction to be given to the training officers and for him to be kept posted on all new rulings of the governing body.
3. The County FA to supply the Referees Association with the necessary basic aids for the training officer to use and to give help towards any finances involved in recruiting and training.
4. The County should arrange periodic refresher courses for training officers to ensure uniformity of application of the Laws.
5. That every recruit should be coached by a training officer before taking his examination.

The Secretary of the Association sent it to the County FA, and as usual we did not hear from the County on the above subject. Training courses were eventually set up and we always considered the information we sent to the County was taken on board. Two members were involved in a week-end seminar on coaching referees set up by the County FA. They were quite prepared to set up a meeting to explain the method they were taught and to teach any candidates on the Laws using the Referees Chart.

June 1965

Charity Cup Matches

Concern was expressed that some referees are declining to take the fee and expenses when officiating at a charity game. When referees do this the fee does not always go the charity, but into the club funds.

The management recommend that referee should take the fee and expenses then return it to the charity concerned. It was brought to the notice of the management of one referee who always turns his fee down and usually ends up having the final every year. Enquiries were made and the answer given was he doesn't charge his fee nor does he claim expenses. When the referee was asked about the complaint he told the person enquiring to mind his own business.

November 1965

The Delegate to the Leamington League requested permission from the Association Management to approach the League at the next meeting to put forward suggestions for improving changing room conditions. They were as follows:-

1   Better washing facilities
2   Better dressing room and separate referee's accommodation
3   Fees & Expenses to be paid before the match
4   Mileage charge to be discussed.
5   Match cards to be given to the Referee, filled in with the team names-at the start of the game which would be returned to the Club after the game with the scores filled in.

Mr Steve Allat FA Speaker from the Football Association panel of speakers

Mr Steve Allot was introduced to the members and he gave an absorbing talk illustrated by colour slides of his tour of East Africa with Middlesex Wanderers F.C .In Uganda, referees did not receive a fee and travelled 30 to 40 miles on foot to attend meetings.   Players never questioned the referee's decisions
In Kenya, crowds were hostile and it was considerably harder and tougher football, but very fair no decisions questioned. There were some excellent shots of the game reserves and of Armond and Michaela Denis's collection of animals.
Mauritius – football fanatics F.A. supplied all officials with new kit, flags, boots etc., at the end of each season. 100% attendance at meetings, all keen to learn and exchange, ideas. Referees were paid £l0.l0s.0d (Ten Guinea's) for top games. More needle in games, decisions sometimes questioned. Members thanked Steve Allat, for giving an excellent and enjoyable talk.

Harry Owen

Mr Sid Sharp acting Chairman, in welcoming members to the meeting told the members that an ex member, Mr. Harry .Owen, who in the past, had given good service to the Association, had died after a short illness. The members were grateful for their officers' prompt action in sending a wreath on their behalf and as a token of respect for Harry .Owen, a minutes' silence was observed.

Life Membership

The three Life Members (see photo) George Pankhurst, Jack Joyner and Tom Story received an engraved Plaque at a buffet Evening. It was presented to the three members by Eric Babington General Secretary Referees Association; also in the photograph is George Dutton and David Clarke Secretary. The three recipients expressed their thanks to the members

Conference 1971

A suggestion that this Association apply for permission to organise the 1971 Conference was put to the meeting. The Secretary put all the information to the members and a discussion took place. It was stressed that it would mean hard work over a continuous period by the majority of members. If you are for the Conference, then vote for it. If you are against the Conference, then vote against. Proposed Harold Hodkinson, seconded John Heywood that the Association make application to organise Conference. George Pankhurst proposed an amendment that the Secretary circulate members with the facts and the decision left in abeyance for one month. Sidney Shuff seconded. Harold. Hodkinson and John Heywood were persuaded to withdraw their proposition and the amendment was carried. Majority of members felt the Association should build up the membership before embarking on staging a Conference

Following the circular sent to all members, a proposition was put to organise the Conference for 1971. It was withdrawn in favour of a motion from .George. Pankhurst He suggested that a sub-committee discuss it again and give a report at the next meeting, on the advisability of running the Conference. This was seconded by Harry. Walton and carried.

Mr Eric Babbington, General Secretary National Referees Association

The meeting was adjourned for the Mr Eric Babington the General Secretary so that he could talk to the members. Instead of talking to the members he began by inviting questions.

He was immediately grilled about Feeder Leagues and the benefit referees would receive when they officiate on the League that has been selected. He told every one the Countics view and explained that most of the information was obtainable from the Football Association, but other points were –

1. Feeder Leagues for following season would be decided in December each year.
2. Incentive for referees entering at 30 appears to have been removed.

3. This system has many pitfalls, but it must be made to work and when it does, it will be a great asset to referees

A discussion on Feeder Leagues followed and it appears that different officials of the F.A. have different views of the scheme, Bill Wall said it must be advantageous for Class 3(three) and Class 2(two) referees to get on the new system and be known as soon as possible George Pankhurst disagreed as he thought this would defeat the object of the scheme. Official information had not been received by the Association, it was decided no recommendations could be made to anyone

Conference 1971

This item was discussed earlier in the season and it was referred back to Management for further discussion, The Chairman and Secretary had been in conversation with Eric Babington on the Conference issue and his advice was looked at very carefully and a full discussion had taken place at the Management Meeting. Notice was given by Secretary that Management had recommended a 75% majority should be obtained for the motion to succeed. (This was adopted unanimously). At the next Council Meeting the Chairman Frank Wall proposed that the Association apply for permission to stage the 1971 Conference this was seconded by Doug Pope. A vote was taken of the members present and it failed to reach the 75% needed, the recommendation was withdrawn with the request to find out more about organising a Conference.

1966

League Reports

Travelling expenses had been discussed and a delegation of four were to meet the League Management. It was explained that one point had been dealt with, which was that all referees should charge the amount they would pay on public transport, no matter how they travel.

Frank Wall reported that the meeting with the League Management Committee was encouraging and the League intended to follow up all points which were put to them by the delegates. Ted Warwick raised the question of the marking system of the League; it does not seem to be working satisfactorily. It seems that referees who only do a few games tend to get good marks, whilst those that do quite a number of games do not get treated as well and they also get different marks. I would like to see all referees treated fairly and consider the Leamington & District Referees Association was best suited to keep a watching brief on the situation

Annual General Meeting May 1966

Meeting held at the **Willoughby Arms.**

President's address George Dutton complimented the members of the Association, despite criticism from one club; He went on to say that the standard and efficiency of referee's in the League was as good as ever. He was sure the Association would continue to enjoy the success it deserved

Chairman's and Treasurer's report were accepted.

Secretary David Clarke tendered his resignation due to pressure of business, and thanked everyone who had helped. He would continue to support the Association in any way he could. Members thanked David Clarke for the work he had done as Secretary

1966-1971

Arnold Rouse was elected Secretary; he was combining both positions as Treasurer and Secretary. Herewith some of the highlights from 1966 to the 1970's

The Feeder and Contributory League system mentioned at various levels is primarily for the benefit of Class 1(one) referees under a certain age who can be promoted on to Senior Leagues. The teething problems that have arisen are being thoroughly discussed by the County Football Association, and further meetings will no doubt be arranged.

The Substitution Law is gradually being brought into use and referees are keeping a watchful eye on the players and Clubs. Assessing is another new suggestion, although the County Members have been assessing referees only when they have County appointments.

A change of headquarters is on the cards as members considered we were being pushed about by the new Management of the Willoughby Arms. The opportunity came when we had an invitation to hold our meetings at the Farmers Club. The Management discussed the offer from George Dutton who was the Steward and decided to send a delegation to the Warwickshire Farmers Club.
The delegation went and met George Dutton, he explained the Rules and Regulations to us, our Meetings would be held every 3rd Friday in the month commencing at 7.45pm the first Meeting to be in December 1966.

After we had met George Dutton the delegation from the Management accepted and thanked him for his offer. We knew that the meetings upstairs would be in pleasant surroundings. We eventually spent 27 years at the Club until the Committee, wanted to turn it into a restaurant. We were disappointed at having to move, we were not the only ones. The Club had a very successful snooker team and they also had to move.

An interesting talk by the County Delegate who was in charge of the referees who officiated in the 1966 World Cup, about the problems they encountered whilst refereeing
We had success in the Six-a-Side Cricket Competitions winning it once and competing in other Finals.
Promotion came to two members of the Association one being placed on the Football League and the other elected to the full list of the Football Combination.

Ex-Class one Referees were being asked to take up Assessing by the County Referees Committee, and Seminars were taking place at the County Football Association on a variety of subjects.
A Mock Commission took place at Leamington with members acting the part of the Player, Secretary, and the Referee. The County FA provided the Disciplinary Commission. A discussion on Neutral Linesmen and the Feeder League situation caused a few problems, meetings were sometimes a little heated but they were interesting,

The Birmingham County Secretary came and talked to the members on the Feeder and Contributory system as well as other issues concerning the County F A
Certificates were being issued to each referee to say that they were registered with the County F.A. and stating what Class they were
Referees marks in the future would be from one to ten and not one to four as it is at the present.

Let us move now to the Election of Officers for 1966 and highlights up to the 1970s

At this Annual General Meeting, the election of a new Secretary would be the third since 1960 and the seventh in since 1948. We at Leamington have been fortunate in that the Secretaries we have had, have done the job well in spite of having a very busy life..
The new Secretary, Arnold Rouse will be the Treasurer as well. The members at the meeting including the President wished him well and advice was offered by George Pankhurst who was a previous Secretary and Treasurer. Another situation arose when it came to elect the Management Committee, four vacancies were available through people resigning or moving to do other jobs in the Association We had six volunteers which resulted in a secret ballot, with two members who were non-voters acting as scrutineers, the first four in the election being elected. All the moves and changes which were happening augur well for the Association at least that was the impression given.
Moving into the second period of the 1960's it is hoped we can see what benefits will be brought into the Association as quite a few of the younger referees have received promotion and have moved on to Senior Leagues.

August 1966

Feeder and Contributory Leagues

The information regarding this new system of moving referees Class 1(one) only on a pyramid system was discussed as a failure, copies of circulars received being out of date.
Secretary informed members that he had received the latest issue of the "Feeder and Contributory Leagues" and had duplicated them for their benefit.

The Secretary stressed he was interested in the system for every member and not only Class 1(one) referees who would benefit now in his opinion all referees should benefit eventually

Secretary of the Leamington Saturday Football League complained about the discourtesy shown by the Organisers who convened a meeting in Coventry on the "Feeder and Contributory Leagues System". He considered the evening was in bad taste as it was an important issue and that referees from Leamington would have been at the meeting had it not clashed with the monthly meeting of the Association.

Doubts were expressed at the legality of the meeting and Secretary was asked to write to the organisers and complain. The Secretary said he would write but you have to remember it was an open meeting it was up to referees if they considered it worth going to. The Management had discussed the issue and had delegated David Clarke to represent the Association. The Secretary also said that everyone who was refereeing was interested in the outcome. At the moment it only affects the Class 1(one) although eventually class 2(two) and class 3 (three) would be involved, if only to obtain experience as linesmen.

Assessment of Referees was discussed by members who said it was unfair, the way the assessors mark referees on the present marking system. It doesn't look very good when a referee's marks from a Club are low. Why not use a marking of (1 to10) (one to ten) creating a clearer scope for officials to work to providing the officials are really fair in their assessments. Ron Locke said that Football League Referees would assess referees much better than Secretaries. Marks are a bone of contention, if Leagues used them constructively all would be well, but most club Secretaries, are prone to mark a referee on one failing only and not on the match as a whole.

Since 1964\65 seasons, the Football Association along with the County Football Associations, have gradually brought into the system, three items to improve and benefit Football Leagues and Referees.

1. The Contributory and Feeder League system will eventually improve the standard of play and help referees to improve as well.
2. Assessment is a method of improving a referee's performance as he gains experience.
3. Substitutes, a new innovation which has been needed for a long time, especially when players get injured. If the injury is serious, the player is removed and this puts the team down to 10 men. If he is capable of carrying on, the player is usually put on the "wing" and is never involved in the game. If substitution had been available, the player could have been taken off and a fresh player would take his place. Questions were asked now that substitution was in force, is it possible or allowed for a trainer to coach during the transitional change of players. It was suggested that the referee use his discretion. Further information on all three subjects would be needed from the County Football Association

Vice-Presidents

Members observed a minutes' silence in respect of two Vice Presidents who had recently passed away, namely Mr Sidney Soden and Mr Richard (Dick) West. Both were Referees in the Association, taking various offices and attaining a very high standard of refereeing. Their service to the R .A was between 1920 –1939 and both had been Vice Presidents for a number of years.

Sidney Soden was one of the Referees who helped to look after the Association during the War and was at the meeting when the Association was reformed. Dick West became involved with the Warwickshire Combination and served on the Committee.

Future Headquarters

Tonight's meeting at the Willoughby Arms will the last one held, we have been using the Willoughby Arms as our headquarters since 1950 when a young "Ken Cox" joined the Association.

His Father was the landlord and with Mrs Cox we were always made very welcome at meetings and social events. Things changed when Mrs Cox died and with the passing of Mr Cox, the new Landlady wanted us out. Our new Headquarters will be the Farmers Club, Willes Road Leamington Spa. And the room is booked from January 1967 to December 1967, all on a Friday evening. The room is also booked for 16th December 1966.

The Management recommend that we meet every month from January to December, this includes June and July. Directions will be placed in the December circular for 1966. The hiring of the room will cost the Association an additional expense and the Treasurer feels we will benefit from being at the Club. The Steward to the Farmers Club is Mr George Dutton

Leamington League Delegation

Once the business had concluded, a delegation from the Leamington and District Sunday Football League was introduced to the members. They were Edward Leddy, Joe.Burnell and the Secretary Ron. Locke Chairman for the discussion John Griffiths. Questions asked to the delegates comprised of changing room facilities, washing facilities referees, marking and Linesmen competition.

The replies given by the delegates, were that most clubs have not the finances to implement those changes that are needed, separate changing facilities for referees was also discussed. It was stated that players' behaviour on a Saturday was exemplary, but will Sunday footballers take it as a serious.

The Leamington & District Referees Association was criticised for not supplying referees for Sunday matches. It was said that there was no approach from the League for referees.

The Secretary said we would welcome referee candidates from the football clubs so we can coach them and they would be able to referee on the Sunday League. Referees who officiate on a Saturday only at the moment do so to achieve a reasonable set of marks they need for promotion to the Senior Leagues The marking of referees varies from Secretary to Secretary.

According to the County Delegate the marks from the Sunday Leagues will eventually be of importance to referees for promotion. Referees should be marked on a separate sheet. The Chairman, John Griffiths was congratulated on his control of the meeting.

Speaker Mr David Schofield - Divisional Representative of the Birmingham and Warwickshire Joint Referees Committee.

He gave members a very enlightened talk on the difficulties that arose from the World Cup with the 9 (nine) Officials all of different nationalities. They were very grateful to the interpreter who was Italian. The team sheet was completed before each game, and players selected for dope test. Balls were chosen from about 12, one was selected after the most stringent test by weight, size and circumference. What was most noticeable among these referees, although very good officials, was the tension when they were lining to a colleague, which was different when they were refereeing. With the language problems it was amazing how well they all blended together and with the Italian interpreter it was a very pleasant exercise, one I thoroughly enjoyed.

A point was made by David, that those junior members when acting as linesmen should take the duties as seriously as when refereeing. David was thanked for his talk to members and so was Ron. Warnke, who gave a short talk on the amount of work that the General Secretary Eric.Babington, was doing for the benefit of the Referees' Association and its members. We are very lucky to have Eric who is an efficient administrator.

1967

Memorandum from the National Referees Association - This concerned the appointment of a full time Secretary. It was proposed by George.Pankhurst and seconded by Secretary Arnold Rouse, that this Association gives full approval to a "full time Secretary" to the National Referees Association. The document is to be returned to the present General Secretary Eric Babington, by 31st January 1967.

Leamington Football League was shocked to learn that the Secretary Mr Ron Locke had resigned from the League. It has been said through insufficient co-operation from his Management Committee. The Chairman Sidney Shuff had also informed people that he was resigning.

Annual Dinner

The Secretary expressed delight that he could say for the first time we have a **FULL HOUSE** of 80- members plus 2 reserves for our Annual Dinner at the Coffee House, Warwick. Everything is booked and we are looking forward to an excellent evening.
February 17th, 1967

Social Evening

A Social Evening organised by John. Sollis – This covered a Quiz on the "laws of the Association Football" between Leamington R.A. and Sutton Coldfield R.A., with Kings Norton acting as question master and judges. Over 50 members were present and it turned out to be a very successful evening. Leamington eventually ran out winners in a close contest. Refreshments were taken and Chairman thanked everyone for attending.

Six-a-Side Cricket

The opportunity to stage the six-a-side Cricket Competition for the Birmingham & Warwickshire Joint Referees Committee was offered to Leamington Referees Association.

The Management had discussed the offer and decided to accept it and informed members that they were interested. A new member Tom Dean told the members that he was attached to the R A F and based at Gaydon. He said he would try and obtain permission to use the facilities of R.A.F. Gaydon on our behalf, the Chairman told him to go ahead. We eventually heard from Tom Dean, who told the Chairman and Secretary to send an official application letter to Group Captain H King OBE RAF Gaydon, and at the same time, thanking him for all the facilities that have been made available to us.
The Sunday dates given to Tom were available; the Secretary in writing to the Group Captain booked the Sunday in June and thanked the Captain for his permission to use all facilities on the day.
The Secretary of the B&WJRCC was informed that Leamington would be staging the Six-a-Side in June and all Associations would receive the information.

A majority of the work at Gaydon was completed by Tom Dean and it seems that the service men at the camp were looking forward to an enjoyable day and offered their help. At the Management Meeting Tom Dean laid out his plans for the Sunday, already two Cricket Pitches had been laid out and rolled, Side shows i.e. Darts and Skittles as well as bowling had been sorted out and all the items were being repainted and repaired.

A few of the Service men at the camp had covered the Tractor and the trailing coaches to become a model train and entertained the youngsters by giving them rides around the perimeter of the airfield. Refreshments were available all the Referees Association had to do was hope for a sunny day and enjoyable Cricket.

The event turned out to be a complete success, the weather was good and we had 20 Teams take part Families all came to be entertained, Tom Dean even found some swings for the Children, which were cleaned and repaired Everything was covered with Insurance, such as public liability and the teams were insured through the entrance fee they paid. We had Boy Scouts tidying up for us and the St Johns Ambulance looked after any injuries.

To make it a great day Leamington Association eventually won the Competition and so were the holders of the Six-a-Side Cup, for the first time, although we had entered it for a number of years I don't think we took it seriously enough, winning it at Gaydon gave the Association the impetus to win it again the following year. In which we did. With regard to the event at Gaydon the Association were complemented on an excellent Competition, a reasonable Profit was made so the Scouts and St Johns also the RAF Benevolent received a few pounds each.

The Association wrote and thanked Group Captain King for his support and for taking part in umpiring a few matches. We did invite the Group Captain to one of our meetings where he gave an excellent talk on his service in the R A F.

The members at that time were still keen to enter further competitions. Having the members so keen was a boost to the Association. Sunday Football was really getting established and we were coaching referees who were very much involved in sporting activities. They were Sports Masters, Teachers, or retired footballers they gave the Association a wider spectrum. We could easily have put out a complete cricket team as well as a very good football eleven

Going back to the Cricket we went to Birmingham as winners to play in the Competition, and one or two incidents cost us the game, firstly the Wicket keeper had misplaced one of his gloves which made it difficult for him to keep wicket and a few runs went astray. When it was our turn to bat one of the opposing bowlers created an incident against one of our batsmen whilst he was bowling. He stopped took the ball from his right hand and placed it in his left hand, at this point he removed the bail and appealed for the player to be given out, because at the point of his bowling, the batsman who was the non striker, was out of his Crease and moving up the wicket. This was correct according to the Cricket Laws, but was considered ungentle manly conduct by the Leamington team who withdrew from the Competition.

The Captain of the opposing team came and apologised and said the bowler should have warned the batsman for encroaching. The Six-a-Side Cricket Competition gradually faded away and the majority of the Associations decided to organise a Six-a-Side Football Competition. Leamington were very successful, we were also able to win the Benevolent Cup Competition, playing Associations like Wolverhampton, Birmingham and Coventry.

This was good for the Association until most of the players we had as referees decided to hang up their boots and stop playing football concentrating on refereeing. Whilst we were successful we had an excellent coach in Alan Windsor who always seemed to get the best out of players. Even with the changes we were still able to raise a team and play in the Competition, and we made sure that the Association was insured whilst playing Football or Cricket, not all Associations did that.

Resignation from League and Referees

Vice –President Sidney Shuff gave the members his reason for resigning from the Leamington &District Sunday Football League and one of the reasons was that he was moving away from Leamington. He also told members that he would still like to belong to the Leamington Referees Association as a Vice-President if the members so generously re-elected him. He said he was sorry about the League Secretary resigning , he felt that it was an unnecessary resignation , he should have waited until the A.G.M Sidney Shuff went on to speak about abusive language by players and the referees attitude towards it.

He congratulated the referee who chastised the whole team for using bad language. This approach had a sobering effect on the game, which finished in a sporting manner.

Henry Hall

A minutes silence was held for Henry Hall, who had passed away after a long illness. Henry joined the Association in 1948 and eventually became the Association Coach, coaching referees on a one to one basis, we cannot recall any candidate failing to pass the exam when they were taught by Henry. He was Regular soldier, leaving the Army in 1947, after 21 year's service, joining as a 15 year old band boy. Henry was not very tall, but it did not make any difference to his refereeing, he had a good reputation of being firm and fair.

Insurance

Lionel Fleet spoke on signing Insurance forms when a player was injured. He asked is this common practice in Leamington. I couldn't remember any incident where a player was injured, although sympathising with the player and the Club Secretary, the form was not delivered to me until four days after the game took place. I wrote a similar statement out to the Club Secretary and returned the form unsigned, for I felt that the statement on the form, "I certify this happened" could not have been true for me to have signed it. Members fully agreed on what Lionel .Fleet had done but Leslie .Ray, who is Chairman of a football club, said that similar things happen to his players where a slight knock, by the Monday turns out more serious than at first thought. Most private insurers do not require referees reports   Members felt that this point should be discussed later on.

Annual General Meeting May 1967

Letter from Vice President Mr.Sidney Shuff resigning from the Association Members moved that under the circumstances we regretfully accept his resignation.

John Heywood in a letter to the Secretary tendered his resignation from the Management as his company are moving to Croydon. Members expressed regret at losing, a very experienced member and wished him well.

The Treasurer gave members a resume on the Balance sheet and explained to the members how their membership fee was used. Out of the first 15s.0d (fifteen shillings) , only 3s.0 (three shillings) was available for expenses and to promote the Association . The remainder was taken up in Fees, Capitation and Affiliation to other bodies (i.e.) the County R.A. and the National Referees Association

Vice-Presidents

With the death of Mr.Richard.West, and Mr Sidney.Soden, Management, proposed that **John Jays, previous Secretary and Group Captain H.King, O.B.E.,**be nominated, this was seconded. Other nominations were put forward and after a serious debate were withdrawn. Before the members approved, an amendment was presented to the meeting, concerning one of the candidates. The issue was that becoming a Vice-President was for people who have supported local football and referees in general. The vote was then taken. The amendment received 6 votes, the original proposition received 12 votes and there were 6 abstentions It was a secret ballot.

This Annual General Meeting was a lengthy affair said the Chairman as he closed the meeting at 10.30 pm

Promotion

Lionel.Fleet - Football League Linesman,
Frank.Wall - Football Combinations Referee

Congratulations to both.

Feeder Leagues

A discussion on Feeder Leagues took place. This also included the letter from the Birmingham County Secretary concerning the disbanding of Warwickshire Combination. Members felt that the Combination could have made a decision earlier enabling referees to move to other Leagues, giving them equal opportunity

The discussion on the Feeder Leagues came from Andy Semple who said referees had been directed on to a league without notification. The members seemed upset at this move by the County FA

It was moved the Secretary write to Eric.Babington giving him a copy of the letter received from the County FA this was rejected. Eric.Davies said the County requested a list from him and other League Secretaries of the referees they are retaining and referees not being retained on the list.

He was very surprised at this move by the County concerning good experienced referees being moved this way .He had no knowledge that they would do this. The Leamington League Secretary would be writing to the referees explaining the County's reasoning.

The Secretary was asked to write to the Secretary of the County FA giving this Association's views on this matter and explaining one or two points that may have been overlooked.

Frank.Wall said what had been done was under the Contributory and Feeder system and if one decided not to accept the County decision, everything they had worked hard for would be lost. Also this Association should bring to the notice of the Leamington Saturday League, now they are a Feeder League the Club Secretary or Assessor has a most important job in football, his fairness in marking referees could make or mar a good referee. On the other hand, favouritism to a bad referee would make a mockery of the system.

The Secretary is to outline a letter for Management's decision at next meeting. The Chairman closed the meeting and thanked everyone for attending. He was pleased to see 14 members at the meeting, but the discussion was important

Warwick Combination

George.Pankhurst spoke on the statement in July minutes concerning the Warwickshire Combination. He felt that referees should not interfere into League activities.

It was pointed out to George.Pankhurst the statement in the minutes was an expression that was used revolving around the Feeder League system. Frank.Wall said no-one intended to criticise the Officers of the Warwickshire Combination he felt they had done everything possible to ensure the League carried on, but its obvious when a League disbands Referees must ultimately suffer.

MrEric.Babington was welcomed with our President George. Dutton,

Eric Babington opened his talk to members and expounded his theory on the Contributory and Feeder League systems, also if time permitted, to talk on the alterations to the Laws of the game.

The Contributory and Feeder League System is in progress, we are now moving in the right direction. Thanks to your President we have an increase of Feeder Leagues in this area at least four more Leagues are in operation. The Referees Committee decided that leagues with referees on the fringe area could be incorporated into the Feeder League system by spreading the leagues over the area.

Leamington was an isolated spot which would benefit the referees in the area, on the proposal of the Leamington Saturday League becoming a. Feeder League, other leagues were written to and information gained regarding the quantity of referees required. We must be fair to the County F.A. Secretary, every referee who is Class 1 under 37 and paid up to the County has been placed on a Feeder League. The Feeder Leagues are of equal standard over the whole Country and Leamington is not and has not been considered a down-graded league.

In the letter to your League Secretary I have explained to him why the referees who were placed on the Local League were not notified by the County. This gave the league Secretary a chance to look at the list and accept the referees on his league.
If the league has difficulties in finding enough matches to give all the Feeder League Referees sufficient marks, they should run a Subsidiary Cup or League Competition to enable the referee to get his full marks
Sunday League Football has been looked into and until the Lord's 0bservance Days Society allows Professionals to play on Sunday with gate money taken, the Football. Association are not interested.
Club Secretaries who send in a report, or mark a referee with a nought, should have to justify that marking, with a report on the match and the reason for the Mark. This finished the talk by Eric.Babington who was then, open to questions.

A point from Eric. Davies- He says Leamington area, including Coventry, is over staffed with leagues, the main stay of all these leagues are the Class lx,(one-x) 2 ((two) and 3(three) referees. Is the Feeder League system fair to referees?
Reply from Eric.Babington -I do not see anything in the league system that stops the referees other than the Feeder League Referee, from having games in the Premier Division. Senior referees are the salt of the earth and we must remember that...

Having finished with the Contributory and Feeder League, a short discussion took place on the alteration of the Laws. Eric Babington told members to ask for the nominated substitutes at the commencement of the game and pointed out one or two additions to the goal keeper taking four steps.

The goal keeper cannot dribble the ball; this was on a circular form that he gave the Secretary to be duplicated. He thanked everyone for listening to him. A vote of thanks was proposed by Frank.Wall, who thanked Eric.Babington for the interesting talk and information he had given. This was seconded by John.Sollis

Mr Cyril Pegg Cambridge Referees Association

Mr Cyril,Pegg, Cambridge Referees, gave a talk on Linesmanship He was Linesman on the F.A.Cup final between Manchester United and Leicester City. The talk given by Cyril.Pegg was stimulating on the efficiency of a Linesman, not only on the field of play, but on their dress and deportment. He stressed that all linesmen should pay strict attention to the instructions of the referee and keep well up with the game. He said a linesman should be able to use both hands when signalling to the referee; this eliminates crossing his body with the flag.

Some of Cyril Pegg's points and remarks aroused a lot on comments from members and questions were asked. In his final analysis, he said it was his intention to be controversial on the Laws concerning linesmen.
A vote of thanks was proposed and everyone said they had enjoyed his talk.

January 1968

Reference was made to the Meritorious Service Award given to referees. We have a member who has asked why he has not been recommended for the Award. The Secretary told the committee that he had been in touch with the Secretary of the Midland Division and the Award is for Service to the Association, not membership, the Secretary also told the member that it would be discussed at the next management meeting. In informing the committee of the request, he also told the committee that certain minutes between 1952 &1960 were missing.
The discussion at management was rather abrasive and the committee members felt that the member concerned was not very supportive or interested in the Association. Before the meeting got out of control the Chairman intervened and said it was unfortunate for a committee member to hold a personal view, but if the member concerned is entitled to the Award then he should be recommended for it.

The Chairman added a rider that the Secretary should investigate further and obtain the information through old records or previous Secretaries.

February 1968

An Association within an Association was the complaint made against the Secretary when a member complained. He said that Association business or the selection of officials for Cup or Football Matches is being discussed at work, which the impression is given to outsiders and members. Another member said officials seemed to be picked before the meeting commenced.
The Secretary said it was poppycock; he had never discussed Association business at work. It is unfortunate for me as there are about eighteen or nineteen active referees working at the same place which is the Lockheed.
The Secretary goes on to say that one has to work somewhere and if the members are not satisfied with me as Secretary we do have Annual General Meetings in May. The Chairman has taxed me on this problem; I resent it and do not accept the accusation that has been made.
It was moved by the Chairman, all appointments to be selected by Management. An amendment was put forward, any Appointments the Association receive, and the officials will be elected by the Chairman, Secretary and one other member. The Chairman withdrew his proposition and seconded the amendment. This became the proposition and the Management members voted in favour.

Concern was expressed by the Management Committee over a resolution submitted to the County FA. It concerned **"Neutral Linesmen"** The resolution was as follows;-"The Birmingham County Football Association in the interest of members of its Affiliated Referees Associations should take immediate steps and mandate its Representatives accordingly to bring before any County Football Association, who restrict any League from further use of neutral linesmen, as it not being in the interest of referees".

Mock Commission

At the conclusion of the monthly business a mock commission was set up to show members what exactly happens at the County Football Association Headquarters, when a player who had been cautioned, or sent off during play for a serious offence. Members who took part were as follows –

David.Clarke	became	Mr Brown -	Referee
Steve. Salter	became	Mr Carter -	Linesman
Frank .Wall	became	Mr Smith -	Club Secretary
Alan .Windsor	became	Adams -	player cautioned
Bill. Alderson	became	Spink -	player sent off

Representing the County Disciplinary Commission were Eric. Brooks, Arthur Guise, and George. Pankhurst. Lionel Fleet acted as County Secretary.

This was a well laid plot to deceive the County Officials, but experience told at the end, and one feels that the exercise was worthwhile and instructive. It shows how a referee should act in all cases. Eric.Brooks spoke to the members and said; when a referee makes out his report to the County, make sure it is correct, readable and concise. He also spoke on the Commission that had just taken place and said he was pleased to take part in a well organised and constructive mock Commission. He hoped members would learn from the exercise.

His words were re-iterated by Arthur Guise and George Pankhurst. Questions were asked on the various points of procedure and how punishment was given. W (Bill) Alderson proposed a vote of thanks to the gentlemen for taking part, seconded by Frank.Wall

March 1968

The Management were very concerned about a letter that was sent to the Chairman of Lockheed Leamington F.C. concerning criticisms of the Club. The person who sent the letter was presumed to be a referee.

This was discussed by management and all the members considered it was a disgraceful letter to send, especially to the Club Chairman. The letter was not signed.

The committee in general felt that less publicity about the letter would be the right thing to do.

One of the senior members who in his position had dealt with a situation and people before similar to the one we are talking about asked the Chairman if he could put a letter together and with Managements approval to send it to the Chairman of the Football Club.

After a brief discussion the management agreed and the letter was sent to the Chairman of Lockheed Leamington.

Annual General Meeting May,1968

Chairman in absence of President was Mr.T.Story

Chairman's Address

 The Chairman opened the meeting and was pleased with the attendance, there were thirty members present and the Secretary said he had received 9(nine) apologies. In his address he congratulated the Management and the Secretary for the success in staging the Six-a-side Cricket Competition and the Association for winning the Cricket Cup.

He said that Leamington Referees was a name to be respected and admired, and quite capable of organising any event successfully. He thanked the R.A. Coach Andy Semple and the Meetings Organiser Lionel Fleet for the amount of work they had done for the Association.

Secretary/Treasurer gave his report and stressed that he was pleased with the attendance on the nine meetings averaging about 69% (sixty nine percent) and thanked everyone for their support.

The income and expenditure showed a seasons profit of £24

Election of Officers

President Mr George Dutton

Vice-Presidents

Two new names were added, namely Mr.Tracey Thomas, Secretary Leamington and District Sunday League and Mr. David Schofield Coventry R.A. and Warwickshire Delegate to the Executive Council. Both were proposed and seconded and both accepted the position as Vice-Presidents of Leamington & District Referees Association.

Chairman

Two nominations were proposed and seconded for the Chairman's position, Tom Story existing Chairman and Frank Wall., each candidate received 13(thirteen) votes . The Vice-Chairman took the chair for the election. Scrutineers Jack Joyner Life Member and. Fred.Tebbs guest from Coventry R.A. Four new members were not allowed to vote they were not registered with the Association.

The acting Chairman declined to use the casting vote available as per rules. The Secretary said it was an unknown precedent, due to the position the Acting Chairman found himself in. This was understood by everyone. The meeting then resulted in stalemate; we could not have two people as Chairman.

The Secretary suggested we follow the Constitution and suspend the meeting The Vice Chairman, Secretary and Treasurer carry on in office until another A.G.M. is called. This was proposed by Lionel.Fleet and seconded by Andy.Semple. The meeting then carried on as a normal monthly Council meeting with the Vice Chairman acting as Chairman..

Adjourned Annual General Meeting June,1968.

Chairman for the A.G.M President George.Dutton.
The minutes of the original A.G.M. were read for information only, to be signed in 1969.

The Secretary with the Chairman's permission spoke on the Rules and the reason for the adjourned Annual General Meeting/
Scrutineers were elected.

Election of Officers for 1968/69 Season

We have already elected the President Mr George Dutton and the Vice-Presidents
We now have to elect the Chairman and remaining Officers.
Two nominations were again proposed and seconded for the position of Chairman.
The election by ballot which resulted in Frank Wall receiving 12(twelve) votes and Tom Story receiving 10(ten) votes, therefore Frank Wall was elected Chairman.
Mr Story was thanked for his services having been Chairman since 1960 as well as Chairman in the 1950's. "You are held in esteem by the members" said the President. The members showed their unanimous approval

The President considered that due to the circumstances, the Rules should be altered to cover all eventualities; normally any Rule alterations should be in the Secretary's hand one month before the A.G.M. The members at the meeting accepted the Presidents guidance.

The proposed alterations to the Rules were then put to the meeting and they were all accepted by the members as follows:-

Rule 3 – Proposed Frank Wall seconded John Sollis - Chairman and Vice-Chairman to hold office for a maximum of 3 years if elected at the A.G.M.
Rule 4 – Approval and Association
Rule 5 – Association, Management and Monthly meetings
Rule 7 Secretary to insert additions and adjust rules accordingly.
Rule 8 Registered with his County F.A.
Rule 11 That the Management Committee are empowered to deal with any matter that is not covered by these rules.

The Secretary is to rewrite the Rules. and obtain copies for the members.
The remaining Rules of the Association were accepted as they were written.
The President closed the meeting.

November 1968

The Secretary was told that he should not have replied to a letter of complaint by one referee against another. The referee who was accused of making remarks about the ability of the referee who was refereeing the match, complained to the Chairman about the terse wording used by the Secretary in the letter he received.
The Secretary was a little concerned about the statement. He admitted writing to the referee who was making and passing remarks and he considered his letter was a private one sent to the referee.

After a general discussion the Secretary was reminded that all correspondence should be discussed at the meeting unless it is an emergency and then the Chairman would be informed. The Secretary was asked to write to the referee on behalf of the Management, he told members that he would write to the referee in question, but he would not apologise for sending the original letter. The Chairman remarked that the matter should now rest and in future wc should ask members for a comment or a reply. A member of the management said he was concerned at the time taken on frivolities at Council meetings. We are not adhering to the Rules and Standing orders.

December 1968

Sports Forum

After any other business, the Chairman welcomed the Sports Forum organised by Lionel Fleet, Guests were George Curtis, Bobby Gould, Coventry City F.C, Tracey Thomas, Leamington League, Mr M.Thomas and Mr Coutts, Blackdown High School, Chairman for the forum Mr. Sid Sharp. The "Forum" was interesting to all members; questions were put to the entire Panel and covered a wide range of subjects of Football from Amateur player to the Professional, also the Professionalism of players. Quite a lot of common sense and ideas came from the session. It seems the majority of Professional Football players would like to see Professional Referees. The Association members objected as they considered that a select band of referees made into professionals would eventually affect referees, especially younger members
A vote of thanks was proposed by Bill.Alderson, who said he enjoyed .listening to the different views, seconded by Bill Wall.

John Sollis Football League

Question were put to John Sollis on Law 12 "Fouls and Misconduct" He said the information, and interpretation, he had received from the Football Referees and Linesmen
Association was such that if all referees adopt the instructions uniformity in all spheres would follow. Members were asked if they would be interested in applying the suggested alterations. The majority were prepared to apply the ruling to the matches they refereed The discussion of uniformity on Law 12,"Fouls and Misconduct," gave the impression to the members, by applying uniformity will mean every referee should fully understand the information and interpretation of Law 12.
This will mean every referee giving a similar decision on a certain type of foul or to penalise or caution. players for misconduct, so players will not be able to say "the referee did not caution me last week" or "he let the opposition get away with it" .The general impression was although most referees will apply the ruling, every match and every referee will be different, as the standard of football also differs

Football Benevolent Cup Competition

Leamington Referees were playing Wolverhampton Referees on Sunday .March 17th 1968, at Flavel's ground, Leamington Spa. The officials controlling the game were from Aldridge Referees Association. The match was a splendid game with Leamington losing by the odd goal in five, excitement and incidents were abound in the game with the home side supporters voicing their disapproval of the referee. In fact one member from Leamington was told to shut up or he would be sent from the ground by the referee.

The person concerned was so irate with the referee, it seemed that every decision he gave was against the Home Team, a penalty appeal was disallowed, some one shouted to the referee to put the lace back into the ball, Even though there seemed to be a problem quite a few members who were watching were having a laugh, the only person who wasn't laughing was the one who was shouting. Eventually things calmed down with Leamington losing.
You could not complain about Wolverhampton who played some excellent Football and the coach Alan Windsor was quite pleased with the way the team played, but not with the result.

As Secretary it was my job to pay the Referee and Linesmen their expenses, I apologised for the unruly behaviour from Leamington, but he just laughed and told me to tell the spectators not to shout so much.

George Pankhurst spoke on his reason for allowing his name to go forward at the A.G.M. of the Birmingham and Warwickshire Joint Referees Committee. He was not upset at being defeated but would like to raise this issue and have this Association place on the agenda of the B & W Referees Committee the following resolution. – "The Birmingham County R.A. in the interest of affiliated members of the Referees Association, should take immediate steps and mandate its representative to bring before any County FA, those .who restrict any league from the use of neutral linesmen, as it is not in the interest of referees". The Secretary remarked it should be discussed in Management.

Various people spoke on the subject and it was proposed that George.Pankhurst be invited to Management to put his resolution forward. The Secretary proposed an amendment which was seconded that George.Pankhurst writes to the management giving them his resolution in detail so the members could discuss the resolution.

The Secretary explained to members if it is written it can be discussed and one cannot deviate from it, but if the resolution is discussed and the one who proposed it was in attendance, it would not allow Management members to talk freely. The voting for the amendment was 17 votes, for the proposition 5 votes. The amendment was carried with no abstentions. Chairman moved business closed.

Group Captain King OBE RAF Gaydon

Meeting suspended to welcome Group Captain Harry King O.B.E., who gave members a very interesting talk on his travels with the R.A.F. He spoke for one hour on everything concerning travelling the world visiting other places with the RAF, unusual sights, and interesting anecdotes. He was asked a question on his refereeing and the Group Captain told members how the NATO Referees Association was formed and the seriousness of the internal games that were played. The members showed their appreciation to Group Captain King for his enjoyable talk. Lionel .Fleet proposed the vote of thanks.

Council Business

Neutral Linesman

This is a continuation of the issue with a resolution by George Pankhurst requesting the Association to place it before the Birmingham &Warwickshire County Referees Committee.

George.Pankhurst who put his resolution to Management said he thanked the Management but he could not accept the proposition they had put forward as it was not in context. Was pleased to hear County report, but would not accept the statement that there would be a shortage of referees. There is a lesson to be learned by being a Linesman to Senior Referees. He did not like the word rumour and the words "Junior Leagues".

A member asked if we had all the facts from George Pankhurst. We could have spent more time discussing the issue, no one on the Management knew that the County F.A. had discussed this position; neither did we know a meeting had been convened with one of the Leagues interested in neutral linesmen.

Lionel.Fleet said George Pankhurst seems to be objecting about the word "rumour." Can we not forget the word and make progress

At this point the Chairman welcomed Mr Eric Babington Chairman of the County Football Association Referees Committee and Ron Warnke who is the Secretary of the Midland Division to the meeting.
Both had been invited by the Chairman as he felt that the issue of Neutral Linesman was at the time a very contentious problem between the Leagues and the County FA.
The problem is the leagues who have missed out on being made Feeder Leagues were struggling to maintain a reasonable standard of referees to their League although they are being told that there is a shortage of referees to fulfil the duties of linesmen. Another point that was made was that referees would be able obtain their promotion to either Class 1(one) or 2(two) providing the marks from the League were good enough After a very lengthy discussion George Pankhurst stated he was not happy with proceedings, suggested we place it on the October agenda to discuss fully.
The Chairman intervened and said that he would like the Chairman of the County Referees Committee to say a few words on the subject.

Eric.Babington – ""we are very pleased to hear George.Pankhurst talk on the welfare of referees and I can assure you all so are the County, promotion can be gained from a League if markings are good enough. The County F.A. would like all leagues to have referees but there are not sufficient men available. Suggest you read the latest minutes of the F.A, We are not interfering with the leagues or competitions, but concerned with Leagues sanctioned by County F.A"

The report which was submitted to County FA is briefly as follows – "You can have linesmen provided the league concerned makes two lists, one for referees, one for linesmen. Young referees would be safeguarded. You can have linesmen who want to run the line only, but they would not be considered for promotion or County appointments.

If a referee takes a line appointment, he must notify the County FA. All the Leagues are on equal planes whether Feeder or non-Contributory".

George.Pankhurst said he was very pleased to hear Eric.Babington's report and would still like to move the resolution is referred to the October meeting, Seconded by Andy Semple.
Lionel.Fleet – "We should make our mind up now. I move an amendment that in view of the Management decision and the report by Eric.Babington, Chairman County F.A. Referees Committee, we accept the reports", Seconded by David Clarke. The amendment was carried by a majority vote...

Meritorious Service Award

We have a member who keeps asking if the Association could find out how the National Executive awards a member the Meritorious Award. The Chairman told the members at the Management that strict rules apply to the awarding of this prestigious award. If we have any one who deserves it we would be proud to recommend the member or members. At the moment we have only one member who has received this award.
The criteria is for 20/21 years service in the Association not membership as some members believe and you have to have held position on Management, or have been the Secretary, Chairman, Treasurer, or even the Coach.
We have a member who thinks he should be entitled to the award and until all the facts and service is collated there is nothing we can do. Acting as Secretary / Treasurer only counts for one item not two, it is difficult to explain the rules and regulations to members and we can understand why they feel aggrieved.
The Chairman told the members that when we get all the information together and if we consider he has not enough service we will inform him.

If we find he is entitled to the award, we will submit his name to the Midland Division and the person concerned will not be told if he is successful, it will be the Executive Council who will inform him before the Conference.

January 1969

The member who is concerned about the M S A has written to the Secretary telling him he was perturbed about the wording of Meritorious service and Active service. The members of the Management considered we had thoroughly discussed the item in 1968. The Secretary was told to contact the National Secretary and get the correct definition of the award.
It was proposed by the management we do not pursue the matter any further.

At the same meeting the members discussed the Meritorious Service Certificate which is an award by the County Referees Joint Committee. The Secretary was asked to write to the Secretary of the Committee and clarify the Award and service required.

The Secretary informed the members of the information he had received about the M.S.C. This was discussed by the members who felt that we would have possibly two or three members who would be eligible for the Certificate. Secretary to obtain the forms and complete them, then return them to the County R A Secretary, with the Chairman's Signature endorsing the forms.

A Referee was accused of swearing at a Linesman at one of the local Football Matches. This was reported in the week-end newspaper. A member of the Management committee who was at the match told the committee that the statement was not correct and the Press have twisted the facts a little.
The Chairman told the members of the Management he would have a word with the referee and make a statement at the Council meeting. He said that all referees should be careful to whom they talk to, especially if anything has happened during the game. It is preferable you only talk to the Association Secretary or Chairman for advice and if they are not available contact the County Football Association.

October 1969

County R.A. Report

The Association has three Assessors according to the County report they are
Jack Joyner, Ron Pemberton, and Arnold Rouse.

The delegate told members if you want an Assessor to come and watch you referee and give advice, then contact them, especially if you are interested in getting promotion. They are doing this job voluntary for your benefit and for the betterment of referees. The reason you should contact your Assessor is that he may not know what type of game you will be refereeing. One referee was concerned he said if he knew he was being watched he could have a bad game. He did not think it right that he should contact the Assessor. The referee was told to take the opportunity whilst it was there. Secretary told the members this was a new venture and it would be in every ones interest to co-operate with the County for this season, contact your Assessor and tell them where you are refereeing.

Ron Pemberton

The Chairman, Frank Wall, told members of the sudden death of Ron Pemberton and the shock it had been when the Secretary had told him. Ron Pemberton was well liked by the members and had recently taken on the position as a County Assessor, Which he was very keen to do. When funeral details are known, a wreath would be sent and the Association would be represented at the Church.

Headquarters

A statement by the President concerning a change of meeting place, this was placed before the members at the April meeting. The Management had discussed the issue and the resolution put to the members telling them we are staying at the Farmers Club and the Secretary and Chairman will visit the Steward of the Club (who is our President) The situation was thoroughly discussed at Management and if we continually move, it will be more difficult to obtain good premises. The Chairman said we are happy here and the envy of other Associations.

Annual General Meeting May 1969

Minutes of the 1968 A.G.M. and the adjourned A.G.M. were signed and both were accepted as a true record.

President's address Mr.George Dutton – spoke on the successful Association we have, it has become an Association to be proud of in this County through its coaching and sporting activities. Very pleased with promotions and good reports of referees

Chairman's report – We have a membership of over fifty, attendance at meetings about 70% Excellent promotions from Class 3 to 2 and 2 to 1. We have had a 100 % success in coaching by Andy Semple.

After the Election, the President before closing the meeting, presented a mounted pen and stand to Tom Dean who was leaving Leamington and moving to Germany with the R.A.F. Tom Dean thanked the President and the members by saying that he had enjoyed his stay at Leamington and thanked everyone for their support.

Feeder and Contributory Leagues

Meeting closed for a discussion on Feeder and Contributory Leagues, also progression through various Leagues. Two referees who had gained promotion to Class 1 (one) had not been placed on a Feeder League. This is wrong when Eric.Babington came to Leamington Referees he promised all Class 1(one) Referees would be placed on Feeder League. The Secretary could write to Secretary Birmingham County F.A. also Eric.Babington.

The formation of the Premier Division in the Works League would result in better matches for Feeder League Referees. It was felt that there is a need for a League between the Feeder and Contributory system, to sustain and give experience to Class 1(one) Feeder League Referees. This would only come if League Secretaries are prepared to accept a change.

John.Sollis said the Football League are now starting an auxiliary list and referees will have six(6) matches during the season, an Assessor will be at every match. This is in Division Four only. If successful, they could be promoted to the Supplementary list.

George.Pankhurst, "This is correct", but I feel Football League has gone back Five years when it had a Supplementary list, where referees had one middle appointment a month. Various views were put by the members; it seemed to be of no advantage gaining Class 1 until you were certain of being promoted. The Class 1x, 2, &3, are the forgotten referees until there is an acute shortage in the lower divisions and smaller Leagues. It is up to us to look after these referees and at the same time encourage the over 50's to continue their refereeing career for the experience they have gained is invaluable to League Secretaries.

Referees Referendum

The Referendum under discussion concerned the National Referees Association financial restraint to improve the Status of the Association in their ability to discuss or negotiate with outside bodies.

The members were asked to put their honest opinion on the form. John Sollis asked if the 20s.0d (twenty shillings) required covering active members who are refereeing would increase the Affiliation Fee from 15s.0d (fifteen shillings) to 35s.0d (thirty five shillings). Secretary informed him that one couldn't say at this point. How many members does it cover? - Every active referee in the Country.

The Secretary gave members the Management opinion. Who considered it would raise the status of the Referees Association Enabling the National Referees Association to negotiate with other bodies on equal terms and remove the impression we are Amateurs. Also there is no cohesion between referees at all levels at the moment.

George Pankhurst – What the Secretary has said could well be right and I hope everyone would support it as it's only factual,

One of the members said "Its all very well for Management to give their opinion, it seems that they are trying to coerce the members to their way of thinking. What happens to the referees locally, why can't they carry on as they have done in the past." What would happen if the Referees Association became fulltime? It would be like the County Football Association. All the old pals etc. "Unnecessary remarks" said the Chairman please remember the officers of the Executive Council are elected annually at the Conference.

Chairman Frank. Wall explained Referendum to members; a question was asked "what happens to part D. when a member belongs to two Associations." You still complete the
Form but make one of the Associations your parent Association.

At this point, the Chairman allowed Eric Davies, Match Secretary; Coventry Works. To give a short talk on the meeting he attended in Birmingham. Covering Feeder Leagues and Contributory Leagues and the difficulties encountered.

Eric Davies-It was a very good meeting and a lot of ground was covered. The Birmingham Referees Committee was in force. Difficulty in running the Feeder League system; About 32 Leagues to one Contributory League, this made Feeder Leagues over funded, and created a limited progression. With the Feeder League marks going to the County F.A. as well as the

Contributory League. It doesn't mean the best Referee gets on to a Contributory League, a lot depends on demand. There were fifty two referees in the County who are Class 1 who did not get on a Feeder or Contributory League.

They would not dismiss a referee for age if he was a good linesman, but after five years promotion is considered if marks are good enough from Feeder League. If not good enough, they are informed by League Secretary. Marking system will change from 1 to 4 to 1 to 10. Possible promotions from January to January; promotion by Regional Areas (we come under Coventry). Eric Davies was thanked for his report by the Chairman.

Mr. John Westmancoat Hon. Secretary B'ham County Football Association

A very interesting talk was given by the new Secretary He covered the new misconduct form, promotion, a new form will be sent to all who applied for promotion and a possible fee of 5s.0d will be asked.

Referees will eventually receive a Certificate which will commence in 1970 season showing their Qualifications. Fees will most probably go up for the next season. On administration, difficulties had been encountered with the new Offices. Things are now getting back to normal.

County Assessors; this is a voluntary job and you should use your Assessors if you want promotion, they did a good job last season. The County Secretary went on to say that a meeting has been arranged for the end of the month. County Handbook should be due out by the middle of November. One further point he made was concerning referees who he considered were letting themselves down by not sending players off when they should have done neither are they cautioning players properly and again they are not sending the reports in to the County Football Association. His final comments were that referees are sending in to the County very poorly written reports concerning misconduct, this is not any criticism of Leamington but it is general all over the County area. I would like to see it improve because we then could penalise the players for the problems they cause in a more positive way.

Nearly four hundred dismissals so far this season, and about seven hundred 'cautions.' A lot of questions were asked the Hon. Secretary who answered them all and clarified various positions. These questions covered mislaid birth certificates, receipts, promotions, Feeder Leagues and how do we get promoted to them. At the end of his talk, the members showed their appreciation in the usual way.

A vote of thanks as proposed by Lionel Fleet, Meetings Organiser, who said it was a pleasure for us to have the Hon Secretary at Leamington. We also have the Chairman and Vice-Chairman of the County as well. Three items emerged from his talk, promotion forms, certificates for referees and the new misconduct forms.

Seconded by Tom Story, who said I endorse the remarks and would like to thank the Secretary for coming. Also my thanks to Lionel Fleet for organising such excellent meetings, as you are aware. We shall be losing Lionel soon, and that will be this Associations loss. The Chairman asked the President George Dutton if he had anything to say.

George Dutton. "Apologies for my absence of late, but I have thoroughly enjoyed the talk and can tell you that the F.A. hold the Birmingham County F.A. in high regard on the way they are running the Feeder and Contributory system".

November 1969

At the Monthly meetings a Member said he was concerned about the lack of contact with the members at the meeting. He asked whether the 30 minute rule is being used to force the minutes and correspondence through without a thorough discussion.

Majority of the members feel that most of the senior members sit at the front of the meeting and try to solve every problem we have instead of allowing free discussion amongst the junior members; after all we are supposed to encourage them to get involved.

The Chairman replied that we can adjust the Agenda, dispense with correspondence, place circulars on the table for every one to read and we do have a senior member available to talk to the young referees if they have problems. The point concerning the 30 minute rule, we will look at it at the next Council meeting.

Lionel Fleet

Every one in the Association was surprised when Lionel told us that he would be moving from Leamington to become the Headmaster of a Large School in East Dereham Norfolk. Quite a few of us knew that Lionel wanted to improve his stature and moving to East Dereham seemed the answer. We all wished him good Luck and hoped he would keep contact with us.

An extra-ordinary meeting (as per Rule 13) took place to elect a new member. David Clarke was proposed and seconded and elected as Meetings Organiser until the A.G.M. in May. This left a vacancy on Management.

Annual General Meeting May 1970

Presidents, Chairman and Secretary's address were read and accepted.
Treasurer's report-
The income and expenditure accounts showed a loss of £14 2s.0d, (fourteen pounds two shillings) this was due to the Conference Levy fund. The Capita should have been paid in 1968. The balance sheet and accounts were accepted.

Election of Officers

The election for the position of Vice- Chairman resulted in two nominations, Andy Semple and Tom Story. After a Ballot Andy Semple was elected, all other officers were the same except the Meetings Organiser. David Clarke was elected to that position.

1970

Refresher Course – The Association are setting up a refresher course for referees to be held on Sunday 28th June, 1970 at the Lockheed, Leamington. Commencing at 10 am. Until about 5.30 p.m. A coffee break and lunch, costing twenty shillings, and a programme giving the schedule for the day would be available, also films and projectionist. All Associations would be informed and we would be dealing with Class 3 and 2 referees. We would appreciate County support, a full report about the Course will be written in the article covering Coaching.

Cricket

A Cricket match was being arranged at Central Hospital Cricket Ground by Sid Sharp for September. The team that had been invited was Gayton from Northampton. Tony Engel introduced us to the Club in the earlier part of the season and the members who went over to Gayton enjoyed the atmosphere and the match.

Although we lost, it was an enjoyable day out, the wicket was a matted strip and well pegged down, and the grass had been cut and some of the players had never played on a matted cricket pitch before. It was good experience for everyone and although we played very well we were not quite good enough. .
The return was being arranged by Sid Sharp at the Central Hospital who at the time had a very nice Cricket ground. The refreshment were organised by Mrs Sharp and they were enjoyable. Leamington considered that they had put out a good cricket team but we still lost by a few runs. We never had the opportunity to play them again their fixture list always seemed full and the players from the Association had moved on.

It would have been nice to have played them again, as they were very sociable and enjoyed their Cricket. It was thanks to Tony Engel who arranged the first match.

League reports – Club Linesmen

Criticism was made at a League on the latitude referees are giving to club linesmen when running the line. The Management suggested all referees follow referees chart on club linesmen. This is and will always be a debatable argument, every referee has is own view on how and what club linesmen should do.

This problem with club linesmen will not go away, everyone has different views, if you stick to the referees chart club linesmen lose interest. In this sphere it seemed that there was still a lot of work to be done before one could lay down a schedule of instructions to junior referees to give to club linesmen. A member said we have discussed this before and I believe a circular and referendum was taken by the County Referees. It would be helpful if we could standardise the issue.

A majority of club linesmen just want to wave the flag. You have to get to know them and judge what they can do and their attitude to the game. The League Secretary said that a complaint came from a club who said the referee used one linesman to the best advantage, but not the other one, who in turn became disillusioned.

The Chairman closed the discussion and suggested the Management take note and discuss at their next meeting and try to produce some positive points regarding Club Linesmen.

Before we move into the 1970-1980 period the latter end of the 1970's proved to be the most instructive period the Association had received. Everything that was talked about was for the benefit of the referee. This meant that the referees would have to work hard to achieve those benefits. Some referees were concerned about the slow movement regarding promotions they say a delay could make it difficult for referees to move into a higher League. The Birmingham County Referees Committee have said that they have everything under control it just takes a little time to send the information out to every referee who has applied for promotion.

Every one was keen to keep moving and refereeing on the various leagues knowing that once all the changes and added benefits had been made and were working. It would be in the referees favour.

When we move into the 1970 to 1980 period we shall find out if it all happens.

Chapter 7

1970 – 1980
The Conference Years

At the end of the last decade club linesmen were causing problems through the Feeder and Contributory League Systems. These were set up to improve football in general and to benefit referees. No one could blame the Leagues for trying to upgrade the standard of football, which they felt would improve the clubs and the league. The trouble was there were more feeder leagues in the County than contributory leagues and this meant promotion for referees would be limited. Some of the leagues were managing to use neutral linesmen in the Premier Division of their League. They were mostly the elderly referees who were quite happy just to be Linesmen on a Saturday afternoon. It benefited the referees on that League, the County were not happy with the situation and the Linesmen knew they would not receive any County Appointments whilst they were on the League.

Another innovation that came about in the latter part of the 1960's was the beginning of Referees Assessors; we were in the forefront at the first inaugural meeting in Birmingham when we had three members elected to serve as Assessors for the County FA. It was unfortunate that Ron Pemberton passed away after a short illness before we could get ourselves organised to go and assess referees. We had quite a number who did not want to be watched by colleagues whilst they were refereeing because they felt they would not be able to concentrate. Once the system was explained to them and they realised the benefits they would gain, no one objected.
The idea of Assessors, according to Eric Babington was for the benefit of referees and as the referees progressed up the ladder possibly to the Football League, by being assessed all the silly mistakes that referees make would be ironed out, at least that was the intention and the County instructed the assessors on those lines. They felt it would make the game enjoyable for the referee and the players. The Birmingham County FA would be setting up seminars for assessors to keep them up to date with all the changes.

In 1970 we had a change of Treasurer with Derek Silk taking over from Derek Locke, the Chairman's position would be changed at the A G M, due to the three year rule,(not a good rule and needed changing) .
Conference was again on the cards and members were very much in favour, a special meeting was called to elect the officers to organise the Conference, funds would have to be raised, and other events would have to be organised.

Andy Semple and Arnold Rouse were quite pleased with the adverts that had placed in the Courier and Advertiser. It was through the advert they had found the first Secretary of the Association. They both went and met Harold Elkington and found out quite a few things about the Association and when it started, who the Chairman was and where they held their meetings.

Complaints about the changing facilities on the public parks in the District, the dressing rooms were being broken into and money and clothes were stolen as well as damage to equipment. The Teams who used the facilities were written to and a letter was sent to the District Councils to see if it could be stamped out

The 1976 Conference was highlighted and a special meeting was called, Arnold Rouse resigned from being Association Secretary over statements made by a Vice–President..
County Quiz Final was being staged in Leamington

Long and Meritorious Service Awards from the National R.A had been awarded to two members, as well as the County Long Service Awards. They were to be presented with other awards at a dinner

Arnold Rouse elected President at the A.G.M

Chris Cairns first lady Referee in Leamington, husband took up refereeing as well to support his wife.

Charity Cup started in memory of George Dutton it would be called the George Dutton Challenge Cup.

Increase in rent at the Farmers Club, Treasurer quite happy to pay, he said we are comfortable here and the rent has not been increased since we came here in 1966. Chairman resigned over a dispute, new Chairman elected

Arnold Rouse received his Meritorious Service Award in 1979 from the National Referees Association.

The above are just some of the highlights from the 70s. With the Conference as well it was a busy time for every one.

We continue with information from the minutes up to 1980.

Derek Locke, who had handled the accounts for three years, told the Committee that he wanted to move on to other things. Derek was thanked by the Association for the service he had given; the new Treasurer would be Derek Silk who is an Accountant

The Chairman's position would change at the AGM, the present Chairman having completed his 3 (three) years as per rule. One can see that particular rule being removed especially when we have difficulty in finding good Chairman.

Various changes were being made and new ideas were being discussed at County Level, although one item "Substitutes" was always talked about this suggestion according to the Chairman of the County FA was highlighted by players being injured in Football matches like the Football Association Challenge Cup, injured players spoiling the game as a spectator sport.

When the FIFA and the FA sanctioned the substitute rule, it was eventually placed in the Referees Chart with certain points that would benefit players.

January 1971

Management members were concerned over club linesmen as the instructions they receive vary from referee to referee. The Secretary asked members if we could do something about it now. It is too late, said Chairman, it would cause further difficulties. We all realise simple instructions are needed. The Referees' Chart states club linesmen should only indicate the Ball is out of play, the referee has to decide if the ball goes over the goal line, whether it is a goal kick or a corner and the same applies if it goes over the touch line, the referee decides whose throw in it is. Majority of Leagues have instructed clubs and referees to instruct club linesmen "ball in and out of play only." Further discussions to take place

Secretary reported that the Association will not be eligible for Cup Final tickets. The reason given is that we are only associate members the referees Benevolent Cup is not a League and we only play a few matches. It is a shock said The Chairman, the County F.A. have left it rather late to inform us, they keep telling everyone that referees are the life blood of football. It was proposed that the Secretary write to the County Football Association. And to Tom Richards Referees Association Delegate concerning the Cup Final ticket issue. It was remarked by a member that we only normally get two tickets and they are the cheapest ones. The committee from the Benevolent Cup were looking at the possibility to see if a League could be formed which would give the committee a little bit more power to discuss the issue with the County FA.

March 1971

At the Management meeting and having further discussions we attempted to collate the fees and expenses in the County. The Secretary is to write to the County FA, giving our views.

One member made the remark, he would like to see the fee and expenses removed and expenses worked on a mileage basis for your own transport where practicable

Other members considered we have the basis for a good discussion with council members. A proposal was put, "all fees and expenses should be standardised by the County FA, relative to the grade of football in each area"
Concern was expressed about the 'fee inclusive' system by some Leagues and compare it with leagues that have 'fee and expenses' in operation. As one member remarked it is a very expensive match when one only gets the inclusive fee after travelling about 30 miles.

November 1971

The Association Secretary is in trouble again, although he was instructed by the County FA to distribute and explain the new forms for assessors. In doing so he had placed the new assessors name on the list that would be circularised to the members, so they could contact him when they wanted to be assessed.
The Chairman remarked that the information should have come from the County FA and the Secretary should have adhered to it. The Secretary was instructed to seek advice first and delete the members name from the circular and referees should be notified that they must give their number (County) and the time of the kick-off when they require assessing.

Fees and Expenses

A lengthy discussion on referees' fees and expenses took place at the meeting. The fees needed stabilising. It was felt that the County should standardise the fees in feeder and contributory Leagues. A member said we should seek out the League that pays the most fees. Most Leagues fix the referee's fee at their AGM. .Senior Leagues have a distribution of expenses which means all clubs pay the same at the end of the season..
The Chairman put the proposals to the members. This was carried and a letter on fees and expenses was sent to the County Football Association, also to the County Referees Delegate to see if they could persuade the County FA to establish a standard of Fees within the County.

Tie Competition

At the August meeting, a member asked about the R. A. neckties. He was told they are about £1 each. The general remark was that they are not very good. It was then proposed to produce our own and a competition was set up for someone to design an Association Tie. The closing date October monthly meeting..
Numerous entries were received by the Secretary and every one was numbered, with the names or identification removed so the Judges would not know who had submitted each entry.
At the October meeting entries were examined and judged by Ron Warnke and David Schofield who decided John Manders design as the winner. Secretary was advised to enquire the cost of producing the tie in various colours.
Before we could place an order, we had to stop trying to produce our own, as it seemed that we infringed the Associations Agreement with a Company who supply the Referees Football Kit and accessories which included the Association Tie.

Once again it was another first for Leamington, it's a shame we were not allowed to proceed with our design, the winning one was super and all the designs were well laid out.

The addition of substitutes at junior football matches was causing a few problems, as referees were using them as club linesman. This was to be stopped said the County Football Association. Substitutes were to be used to replace injured players so the team would have eleven fit players on the field of play. This would allow the injured player to receive treatment. Once the substitution had taken place, the player substituted would not be able to

take any further part in the game. They were not to be used as club linesman.. Some members are of the opinion that they should be allowed to be used as linesmen they would help the referee. Quite a few leagues have placed it in their handbook that substitutes are not to be used as linesmen.

David Schofield, Birmingham and Joint Warwickshire Referees Committee, told members that junior referees were not bound by instructions that were given to football league referees in his talk he asked them to use common sense. It seems that some junior referees were cautioning and sending players from the match and getting into trouble writing out reports which were incorrect.

1972

Speaker – Mr Eddie Hapgood

Mr Eddie Hapgood was introduced by Mr Frank Wall. Eddie Hapgood was Captain of England Football Team as well playing for Arsenal F.C in the 1930s.. He was called an Ambassador of Football because he as one of the many stars in the Lucky Arsenal side, he started his talk by telling the members that he was always into trouble kicking a ball about when he was a youngster and he finally played for Kettering town, although he mentioned that Bristol Rovers were interested in signing him but he went to Arsenal instead winning five Championship medals and two Cup Winners' medals. His International career was shortened due to the War, which only allowed him to collect 30 International Caps. The International matches he played before the War and the ones against Scotland that were organised during the War, were the ones he talked about and the type of players he came across and the antics they used to gain free kicks.

One game he mentioned which caused a few problems was when England played the German National Team in the 1938 Olympics, He said problems arose with playing the National Anthem of either Country he did not say much more about it and nobody questioned him, but one or two of us found out the reason by reading various books. It seems it concerned the respect to both countries National Anthems. The Germans would stand to Attention when the English National Anthem was played and the England players would give the Nazi salute as demanded by the host nation. .
He talked to us about the standard of referees who were officiating before the war and since, in his opinion he considered referees were not fit enough and they did not train hard enough. He was surprised to find that Football League Clubs were not prepared to help referees. During his talk he spoke about Herbert Chapman the Manager who signed him along with other players during the 1930s, he said he only brought players to do a job at Arsenal and from that he gave us an insight into the training the players did and how hard they worked at it. He also talked about tactics and how they improved the defence cover which allowed defenders to break from the deep into an attacking mode. The whole talk kept members spellbound as Mr Hapgood danced around on his feet, it was obvious to us, even though he was over 60 years old, he was still fit and his feet were tiny. I think he only took a size 6(six) shoe.

He said he became a Manager. I believe it was "Watford F.C." after the war instead of carrying on playing. It was not a happy time. He talked of being in the R.A.F. and travelling around playing football when they were allowed to during the war especially contests against old colleagues who were playing for professional Clubs, because they were stationed in the area, he mentioned some of the players who became Football Managers.

After two hours of non-stop football, he told the members he was also a qualified Tennis Coach and enjoyed playing tennis, good for reflexes he said. At 10.15p.m, we had to call a halt to his talk and thank him for coming to the meeting and talking about his football. We were hoping to invite him again because he was living in Leamington, but it was not to be. Unfortunately Eddie Hapgood passed away after a short illness and was buried in Leamington in 1973

May 1972

A Coventry League has reported a referee to the Birmingham County FA, requesting ratification of their Leagues decision to remove the referee from their list of referees for his alleged failure on three occasions to officiate at games allocated to him. A copy of the letter was received by the Secretary of his Association.

After a discussion the Secretary was asked to write to the League Secretary asking whether the referee concerned has been given the opportunity to answer the allegations.
At a later Management meeting the Secretary informed the Committee that he had not heard from the League concerning the Associations request.

Conference 1976

Vice Chairman David Clarke gave members a resume on the Conference he asked members to vote on management's recommendation that we accept Midland Division's invitation to run the 1976 Conference.
It was moved by Tom Story- seconded by Frank Wall. we accept Midland Division invitation- voting 18 for- 2 against with 4 abstentions. Questions were asked and nobody really knew the answers, the members were told it would mean a lot of hard work and a very strong committee would be needed. (More information on the Conference is in the chapter on the 1976 Conference). In accepting the Midland Divisions invitation to organise the 1976 Conference a special meeting would have to be called .to elect the committee.

First Secretary of the Association

Information about the Association and how the Association was formed was given to the Secretary, when the daughter of the first Secretary Harold Elkington phoned him. With Andy Semple they went to Budbrooke where Mr Elkington was living with his Daughter. In meeting Mr Elkington (Harold as he liked to be called) we also found out that the Chairman was a Pepper Talbot who was also Secretary of the Warwick and District Football League. In talking to Harold we could not push him too far when we realised he was well into his late Eighties. He did mention George Dutton and others whose names are mentioned in the first Chapter. It was thanks to the report in the Warwick Advertiser that we had good information to work on. We also found out that Harold was a very keen player of draughts and even at his age plays in competitions.

While the vote was unusual and the fact that Harold Elkington was a member over 80 years ago, he was responsible for the Association being formed in 1921. It must have been a very difficult to have organised the referees to form an Association.

Chairman and Secretary told members of their enquiries and the success they had, in finding when the Association was started after visiting George Dutton, it was noticed he had a chiming clock for being 'Chairman from 1926 to 1933.' The Secretary told the members that after seeing the Clock in Mr Duttons house he was under the impression that the Association had started years earlier. With the Chairman Andy Semple we tried to get an article in the local newspaper, to see if anyone could remember the early years of the Leamington Referees Association. We have approached a reporter from the Leamington Spa Courier and the Warwickshire Advertiser to help us. This has proved successful.

Extra-Ordinary meeting – Harold Elkington – proposed Arnold Rouse, seconded A (Pat) Gwynne, that Harold Elkington be made a Life Member- of the Association and a Vice-President, the voting was unanimous.

General Information

The Meetings Organiser Arnold Rouse gave members a talk on the planned programme of speakers and demonstrations for the next twelve months. All members received a pre-printed card with all the relevant dates.

The Association has been attempting to stage films of previous World Cup and Cup Finals at the Spa Centre. Restrictions have been placed on the organisation involving number of tickets sold and in November 1972.

The Secretary reported no further progress had been made due to technical difficulties that had arisen between the \Leamington Corporation, the British Film Industry and Theatre Management. The film show is now unlikely to take place until next year.

Frank Wall reported that for personal reasons. John Sollis had decided to resign from the Football League. It was regretted it had been necessary for this decision to be taken and a vote of thanks was expressed to John Sollis for the honour he had brought to the Association. Quite a few of the older members were disappointed in John retiring, because they all felt that he was a good Referee who should have reached the middle of the Football League.

Concern was expressed by members with regard to the incident reported by a member when officiating at the Lockheed Works ground. This resulted in a loss of a small amount of cash, damage to clothes, etc. It was agreed that as there were no disclaimer notices displayed by the Sports and Social Club, the Secretary should write to the Lockheed Sports Club submitting a copy of the referee's claim and requesting action should be taken by the club to prevent the repetition of an incident of this nature. This was proposed and seconded and unanimously accepted by all members present.

Expenses- this was stated in February management that we attempt to collate fees and expenses in the county. We should write to County FA with the Secretary giving our views. One member said he would like to see fees and expenses removed and expenses worked out on mileage basis using your own transport where practicable. It was recommended all fees and expenses should be standardised. It becomes very expensive when you travel 30 + miles and only get an inclusive standard fee.

Quiz Cancellation

The Association received a letter from Sutton Coldfield RA requesting an explanation with regard to the cancellation of the quiz competition, which resulted in a wasted journey to Leamington for Sutton RA

The Secretary explained that the Quiz had been cancelled at short notice by Mr L Robinson (Organising Secretary) as the date we had mutually agreed with Sutton was one day past the deadline date he had stipulated. The Secretary stated he had not contacted Sutton Coldfield RA because Mr Robinson had informed him that Mr Gibbs (Chairman of Sutton RA) was already aware of the cancellation. It was agreed by management after a lengthy discussion that a letter should be sent to the Secretary of Sutton Coldfield RA, and also to the Birmingham &Warwickshire Joint Referees County Committee. It was also agreed that the matter be raised at the AGM of the B & W J R C C in May 1973.

Coventry Benevolent Cup Final 1972

Leamington Football Team who was the holders of the Cup was held to a draw by a very strong Birmingham Team. There was no score at full time and 15 minutes extra time was played with the result remained the same. The Trophy will be held for 6 months each. This was the only second occasion that the Cup had been shared since the first final in 1940. In 1956 Leamington and Stratford fought out a goal-less draw after extra time.

Leamington Team J .R .Sharp; P Murphy; R. G. Frisk; C. Lloyd; D. Windsor; D. Morris; R. Inskip; B. Robinson; A.Fearn; J. Collins; M.Windsor; substitute; J Pawalic.

The match was played at Wilmot Breeders' Sports Ground Elmdon, Birmingham, on Sunday 14th May 1972.

Lockheed Leamington won the Senior Cup that year and Westlea Wanderer won the Junior Cup.

Assessing

The Secretary gave a resume' on the course the assessors attended at Birmingham and various points were discussed. How assessors approach referees, what to look for and a general assessment of young referees. A question was asked – "are feeder league referees assessed" the reply was given only by the. 'County Referees Committee' who mark each referee and the marks have to be maintained. Two different forms are used, one by the county assessor the other by club Secretaries.

In his talk the Secretary explained about the new form which gives a breakdown on the way the referee handled the game, each game is different, the ground conditions, plus the weather will make it difficult for the referee to be assessed, but all these conditions are taken into account and referees must give their County number to either the Assessor or to the Assessment Officer when requesting an assessment..

August 1973.

Valuables

Referees were warned not to leave valuables, money, watches, etc in the referees changing rooms; it doesn't matter where you are refereeing. One of our members had his wallet and other items stolen from the referees changing room whilst he was refereeing a match. It was reported to the Club and it is doubtful if anything can be done because Disclaimer notices are posted around the ground. The item was discussed at the Sports & Social Meeting of the Club concerned, but no action was taken.

Mr Gordon Milne, Manager Coventry F.C.

Gordon Milne proved to be a very able speaker and gave members a brief resume of his activities as Manager of England's Youth Team. This followed by a general discussion on football problems; everyone enjoyed the talk that Gordon gave to the members and the competent manner in the way it was given. A vote of thanks was expressed to Gordon Milne and endorsed by all members.

Monthly Speaker Mr Holland

Speaker – A complete change of the format was made when the Speaker for the evening was introduced to the members. Instead of football or refereeing, Mr.Holland (Secretary of the Warwickshire Branch of Conservationists) gave members an interesting talk on the subject of "Conservation" which covered a large field, including the food problem created by population growth, pollution (sewage, air, sea pollution etc)., usage of materials (E.G. Oil), loss of land (i.e. deserts etc).

Mr Holland was thanked for his lively talk and members enjoyed the question and answer session. This was a change from the normal speaker who had to cancel at short notice.

Monthly Meeting

Letter from Mr. Eddie Reynolds stating that two members from Leamington have qualified for the Birmingham County Football Association Awards, having completed 21 years active service as a referee; they are Arnold Rouse 5403 and Tom Story 4294

A busy time fundraising and sporting events for the Association.
Fund raising is always a problem, according to Bill Alderson. The Association has made a profit of £60 for 10 weeks sale of W.B.A. tickets, also the Association would be receiving £175 in respect of tickets sold for the Birmingham County Football Association.

Local League Secretary stated that he was not receiving notification from referees regarding their non-attendance at matches- there had been five such cases on Sunday. It was agreed that the Secretary should remind the members on the December circular that if they were unable to officiate in the matches they have been appointed to, they should advise the officials concerned

The Meetings Organiser had made arrangements for several club officials from the Saturday League; for a general discussion between the clubs and referees, to express their views and the players to find out what they look for and expect from referees. The Secretary of the League Tracey Thomas acted as Chairman. He introduced the following – Brian Robertson and John Stefani (Hampton Magna F.C). Neil Stonell (F.C.Crusaders), George Slatter (Rail Wanderers F.C.)Each member expressed his own personal view with regard to referees.

Points raised were –

1. Immediate control
2. Treatment of players as adults.
3. Explanation of decisions given
Conformity; with regards to penalising of players for verbal dissent

A lively discussion ensued with a majority of members participating. A vote of thanks was given to Tracey Thomas and his colleagues for coming to the referees' meeting and giving everyone the opportunity to discuss issues concerning local football. they were thanked by David Clarke.

January 1974

Expenses for Assessors

Travelling expenses for Assessors was referred back to Management after due consideration and discussion. It was agreed the Secretary should write to the Birmingham & Warwickshire Joint Referees County Committee, to enquire whether assessors can be compensated for their travelling expenses particularly with the present high cost of petrol. A copy of the letter has been sent to the B C F A.

The period between 1972 and 1976 was having a quiet spell as far as reporting the management minutes, not because of any problems but the fact that everyone is geared to the Conference.

The Association during this time was still efficiently organised and the members were supporting everything that was being done, you will notice some of the items concerning the Management and the Association move forward as much as twelve months.

1974
Leamington League

Letter received from the Leamington League Secretary giving details of misconduct points system which clubs in the league have agreed to operate. The Secretary would be pleased to receive observations that the Association would like to make. Members were reminded that to ensure the success of the system all cautions – dismissals, must be reported to the League.

The proposed misconduct points system is awaiting approval from the B.C.F.A. Referees are requested to report all cautions/dismissals also the actual kick-off times are recorded on the match forms. If the kick-off is late, report the reason for delay.

Speakers –

John Jarman FA Regional Coach for the West Midlands

Meeting Organiser had arranged a speaker to give members a talk on player/referee relations
George Pankhurst introduced the speaker Mr. John Jarman, to members. Mr Jarman is the present F.A. Regional Coach for the West Midlands – he has been appointed Director of coaching for the F.A.of Ireland. As a player, he played for Wolves, Barnsley, and Walsall. With his wealth of experience Mr Jarman was able to deal competently with his topic and his talk was enthusiastically received by the members. He talked of "Win at all costs" attitude by clubs, the pace of the present game, the necessity for close co-operation, between players and referees. After his talk, a question and answer session was allowed, this gave every member the opportunity to air their views and John Jarman gave each question that was put to him the right answer which pleased the member who had asked the question, it was a very lively evening and thanks were expressed to John Jarman for giving his time to come to Leamington and also to George Pankhurst for inviting John.

Mr Jim Simms Football League

Meeting Organiser had arranged for Mr. Roger Kirkpatrick as a Guest Speaker. Apologies from Mr. Kirkpatrick, he was unable to fulfil the commitment. Mr.Jim Simms, Football League, Leicester R.A., stood in for his colleague. Jim Simms proved to be a very able speaker, his subject being the problems facing referees and in particular, junior referees. He high-lighted problems and provided much useful advice. The necessity for effective man-management to obtain respect and co-operation of players was stressed. A lively question and answer session took place. A vote of thanks to Jim was given and appreciated by all

A.G.M May 1974

Andy Semple had completed his 3 years as Chairman; the new Chairman was Arnold Rouse. The Meeting Organiser was Fred Tebbs. There was no change in any of the other positions. Dennis Reynolds remained as Secretary and Derek Silk as Treasurer. The Auditors and the delegates to the various Leagues and County Committees were re-elected.

Monthly Meeting

The Benevolent Cup has a new Committee Chairman, Ken Anderton. No promotions for the referees at Leamington from Class 2 to Class 1, and very few from Class3 to Class2.
Yet another disappointment for Leamington Referees - no promotions again! We do not seem to have anyone speak up for the members at the County Football Association. George Dutton was asked why we are always losing out in the promotion race. He told members he would look into the promotion selection and speak to the Referees Committee. He also requested the names of all the referees who had applied for promotion.

Conference Gateshead 1974

The delegate said the proceedings were marred by the collapse and death of Captain George Allen, Treasurer of the National Referees Association who collapsed whilst waiting at the Station for his Train to the Conference at Gateshead. Captain George Allen was a remarkable man and was greatly respected by every one in the Referees Association. His talks to the members when he came to Leamington were always interesting and full of anecdotes; he will be missed. When the information reached Leamington after the Conference a minute silence was held in respect to Captain Allen
According to the Delegate, the Conference at Gateshead was well organised.

Conference 1976

The 1976 Conference at Leamington is struggling with fund raising to keep up with costs. These have escalated to £3,500, now a rise of about £1,000 in 12 months. More on report in "Conference 1976"

A donation of £5 was made to the Neville Pipkin Fund Appeal.

Members are advised to inform the assessors of any changes in match fixtures, if they are seeking promotion. Coaching at St. John Headquarters, Warwick, the first week in September. Shortage of referees, still 10 or 12 short each week said League Secretary.

Mr. Roger Kirkpatrick

The Chairman welcomed Roger Kirkpatrick who was the speaker for the evening and informed members the business would be reduced to enable everyone to listen to the guest speaker.
Roger Kirkpatrick presented members with an interesting talk on his refereeing experiences to a well supported meeting. His forthright manner and unconventional approach to refereeing problems certainly held the attention of his audience. When Roger had concluded his talk, a short break ensued whilst members of the 'Multiple Sclerosis Society' were introduced to Roger Kirkpatrick. This enabled the Conference Committee, through Roger Kirkpatrick, to present the Society with a cheque for £500, raised in the Joint Sponsored Walk, organised by the Conference. A vote of thanks to Roger Kirkpatrick and the Multiple Sclerosis Society by the members was heartily endorsed.

Monthly Meeting

Complaints by Clubs, concerning overcharging on travelling expenses by referees; it is three pence per mile max, as per League Handbook, said Coventry and Suburban delegate. Permission has been granted from the B.C.F.A. to compile a list of Linesmen for Premier Division One

Travelling expenses, as the cost of petrol had now risen to 70p per gallon, it was agreed the Secretary write to all Leagues and other Referee Associations suggesting, the sum of 4p per mile be considered for travel by private transport.

1975 Guest Speaker – Mr. Geoffrey Thompson .

The Chairman welcomed our Guest Speaker Geoffrey Thompson, Secretary Birmingham County Football .Association.

Geoffrey Thompson is now the Chairman of the Football Association and a Vice-President of UEFA.

The Secretary had to apologise to the speaker and the other County members who had travelled to Leamington for having to have the meeting in the Lounge Bar. Fortunately the Steward was able to close the bar, it enabled the Association to continue with their meeting and having a full house everyone was standing around the room listening to Geoffrey Thompson. The problem was due to alterations to the meeting rooms upstairs.

He gave a talk of interest to all referees; this covered all aspects of refereeing, qualities of a good referee (knowledge of the Laws of the game, physical fitness, self reliance, personality etc) correct method of applying cautions and dismissals. Preparation of misconduct reports (brief but precise and accurate) acknowledgement of appointments, particularly County Appointments, promotional system for referees (aim is that all Class 1 Referees under 37 years of age should be on a Feeder League)

This was followed by question time, the Chairman allowed members to put one question to Geoffrey Thompson. A vote of thanks was proposed and heartily endorsed by the members present. The other Guests present were David Schofield who was always welcomed at Leamington and his words of advice were always taken aboard by the members, we also had Mr Fred Newbold from Birmingham who was Secretary of the Birmingham Works League, and our President George Dutton. Mr Fred Newbold was a very good friend to referees; his little talk went down reasonably well with the members who were at the meeting. It was a very informative meeting and every one enjoyed being there.

***Tom and George Receiving Their Meritorious Service Awards
From Eric Babbington***

August 1975

Premier Division games in the Leamington & District Sunday League. The change in appointing referees to the Leagues Premier Division was explained to the members and their re-action to the payment of a higher fee to referees. With the referees being selected by the league, the marks received during the previous month would be considered by the league, this move was not very well received. It was stated that certain referees will always get more marks than other referees and a general discussion took place on the proposals, the League Secretary said the reaction of members both for and against the proposals would be referred back to his committee. No vote was taken.

Monthly Meeting

A serious complaint was made by the Coventry Suburban Alliance League about a referee not honouring appointments and failing to inform the clubs of his non-availability, it was unfortunate that the referee concerned was a member of the Leamington Association, the Secretary was asked to write to the referee about the complaint from Coventry.
Strict rules now being applied by the County Football Association, this concerns referees who allow their registration to elapse and wish to re-register.

Class 1 (one)   between 2 to 4 years will be re-registered as Class 2. Over 4 years to be re-examined.
Class 2 (two) between 2 to 4 years will be re-registered as Class 3   Over 4 years will be re-examined.

One of the younger refereeing members informed the meeting for reference purpose of the reply, he had received from the Birmingham County F.A. regarding his recent decision to caution instead of dismissing a player for his misconduct, his decision having been guided by the action taken in a similar situation by a football league referee. The ruling of the B.C.F.A. was that referees should act in accordance with the Referees Chart.

Female Referees – In an answer to an enquiry regarding women referees. It was pointed out that they were eligible to referee schoolboy, youth and Ladies Football

The meeting was preceded by an 'Extraordinary General Meeting' called to elect two Delegates to the Coventry and Suburban and Football Alliance. Proposed by Arnold Rouse,
seconded by W (Bill) Alderson, that Derek Evans and Brian Hackleton be elected to replace colleagues who had left the Association.
Leamington & District Saturday League Secretary Guy Reeve, complained about referees failing to honour appointments. If they do not receive notification from the home club, the referee should still attend the match and if necessary, claim his fee and expenses from the league.

September 1975

Meritorious Service Awards & County Awards

Notification has been received by the Secretary concerning the Referees Association Long and Meritorious Service Award, the application placed before the Midland Division on behalf
of George Pankhurst and Tom Story had been successful and approved at the 1975 Conference.
A special event should be arranged to cover the official presentation of these awards. A date was agreed and February 1976 was suggested. The Chairman said he would sort out a few venues and report back to the Management.

At the September Management the Manor House was booked and all arrangements were made. The Association decided to subsidise by paying for the Band.
Ticket will cost about £3.50 pence each for members

Guests were nominated and to be no more than 10(ten) and the minimum number to break even would be 80, max 140 (one hundred & forty)
Guests to be invited would be the President and Secretary of the National Referees Association, plus the President of the Leamington Referees Association.
The two recipients of the Awards plus their Wives i.e. Mr & Mrs Pankhurst, Mr & Mrs Story,
The Chairman and his wife were also invited as guests.
The band booked was the "In Swingers"
Invitations were extended to other bodies including local Football Leagues. As well as receiving the Referee Award Tom Story and Arnold Rouse are to receive the 21 year Award from the County Football Association.

Conference Levy

The Referees Association at a recent Conference imposed a levy on all registered members of 50 pence per head commencing in April 1976.
This is in addition to the affiliation members pay to the National Referees Association. The amount of Subscription is £1.30 (one-pound thirty pence).
Associations were not very happy about the increase and intend to show their displeasure by making a complaint through the Birmingham &Warwickshire Joint Referees County Committee.

November 1975

Referees overcharging on Fee & Expenses, is unusual in Leamington remarked the Chairman as the Secretary read out the letter of complaint from a local Club. The Club has complained to the League who forwarded the letter to the Association.

At the same time a Club from the lower divisions has complained about a referee and his ability to referee football games. Complaints have been made about the same referee from another League.

In dealing with the first complaint a short discussion took place and the Secretary was asked to write to the referee asking him to substantiate his expenses and let the Secretary know as soon as possible.

With the other complaint from the two Leagues, the members had the complaints read out to them. It seems that he has been cautioning players, taking their names and not reporting them to the County FA. He has also been sending player from the 'Field of Play' for offences he considered warranted being sent off, not for the offences they may have committed.
None of the players concerned have been reported to the County FA.

Other complaints and accusations had arisen from the original complaint; these were not proved by the Leagues concerned. The Referee has been reported to the County Football Association who requested the Referee to travel to Birmingham so they could assess him and question him on the 'Laws of the Game.' As he would not go to the County Offices, the County decided to withdraw his Licence and stopped him from refereeing.
This did not make any difference to the referee; he immediately joined another Referees Association outside the area of the Birmingham County FA and registered with another County Football Association and continued refereeing.

1976.

Celebration Dinner/Dance- Presentation Evening .

At the commencement of the Dinner before grace was spoken the Chairman asked members and Guests to stand for a minutes silence in memory of George Dutton who passed away in Hospital and William Day who died following an accident on the Fosse Way.
The event was held at the, 'Manor House Hotel, Leamington Spa.' This was accepted as being successful, although some criticism was expressed regarding the time taken up for speeches, and the presentation of awards. It was accepted that this was due to the exceptional circumstances brought about by the presentation of the two Referees Association "Meritorious Service Awards" to George Pankhurst and Tom Story also included the B.C.F.A. "Long Service Awards to Arnold Rouse and Tom Story. Chairman and Organiser were thanked by the members.

Roger Smith, Leicester & Loughborough Referees Associations,

Before the meeting commenced, the Chairman Arnold Rouse requested members to stand for a minutes silence in respect of our President George Dutton, who has passed away in hospital and to William Day (Lighthorne) a young member who had died following an accident on the Fosse Way. Letters of condolence have been sent to all concerned. After the minute's silence the speaker was introduced to the members. Roger gave the members a well presented talk on "Law 5 Referees" he put forward several controversial points of view. His talk was illustrated by pictures and a lively discussion ensued at the end in which the members present participated, this made it an enjoyable meeting and Roger who is involved with Loughborough Association offered his and his Associations condolences in Leamington's loss.

AGM May 1976

At the Annual General Meeting, when all the Association business and the Accounts had been accepted. The Association came to the election of President. To replace George Dutton who had passed away in February after a short illness.

Before the voting could take place, the Chairman asked for nominations. It was proposed by David Clarke and seconded by Tony Engel that Arnold Rouse be elected President of the Association. It was a unanimous decision.

Andy Semple was elected Chairman, and Dennis Reynolds was elected Secretary.

Chairman, Andy Semple, welcomed Mrs Chris Cairns as the first lady member of the Association and wished her well in her refereeing career. Mrs Cairns was accompanied by her husband who is considering becoming a referee himself.

Recommendation from management that the Association take over responsibility for organising the "Leamington Referees Shield" (six-a-side) Competition; for the Referees Benevolent Cup (Charity) Competition. This was approved by all.

League Report – The Delegate reported that match fees had been increased from £1 to £1.25p (One pound and twenty five pence)

A Charity Football Cup was put in motion by Arnold Rouse and Andy Semple in memory of George Dutton. It would be called the 'George Dutton Challenge Cup' – the Chairman Andy Semple had reported that a Cup valued at approx £90 had been donated by a Coventry Firm.

At a meeting of the Steering Committee. Four Leagues have expressed interest to date. We eventually hope to have 8 Saturday and 8 Sunday teams represented.

Promotions – Referees Committee B.C.F.A. David .Schofield, Vice Chairman, said that three meetings had recently been devoted to the new system of dealing with promotions and to referee appointments. This new system will enable promotions to be made by the end of March. Appointments will in future be made by members of the referees committee.

A special effort is to be made to recruit registered referees into the Referees Association. The Vice Chairman said that a list will be circulated to every one.

Referees coaching were again very successful, with Andy Semple as the coach, helped by Arnold Rouse. Most courses were held at Blackdown High School Leamington and Andy who had done the coaching for a number of years, decided to ease down, this allowed Arnold Rouse to take over. In future the coaching courses would be at the St John's Headquarters Emscote Road Warwick,

Superintendent Whittaker Coventry Police

A very interesting and entertaining talk was given by Superintendent Whittaker on Hooliganism, crowd control, and on the procedures adopted by the Coventry City Police Task Force; to overcome these problems.

It was a very enjoyable evening and the explanation given by the Superintendent was brilliant. He explained how the police infiltrated the trouble areas and controlled the supporters in groups, also how they met trains and buses bringing supporters to the ground and how they controlled their movement.

It gave one the impression that as a genuine supporter, you could enjoy the match. A vote of thanks was expressed and endorsed by the members.

League Reports

A player had been sent from the "Field of Play" by the referee for abusive language. The player was on the touchline, waiting to enter the field of play as a substitute. The referee ordered him away from the ground. This situation created a problem, the Club were informed that they could not replace the player, who was a substitute and had not been used. This left them with two substitutes to use. Even though they had eleven players on the field, everyone was told that all players including substitutes were under the jurisdiction of the referee.

The delegate reported that during the recent spell of adverse weather conditions, a number of referees had arrived late and cancelled matches after the teams had changed and were out on the pitch, members were requested to arrive at least 30 minutes beforehand to avoid this problem, matches may be played on Sunday afternoon by mutual agreement (only applicable for this season due to adverse weather conditions).
Arnold Rouse has been appointed Vice-Chairman of the Leamington & District Sunday League.

Warwickshire Farmers Club –

Association Headquarters – Information was received by the Secretary at the proposed rent increase, due to overheads and inflation from the present £2 50p per meeting to £4.40p –
Treasurer stated that the hire charges had not been increased for approx 10 years also it would be difficult to obtain suitable alternative accommodation. It was proposed and seconded that the increased charges of £4.40p per meeting be accepted, this was carried. It was suggested that April and December be discontinued to save money, referred to management.

League Reports

A member remarked on referees failing to honour appointments or arriving late. It was suggested that leagues should have the right to discipline referees in a similar manner to players. Vic Shepherd referred to the F.A. minute which reads "In Competitions where rules permit fines to be imposed on Clubs, for lateness, the same rule may be applied to referees provided the rules of the competition allow. It was agreed that this matter be referred to management for their consideration.

Prior to the commencement of the Council meeting Arnold Rouse read out a letter the Secretary had received from Andy Semple informing him of his decision to resign as Chairman of the Association. Andy Semple referred to the lack of participation and interest shown by members at Council meetings and for social events organised on their behalf. He also referred to the lack of support from members for the six-a-side competition held on 12th June and the difficulty entailed in getting 6 (Six) members for a team. Finally he referred to the poor attendance at the August Council meeting where only eight of the twelve members who attended had remained to listen to the speaker, Maurice Pulley from Coventry. He felt that his own recent lack of enthusiasm could be partially to blame for this unsatisfactory state
of affairs. He had therefore decided to resign as he felt that with a new Chairman to give a more enthusiastic lead, a livelier R.A. might emerge.

Arnold Rouse explained to the Management Committee members that he had been unable to persuade Andy Semple to re-consider his decision. Acceptance of his decision was therefore moved by Berkely Bugg. The Secretary was asked to write to Andy Semple expressing the regret of members at his decision and to thank him for his past efforts on their behalf, also to express the hope that we shall see him at our future meetings.

An Extra-ordinary General Meeting to be held before the October meeting; to elect a new Chairman. This was called and the President who chaired the meeting explained the reasons to the members, he then asked members for nominations. It was proposed Duncan Macauley be elected, seconded by John .Austin. There were no other nominations, so Duncan was elected Chairman until the A.G.M.in May, 1978.

County R.A. reports

Referees can register with the B.C.F.A. at the age of 17 years and referees who wear glasses can now apply to be Class I (one) referees, concern was expressed regarding non- appearance of referees at personal hearings.

Prior to the commencement of the meeting members were informed of the recent death of Ron Warnke (Vice-President) and in his memory the members stood and observed one minute's silence. The death of Ron Warnke was a blow to Leamington members, having known Ron for as long as one can remember, he always seemed to be there when needed. Ron was instrumental in suggesting the move to Solihull for our Conference in 1976. Condolences were sent to Mrs. Warnke on her sad loss (more about Mr.Warnke in Conference 1976).

Referees travelling expenses

Referees travelling expenses – It was recommended from management that the charge should be 5p per mile. This was accepted by members where the rule of League Competitions does not specify the actual travelling expenses which will be paid.
Travelling expenses claimed should be assessed as follows –The actual fares incurred (if travelling by public transport) or if by own transport 5p per mile. The Secretary was requested to include this information, which will be effectual from 1st January 1978, on the January circular, also to inform local Leagues.

1978

Monthly Meeting

Promotions have been more closely vetted and take into account total matches officiated, average marks also any County F.A. appointments taken, next season's registration forms will have a section set aside for referees applying for promotions to cover questions such as –
"When did you first apply for promotion, have you been on a Bilberry Course etc (coaching)".
All referees who have failed to obtain Class 1 (one). Will be notified by letter together with an indication of the reasons why they have not been promoted. Various reasons were suggested at the Meeting by the members who have been promoted. Not enough games, marks not up to County standard and the County Assessors were not informed..

Brian Hackleton informed members that he has accepted an appointment in Nigeria from the end of April for a period of 12 months. He rendered his apology for absence from meetings until his return. Brian has just been promoted to a Class 1 (one) status. Best wishes were expressed to Brian by the Chairman on behalf of the members.

Report from the Football Association, giving details of the new Referees Charts, which will contain Laws and Amendments; alterations, illustrations of the signals used by the referee and linesman

Fred Tebbs requested consideration be given to the conference committee's recommendation that a chain of office be provided for the President and Chairman, referred back for consideration at the September Management meeting.

County RA Reports

Disciplinary reports - Incorrectly written out reports presenting problems -.County FA has said this needs addressing and members are asked to seek advice when dealing with (misconduct or dismissal) of players and sending in reports. Seek advice if you think it is needed.

County Appointments – reason for non-acceptance of appointments must be confirmed in writing.

Insurance – proposed new scheme being sought where all registered referees will be covered when travelling to and from matches as well as officiating. The cost is to be implemented, within the framework of the affiliation fee to the National Referees Association.

Complaints have been received about referees not honouring appointments. The League Secretary should be informed and if the information is correct the referees should be admonished and removed from the League list.

The delegate to the Coventry Leagues requested referees to ensure that when they receive the match forms before the game, they are signed correctly with the date, division, team and linesmen's names, referees to sign their name and registration number, enter score and indicate linesmen's marks

December 1978

George Dutton Challenge Cup

Following an enquiry into the circumstances relating to the postponement of the match between G.N.P v Pinvin Utd, it was unanimously agreed that the Referee should have overruled the protest made by the Officials of one Club with regards to the marking out of the pitch and the statement made that it was not up to the Football Association standards.

It was decided that arrangements should be made for the match to be played in Coventry with a different Referee. The match was arranged for the Conference Sunday in January 1979 at the home ground of G N P FC.

The weather for that Week-end was cold and frosty, and when Pinvin FC arrived at the ground they found the goal posts damaged and parts of the pitch rutted. They refused to play on the pitch. The referee had earlier called the game off. The home Club failed to contact Pinvin to tell them the game was off.

Pinvin made an appeal to the County that the Football grounds were not up to FA standard and they were claiming financial loss by travelling to Coventry twice and not playing. They also demanded that the game be transferred to Pinvin.

The Hearing was due to be held at the Midland Hotel Birmingham on February 12th 1979 at 7.30pm.

Efforts were being made for the match to be played at Kenilworth Rangers ground, this unfortunately was also called off due to the weather. The final arrangement for the match to take place was at Warwick County Council Staff Club on Sunday 15th April 1979.

March 1979

The committee of the George Dutton Charity Cup were not very happy at having to go to Birmingham to respond to the charge that we were not being fair to Pinvin FC. The committee considered that they had done their best to have the match played; it was the weather that interfered with the arrangements. The Chairman Sid Sharpe said he would go with the Secretary and the County Delegate from the League would also be present. At the meeting in Birmingham the committee from the County introduced them selves to everyone and it also included the Secretary of Worcester Football Association who was an observer because Pinvin was registered with them.

The Chairman of the Birmingham County who opened the meeting allowed Pinvin and the George Dutton Committee to put their points although at separate times. When they had made a decision we were allowed in the room together and the County Decision was given in our favour. We had a good talk with Pinvin and with the Secretary from the Worcester FA it was pleasing that there was no animosity over the incident and the Secretary wished the competition good fortune.
The match v G N P was played and Pinvin went on to play in the Final, against Bartley Green, at Racing Club Warwick, and lost 1-0.

1979

The Secretary Dennis Reynolds, will be standing down at the Annual General Meeting. All the other officers will be prepared to offer themselves for re-election. John Austin, will be prepared to stand for the office of Secretary.
The following proposals from Management were proposed and seconded and unanimously agreed by members present:
(a) The position of Meetings Organiser and Press Secretary should be rescinded with management taking over the responsibility of these positions.
(b) The number of management be increased from 4(four) to 6(six).
(c) The subscription rate for 1979/80 season should be increased from £2 .50p to £3 .

Leamington Saturday League

With the collapse of the Leamington Saturday League at the end of last season, several clubs had moved into the Coventry North Warwickshire League, also the Coventry Alliance and Suburban League.
A serious complaint was made by spectators against the use of foul and abusive language by clubs, on council pitches. Referees were urged to do all they could to stamp it out. It has been said that clubs could easily lose the use of council pitches or private grounds if the abuse continues. Another case was brought to light, about the referee using foul language. The complaint was not from a team, but a member of the public. The Association felt it was a serious matter and appealed to all referees to stamp it out
Members were informed that Arnold Rouse had received his Meritorious Service Award at the 1979 Conference and a presentation would take place at Dinner/Dance. Congratulations were offered.

Secretary's Report

Letters concerning the assault on two of our referees read for information. A discussion took place on the whole question of assault and the action that should be taken. All members agreed the referees must get the backing of the Disciplinary Commission when issuing punishment for this serious offence and a recent case in our opinion did not show this was happening. Members found it difficult to understand why the referee was not at the disciplinary hearing. Our representatives to the Birmingham and Warwickshire JCC were asked to take the matter further which they agreed to do. It was pointed out to members,
This was an isolated case and they should not be put off refereeing because of it.

A letter from Frank Wall retiring from the R.A was received and read; members expressed their disappointment at Frank Wall's decision. The Secretary was asked to write to Frank Wall expressing the committee's thanks for all his hard work over the past 20 years.

This was a surprise to quite a few of the members and having known Frank since the 1957 period, and the amount of work he put into the Association. It seems that all the senior referees who were involved with the Conference have moved on; let us hope that the younger members who have taken office now carry on the good work. I know they will and it will be rewarding for the Association to have members reach the standard to referee on the Football League.

Leslie Staite thanked the players who turned out for the Coventry Benevolent Cup Final which we lost but nevertheless put up a good fight. We received the runners up trophy which was displayed at the meeting. It was decided to find out date of next year's competition as soon as possible so that we can get things under way.
Bill Burnell reported on the state of the George Dutton Cup for this season. It was pointed out that a vacancy appeared on the management following Frank Wall's resignation. John Birch was elected.

Arnold Rouse who has been doing the Coaching for the Association and had been having plenty of success with referee candidates taking the examination at the Sidney Singer School in Coventry passing out with very good marks, due to other events taking place he approached John Mander to see if he would take over the coaching whilst he was involved with the other issues. John agreed and became the coaching officer to the Association

Success came his way and the members who he coached were soon refereeing. John went on to take up the new Licensed Instructors courses set up by the Football Association. He progressed so well that he became the Area Officer and gradually recommended other members to take the course, (a further article will be written about licensed instructors in Coaching)

December 1979

It was reported that the matter concerning assaults on a local referee was being taken up with the County Football Association by the representative from the County Referees Committee. The delegate requested that referees keep copies of all their reports.
Two Referees suspended this year. Eight cases of Assaults reported to the B.C.F.A. Two cases have not been confirmed, one case still under review.

The ending in 1979 was not one you would expect with Christmas on its way. The latter part of the 70's seemed to be where members who had been in the Association a long time were beginning to leave or retire and move on. When I spoke to them over leaving or resigning, they all said they had enjoyed the years in the Association and the friendship they had made and felt it was time to leave, although they all said the interest of the Association would always be there. It was a sad feeling to me because the majority had been in the Association since the middle or late 1950's and we were all involved with the Conference. Still time must move on and we will see what the period between 1980 and 1999 brings and that will depend on the Officers and the support they receive from the members.

The National Referees Association 58th Conference 1976

Staged at St John's Hotel Solihull

Organised by the

Leamington &District Referees Association
for the 11th 12th and 13th June 1976.

The National Referees Association Conferences have been organised through the Divisions since the formation in 1908. Leamington staged the 58th in 1976.

The Conference is a special event to referees. A great deal of importance is attached to it. It is an event that one Society or Association has the privilege of organising the three days of activity. As well as fund raising you had to find accommodation for about 600 people, a venue for the Conference, and entertainment with suitable meals for all.

Leamington was one such Association and at least two attempts were suggested before the council members were in favour.

The following is Leamington's effort in staging the 58th Conference: -

The next time the conference was mentioned was when the Midland Division in 1966 were looking for someone to take on the 1971 Conference. Two members of the management did show an interest and a request went out to the members to see what the response would be to stage the 1971 Conference at Leamington. This was thrown out by the members at a meeting and it seems that insufficient time had been given to the event also members felt that they were being rushed.It was suggested that the management find out as much as they can from other Associations who had organised a Conference, if members agree it has to be with at least a 75% majority. When it was raised again the voting did not reach the 75% required so the issue on the conference was dropped, five years later it was again, the turn of the, Midland Division to stage the Conference. The Association was given the opportunity to organise the conference and the management committee were a little bit more prepared and they had within reason done their homework. Eventually the management committee decided to go to the monthly meeting and seek support from the members to stage the 1976 Conference.

After a general discussion at the meeting most of the members were in favour and suggested the management obtain the following information:

1. **The overall costs,**
2. **Who would pay for the delegates expenses**
3. **Do members attending pay for their own Hotel Accommodation?**
4. **What size Committee would be required.**
5. **And would the Association benefit from staging this Conference.**

Members of the Management arranged a meeting with the Midland Divisional Representatives, David Schofield and Ron Warnke. At the meeting they were told:

1. **Delegates attending the Conference would pay a Levy,**
2. **The amount decided by the EC Council.**
3. **Delegates would pay for their own Hotel Accommodation**
4. **All the Conference Committee would have to find, would be a suitable Hotel to accommodate all the members of the National Executive Council. In one Hotel if possible. This was the basic requirement**
5. The Committee would also have to find funds for entertainment and other items such as Transport to and from the Conference Hall. Sponsors would help if a brochure were to be produced, advertising their business.

December 1971

At the next Council meeting a summary of the meeting with the Midland Divisional representatives was put to the members and the Chairman asked them to vote as they felt, remembering "if you vote in favour, there is a lot of hard work to be done": - members were informed at this point, 'it is only a tentative enquiry'. The Conference will cover three days of activities, the proposition was seconded, and the voting was in favour. The Secretary was asked to write to the, 'Midland Divisional Secretary, suggesting that Leamington & District Referees Association was a possible venue to stage the 1976 Conference. The committee would need the members' support during the next four years if the proposal was accepted. The proposition was sent to the, Midland Divisional Secretary.

.

In 1972 after the Midland Division had held their meeting, the final go ahead was given to the Leamington Referees Association to stage the 1976 Conference. A meeting was finally called on Friday 14th April, 1972. The extraordinary meeting took place with 19 members present. David Schofield outlined the procedures and said, "You will need a Chairman, Secretary, Treasurer, plus an Accommodation Secretary, and Committee".
David Clarke chaired the meeting and he allowed everyone to put their points of view concerning the Conference. The Chairman was elected, nominations were then moved for the Secretary, one of the Vice-Presidents was determined to highlight the abilities of a colleague when he nominated David Clarke, telling every one the he would be the best man for the job. The Secretary of the Association who had also had his name put forward, wasn't very pleased, the voting resulted in David Clarke being elected.

One member was concerned over the Association, if any of the present officers were elected to the Conference Committee. If this happened, would the association suffer and he was suggesting the officers of the Association should not hold office in the Conference committee. The suggestion was rejected and left to be raised again at the AGM. The County representative said most officers of an association are the ones who get involved with conference.

The following Officers were elected:-

Chairman – Mr.Frank Wall
Secretary - Mr David Clarke
Treasurer - Mr. Derek Silk
Mr.F.Tebbs - elected Assistant Treasurer

The Election of Accommodation Secretary was left on the table. Arnold Rouse was asked, he said he needed time to consider, but was elected on to the Committee.
At a Meeting later on, additional Committee Members were elected they were Bill Alderson, Bob Field, Andy Semple, and Vince Slark.
Events conspired to create difficulties for Leamington Referees Association because at the Annual General Meeting in May the Association Secretary resigned from holding office due to health problems and he finally went into hospital for a serious operation and it took him nearly 12 months to recover.

Fund raising was essential and first on the list was a sponsored walk, this was held at South Leamington Football Ground and majority of the walkers were referees. A certain amount of money was raised. The Chairman obtained a Gentleman's Wrist Watch which was donated and the time was set, tickets were sold to guess the time it finally stopped. The committee were meeting quite regularly and fund raising was going along steady, little did the committee or the officers realise the problems that were in store.

The Chairman Frank Wall gave members at the January 1973 Council Meeting, the requirements and responsibilities to be covered by the Committee. The cost of organising the conference would be in the region of £2,000 to £2,500. At the moment, we have raised £700 and a certain amount will be raised by the levy to members attending.

The Spa Centre had been booked for the conference. Accommodation, transport and booking forms will be part of the organisation. Other issues were the Friday evening reception, entertainment on Friday and Saturday. The conference lunch and Ladies outing were all to be organised. The Chairman and Secretary went and booked one or two Hotels and Guest Houses in Leamington

Eventually the first hiccup occurred in the staging of the conference, after booking the Spa Centre for the Conference business. It was realised there was not a facility in Leamington that could possibly provide a function room large enough for between 400 to 600 people. It meant the conference and conference luncheon would have to be held at the Lockheed, with the evening function at the Chesford Lion, subject to both facilities availability. Transport would have to be arranged to transport members to the various Hotels or Guest Houses, which had been booked.

As well as raising funds, a desperate issue rocked the boat. The Chesford Lion collapsed, the reason was not known, but the owner cancelled our booking for the evening function and the hotel accommodation. The events that happened were a headache for the Chairman and Secretary until Ron Warnke suggested, the 'St John's Hotel in Solihull', the Chairman, Secretary and the Divisional Vice-President Ron Warnke went and had a look at the Hotel. They were quite pleased with all the facilities It was large enough to accommodate the conference, luncheon and evening function. Space was also available for the executive to hold their meetings.

Accommodation was excellent when nearly 75% of members attending could be housed in the one Hotel. On returning to give this information to the meeting, the committee were unanimous we move to Solihull. The Secretary then booked the hotel.

The committee set up a plan to cover everything with the move and cancelling the Hotels, and Guest Houses, booked in Leamington and surrounding Districts. Hotel Managers or Owners would have to be visited and apologies given for having to cancel, and giving them reason why, the Lockheed was cancelled, reference the Conference and Luncheon. Arnold Rouse having recovered from his illness was elected Accommodation Secretary.

He was responsible in cancelling the various hotels and guest houses that had been booked. Before doing so he paid a visit to the St Johns Hotel with the Chairman and Secretary to look at facilities and Accommodation. At the meeting all the rooms in the old part of the Hotel were provisionally booked, also the newly built part, with all bedrooms en-suite, were booked. This gave the committee about 65% of total accommodation needed. The price per en-suite room was quoted and confirmed with the Secretary at £10 bed and breakfast, per night booked from Thursday to Sunday. To make sure that accommodation would be available within the vicinity of St John's the accommodation secretary paid a visit to the hotels in Olton, Knowle and Dorrage. Each hotel was checked for the number of rooms available, cost, and if it was B&B or not, when we visited each hotel or guest house we were made welcome, the rooms were kept in good order, pleasant and well decorated.

This exercise took about 3 weeks, various hotels and small guest houses were visited and suitable ones were provisionally booked for the three nights with the total rooms and prices quoted, the prices were from; single room - £3, single room with shower - £5, double room en suite - £7 or £8, and a double bedroom - £6. These prices varied depending on the hotel.

Before booking the hotels all prices were checked with the committee. Everyone seemed happy so we wrote to each hotel and guesthouse, booking them for the three nights at the prices quoted and in doing so we made it perfectly clear that the delegates attending were responsible for their own booking and no financial responsibility would be accepted by the committee. Once the hotels had been booked the Accommodation Secretary had the job of cancelling all the guesthouses and hotels in the Leamington and surrounding area, every hotel and guest house was visited and the situation was explained to them. No one complained although one or two of the Hotels had lost other contracts when the Chesford closed down.

This enabled the Committee to set up the Booking Forms for the Conference. We used a coloured chart system for Accommodation. On the booking form members had a choice depending what they could pay and it was first come, first served. It was amusing, we had two members who only paid for the evening functions, and one parked his caravan outside Knowle and with his wife went by car to St. John's. They used toilet facilities to wash and change, another couple parked their caravan behind the hotel, no one from the hotel realised what was going on until he drove away on the Sunday morning.

We were very fortunate in our dealings in the Solihull area, we managed to get our bookings to the hotels signed and sealed before the 'National Exhibition Centre' was completed, once it was opened hotel accommodation became very scarce. A system of transport for the delegates had to be set up and Vince Slark who was the organiser set about this task, the first thing he had to do was check all the hotels and route to St Johns Solihull. He then wrote to a bus company for quotes. Once that was completed he put his dossier to the committee who selected the Midland Red Bus Company.

The transport from Conference to the Hotels and back on Friday and Saturday worked like a dream, the Buses were punctual picking up the Delegates and their wives and taking them back to their Hotels, the drivers were always pleasant.

In each hotel we had a committee member and his wife staying and the Hotels used were the St Johns Solihull, The Flemings at Olton, The Greswolde and Bank at Knowle, and the Forest at Dorridge plus two Guest Houses one locally, and one at Acocks Green, each member had a list of guests staying at the Hotels. Arrangements were made at one Guest Houses a Taxi was used. The Transport system enabled the committee members to keep every one under control.

A young Irish couple ran the Guest House in Acocks green and they were brilliant. We had Americans from Upper Heyford who were referees and wanted to come to the Conference but their wives also wanted to visit Birmingham to go shopping. To accommodate them I put the five couples in the guesthouse, one of the American referees informed me that they had enjoyed the week-end and were staying on for the week

A few problems did arise with the accommodation. One was on Friday evening when a complaint was made against the smallness of the room allocated to them. On investigation we were told that the Hotel had put them into a box room by mistake. We contacted another Hotel which had held back two rooms for us and checked whether one of them was available. The answer was "yes" so I booked on behalf of the couple and arranged for a committee member to sort it out once they had returned to their Hotel. This was done to everyone's satisfaction.

Funds still had to be raised, waste paper was paying dividends and a joint sponsored walk with the Multiple Sclerosis Society left us with a clear £1000 which was split 50/50. At the meeting, various suggestions were forthcoming, it was suggested we try to raffle a Car. One or two of us had helped local boys clubs sell tickets for a car, the suggestion was looked at, whilst members were talking about fund raising, the Secretary told us of the concern that was being expressed by the National Secretary and other members of the rapid rise in the Cost of Living, it seems that OPEC were putting the Barrels of oil up every day.

The Secretary told the National Committee that we had discussed other ideas and was making progress. At that point he told us that the Birmingham & Warwickshire J C Committee under Ken Anderton was prepared to set up a separate committee to raise funds to help the conference committee and with his committee from Coventry the Car Raffle war organised. We obtained the Car which was a Mini from Pitkin Motors in Leamington and other prizes were obtained in Coventry.

The raffle books were sold on a 50/50 basis and were sent to all Referees Association's or Societies in the Country, the competition finally cleared sufficient to pay for the Conference. All credit is given to Ken Anderton, Alan Richardson, Alan Richards and Kieron Barrett who formed the Committee and it was suggested later it could be used for the National Referees Association in general. The Conference Committee really appreciated the amount of work that Ken and his colleagues did for the Conference.

Another event to raise funds for the Conference was the Six-a-Side Football Competition started in June 1973 at Harbury. David Clarke obtained Sponsors for this, they provided a very nice looking Shield to present to the Winners, this six-a-side, was the first one we organised. Every match was refereed by officials from the Football League who supported the committee, it was an excellent day. The event became an annual one with funds generated going to the conference. After the conference had finished all the funds raised went to the Referees Benevolent Fund and since that date it has benefited considerably and over the years.

Other fund raising events were being considered, such as a treble's competition, this was set up and finally brought in £250(Pounds). The Local Sunday Football League handed over a Cheque for £73(Pounds), this was from each player paying a registration fee to the league, which was then handed over to the committee to raise extra money. We built the Six-a-Side into a Sports day with a fete and side stalls, similar to the one we organised at RAF Gaydon for our Six-a-Side Cricket match.

Conference Report August 1975

David Clarke reported he had now sold off approximately 6 tons of waste paper and the collection of further supplies had now been discontinued. A Conference Committee Meeting with the Executive Council would be held the next week.
Pat Gywnne expressed a general disappointment of members at the decision to change the venue for the Conference from the Chesford Lion to the St Johns Hotel Solihull. David Clarke fully explained the circumstances leading to this decision and stated the alternative venue had been determined by the size of the hall required to accommodate people attending the conference. He emphasised the conference was still being run by Leamington Referees. Legal action against the Chesford Lion was under consideration with a view to obtaining compensation for the inconvenience and extra costs involved.

He asked members for their continued support for this event particularly in view of the extra work now entailed due to circumstances beyond Conference Committee's control.
Members then indicated their acceptance of these circumstances and expressed their appreciation of the efforts of the conference committee in re-organising the arrangements at such short notice.

The Secretary gave brief details of the report being submitted to the Midland Division Council Meeting in September, giving details of the setback that occurred in 'May.' A conference hand-out was made available to all members at the Council Meeting. Herewith the report that David gave to the Midland Division

Leamington Referees Association Conference Committee
September 20th 1975 Report to the Midland Division Council Meeting
Conference 1976

At the last meeting in March it was reported that considerable progress had been made and this has continued. Unfortunately a major setback occurred on 17th May 1975, when a letter was received from the 'Chesford Lion' cancelling the booking we had made twelve months earlier. As this Hotel is the only one near to Leamington which has a Ballroom large enough for a gathering the size of the RA Conference it was obvious, that unless they reversed their decision all the arrangements made with Hotels, Conference Halls, Transport and local Authorities would have to be cancelled.

A meeting was arranged on Thursday 22nd May, with the Chairman and Finance Director of the 'Chesford Lion,' with the Divisional Vice-President Mr R Warnke present. No promise could be obtained from the hotel to reverse the decision to cancel the booking with no explanation other than "the present economic situation" was made a.short discussion afterwards between the committee was all that was needed to conclude that even if legal measures were taken to force the Chesford Lion to honour their commitment their attitude on the day could well ruin a very important occasion. It was agreed therefore an alternative venue should be sought and the question of damages be investigated if the need arose.

The President was kept informed of the situation by Mr Warnke. The Conference Committee with the assistance of Mr Warnke considered that the St John's Hotel would be a suitable venue for the Conference, As it is within a reasonable distance from Leamington. An appointment was made for Tuesday May 25th with the Manager when the Committee agreed to book the Hotel for the Conference. Since that date agreement had been reached on the cost of the Buffets, Luncheons, provision of Bands, use of all Hotel facilities etc.

Most of the work already carried out in organising the Conference in Leamington has been cancelled, a major proportion of this unpleasant task having fallen on our Accommodation Secretary Mr Arnold Rouse.
The Conference handout was prepared with a bit of a rush, but we were pleased with the reception it received from the delegates at the 1975 Conference in Torquay.

Conference Fund (Finances)

1   We have held the Six-a-Side Football Competition again this year and it has proved a highly successful social occasion but the net money raised was lower than last year due to increased expenditure.
2   The sponsored walk in1976 had to be cancelled due to a surplus of walks in the area.

3   County R.A Raffle

The draw has taken place and we understand that a profit will be made of around £1,400.00(one thousand four hundred pounds). Our Committee would like to place on record our thanks to the Birmingham & Warwickshire Referees Joint Committee for organising this raffle which should cure the problems of inflation which was not envisaged when the job of providing the conference facilities was undertaken.

Conference Report February 1976

A concise report provided by David Clarke

Booking Forms now distributed, guests invited and details of acceptances to date provided- Conference Committee to invite their own guests in due course.

Financial situation £3000 (Pounds) plus booking form fees (approx, £1100 (eleven hundred pounds) received to date)

Mayor of Solihull has been invited to open the Conference.

Catering arrangements have been finalised.

Leamington Silver Band and Barry Jons engaged for the Friday Evening.

Transport is to be provided by the Midland Red Company.

Ladies Lunch and outings (shopping or a visit to Charlecote Park) have been arranged.

Members, who had offered to assist at Conference, were requested to be in attendance at 8.15am prompt at Solihull on Saturday 12th June 1976. Each one received a detailed schedule of the events that would take place during the day, each had slightly different duties to perform, and they were as follows:

8.15 am meet for briefing with Secretary.

Supervising signing of register for Delegates / Directing Officers to the stage,

Collect Containers for Silver collection at Lunch time, after lunch direct Delegates back to the Conference Hall, remain in Hall, in case required for help.

There were slight variations to one or two schedules; for instance one member was asked to assist the General Secretary during Conference if needed it meant he would be stationed by the side of the stage. The members who offered to assist seemed to enjoy the work they did and the pleasant way they oot about the tasks made everything worth while.

The actual Committee members had a complete Itinerary of the events for Friday and Saturday which detailed the jobs and timing they would be doing. Everything depended on how well the Committee worked together and knowing the effort everyone had put into the Conference since 1972 the Chairman and Secretary had no worries.

The Itinerary for the Friday was a very busy one and when all the delegates had booked in at St John's a quick check by phone to all the other hotels confirmed that everything was okay and all guests had arrived. With the two bands and a meal the evening was a success.

The Saturday would be very busy in the morning, with the Chairman and Secretary welcoming the Guests to the Conference. This included the Mayor of Solihull and when he had welcomed the Conference to Solihull to make sure he is escorted out. A quick check to see that all the Tellers were in position and that all delegates, wives and partners were in attendance, the Ladies were briefed by the Ladies Committee, when the Long & Meritorious Service Awards and the Life-Membership Awards had been presented. The Ladies would then move from the Conference Hall and join the coaches taking them on the organised day trip. This took them to Charlecote and then on to Leamington, where they had lunch at the Manor Hotel. This was a successful day out.

Once the Conference had started, only a few of the Committee would be busy, helping out with the collection and setting up the Tombola stall for the evening. The committee members, who were responsible for the transport to the various Hotels, would be busy making sure that everyone caught the coaches back to St Johns Hotel for the evening's entertainment.

After the report the Secretary gave in February, the committee still had a lot of work to do before the final day came. Fund raising was still going on and small amounts were given to the Treasurer.

The final Conference report was given to the Council Meeting on the 7th May 1976. In the report the Secretary told the members we now have approximately £6,000 (pounds) available. Accommodation will be required for approximately 500 people from outside the Midlands area with representatives from the Midlands bringing the total up to the 600 mark.

Conference starts at 9.00am prompt on Saturday morning and after a break for Lunch, a silver collection for the Benevolent Fund will be made.
After Lunch the Conference will resume on the subject of 'Disciplinary Matters' with talks being given by Sidney Stokes, Alf Gray and Ken Walker.

The Evening function, at which the Referees Association Conference Draw will be made, will commence at 8.00 (20.00 hrs) with two bands (one a Calypso band) the other a (seven piece Dance Band.) provided by the Hotel. They will entertain the delegates for the whole of the Evening function.
The Tombola stall on behalf of the Conference Funds is being organised by Leamington Referees Association.

Transport has been laid on for collecting delegates and their Ladies from outlying hotels and Five Coaches have been booked for the Ladies outing.
All Accommodation arrangements have been finalised by Arnold Rouse and a display has been organised by Andy Semple and Pat Wright to show delegates some of the History of Leamington Referees.
Eight Scrutineers will be required and also assistance to cover the allocation of conference magazines and the signing of the attendance register.

Before we get to the final conference report, let us pay a tribute to the Ladies Committee who organised the Ladies Outing and Hotel Luncheon on Conference Day. The Committee under Mrs Clarke helped to raise funds for the Conference by promoting events in Harbury. They made all the arrangements for the Ladies trip to Charlecote and. The Luncheon at the Manor Hotel the whole day's outing was deemed by the guests as excellent and a real success.

The Final Conference Report

A short report was presented by David Clarke, which is as follows:- "The Friday evening buffet/dance featuring the Leamington Silver Band and the Barry Jonn's Trio, was very successful."
On Saturday every one was kept very busy arranging the distribution of Conference Folders, signing-in the visitors, organisation of the ladies outing etc.
The Conference was very successful, with Frank Wall Chairman of the Conference Committee proposing a vote of thanks to the retiring Officers of the National R A
At the Dinner/Dance entertainment was given by the two Bands provided by St Johns Hotel. During the course of the evening the Draw was made for the Mini motorcar, as a fund raiser with the Tombola, organised by Bill Alderson both were highly successful.

Congratulations to the Conference Committee on the very high standard attained, this was expressed by many of the visitors, some who considered it the best function they had attended. Well over 30 letters were received by the Secretary, congratulating the Association on a successful Conference, all the Letters from the various Individuals and Associations were placed in book form for any member to read and at the end of this chapter a brief resume' of the letters received will be printed.

Frank Wall Chairman thanked the Conference Committee for their efforts which had resulted in such a good job being well done by Leamington R.A.

The Conference was an occasion that members who were involved could talk about for years and when a few of us meet we usually do. It was the biggest undertaking that a small Association like Leamington had attempted and the Committee with the Officers like;- Frank Wall, David Clarke ,Derek Silk, Arnold Rouse, Andy Semple, Vince Slark, Fred Tebbs, Robert Field and Bill Alderson, could still feel proud for the amount of work that was done to make it a success. We had a considerable amount of help from people like the National Secretary Ron Warnke and previously Eric Babington who had retired from being the National Secretary, we had David Schofield from the Midland Division also the Birmingham &Warwickshire J C C. Ken Anderton with Colleagues from Coventry. We also had members from our own Association either helping over the Week-end or just coming for the day: here are a few names, Brian Hackleton, Dennis Reynolds, Pat Wright, Duncan MacAulay and Keith Hunt.

We must also mention the Ladies Committee. It is explained how they set about raising funds for the Ladies Outing and they should all be mentioned: Mrs Pam Clarke, (Chairman) Mrs Jennie Silk, Mrs Moira Slark (Secretary), Mrs Helen Wright, Mrs Pat Semple, Mrs Ann Hyam, Mrs May Field and helpers M/s Christine Clarke & Andrea Slark.

After the Conference had finished and on Sunday morning everyone started to leave and travel to what ever part of the Country they came from. On the way out we had compliments galore, and word such as well done, thoroughly enjoyed the week –end, best we have ever been to, with these plaudits ringing in our ears we finally settled down.

Herewith a few of the pleasing remarks made by the President and the Delegates from the Various A S B's to David Clarke Secretary which is compiled in a Book.

K Burns Esq President National Referees Association:-
"Dear David speaking for all members of the Council to thank you, your committee and the Ladies for making the Conference the success it was"

Mrs Ken Burns to Mrs Pam Clarke Secretary of the Ladies Committee: - Congratulations and many thanks for a marvellous week-end thoroughly enjoyed by one and all.

AH Lavender Esq Immediate Past President:- Thanks to you all for a wonderful job, well done.

R Warnke General Secretary Referees Association:-
Congratulations in overcoming all your difficulties and the endeavour by Leamington RA **"TO MAKE A GO OF IT"** resulted in one of the most successful Conferences I have ever known.

E Adams Secretary Midland Division:-
"Congratulations on the excellent arrangements made for the Conference Leamington RA will be remembered by all for many years to come for their work and devotion."

Alan Robinson Overseas Secretary:-
"May we from Portsmouth offer you and your committee our congratulations for a well organised Conference, it was a terrific week –end for the Ladies outing .Well done!!"

David Schofield Warwickshire Delegate:-
"Please convey to the committee and the 'Ladies team' my warmest congratulations and personal thanks for a wonderful Conference"

William M Alexander Vice- President National Referees Western Division:-
Congratulations to you and your committee for your excellently arranged Conference, it was first class 'Well done.'

Edward Ring National Referees Association & Magazine:-
"A great job, by a great team."

Norman Rippon Durham County Society:-
"May I commit in writing my most sincere congratulations to you, your wife and committee for a well organised Conference."

W F Pennick General Secretary BCFA:-
"Dear David would you convey to all members of your committee the thanks of myself and my wife for a most enjoyable week-end at Conference."

Tracy Thomas Secretary Leamington & District Sunday League:-
Dear David please convey to your committee the sincere thanks of my President, my wife and myself for the excellent evening we enjoyed in pleasant company at your Conference Hotel on the 12th June 76.

Wilfred Eastwood Birmingham & Warwickshire Referees Delegates:-
"What a wonderful Conference, you and your committee must feel very proud. In all sincerity I think it was one of the best conferences I have attended".

Brian Chester Secretary Doncaster &District Referees Society:-
Congratulations for staging the 1976 Conference in such a successful manner, an excellent week-end for everyone.

E G Reynolds Secretary Birmingham & Warwickshire Joint County Committee:-
Congratulations I am sure the loud and sustained applause you and your fellow committee received at the Saturday night function, said it all far more efficiently than words of mine can.

Jim Sims Leicester Referees Association:-
Dear David on behalf of Audrey and myself I write to thank you and your Committee for the hard work and organisation in making the 76 Conference so enjoyable.

John Marsh Hon Secretary Brecon and District Referees Society:-
On behalf of our members may I offer a big 'Thank You' for the success of the Conference, the friendliness of your committee and the happy atmosphere they created, especially our guide Fred Tebbs, his smiling face was a joy to behold.

Brian More Secretary Milton Keynes& District Referees Association:-
After attending Conference 76 I must write and send our thanks to you and your committee for all the hard work you put in to make the Conference a success, congratulations to every one concerned.

This one is from Eric Babington who was the General Secretary of the Referees Association and was instrumental in guiding the Association in the right direction as far as the Conference was concerned and he was also a very good supporter to Leamington whilst he was on the County Referees committee. Eric had resigned from being Secretary of the National Referees Association and David Clarke Conference Secretary wrote to Eric after the Conference and in his reply to David was one of appreciation and pleased that in some small way he had helped Leamington to organise a successful Conference.

Herewith the names of the Association or Society, or even personal notes:-

D T Jackson Secretary Kings Norton Referees Association: - "Excellent week-end".

Northamptonshire County Referees Association: - "Congratulations to a well organised Conference."

Alan Tate Secretary Slough &District Referees Association: - "First Class arrangements for a wonderful Conference."

Gerry Taylor Secretary High Wycombe Referees Association: - "A Truly Magnificent Conference."

H G Ivie Secretary Ilford Society OF Association Football Referees: - "An enjoyable and efficient Conference."

A J Allright Secretary West Middlesex Referees Society: - "Congratulations on a well organised Conference."

W Lawrence Woolwich Referees Society (London):- "A most Excellent Conference."

B B Bradford Sussex Referees Delegate:- "Thanks for staging a wonderful Conference at Solihull."

G Pankhurst: - "Well done to the success of the 76 Conference, an excellent week-end."

T Lattimore Secretary Harrow & District Referees Society: - "Congratulation on the way you presented the 58th Conference."

T Lewins Coventry: - "Congratulations on a well organised Conference."

R Drake Secretary Portsmouth Referees Society: - "What a wonderful week-end every one enjoyed at the Conference well done to you all."

T Miller E C Devon County Referees: - "Enjoyable week-end and congratulations on achieving a very high standard, many thanks to all your Committee."

O Venning Hon Treasurer The Referees Association: - "it was a memorable week-end and well organised, my wife and myself send you our Congratulations".

The Collection taken at Conference of £67,30p was a Conference record.

After all the hard work and enjoyment the Association had over those three or four days serious activity, it was pleasing to settle down to normal business. After a short break David Clarke organised a small get together for the officers from the National R A and the Committee. Every one had a enjoyable meal and a good chin wag, and again the Committee was Congratulated by the President Ken Burns for a job really well done. So ends the 1976 Conference. .

Chapter 8

ASSESSORS

Junior& Senior Referees

Assessing referees is very important. In the early days no one was able to tell a referee that he was not in the right position or that he was not using his diagonal properly, according to Harold Elkington the only time we had any information was when we had the occasional visit from the Birmingham County Referees Committee Members.

This situation must have been very similar to the way the members were coached during the earlier days and up to 1939. Harold told us, to actually receive any benefits you had to belong to a large Association where members were able to get elected to the various Committees.

It was obvious that changes were needed and majority of referees in the 1940s and up to the 1960's would not be able to say that they had been Assessed, in fact if you had spoken to referees about being assessed by a fellow referee, they might not have known what you were talking about

During the 1950s a few referees had Senior members watch them and general advice was often given. One referee we knew had a Senior referee who was on the Football League watch him at a match and all he said to the young referee "what is wrong with your whistle." He did not give any explanation and we don't think the young referee ever learned anything from that statement.

It wasn't until the late 1960's that general information was being "circulated" to the referees Associations from the County Referee's Committee. The talk was about Assessing and how it would be started. The Association were asked to discuss the issue and send nominatons to the County Football Association when a Seminar would be held to discuss the whole issue of Assessments and how the referee could be marked. Leamington Referees sent in three names and they were Jack Joyner, Ron Pemberton, and Arnold Rouse, they were all Class 1(one) and had been on a Senior League. Jack Joyner and Ron Pemberton had retired from active refereeing and Arnold Rouse had retired from the Senior League although still refereeing in junior football

The Chairman of the County Referees Committee Eric Babington invited all three members over to Birmingham to the Seminar which was held on a Sunday. At the start of the day he explained everything to us and what the County was trying to do, he told us that he had been in contact with as many of the County Football Associations as he could to find out how they had been assessing referees and what success they had. The directive for this approach came from the Football Association and Eric Babbington told everyone that very few Counties were actually assessing referees or even attempted to do so. From that introduction we were then formed into groups with a Leader who was from the Referees Committee, we were given a subject and a pile of forms to sort out and find the best one available. Most of the forms had general information that was needed.

At the end of the day we had a talk from Eric Babington and David Scofield. This covered the work we had been doing during the day and what the County were hoping to gain from the seminars, he told us that another one would be held shortly, as far as assessing was concerned we would hear from the County Association. This information eventualy came and the three names sent to the County Football Association were nominated as assessors, we were sent a list of referees who were applying to the County for promotion from Class 3(three) to 2(two) and Class 2(two) to 1(one).

The referees were not informed neither did they have to inform the assessors of who they were refereeing, or what type of match it was, this information the assessor had to find out for himself.

All this was happening in 1969 and when the information was given to the members at a monthly meeting and they were told who the assessors were, there was no objection to the newly appointed assessors, the problem was from some referees, being watched for promotion. What happens if one has a bad game?. The only answer the Secretary could give the members was that the assessor would have another look at the referee again.The system was again explained to the members and they were assured that the assessors were not setting out to criticise a referee but to help him rectify any faults he might have.

The Secretary went on to explain to the members the way the Chairman of the County Referees Committee wanted referees who were applying for promotion from Class 3(three) to be assessed. The Secretary told the members that co-operation with the League Secretary was essential, so the referee would be assessed on a suitable match. This would test the referees ability and knowledge of the game without putting him under pressure.

The marking system was such that only a number of faults would be registered, any general information for the benefit of the referee would be separate. The form would then be sent to the County Football Association and a copy would be sent to the referee. The same system would be used for referees seeking promotion from Class 2(two) to 1(one). At this time the system did not have Area Assessment Officers-they were brought into the system later on.

Once the system was started at Leamington we had a sad beginning. One of the assessors Ron Pemberton collapsed and died of "a heart attack" this left us one member short and it seemed that three assessors were needed to benefit the Association. With the referees on the Feeder and Contributory system refereeing on a Saturday and the increase of Sunday football for senior and junior football, the boys League needing referees it meant a busy time for assessors. At the next meeting we asked if any one was interested in becoming an assessor. Sid Sharp was the only one interested and he was a Class 1(one) Referee, his name was sent to the County F A and he was accepted.

We were into the 1970s now and changes were already taking place. An Area Officer was nominated who was Cyril Gould from Coventry and he was covering Kenilworth, Leamington and Warwick area.The referee would be assessed by the Assessor, his assessment would be sent to Cyril Gould who would take two copies removing the marks the assessor had awarded the referee and he would send one back to the Referee and keep one for himself, the original form would be sent to the Birmingham County Referees Committee so it could be used when the Promotion Committee meet.

Further Seminars were organised by the County Referee's Committee which always turned out to be full of interest, with plenty of interesting discussions taking place, when the final conclusons were reached it was amazing how compact the answers were from all the groups.

We had a problem with one of our assessors. He was told not to referee any more football matches. If he did he would be removed from the assessors list, as they considered his refereeing would not benefit assessing. The colleague was very upset and when we found out who had complained about him, we were disgusted. The assessor then retired from. refereeing on a Sunday afternoon and concentrated on just assessing referees, it was a petty complaint and the Under 10 and 11 boys were left without a good referee. Since that issue the Chairman of the County Referees Committee was told what had happened the situation changed and assessors with senior experience were allowed to referee at a lower level.

This Article is from John Austin The Area Assessment Officer.

Assessing has gone on by individuals on their performance since refereeing started no one is more critical than the referee himself, this should still be the case but it always helps to have an independent view of one's performance.

The aim was and always will be to try and advise the referee how his performance can be improved and should never be destructive, always constructive to encourage new up and coming referees.

I recall in my early days as a Class 3 referee, tales of assessors hiding behind trees watching referees, trying not to be noticed, were common, but that was not always the case, the majority of assessors like to meet and see the referee. I was assisted greatly by the advice and comments made by the assessors and during the three seasons I was assessed for promotion I found the comments nothing but positive.

Over the years assessing has become more important to the referee and you can be sure the more you progress the more you will be assessed.

Club marks were, in the early days, the main feature of promotion with assessment never really being considered by the referee's committee when promotions were made.

That has changed and the present criteria for promotion have changed. The refereeing year now runs from March through to the end of February, promotions being made at the beginning of March.

To gain promotion you must send a list of matches to the Area Assessment Officer who should report the fact if you fail to do so, to the County F.A.

You must complete at least 20 matches in open age football during a season preferably in different leagues, this will give the referee a variety of matches to referee, it will also give the assessor a better opportunity to assess the referee..

An accelerated promotion system is available where you have to complete the first year's criteria Level 6 to 5 by October and the second year's criteria Level 5 to 4 by the end of February.

To be considered for a level four promotion you should also complete at least five appointments as an assistant.

You must also attend a seminar for one day and be assessed at least three times.

The promotion panel considers all these elements and failure to comply with any aspect will result in the non-consideration for promotion.

In the early days Warwick, Leamington and Stratford areas came under the Coventry assessment officer. Around 1990 the County agreed to South Warwickshire having their own Assessment Officer and John Mander the Association Licensed Instructor became the Area Assessment Officer as well. I took over from John some three years later. The object being, to ensure the referees within the Leamington area were properly looked after.

With a team of assistants which have included Arnold Rouse, Pat Wright, Brian Field, Andy Dalziel, John Sharp and several others, we have assessed many up and coming referees which has included females referees as well.

Referees now wanting promotion from Level 7(seven) to 6(six) and 6(six) to 5(five) need at least three assessments during a season.

This is part of the promotion criteria.

To achieve this, match details must be sent to the Area Assessment Officer who will appoint an assessor to the match of his choosing.

Once the match has been completed the assessor will compile a report, a copy of which goes to the referee and the other copy to the County Football Association.

At the end of the season the Area Assessment Officer completes an overall report for the referees' committee's consideration when promotions are made.

Comments on the referee's suitability for promotion, and his co-operation with the assessors is made and may well have an effect on the promotion for that referee.

More and more emphasis is now being placed on assessments and this involvement will only increase.

Assessors now have to train in the art of assessing to try and ensure a good quality and consistent system.

They have to re-license every five years to keep them up to date with Law changes and without a license cannot go and assess referees..

They also need to have a good solid refereeing background to understand the pressure and problems that referees encounter and need to have the right type of personality to ensure constructive advice is given.

Once a Referee has attained level 5 he may never ever be assessed again unless he progresses further.

This is not always a good idea, as we can never stop learning and improving our trade.

Once a Referee is promoted on to feeder leagues as assistant or referee they will be assessed regularly with a view to maintaining League standards the progression of the referee.

What are assessors looking for? The list is endless but in the first instance the correct interpretation of the laws is very important along with position and movement to ensure you are in the correct place to make your judgment. Management of players and officials along with self-management and ensuring that equipment conforms to the laws are all very important.

Many more points are observed by the assessor with a view to offering advice and suggestions.

Referees should remember that the assessor is not the enemy and can be your best ally.

The whole system of assessing has been altered and streamlined over recent years.

A new contributory list of assessors has been created to cover all leagues and officials wishing to move up the ladder. This scheme is run by the Football Association and covers leagues such as the Conference and Southern Leagues. Assessors are not tied to one league and the FA appoints the assessor.

Referee assessments continue right up through the ranks into Football League, Premier League and Europe. The higher you go the more in depth the assessments are and the referees just starting out to referee locally will need different advice to the referees who referee on the Senior Professional Leagues although often the mistakes are the same.

It is clear to see that assessing which started out as an aid to promotion has become an integral part of the game.

What rewards are there for assessors? The answer is very minimal. It's nice to pass on some of the knowledge gained over the years and hopefully see an up and coming referee progress with a little advice from the assessor. Being assessed is only one part of the steps to promotion, once the referee has reached a standard such as Class 1(one) or Level 6(six) to 5(five) he still has to work hard to reach the Top.

John Austin (Area Assessment Officer)

The article John Austin has written covers the method being used to train assessors, since the beginning when everything was a slight hit or miss affair, the system has gradually improved, the forms that were used were updated and the Area Officers made the system more efficient which was a good thing. This meant the assessor did not have to spend time seeking out the referee he was to assess.

John also mentioned a few of the assessors? That were currently assessing in the 80s and the 90s in fact they were still assessing in the 21st Century, except one member who retired from active assessing in 1997. Some of the earlier assessors from the 70's were Harry Boardman who assessed locally as well as the Southern League, Sidney Sharp, Alan Windsor and Arnold Rouse.

In the article at the beginning John mentions the Classification of referees as Class 3(three) 2(two) or 1(one) and then moves on to the term **Level.** All these changes are mentioned in the Chapter 2000 to 2004.

A pamphlet is produced giving information of the type of guidance the assessor receives also the type of form for the referee who is being assessed.

The guidance is about the uniformity of assessments, advice and information the Area Assessment Officer will send to you concerning the referees you will be assessing, also advice on how to use the forms, and to make sure you have your County FA pass with you. It is essential that you read the pamphlet.

When you have assessed the referee, you have to complete two Assessment forms, both are identical.

You indicate your mark for the referee on **ONE** form only, on the reverse side of both forms the assessment officer has to complete the section giving his advice to the referee he has assessed.

Both forms are then sent to the Area Assessment Officer, who checks the advice that's given and makes sure the Assessor has signed both forms,

The one form that has the referee's mark from the assessor is sent to the County Football Association. The other form giving the referee all the information he requires to improve his refereeing is sent to the referee concerned,

When the referee is being assessed there are certain items from the 'Laws of the Game' that have to be observed. The majority of assessors have their own way of doing this, some jot down notes, quite a few tape the whole match, and a few assessors rely on memory and only record the important points, or if any problems occur. It doesn't matter what the assessors use or how they record an assessment, they very rarely give a referee a bad report. The assessors have to remember it depends on the classification of the referee they have to assess.

Herewith the 9 items from the, 'Laws of the Game'

1   Appearance
2   Signals
3   Stoppages
4   Advantage
5   Co-operation with Assistant Linesmen
6   Application of the Laws
7   Positioning and Movement
8   Overall Control and Authority
9   General Control and Constructive Advice

On the reverse side of this form are 36 sentences covering the above 9 sections and the assessor is recommended to tick up to a maximum of six points which he thinks would help the referee to improve his performance.

Each Assessor when he has completed the form has to sign it and give the date. Most assessors would have taken a copy for themselves mainly for reference purpose. Another form was available for the Junior Referee if he required gaining further knowledge. It was called a 'Self Check List for Referees' all it does is give the referee a list of 47 questions that he can read and check his own faults and then correct them.

The higher the referee attains on the new Level System the more direct and firmer will be the Assessments he will receive, at one point the referee may need a Mentor.

Referees on the Premier League and the Nationwide are Assessed every match and they have a Mentor as well.

The County Mentor Scheme

The County Mentor Scheme. A booklet has been produced for the scheme which is for the newly qualified referees, it gives you all the knowledge you need to know. The person who will be your Mentor has in all probability taken a course with the County Football Association. You have to be a Senior Referee to become a Mentor. The mentor will be someone you can talk to if you have any problems and he may want to watch you referee a football match, if that person cannot find the time to watch you possibly due to football appointments, he will have a colleague who may have actually retired from refereeing and would be available to watch you over a number of games and give a good clear and concise report about you. They are usually called 'Mentor's Assistants' .

The ten items you will be marked on are as follows:-

1	**APPEARANCE**
2	**SIGNALS**
3	**STOPPAGES**
4	**MOVEMENT**
5	**POSITIONING**
6	**ADVANTAGE**
7	**CO-OPERATION WITH CLUB LINESMAN**
8	**APPLICATION OF LAW**
9	**CONTROL**
10	**MISCONDUCT.**

Referees will be marked on the above Items, on the following symbols below
G –Good, S- Satisfactory, and N-Needs Consideration
The Mentor will usually discuss the sheet with the Referee and a copy will be sent to the Training Officer.

Retain and Retention

Once the referee has passed the Examination and has been seen by the Mentor or his Assistant, there is not a lot the Referees Association can do. The candidate before he takes the Exam is told all about the Association and why it is best to be a member, if only to be covered by Insurance. The referee is also bombarded by the Football Association and told he is a member of FAMOA. (This is explained more in the Chapter 2000-2004)

You cannot force any candidate referees to join the Association you have to leave it to them to make up their mind. Everything has been tried by the Officers over the years to encourage the youngsters; we have paid their first years membership to help them financially. Sometimes we are successful, we then encourage them to take an interest in the Association and hope they continue in membership.

It is entirely up to the referees who have just passed the Examination.

The Cooper System

This is a system that was brought into refereeing in the beginning of the 1990s and used to confirm the fitness of Referees and Linesmen on the Semi- Professional and Professional Leagues.

It started with a running distance to be covered in a certain time, a slight alteration was made to allow for age difference, so that if you were a 20 year old referee you would be expected to complete the course in the time stated, if by chance you had finished running the distance within the time limit you would be expected to continue running until you reached that time. If you were older than 20 years the time was extended to compensate the age difference and it was only extended by so many seconds.

Sprinting was another factor and again a certain distance was used, this had to be completed in so many seconds and you had to return to the start within a specific time and complete three more sprint distances each time within the time allowed and returned to the start within a certain time..

In all these tests you were not allowed to walk. If you did at any time you were penalized with extra sprints.

Herewith the distance and minimum time allowed.

2,060 metres to be completed within 12 minutes, the age allowance would have been in added seconds.

The sprint session was as follows;-

70 metres sprint in 7.5 seconds returning to the start within 15 seconds, to complete three more sprint sessions finishing at the start each time.

The referees on the Semi-Professional Leagues have found that the actual test was difficult to complete, you had to make sure you were at a reasonable fitness level before you competed in the tests.

After a number of years the Leagues altered the system by increasing the distance and they also brought in a 200 metre sprint to be covered in 32 seconds whilst all this was taking place,

You were not allowed any time wasting. Evidently the 200 metres was a killer blow to a number of referees and linesmen.

In one instance the failure rate was at least 50% and quite a number of referees and linesmen were allowed a second chance at completing the course, if they failed a second time they were removed from the League they operated on.

Some of the Semi-Pro Leagues allowed an extension of time on some of the tests this allowed the referees and linesmen who had failed the first time a little leeway to obtain the extra fitness needed, so they could continue officiating on the League.

One League did not allow that to happen, they considered the allotted time was fair enough, especially when all ages had to compete the same distance in the same minutes or seconds, and as they stated a number of the Leagues Officials over 40 years old had completed all section of the test.

The above system with distances and time was given to me by colleagues who have been through the whole system to attain fitness on the Leagues they have been officiating on. The times and distances may have altered since that date.

Chapter 9

Licensed Instructors & Coaching

Coaching referee candidates was according to Harold Elkington was very difficult. We were very fortunate to have been able to talk to Harold who told us that majority of the referees either taught themselves or had a colleague asking them questions. They used the Referees Chart and asked questions on the 'Laws of the Game.' There were 17 Laws for them to learn. If they took an examination it would have been held in Coventry and after passing they would have been asked to join the Birmingham County Football Association for a small fee. This would register them with the County and allow the candidates to referee officially.

This system seemed to be in operation in the 1930s, when members were invited to join the Association then coached through the Referees Chart. They were then allowed to take the referee's examination in Coventry. It seems that George Dutton who worked in Coventry and was well informed on County matters, may have been the person who was responsible.

When the Association was reformed in 1948 an attempt to set up a coaching session was very difficult, although George Pankhurst did try to set one up at the Leamington Boys Club. The difficulty was getting the candidates to turn up to the coaching sessions, the members who did the coaching were Alec Walters and Henry Hall they either coached together in the local Public house or at Alec Walters house during the week. In most cases all coaching would be done individually, it did not matter which way the candidate was taught, they never had any failures and majority went on to reach a good standard of refereeing.

A gradual change took place at the beginning of the 1960s' when John Jays the Secretary set up a coaching session for candidates at the Association Headquarters. Every officer and the members who made up the Management formed the committee taking it in turns to coach the candidates who took the Examination at the Willoughby Arms by members from the Birmingham County FA. We were successful every one passed.

Whether they all took up refereeing is another story. One member who helped John Jays was Frank Wall who coached members when John Jays retired.
He went to Birmingham on a Week-end course with David Clarke arranged by the Referees Committee from the County Football Association. The idea was for the members who went on this course to use the information they received and coach the referee candidates on that syllabus. At the next council meeting they gave members a resume of the type of information they received from the Referees Committee. This would enable them to coach referee candidates through to the Examination.
Frank eventually coached on his own until about 1966 when Andy Semple took over the coaching. He had support from Arnold Rouse and this continued every year until the 1976/77 season when Andy retired from coaching. Arnold Rouse became the coach until circumstances made him look for someone to take over coaching on a more permanent basis, this eventually came about as you will read later on.

Whilst Andy Semple was coaching he was very keen to go to Lilleshall so that he could improve the way he coached the candidates, with improvements to the syllabus it would make it interesting. These courses were approved by the Birmingham County Football Association. You either went for a week, or possibly longer and the person going had to be recommended by the Association.

Andy Semple was well known as a good coach and was appreciated by the County Referees Committee. It was no trouble for Andy to go on these courses; it was very valuable to any one who helped Andy with his coaching.

When he did the course at Blackdown High School, what he had been taught at Lilleshall did show and the candidates were being instructed the way the Football Association required referees to officiate.

All the time he was coaching he had in his mind to set up a Seminar for the referees he had coached over the years to see how they were getting on in the refereeing world. This came about in 1970 when Andy had put together a programme with times and points to be discussed also the type of person he would like to be the course leader. It was eventually discussed by the Management Committee and approved.

Referee's Refresher Course 1970

This course was set up by Leamington & District Referees Association and was the brainchild of the Association coach Andy Semple. This again was another first for Leamington.

Andy informed the members at a Management meeting the idea in setting up the refresher for Class 2(two) and Class3(three) referees to obtain some idea of their progress and to bring them up to date on certain parts of the Laws of the Game. He outlined his idea and suggested the people he would like to have demonstrated and lecture to the referees' attending. Andy showed the members the group schedule for discussion; they were Advantage, Dangerous Play, Off-side, Postponements Suspensions and Abandonment's, Referee and Linesmen Co-operation.

After a discussion the Management approved and the Secretary was asked to find a reasonable venue, the cost and dates available. Once we had the venue and a selection of dates the sub-committee went ahead.

The secretary in looking for venues decided to have a word with a Mr Elliott, the Manager of the Sports and Social Club at the Lockheed and after making an appointment the Secretary went to see Mr Elliott and discussed the possibility of using the Staff Canteen and the Ballroom for discussion and the use of films. He told me to put it all in writing and send it to him, also to go and see Mr Stratten who was in charge of the Canteen and explain to him what we wanted in the way of food and use of the Staff Canteen.

The meeting with Mr Elliott was a success and during our conversation about the refresher course the subject of Cricket was discussed and Mr Elliott was very knowledgeable having played Cricket as the Wicket keeper for Derby County CC. He was quite pleased and I believe talking to him helped our cause. After that meeting a letter was sent giving all the details and dates to the Sports and Social Club, and another letter to Mr Stratton.

We eventually received permission to use all the facilities, even the pitch outside if we needed it and I was told it would be marked out. From that information we went ahead and fixed the date, which was Sunday the 28th June 1970. Confirmed with Mr Stratten the date of the Seminar and requested the cost of food for the day.

The next step was to write to the Secretary of the Football Association for permission to book an F A speaker for the day and to hire two films. We eventually received notice that we had to liase with the FA speaker Steve Allatt from Birmingham who acquired the films that we needed, also Steve was available on the Sunday we had chosen.

Hiring a projectionist to show the 16 m/m film was thought to be a problem, fortunately Andy Semple had found that a gentleman from Cubbington had all the equipment and would hire it out to us, we did better than that we asked him if he would set the films up and display them at a reasonable cost, and agreement was reached.

We also had to pay for a member of staff to be in attendance at all times in case of Fire or other related problems, all these little things were added to the cost, fortunately the staff member was reasonable and only charged us a small amount, we also had to pay for the Hire of the films and pay postage for their return to the FA

In putting all the items together a costing was worked out by the Treasurer and even though the Association would be able to give us a reasonable grant other sources would have to be found to find the money for it to function, the referees who would take part would have to pay for their meal which we worked out at about £1(one pound) each.

At this point the committee decided to write to the Birmingham County F A and ask them for some financial support, we had a letter from the County asking for more information, this was sent to them and we eventually heard from the Secretary that a certain grant would be given to us, to carry this out we had to invite Eric Babington, David Schofield, and Ron Warnke.

Andy Semple was going to invite Eric and David to give a short talk to the members, Ron Warnke as Secretary to the Midland Division would have been invited anyway.

With the grant from the County F A and money coming in from the members who attended it meant that we should be able to balance the books.

The next thing the Management required was a schedule and a programme for the day with all the information necessary so that every one who would be there would know what they would be doing.

This was left to Andy Semple who laid out a time table for the day as follows:

9.30am	ASSEMBLE
9.45am	Opening of course by Eric Babington Introducing the Team Leader Steve Allatt
10.00am	Group 1 Discussion
10.30am	Group 2 Discussion
11.00am	Coffee
11.20am	Lecture and film by the Leader
12.30pm	Lunch
1.30 to 2.30 pm	Groups 3 and 4 Discussion
2.30pm	Lecture by Eric Babington and David Schofield
3.15pm	Groups with group leader thrash out points from the Discussions
4.00pm	Tea
4.20pm	Open Discussion with Leader and Group Leaders
5.00pm	Course Finishes.

The above was sent to all concerned and all Associations in the Midland Division were written to and a majority of the Class 2 (two) and Class 3 (three) in the local Associations were written to. We had to do a little bit of chasing on the week before the event took place even then we had a total of 70 people including a few of the Senior members who came along. All the referees were split into Groups of 4(four) from there a Leader of each group i.e. Chairman was selected who would put all the points together and present them to the course Leader for Discussion. Each group discussed a different subject which was approved by the Team Leader. They were as follows:-

Group 1	**Covered Advantage**
Group 2	**Covered Dangerous Play**
Group 3	**Covered Offside**
Group 4	**Covered Postponements, Suspensions, Abandonment's.**
Group 5	**This was in reserve, and used by the Team Leader, it covered Referee and Linesman Co-operation, with Club and Neutral Linesman.**

It turned out to be a very good day and well organised, the County were quite pleased with the report sent in by Steve Allatt and from Eric Babington who sits on the County Referees Committee. It was a first for Leamington and the Secretary received a letter from the County Secretary congratulating the Association for its forward thinking, but they reminded us that all future Seminars for Class 2 and 3 referees would be organised by the County Referees Committee and Bilberry would be made more use of.

The above was the brain child of Andy Semple and it proved very successful.

From then on the coaching from Leamington seemed to take an upturn and the Candidates who were coached by Andy and others had no trouble in passing the Examination and the majority made good referees.

We have had only six members do the coaching since the 1960 period, we have had plenty of support from Senior Members who come along and help the coach in giving instructions and advice, and more will be mentioned when we move into the 1980s.

When Andy decided to retire all efforts were made to encourage him to stay on but he declined.

Arnold Rouse decided to take over although he had not been to any of the courses at Birmingham or Lilleshall he had coached quite a number of candidates who had passed the Examination.

The first thing he did was to look for a place locally to teach the candidates and the St Johns Ambulance Headquarters was available .Getting permission to use a room was no problem and a small rent was discussed paid as a donation. The room itself was ideal but the condition left a lot to be desired, it was damp and cold with only Electric heaters to use. Before a meeting could start the heating was switched on at least half an hour earlier to warm the room up.

Once the candidates arrived we were okay and the room was used for three years whilst candidates were being coached. All the candidates once they had finished the course had to go to the Sidney Stringer School in Coventry to take the Examination, this was a successful event because I had only one candidate fail and the reason given was that he could not write properly. That was not a problem; one of the County Committee members sat him down and asked the Questions. He answered every one so they told him he had passed the Examination. We were very sorry to find out that he did not take up refereeing he said he was a little concerned about filling up forms, he would have made a good referee; even though he could not write properly he could talk and argue on any point.

Most of the referees who were coached by Andy Semple and me reached a very high standard of refereeing officiating on the Football Combination and the Southern League and quite a few officiated on the Midland Combination.

The coaching session I was involved with slowly came to a halt when Sheila my wife who was a Councillor and a member of the Warwick Town Council was in a position to become the Mayor of Warwick which was an honour for Sheila. This situation meant that we had to find some one to take over the coaching whilst I helped and supported my wife.

I had a person in mind namely, **'John Mander'** and decided to approach him to find out if he was interested. When John was asked if he would be interested to my surprise he said 'yes,' we had a talk and arranged to meet at the beginning of the next coaching session at the St Johns Headquarters.

There was only one thing I forgot to tell John was that the equipment we had to use was basically a piece of hardboard with the pitch marked out and a box of miniature players, plus the Referees Chart. Everything else was made by the coach, sketches and drawings were used, even so the candidates were well taught. When John took over he was in a position where he was able to improve the equipment he was using, this must have helped in the way he coached.

This is **John Manders** view on how he became the Association Coach and held that position for 17 (seventeen years)

The other day after speaking to Arnold Rouse, I began to think how certain things happen by chance and change your life.

Way back in 1968 my playing days in football were coming to an end and I was starting to think of what I could do when I finally "Hang up my boots". I decided to try my hand at coaching, and then I found out that I would have to wait about six months before I could get on a course. I was told that part of the coaching included a test on the laws of the game and as I had so long to wait I was persuaded by a local referee Derek Lock to attend a refereeing course.

This took place in Derek's front room at his home in Rugby road; the course was led by Andy Semple and consisted of reading the Referee's Chart, with Andy and Derek interpreting the Laws as they should be applied on the field. Some weeks later after passing the exam held in Coventry. I found myself a Class 3(three) Referee and joined Leamington & District Referees Association.

Such was the enthusiasm shown by Andy and Derek for refereeing that I decided to referee a few games, the rest is history, and needless to say I never did attend that coaching course.

In 1979 having been a Class1(one) Referee for a number of years I was persuaded by Arnold Rouse to help on the referee coaching course that he was about to start, I agreed, a decision that was later to bring about a change in my life.

The coaching courses were at that time held at the St John's Ambulance Headquarters in Warwick. After the first course Arnold left me to it and I assumed the role of coaching officer for Leamington RA.

It was in this role that I was invited to attend a meeting in Coventry, the speaker was Mr Jim Sims from Leicester, Jim was an ex Football League Referee and a Football Association Licenced Instructor and a stalwart member of the Referees Association. I was very impressed by what Jim had to say, and I realised just how little I knew about how to instruct and how so much more could be done to make the course better.

After the meeting I had chance to speak to Jim and was able to tell him how impressed I was with his talk, and how I would like to be able to improve the courses that I ran. He suggested that I should apply to go on an Instructors course run by the Football Association.

I did apply and through the Referees Association and I was granted a place on the week long course to be held at Lilleshall in August 1987.

What a course, work all day and then spending the evenings preparing your presentation for the next day, I said evenings but sometimes we worked into the early hours of the morning. Ask anyone who has been on the course. I was glad when Friday came and I was told that I had been successful and I would become a Registered Instructor.

It was only when I came home and later began to read through my course notes and material that I realised just how much I had learnt throughout the week.

I now began to put into practice the things I had learnt and started to improve the courses run by Leamington RA. As a registered Instructor I was invited to join the County instructional team, this was led by the Area Adviser Wilf Coffman and I assisted in the running of seminars held throughout the Birmingham County area.

The following year I was invited by the Football Association to take the second week of instruction in order to obtain my Licence. This second week took place at Wallsall and although it was again hard work, I felt because I knew what was coming the time passed very quickly I was again successful and became a Football Licensed Instructor. I was now able to instruct at County Level and became a full member of the County instructional team, I also carried on the basic training for Leamington Referees.

I was at this time employed by Benford Ltd as a Foreman Electrician; there came a vacancy for the position of Training Manager. Because of the in depth training I had received from the Football Association and my knowledge of the Construction Industry I applied for the position and was appointed Training Manager, a position I would not have been able to apply for, had it not been for Arnold Rouse persuading me to take over the Coaching at Leamington.

On the County training side I was appointed as deputy to Wilf Coffman and helped to promote and work on the County residential courses at Bilberry and later at Hillscourt. I also assisted Wilf in the counties of Staffordshire, Herefordshire and Worcestershire with "in-service" training programmes. In 1994 Wilf Coffman resigned his position as Area Advisor because of his wife's ill health and left the area. Wilf now lives in Chepstow.

With Wilf's resignation I was appointed to the position of Area Advisor for the Football Association by the Director of Refereeing Ken Ridden, and given the responsibility for the training of referees in the counties of Worcestershire, Herefordshire and Birmingham County
In my role as Area Adviser I joined the team of Advisers operating throughout the Country. We were responsible for not only the training within our own areas, but interpreting Law amendments and producing all the books assisting referees i.e. Report Writing, FA
Memorandum and Referees check lists, and I was able to attend meetings held at the then Headquarters of the Football Association, Lancaster Gate London.

I was also on the F A Panel of speakers and spoke at most of the R A Society meetings throughout the three counties. With such a heavy workload I needed help with the courses in the Leamington Association and obtained the help of John Sharp.
John proved to be an excellent Instructor, and has since obtained his licence and as you well know is the Leamington R A Licensed Instructor. We also had another John involved with the coaching that was John Austin. He also took the courses and became a Licensed Instructor.

As its said, all good things come to an end and when Ken Ridden retired the F A disbanded the Area Advisor scheme and replaced it with paid Managers (Oh to be young). I still hold my Instructors Licence, and was recently made a F A Honorary Instructor, I also in 1998 received a certificate for 10 years service as an Instructor.
As I said at the start certain things happen and change your life, if I had not accepted Arnold's invitation to help with the course I would not have held the position of Training Manager for the firm I worked for, nor would I have tasted life at the top of the refereeing administration world.
So remember next time someone asks you to take up a position in the Referees Association, think about it, you never know were it might lead you to.
The above article was written by John Mander.

John Mander continued giving that service to the County and travelled extensively from Association to Association. He was always able to give a lecture on the Laws of the Game, whilst John was involved with the County we were very fortunate to have two more members go through the Instructional Courses to become Licensed Instructors, they were John Sharp and John Austin. Both coached the Association members and when John Mander resigned in1998, at the A G M.

John Sharp was elected to become the Instructor to the Association. He has followed on with the same success as John Mander. John Austin is another Instructor and has had success at Leamington and Stratford. John transferred his allegiance to Stratford Referees Association although he still does the Assessing for Leamington. Our loss was Stratford's gain.

When John Sharp became the Association Coach changes at the Football Association were about to take place. Ken Ridden Director of Coaching had retired and John Baker became the new Director of Coaching with a number of changes that would affect every referee.

The change meant that a different view would be taking place. It would be out with the old and in with the new, by saying that his ideas would in one way revolutionise referees. The coaching methods would be different and the Licensed Instructors would still be needed. Referees would not be known by the classification that has always been the trade mark, when you became a referee with the County Football Association you had to register with them. You would then become a Class 3 (three) referee. Within two years you should be in line for promotion to become a Class 2(two) referee. Once you received your promotion you would be able to receive County Appointments, promotion towards a Class 1(one) status is entirely up to you the referee. When you are classified as a Class 1x it means you are over 50 years old and could referee only up to a certain standard. The new system that came into being in 2001 is the Level referees would attain as the move through the system and referees would be classified from 10 up to 1. (More about the system in 2000 to 2004)

Licensed Instructors for the 21st Century

John Sharp who was again elected the Association Coach at the 2004 A G M has penned his views on the coaching courses he attended to become Qualified.
John Austin also has had to attend these seminars to Qualify. John is the Area Assessment Officer as well and he has produced an Article on how referees are assessed. (This is in another Chapter).

John Sharp started by saying that he had been helping John Mander with Coaching Courses at Leamington RA for some time when he was asked by the Birmingham County FA to attend a Licensed Instructors training course. Each year the County FA are allowed to send two candidates to the Instructors course run by the FA, these courses were held at Bishop Grosseteste College, which is a Teacher Training College in Lincoln.

This is Johns view on the way the Seminars are organised with Ken Ridden as Director of Refereeing heading the course. The course Instructors were Derek Bray, John Baker, and John Davies. The course ran from Saturday afternoon to the following Friday and was divided into two parts. On successful completion of the first year, you became a Registered Referee Instructor and then you were invited back the following year to complete another weeks training to become a fully Licensed Instructor. The Licence is valid for 5 years, after which time you are required to attend for a week-end re-licensing course to prove that you still have the necessary capabilities to continue for another 5 years.

On arrival at Lincoln, you are allocated a room and given a timetable of events for the week. At dinner that evening you met the other members of your group .The first year I was in a very mixed group consisting of one Football League Assistant, one ex-player, a musician from the RAF, two lads on senior leagues in the north and two others like myself operating on the local Leagues. Mike Weakley from the Birmingham County FA was the group tutor. Later on that evening we were introduced to the Course Staff. We then broke into our tutor groups for a demonstration lecture from the tutor, we were all given a different topic on which to go and prepare a lecture for 9 o'clock the next morning.

The lecture that we presented each day had to be a specific length, the first one for seven minutes working up to fifteen minutes for our final lecture on the Thursday and we were only allowed a few seconds leeway. As well as preparing what we were actually going to say, we had to produce all our training aids, although in the first year we were restricted to use "flash cards" and a magnetic or Velcro field of play. Each day the lectures we gave were watched by a least one of the course leaders and we were given a critique of our performance and expected to improve by the following day. The two things that I was regularly pulled up for, was being too static and not speaking clearly enough.

The lecture we gave on the Wednesday was the same one that we had to give on the final Thursday, so after receiving the critique for the lecture we gave on Wednesday, much midnight oil was burned getting the lecture up to scratch for the next day. On Thursday morning we did our normal course work, and in the afternoon we had to deliver our final pass or fail the lecture. This lecture had to be delivered to a different Tutor Group to the one in which you had been working with and two course leaders were in attendance to assess. Later on that day we were given feedback from our lecture and told if we had passed or failed. I am pleased to say that the entire group were successful. The next day we attended one final course session, said goodbye to new made friends and headed for home and back to the Association as a Football Association Registered Instructor.

That is the first part of John Sharp's story on how he became a Registered Instructor and in the second part John returns to Lincoln for more hard work and hoping to return as a fully qualified Licensed Instructor.

In 1998 just two weeks after moving house, I was back to Lincoln for the second part of the course. On arriving at Lincoln this time there were a number of familiar faces from the previous year. Although no one from last year's group was in my group this year. Most of them were experienced referees except one from Surrey who was a class 3(level 7) this was unusual.
Ken Ridden again headed the course with John Baker, Ron Groves and Derek Bray as course instructors, with John Mander one of the group tutors.
Our Group Instructor was Ray Payne a headmaster, who had a good supply of Irish jokes. These kept us amused in the bar, on the odd occasion we were able to get there.

The format in the second year was similar to the previous year except that the lectures we had to present were longer and had to be a standard that could be delivered to referees on higher leagues as part of their development. We were now allowed to use overhead projectors as well as magnetic boards etc, laptops; data projectors and power point were very much in their infancy those days. Many of us took our own computers to help with the preparation of our lectures and they were a great help.

A special lecture this year was in the form of a demonstration by the Nottingham FA demonstration team, who actually put on a full scale football match, that had so much going on the 'referee' had little or no chance of keeping control and our task was to review this game and decide what advice we would give to this referee to help him improve. So realistic was the match that several of the residents of nearby houses came to the college to complain about the language.

As the week progressed the stress levels rose in preparation for our final lecture to be delivered on the Thursday and highly scrutinised by the Course Instructors, the lecture as in the previous year was delivered to a different Tutor Group, with the course Instructors looking on. I was third on and had to watch two other members deliver their lectures, one was over the time allocated and the other member just dried up after about 15 minutes. The subject of my lecture was Positioning at Free Kicks and I completed it in 21 minutes and 9 seconds, this was one of the best lecture that I had delivered time wise and was given a pass, all the remaining members of my group except one passed, so it was out into Lincoln that night to celebrate.

For the next five years I set about running candidate courses for Leamington RA and helping out on the County FA seminars when asked. The work was very rewarding, especially when you see new referees taking up the whistle and becoming members of Leamington Referees Association. Unfortunately not too many seem to have lasted very long.
After five years you are required to attend a re-licensing course to make sure that you are still up to the required standard. This is a weekend course which is held as are all FA seminars at Staverton.

For this week-end you are given the topics for your two lectures well in advance so that you can come prepared to deliver your first lecture on the Saturday afternoon. As before you were given a critique and expected to improve by the time you delivered your next lecture on the Sunday morning. With this hurdle safely negotiated, your license is extended for another five years and you are given a written report on your performance and sent back out in the world to train more referees.

Whilst at Staverton there was considerable debate on the method of re-licensing and more people seem to be in favour of being assessed whilst delivering lectures out in the field, rather than having to attend a specific course. As with all arguments there are points both for and against that method. The biggest argument against is that it is easier for the FA to keep Instructors informed of changes etc if they are all together on the same site for a couple of days, but this can be offset against the distance some people have to travel to get to a course.

Since qualifying as a Licensed Instructor, I have concentrated on training new referees and have been involved in some very enjoyable courses. Almost 100 referees have passed the examination with only four failures. Only about 10% have taken up the whistle and are still around today. It can be quite disheartening when running a course to realise that the participants will never take up refereeing and are only there because they needed to referee by their club on the odd occasion or are doing it because they need it for their Duke of Edinburgh Award.

In an effort to alleviate this problem, the FA a few years age decided to change the way in which courses are run. It was decided to run four week courses, with an exam at the end, for those people who just wanted a basic knowledge of the laws and then those who wished to continue to qualify as a referee have a further four weeks tuition during which time they are actually required to referee three matches, with another exam at the end.

The main problem with this system is that when the candidates go out to referee their three matches, they have to have a Mentor with them with whom they are able to meet after the game to discuss their performance.
With a small Association such as Leamington it is not possible to find enough members prepared to be mentors, so to date I have remained with the basic course of around 10 weeks.

Another task that comes the way of Licensed Instructors is to invigilate at candidate referee exams; this is something I find very enjoyable. The exams these days are split into two parts, the written and the oral, In the written part a candidate answers about twenty questions as laid down by the FA and the oral, is a one to one session with the invigilator again answering a number of questions set down by the FA. The two marks are then totalled and divided by two, the candidate has to obtain an overall mark of at least 75%. If a candidate scores between 70 & 74 %, we can go through their written paper with them to see if we can get them to give a bit more information that would result in them scoring enough marks to pass the exam.

Our remit especially on the oral part of the exam, is to try and extract as much knowledge as we can out of each candidate. Often when you put the question to them they will give an answer that is probably only 50% correct, by putting the question in a different way or getting them to think about exactly what they would do on the field of play we can usually get an acceptable answer.
Part of the work of a Licensed Instructor is the development of all referees from Level seven upwards. As most of this work in our County takes place in Birmingham area it can be difficult to be available for these sessions and the FA are now saying that if we do not get involved in referee development then we will be "demoted" to Registered Instructors. This has obviously caused considerable amount of consternation amongst the Licensed Instructors and our feelings have been made known to the FA

The past seven years as a Licensed Instructor have been very enjoyable; I have met many people that I would not have done if I had not been Instructing. You find a great deal of satisfaction when your candidate pass the exam and even more when you see them out on the field of play with the whistle. My only regret is that so many of the candidates that have passed the exam are no longer refereeing. Speaking to other Instructors this would appear to be a countrywide problem and one which we need to address to stop the number of referees declining even further.

Article written by John Sharp (Licensed Instructor)

The end of the second term at the College in which John explained how hard the course was and the lectures he had to produce were of a higher standard, all this augers well for any referee candidate who wishes to be a referee.

John carries on and explains the week-end course seminar to see if he was still able to Coach; it was pleasing to note that he passed that test for another five years. The remarks that John Mander made to both of the Instructors proved to be correct, that it would be a week of intense pressure and full of lectures morning, noon and night.

In the last section John explained some of the problems that Licensed Instructors can be up against and by reasonable dialogue they can be overcome. He also talks about coaching referee candidates and the amount of work being done to keep candidates interested and involved in refereeing. The answer to the question is entirely up to the referees who have been coached to the standard the Instructor required, once they start refereeing they are on their own although we have a Mentor system that can help the referee and give him good advice.

Any referee who has been coached on the 'Laws of the Game' by any of the Licensed Instructors from Leamington have been given first class service and if they do take up the opportunity to actually become Referees they would have had a good grounding to start with, and they would be able to receive advice if needed..

Chapter 10

The Referee Association

How the Divisional System Operated

One of the problems for ordinary members of The Referees' Association under the system which served for almost a century until its replacement by what we have today was that so few of them really understood it. Having been involved for a reasonable number of years at Council level, because of my commitment to the editorial aspects of "The Football Referee," I am convinced that most members were either not interested in how the system worked or, if they were, they couldn't be bothered to ask the relevant questions.

Let us look at it in a simple manner, starting at Association, Society or Branch level and working our way to National Council level.

Each ASB sent at least one delegate to the regular meetings of the local County Referees Association. This ensured that all ASBs could officially represent meetings via the RA within their local County FA area. Many problems were easily resolved this way.

Then, each County RA elected one person to represent that body at divisional level. These were known as Executive Members and, obviously, they would represent all county-level interests at the next higher level of the divisional structure. There were five English Divisions: North East, North West, Midland, Southern and Western. There was also the Welsh Division, Northern Ireland was represented via the North West Division. There also existed an Overseas and Services Division, though it did not have regular full meetings like the other divisions, for obvious logistical and financial reasons.

Each of the 'home' divisions was guided by its elected Vice President and Secretary. These people duly took their seats on the national RA Council. These twelve elected officers join up with the National President, the Immediate Past President, the RA's General Secretary, the Overseas and Services Secretary and the Editor of the national magazine. In times past there was also a Treasurer and a Supplies Officer, but since 1977- when the RA introduced a paid administration- these two offices have been provided via the RA Office. The Office was originally at Kingswinford and is now at Coventry

The RA Council, as the top tier of the administration, was ultimately responsible for maintaining the Association on an even keel. Major decisions were agreed at the Annual Conference weekend in June. On the Friday afternoon of the Conference week-end, the members of the Council and the Executive Members from all the counties would meet together to review progress and discuss fresh ideas to help the Association

The RA Council members each took part on at least one sub-committee, these being concerned with Finance, with Administration and Policy, with Instruction and Publication and with Conference. Each of these sub-committes had the power to co-op other RA members for their expertise.

This hierarchy—from Council to Division to ASB's to Individual Member—had its uses, but it also had its problems, many of which centred around the concepts of 'remoteness' and 'slowness of action and reaction'

The 'old' system was eventually replaced at the Annual Conference at Cardiff in 2004 and nowadays the individual member in an English RA association, society or branch, belongs in fact to the RAE (the RA of England). "The Referees' Association" today embraces three National

Associations, one each for England, Wales, and Northen Ireland and it is 'The RA' which provides the overall administrative support. Scotland has never featured in the RA set-up.

The article above was written and sent to me by Mr Ted Ring who has been involved with the National Council for a considerable number of years, he was also involved with the Referees Magazine. It has shown how the Association functioned, it also emphasises how important is is to have Delegates representing the ASB's at the County Referees Committees.
The Birmingham & Warwickshire is a combination of two separate sections joined together and it meant that we had two delegates representing members on the Midland Division.
Since the change we are still fortunate in that we had two members from the B&WJRCC elected to the new ' Board of Management'

.

This section of the book is very important to Leamington as well as other A.S.B's. At the Annual General Meeting where the officers and delegates are elected, we have to elect a delegate to the Birmingham & Warwickshire Joint Referees County Committee. Normally two members are elected although only one will have a vote at the meeting. The reason two are elected is make sure that we are represented, most meetings are held in Birmingham and they are by-monthly, it is a lot of travelling for the delegates. They have tried other areas in the County to have the meetings, this hasn't been very successful.

Birmingham & Warwickshire Joint Referees County Committee will have been mentioned quite a number of times as you read through the book. It may not be the same title and Leamington were first mentiond when it was called County Referees Committee and John Wildsmith from Leamington was the first Chairman. We had other members on the committee, in 1930s. There was a temporary slow down during the War. When it reformed after the War and eventually after a few changes it finished as it is now
The B& W J R C C cover all the Referees Associations in the Birmingham and Warwickshire area, one group of ASBs represent the Birmingham area and the other group represent Warwickshire. Both of the elected representatives were elected to serve on the Midland Division of Referees Association.

The Birmingham &Warwickshire Joint Referees County Committee rely on a capitation fee of the previous season's membership from every ASB's in Birmingham & Warwickshire to fund the work they do. The officers who are elected are the Chairman, Secretary and a Treasurer in recent years they have elected a President.

The Birmingham & Warwickshire Committee as well as having two delegates elected to the,'Board of Management'. have a member who represents the Committee on the County Football Association Referees Committee, so problems when they arise can be dealt with by the County Football Association.. There are about 20 Referees Associations who are members of the B & W J R CC and the meetings are usually full of interesting items.

In 2004 we saw the end of the Referees Association which was formed in 1908, the Midland Division also disappeared, 96 years of work and endeavour were gradually pushed aside.The new Referees Association took over.(There is a comprehensive report on the change that was made from 2000 to 2004 called the Future and 2004 to 2005 is called the new Referees Association and the Referees Association of (England) at the end of this book.

Association Newsletter

The Newsletter was one way to notify the members of the future activities and to keep the members informed on general business. In the 1960 to the 1970 period a single newsheet was sent out to paid up members giving notice of the date of the Meeting and whether Speakers had been organised, gradually the newsletter ceased to function and it wasn't until the 1987 period when the Management decided to print a 20 page Newsletter. The first one was produced in August 1987 and continued from there. John Mander was the Editor and general information was placed in the newsletter along with the Management and Council Minutes which more or less filled the pages, articles from Simon Rogers helped and so did reports from the various speakers who attended the monthly meeting.

The Newsletter was enjoyed by the members who appreciated the informaton being sent to them, this was on a monthly basis. After a while the newsletter ran into problems which made printing difficult. The Editor as well as producing the newsletter was also the Coach and involved with Management, this meant that he was finding it difficult to find the time to put articles together and he sought help with someone taking over.

Eventually Brian Hackleton became the Editor and he found it very difficult especially travelling long distances to work and back, which limited his time. The next member to try and produce the Newsletter was Ray Morgan who also found it very difficult to produce a monthly issue. The problem was putting articles together in your spare time, if you were working full time it became very difficult, Ray was using the same format as the other members, but he finally had to retire from trying to produce a monthly issue. This is when when Tom Prendergast took over in 1992 producing the newsletter, and he like all the others began to find it time consuming. Tom did have a little more help in the production of the newsletter, he had encouraged his firm to sponsor him and the Association, they also allowed him to use his Secretary to type the articles and print the complete layout.

This carried on until about 1995 when his Company was going through a change, this meant that the newsletter was again seeking someone to become the Editor. All this change was brought up at the Annual General Meeting in February. No one offered their services, and when the President said that it would be a shame if it was finished for good, still no one offered to have a go.

Once the AGM was finished the President Arnold Rouse told the Chairman he would have a look at it and see if it was possible to carry on, he was offered advice by Tom Prendergast and Steve Portch offered to set up the Master copy on his Computer so that they could be printed off. Not having any knowledge of setting up a Magazine or a Newsletter and certainly no computer experience we should have to do the best we could. Arrangements were made with Steve who would put the articles into the Newsletter and let me know when it would be ready. He said not to worry if the articles were hand written or from a newspaper he would type them up on his computor, the only trouble was it meant fetching it from his home at Kineton

It was fortunate that Steve Portch was involved with computers which was a help. The first edition was about to be produced and the articles written to be placed in the Newsletter were ready. The problem was the articles had to be delivered to Steve's home at Kineton, the Master copy was returned and then taken to Ray Morgan who was going to get it printed for me. This situation with moving from one to the other did not work very well, unfortunately it was the only way at the moment and to produce monthly it had to be done. After about the third month it was getting difficult to have the finished articles ready for posting, in time for the meeting.

Having realised the difficulties we would have, the Editor decided to see if he could find somewhere where the newsletter could be photocopied at a reasonable cost, this was proving difficult, working on a basis of 70 or 80 copies. Most Photocopiers were charging 5p per A4 copy and having printing both sides would make it 10p a copy. Then multiply the number by 10 again to give you a 20page newsletter the cost per month would be between £70 or £80 pounds this would be too expensive for the Association to support and members would not pay £1 per copy.

The third newsletter under the new Editor was produced in 'Coventry as a one off situation and it left the Editor and Steve Portch looking further afield for help and possibly sponsors. The Editor having been friendly with the Directors at Nicolet Instruments decided to go and have a talk to them, he went and saw the Manager who said he would be quite pleased to help.

When we came to the next month's issue most of our problems were solved and the printing was not a hassle. This support and sponsorship from the Advertisers who never quibbled when they were approached for an x amount for the season's advertising, in fact from one Advertiser we received vouchers or a Donation to our Christmas Quiz and another told me if we had any trouble in printing he would help me, also members received a discount from most of the others.

The Newsletter was being distributed further afield and the format was still very similar to when it started. Once the new Editor had settled down and slightly changed articles around the first move he made was by not putting in the Monthly and the Management minutes. He felt the members should try to attend the meeting. Articles were found from numerous places and if they were from a Daily Newspaper he always phoned or wrote to them for permission to use and only once was he refused to use the article. The reason given was the writer who was a Football Referee was under contract to them.

Another blow came about when Steve Portch withdrew his support mainly through his business having to travel abroad. This left the Editor needing help, at the Annual General Meeting. Peter Liddington stepped in to see if he could help, we had a chat and he suggested putting all the draft pieces together and let him have them. He would then set them up to produce the 20 page newsletter A5. This to me was a big help. It meant I would only have to deliver the draft to Peter and he would return the finished article ready for printing.

Everything was now set up for a good run and I was getting more used to the computer.But like all stories there is an end to it, with Peters employment it was getting difficult for him to help where the amount of work he was doing was gradually increasing and it meant calling time on his support. This situation meant that I had to have a go and do the spade work and produce the articles for the Newsletter.

After a few splutters the newsletter was printed and one can admit that a few errors arose in some of the printed work. But after working hard and checking my printing with the spell check everything seemed to come out okay, the Printing margins and numbering made the Newsletter easier to produce. With articles used from other sources they only had to be typed in situ, a few articles from the members helped which were well written, if mistakes were made no one told the Editor.

Over the years that the Newsletter has been printed a number of excellent written articles from the members and from people outside have been used and it may be possible to reprint them again. One thing that has helped me in finding and using articles, has been the Magazines received from other Associations. Even the "Football Referee" has been a good source of information.

A major blow to the printing of the newsletter was being informed by the Manager of Nicolet Instruments. that the Company would be closing down in March 2002 and going to Cambridge.

This meant that again we would have to start looking for someone to help with the printing. One of the Advertisers had offered before and he was phoned to see if he could help. No problems he said bring it over. This seemed a good opportunity to take up so I went and saw Norman Stephens and took a ream of paper with me, we printed the newsletter on his small Printer and it was folded and stapled at home and then posted to the members.

We were very grateful to Norman for his help in producing the newsletter, we needed a more permanent home if were are to carry on. In talking to Ray Morgan he said he would approach his firm to see if they could help, later on the next day Ray told me to bring the next issue to his firm and he would have it printed for us. This is exatly what happened and Dafferns were thanked for their support, from that month the Newsletter was printed by the Company until 2004 when the Editor was finding it difficult to carry on. Once again an appeal was made and no one has offered any help or offers to continue printing the Newsletter. So it was finally laid to rest.

The Referee and the Laws of Association Football

In this book you will have noticed that various chapters have mentioned subjects, such as Coaching, Assessors, Football Leagues, Football Referees, Charities they are all part of being a referee.
This section concerns the Laws of Association Football or LOAF as it is called..To become a referee you will have to have a certain lnowledge of the Laws of the game.You may think how do we get all this knowledge, is it very difficult? To answer the question it is not difficult at all, you do not have to have a degree. A good knowledge of Football does help and if you have played for a team over a number of years that's better stlll. If you have never been involved in football at all, it is not a deterrent, in fact some candidates who have never played football generally turn out to be good referees. In any situation every candidate has to take the 10 week course set up by the County Football Asociation and delivered by the Licensed Instructor who is fully qualified and in all probability a very experienced referee.

When a person whether male or female decides to become a referee, you need to get in touch with the local Referees Association. If that is not possible, the local Football League will help, or better still contact a referee who lives locally. Once you have made contact, the Licensed Instructor will contact you and inform you when the next coaching course is to take place. You will be given all the information you require, as well as the cost. When you attend the first session The instructor will give you a form to complete and he will also ask for payment, this will go to the County Football Association to make sure you are registered. It will also pay for the coaching given to you by the Licenced Instructor and allow you to sit the Examination. If you pass he will advise you and give instructions for you to contact the nearest Football League Secretary.

There are two different types of courses that you can be coached on. One is for 4(four) weekly sessions, this one just gives you a brief knowledge of the Laws of Association Football. The other is a 10 (ten) weekly sessions, resulting in the candidate being able to take the Examination set by the County FA. Once you have passed the examination you will be classed as a referee, with the classification of a Class 3(three), or with the new system now being used by the Football Association and County Associations. If you are under 16 (sixteen) you would be classed at a Level 8(eight), once you reach the age of 16(sixteen) you are then moved up to Level 7(seven). If you were over 16(sixteen) when taking the exam, you would automatically become a Level 7(seven).
Whilst you are training you are placed on Level 9(nine) irrespective of age. This covers every one for public liability Insurance.

The Licensed Instructor will take you through the, 'Laws of Association Football' concentrating on one or two sections as each week progresses, when he is of the opinion that you have had sufficient lectures. He will start asking you questions and expect answers. When you have a reasonable number of Candidates taking the examination, you get to know your colleagues and slowly build a rapport between each other. When that happens you will really start to digest the Laws as they are being unfolded by the Instructor, you can rest assured he will make it interesting. When you sit the examination it may be in the local area, this depends on the number of candidates..You might have to take your Birth Certificate with you and another possibility is that you may have to be cleared through the Child Protection Scheme the Instructor will advise you on all those items.

The 17 (seventeen) Advice on the Laws of the Game are listed as follows:-

Law 1   The Field of Play
Law 2   The Ball
Law 3   The Number of Players
Law 4   The Players Equipment
Law 5   The Referee
Law 6   The Assistant Referee
Law 7   The Duration of the Match
Law 8   The Start and Restart of Play
Law 9   The Ball in and Out of Play
Law 10   The Method of Scoring
Law 11   Offside
Law 12   Fouls and Misconduct
Law 13   Free Kick (Direct & Indirect)
Law 14   The Penalty Kick
Law 15   The Throw-in
Law 16   The Goal Kick
Law 17   The Corner Kick

The above was taken from the Referees Chart 1956 and the additions were as follows:-
Specimen Report regarding Misconduct
Co-operation between Referees and Linesmen
The Diagonal System of Control
Diagrams Illustrating Points in Connection with Offside.

The recent issue of the Referees Chart is now called 'LOAF' which is an abbrevation for the 'Laws of Association Football'
The Seventeen Laws still have the same title although the actual Laws themselves have been updated or modified to suit the modern game.
After the seventeen Laws in the 2004/2005 LOAF there are eight sections which involve the Referee, Assistant Referee and the Fourth Official. The Licensed Instructor will take each Candidate through that part so that when you have passed the Examination to become a Referee you will be prepared to implement them as you Referee various League or Cup Games.
In producing this short article on the Referee and the Laws of Association Football my intention is to write about Substitutes, Procedures to Determine the Winner of a Match (Kicks from the penalty spot).and the Fourth Official. This will show you what a referee has to do when he becomes a referee, the instructor will enlighten the candidates further when he talks about coaching assessing, the mentor system. A brief look at FAMOAand the new system of classifying referee will be mentioned and the Child Protection situation will be explained to you.

Substitutes Law 3

Substitution was talked about in the 1965 period and gradually brought into use. Thefirst time they were used only one player could be substituted after a few years it gradually went to three players.These were nominated to the referee before the game had started, this was always difficult in junior football. Most teams only managed to have enough players to form the team, a number of teams gave the names of players to confirm with the Laws and rules of the Competition. As long as they turned up to the match and before the final whistle was blown they were eligible to play.

Changes have been made since the early days and referees were expected to study the rules of all the competitions the matches were played under. In all cases only three players can be used, this can be from a selection of five players. In friendly matches substitutes can be nominated from three up to seven players, providing the teams agree to a number.

Substitution Procedure

This is in Law 3 and to replace a player by substitution certain conditions must be observed.
One is that the Referee is informed before any substitution takes place.
The names are given to the Referee before the match. The substitution takes place on the half-way line and it is completed when the substitute enters the field of play, who then becomes a player.
The player who leaves the field of play ceases to be a player and takes no further part in the game.
In all cases the player being substituted must leave the Field of Play before the player taking his place can enter.
If the referee is not informed of the Substitution and the player enters the field of play, the Referee will caution the player with a Yellow Card. There are other infringements in which the Instructor will inform the Candidates as they are being coached. .
All substitutes are subject to the Authority of the Referee whether called upon to play or not.

In boys and youth football the Substitution is different in that they have a system of roll-- on and off. There doesn't seem to be a set number and players can be substituted and eventually sent back on to play, it sounds difficult but some young players put in a very good session of football and then tire easily, the Coach is usually aware of this so he uses the sytsem to rest his players and when they have had a rest and possibly the game needs a change they are sent back on to play.

Procedures to determine the winner of a match

The procedures to determine the team that wins a match is the same for the local Cup or League subject to the Rules of the Competition. The same rules apply to the Professional Leagues and Competitions. After 90 minutes football, Extra-Time of 15 minutes each -way is played and if the match is still a draw then if the Competition rules allow Kicks from the Penalty mark are taken. In most of the Competitions in the Professional League's an Away goal does sometimes eliminate the taking of Penalty Kicks where the goals scored are counted as double. That method is not used in Local Cup Competitions

Another method was tried and that was the Golden Goal. This was played out in Extra –Time, that method has been moved on, it was used in local Cup Finals to ease the fixture congestion. A few years ago the method used today was not thought of, if you had a Cup match and it was a Draw after 90 minutes you had a replay, extra time was not considered until the second match and then you played the normal 90 minutes plus the extra time of 15 minutes each way. If it was still a draw the match was played on a neutral ground, and even then we had problems, especially if it was coming to the end of the season and fixtures were beginning to build up. This happened to one of the Charity Cups organised by the Referees, both teams had played three times drawing each time when they played for the fourth time, we had to go to the drawing of Lots' to get a result and with the Final arranged on a certain date the Committee had no alternative.

The team that drew the winning lot played in the Final on the Sunday and unfortunatly they lost and most of the players were dissapointed, but remarked that they felt very tired, They had played seven matches in 14 days. The problem was the weather which during the season caused matches to be cancelled.

Kicks from the penalty mark

This is the method now used to determine a winning team and it is just as heart breaking to players who lose the match from the kicks when you consider the effort they put into the game.

Procedures are as follows ;-

- The Referee chooses which goal the kicks are taken from.
- One Linesman (AR) moves to the Penalty area where the kick is being taken from. The other Linesman (AR) remains in the centre circle.
- This is where all the player from both teams who will be taking the Kick have to stay.
- The Referee makes sure both teams are equal in number and only the players who were on the field of play at 90 minutes are allowed to take the Kick.
- The referee takes the names of the Five players from each team who will be taking the Kick. He will then toss the coin between the two teams and the winner has a choice of going first or second. The Referee will also keep the score.
- Both teams take 5 Kicks and they are taken alternatively and by different players
- The team that scores the most goals after five have been taken is declared the winner.
- The goalkeeper from each team must stay in the penalty area where the kicks are being taken, each goalkeeper takes it in turn to go in the goal when his opponent is taking the Kick
- If the ball is stopped by the goalkeeper, or it misses the goal completely, or it hits the crossbar or the uprights and rebounds into play, that is the finish of the Kick
- After 5 Kicks and the score is equal whether goals were scored or not, the players who were not nominated as the first five, continue to take the penalty Kick alternatly until a result is reached.
- Only the players and officials are allowed to remain on the field of play, when the kicks are being taken

That is the extent of the Procedure to determine the winner of a match

Fourth Official

The fourth official may be appointed under the Competition rules and he can officiate if any of the three match officials is unable to continue , His job is to assist the referee at all times. The fourth official covers most things during the match such as looking after the match ball, substitution and if there are any problems within the Technical area, he also informs the referee if an incident occours and the referee has missed it and he must report any incident to the appropriate body and at the same time let the referee know what he has done.

This is only a brief introduction to the position of the Fourth Official and at the moment it is only the Professional Leagues that have a fourth official at the game every week.

In local Football the fourth official would only be used as a Linesman (AR) in Cup matches, unless it was an important match where a result is required. .

Since the Laws of Association Football were written in 1846 at Cambridge University, alterations have been made, the first one was in 1872, when the size of the ball was fixed. The next one was in 1875 when the crossbar was put in place instead of using tape as they did. In1878 the referees were involved with the change, when they were allowed to use whistles for the first time. After that we had the introduction two handed throw–in first used in 1882, goal nets in 1890 these were designed by a Mr Brodie from Liverpool and they were first used in the FA Cup Final between WBA and Aston Villa in 1892. In 1891 a double addition was made with the penalty kick being introduced, and Referees and Linesmen used instead of Umpires. In 1905 Goalkeepers ordered to remain on the goal-line for penalty kicks, and 1912 Goalkeepers' use of hands restricted to the penalty area.

The Offside Rule was changed in 1925 from three to two defenders between the attacker and the goal-line. There were plenty more additions or alterations made to the Laws of Association Football and even now certain changes are being made.

As a candidate being coached you will be told about the changes that will affect you, the e.g. Red card and the Yellow card you will learn more about whilst you are going through the course.

Here is the information on the Red and Yellow cards..

The Red card was first used on the Football League about 1982 and after a short life they were removed by FIFA. Which was a disappointment to referees who were itching to show the red card to players who commit serious offences,

Eventually they were returned to the Football League in 1987 and along with the yellow card, this was for referees to caution a player for technical offences or for showing dissent, if the player committed two such offences he could be dismissed from the field of play by showing him the second Yellow card and then the Red one.

The junior referee was not allowed to use these cards at the time they were introduced, it was only after the FA were satisfied that the system was working, they were eventually introduced into all levels of football.

When the candidate has passed the referee examination he immediatly becomes a member of FAMOA and receives an amount of information from the Football Association he is encouraged to go out and start refereeing. All the equipment and kit he needs to start is available from the Referees Association and each Referees Association has a supplies officer who will kit the referee out.

Chapter 11

Charity Cup Competitions

Charity Football Competitions are just as important to the referee as a normal football match, with the Charity being a little more competitive. Majority of referee's enjoy taking part for most of them it is a privilege to referee and they do give their support to the charities. We do have one or two organisations who donate the money they make to the larger Charitable Groups. We also have the small Charity Competitions which set out to raise money for the elderly the sick and needy.

Various Charity Cup Competitions have been mentioned, to determine when they started has been a difficult task. A few were being played for before the 20th Century and others may have started later on, it is not easy to say who was the earliest. There are three Cups that could vie for the fist position and each one has a unique story to tell, although one will be told with a little tongue in cheek. It was only by talking to Harold Elkington when the Chairman Andy Semple and I visited him in 1972 that the information came about.

Each Cup or Competition was always set out to raise funds for a particular Charity and the first one was no exception. 'The Leamington Hospital Charity Cup' was bought to raise funds for the, Hospitals in Leamington and Warwick. It transpires that the Cup was made in London and purchased by a Gentleman from Leamington, who gave it to the "Hospital Committee" to raise funds that were badly needed by both Hospitals. This purchase and setting up of the Committee was in the latter part of the 19th Century the date I was given was about 1895 and the cost of the Cup was presumed to be about £100(pounds). With the Cup the Committee raised quite a reasonable amount of money.

The Southam and Stockton Charity Cups were unique in that one was donated to the village after the organisation disbanded. The Stockton Cup was for teams that played 'Polo' in competition. The Southam Cup is unique. It is a Cup with three handles.

Herewith a list of Charity Cups and each one will be mentioned with as much information as possible, they are not in alphabetical order, but in the order when it was presumed they started, the majority belong to organisations outside the structure of Football Leagues. We do have a few that are played for within the rules of the League.

Leamington Hospital Charity Cup.
Southam Charity Cup
Stockton Charity Cup
Whitnash Charity Cup
Warwick Cinderella Charity Cup
Wellesbourne Hospital Charity Cup
Jockey & Hounds Charity Cup (Southam)
Leamington Invitation Charity Cup
Cancer Charity Cup & Supplementary Cup
Warwick League of Friend Charity Cup
The Sean Horgan Cup
George Dutton Charity Cup
Andy Campbell Charity Cup
Joe Burnell Supplementary Charity Cup
The Maurice Billington Cup
Coventry Referees Benevolent Charity Cup

Leamington Hospital Charity Cups

The Invitation and Charity

Earlier on it was said that one of the Cups mentioned would be told with tongue in cheek. The information we received from Harold Elkington was that the Cup was purchased in London by a gentleman named Smith. It was brought back to Leamington and given to the Committee. This Committee had been set up to organise ways of raising money for both Hospitals yet the Warneford was mentioned quite often.

Dates that were mentioned seemed to vary and one article was found in the local Warwick & Warwickshire Gazette in 1933. The Chairman Mr Tom Hemmins was retiring from the position having completed 37 years that would put the Hospital Cup starting about 1895. This was mentioned in our talk with Harold: a fair amount of money would have been raised since the competition started.

In talking about the Cup, it transpires that there were two Cups concerning the Hospital one was called the Leamington Hospital Invitation Cup in which teams were invited to enter and on being knocked out in the 1st round were entered into the Supplementary Cup called the Joe Burnell Cup .The Invitation Cup is at present being held by Rugby United F C. The other Cup which is called the Leamington Charity Cup is at present with the Committee.

Since the earlier information was passed on to me it seems that at one stage the second Cup was introduced and this would have been before 1939 when George Dutton was the Secretary and he eventually handed both Cups over to Guy Reeves and Brian Knibb.

This additional piece of information was sent to me by Brian Knibb, it does clear up the issue of the Two Hospital Cups, the information was written in the Programme for the Final of the Leamington Invitation Charity Cup Stratford Town v Racing Club Warwick. The Final was played on May 20th 1983

The Hospital Cup is reported to be one of the most valuable and oldest Trophies in Football. It was first competed for in 1895. Proceeds in those days were solely given to the Leamington Warneford Hospital.

Herewith a list of recorded winners from 1895 to 1910:

1895	Redditch Excelsior	
1896	Leamington Town	
1897	Atherstone&Stockingford	(Joint Holders)
1898	Rudge Coventry	
1899	Leamington Town	
1900	Atherstone	
1901	Redditch Excelsior	
1902	Coleshill Great Heath	
1904	Herberts Athletic Coventry	
1906	Leamington Town	
1907	Herberts Athletic Coventry	
1908	Leamington Town	
1909	Leamington Town	
1910	Lord Street	

In 1937 the Charity Cup Competition decided to purchase another Challenge Cup to commemorate the Coronation of King George V1 and Queen Elizabeth. This Cup is the current Leamington Charity Cup. The old Cup was withdrawn and registered with the County Football Association as an Invitation Cup.

In those heady days of Football large crowds witnessed some incredible matches. One instant was when Portsmouth brought their 1939 Football Association Cup winning side to Leamington to play a Charity game.

The programme goes on to say that although the magic of yesteryear football has gone. Some stirring games involving Coventry City, Leicester City and Lockheed-Leamington have been witnessed at the Windmill Ground in the late 60's and early 70's and the Invitation Cup has been graced with some well known Referees. Eric Jennings was one who refereed the year he was compulsory retired after refereeing the FA Cup Final. Roger Kirkpatrick the extrovert from Leicester was another.

Recent Winners from 1978 to 1982 are:

1978/1979	**Kineton Sports**
1979/1980	**Long Itchington Sports**
1980/1981	**Long Itchington Sports**
1981/1982	**Racing Club Warwick.**

The Joe Burnell Cup was implemented in the 1970 or 1980 period. To give the Competition the extra edge in fund raising
The Cups themselves are Magnificent Trophies and well worth winning

Southam Charity Cup

The Southam Charity Cup came into being in 1905 and it was unique in that it was one of the Three Handed Cup in existence. A competition was organised during the season and money was raised for the welfare of the elderly and as a Christmas bonus.

The Competitions were always well supported and if Southam reached the final. The crowd could easily reach a figure of 2,000 and if they won the Cup it was paraded around Southam behind the Southam Town Band. Every pub would receive a visit from the Team and no doubt the Cup would be filled time and time again

The Chairman was Mr Victor Hodges of the Charity Cup Competition as well as Chairman of the Football Club, With Mr Lesley Amour as the Treasurer.

Gordon Seaton was the Secretary for twenty years after the War and a Mr Roy Gulliver took over as Chairman from Mr Hodges,

The Charity Cup is still in Southam and moves have been made to set up a Charity Competition. Information concerning the Cup was found in the Leamington Spa Courier dated September 1st 1905. At the Annual General Meeting of the Southam association football Club which was held at the Bull Hotel. There were 40 members present and the Treasurer told everyone that the accounts were in a satisfactory condition. The following Officers were elected Hon Secretary, Bert Usher, Captain, J Hearne, Vice-Captain, W Powell, Committee Messrs, J Carter, A Hancocks, H Morby, G Baldwin, F Evetts, M Badger, T Fletcher and W King. The Hon Secretary told the members present that the Committee had purchased a handsome Challenge Cup. Which they desire to thank all who so generously subscribed to the fund.

All ready 10 Clubs have decided to compete for the Cup. One of the Rules expressly stipulates that he final shall be played on the Southam ground, and the gate money, after payment for expenses, distributed as a Charity to the deserving poor of the Parish.

The Committee have arranged with Mr J Rose for the use of the old Rugby Football field.
It might be mentioned that no playing members are to be on the Cup Committee of Management.
Thanks to the Courier and Simon Steele (Sports Editor)

Stockton Charity Cup

Stockton Charity Cup is another unique Cup that for years has been raising money for Charity before it was used as a Charity Cup Competition the Cup belonging to the Garland family, it was known as the Garland Invitation Cup and was usually played for by Polo teams at Moreton Morrell. The Garland family originally came from America but had settled in the area. The transition from a polo trophy to a football one is unclear
Stockton Workings Men Club won the Cup on three successive occasions between 1905 and 1908, and as it was the custom in those days the winning team were allowed to keep the Cup. Evidently intense rivalry occurred between Southam and Stockton especially if Stockton were the winners. The Final was always played at Stockton.
Having won the Cup outright it was renamed 'The Stockton Charity Cup' a separate Committee was formed and money raised went to deserving causes from the village .The Charity Cup Committee were not allowed to hold their meetings at the headquarters of the Football Club, the new headquarters for the new committee was the Kings Arms Public House where it remained until the Pub was demolished in 1964. The Barley Mow became its new home until 1988 and the present headquarters is the Crown Inn.

The names of the committee members pre-war are not available, yet we have the names of the players who participated in the three finals and they were :- T Rawbone, J Baldwin, C Bicknell, S Love, W Rawbone, W Noon, H Greenfield, G Baldwin, E Windsor, T Gulliver, E Smith, H Warner, W Warner.
It seems that George Bicknell was the Secretary from 1946 until 1965; other committee members at that time were T Hawker, B Tompkins, WHC Bicknell, and G Finch. It was the latter named George Finch who took over as Secretary, a post he held until retiring in 1988, his wife Anne was evidently a great help during the years he was Secretary. Brian Skidmore took over the Secretary's job in 1988 and still holds that position.
During George Finch's time as Secretary a Bert Bishop joined the Committee and presented a Charity Cup, known as the 'Bert Bishop Shield' which is awarded to the man of the match after the final, the player holds the trophy for twelve months but also gets a trophy to keep
George Finch died in 1991, and in a mark of respect the competing clubs made donations enabling the committee to buy what is now the 'George Finch Memorial Trophy.' This is awarded to the runners- up in the Final.

The very first Final was played on Easter Monday afternoon and this tradition has continued with large Bank Holiday crowds recorded in the early years.
The success of the Charity Cup must be due to the amount of work and effort put into competition by the Secretaries such as George Finch and Brian Skidmore.   .

Whitnash Charity Cup

This is another Charity Cup that was very prominent during the 1920 to the 1939 period and information passed to me is that the Whitnash Cup started about 1909 and a photograph is supposed to confirm this. The Committee was raising money for local organisations and the Final was usually played on a field called the Bulldog which was up by the Railway Line.

When Lockheed played at the Windmill, the Competition was given permission to stage the Final at the ground to raise extra funds.

The Cup eventually has been found; a gentleman informed the Club that he had found it in his Loft, although the base is missing. A Photograph of the Cup is displayed in the Photographs Pre – War (Leamington All Saints winning the Cup in 1923-24

It has again been impossible to find anything more about the Cup, the only information I have been able to find out is through the minutes of 1930's where it seems that the Charity Cup Competition were not happy with Leamington Referees at the time and went elsewhere..

The Charity Competition was being played for in the 1950's but then gradually faded out.

Warwick League of Friends Charity Cup

This Cup was started in the 1953/54 season. The Cup was presented it to the Committee and reported to have come from the Hospital. The competition was started by [Herbert Waldron and Charlie Wiseman.]

Tom Story and Arnold Rouse were invited on to the Committee with the idea to help raise funds for the Hospital. At the first Final which was held at the Lockheed Leamington's ground was financially a great success, we had Nurses selling raffle tickets at the Final which helped to swell the funds. Once the Competition was set up the standard was quite good, we had a very good selection of teams from Coventry, Nuneaton, the Warwickshire Combination and local Clubs. The first Finalist was Southam United they played Longford Rangers who at that time had one or two ex Coventry Players playing for them.

Herbert Waldron who was the Secretary eventually had to resign through business pressure and Bill Jackson took over and continued to raise money for the Hospital, although it was getting difficult with other Charity Cups being played for and various Leagues in the District had tightened their Rules to limit outside Cup Competitions.

The Committee gradually broke up mainly due to pressure of work and it became difficult to organise a competition with clubs declining or unable to enter. The Secretary tried to organise it on his own, but found it difficult, the Competition eventually closed down.

The Warwick Cinderella Cup

This is a Warwick Charity Cup and teams from Warwick & District Football League played in the competition between the turn of the Century and up to the 1939 era, not a great deal is mentioned about the Charity, but it was an essential part of Warwick especially to the poor. The money raised from the competition was used to purchase boots and shoes from various places so that the very poor children and families who applied to the Committee were able to go through the winter with shoes on their feet.

The Charity was in being before the First World War; it may have been in operation before the turn of the century. Browsing through the micra films of the Warwick & Warwickshire Advertiser in the earlier 1900s mention was made of a football match being played and it eventually closed down during the1939 conflict.

It seems that the earlier mention of Pepper Talbot secretary of the Warwick Football League was very involved with the Charity and so was a Mr Bartlett who was my wife's Grandfather. It was a separate Committee which organised the Competition for the teams and arranged the matches as well. The referees from Leamington and Warwick refereed matches in the Competition as they did for other charity competitions before the War

Wellesbourne Hospital Cup

Enquiries have been made to people from Wellesbourne about this Cup, it is in existence but where no one knows where it is.

The Cup was mentioned in the Warwick & Warwickshire Advertiser in the 1920 period when a match was played at Wellesbourne. This match raised a reasonable amount of money for Stratford Hospital.

Jockey & Hounds Charity Cup

This Cup was named after the Public House that organised the matches, according to the report in the Warwick &Warwickshire Advertiser in the 1920s. There were problems at the match and this was reported giving all the fact and the reason why the match did not finish on time.

The whole issue was reported to the Committee and it transpired that the Referee had an argument with the goalkeeper who would not leave the field the referee refused to restart until he did; eventually another person took over and refereed the match to a finish.

At the meeting to discuss the problem, the Chairman said we are in a difficult position with this match. The reason being we have not had the Competition sanctioned by the County FA. The Chairman said we must make a decision and stick by it, after a discussion the Committee ordered the match to be replayed with a different Referee and the goalkeeper was not allowed to play in the Competition.

The Charity Cup evidently raised money for the local people in need.

Cancer Cup and Supplementary Cup

The Cancer Charity started to raise funds for Cancer research from the 1950s when the Committee was organised by Sidney Jackson, and Brian Knibb. They raised money from the Cricket Competitions during the season. To start the Competition off with trophies.The Jewellers named Grayson in Leamington presented a Shield to the committee for the Winning Team, and the Directors from Automotive Products presented a Cup for the Runners-up. Eventually Mr Emmott one of the Directors from AP gave the committee two Cups for the Competition, one was for the best Bowler taking the most wickets, and the other was for the Batsman who made the most runs. In talking to Sidney Jackson he said he had no idea who would have the Shield now or the Cups, they could well be gathering dust in a Cricket Clubhouse.

The Competition to raise funds for Cancer Research was handed over to Tracey Thomas. He also had a Cup donated to the Competition which came from a firm called, 'Karobes' from Leamington the firm dealt with ancillaries for the car interior. Tracey Thomas then set up a Football Competition with teams from Coventry, Nuneaton moving on down to Redditch. Arranging fixtures became a problem, because of the distance and travelling to the various grounds, the teams played on a Saturday but co-ordinating the Conference dates between each League made things difficult.

When Tracey Thomas became Secretary of the Leamington & District Sunday League, the Cancer Cup became part of the League although it had its own Committee. Majority of the teams were from the Sunday League and the Cup was by Invitation only. The Competition was a success straight away even though teams had the choice they still paid their fee and entered. After the initial success a Supplementary Cup was brought into play this was the idea of one of the Committee members, the Supplementary Cup was donated by the Lockheed Football Assistance Committee.

It seems that this Committee raised quite a lot of money without actually being tied to the Lockheed Football Club. The name of the trophy was called, 'The Lockheed Football Assistance Cup' and this made the Cancer Cup Competition a success

Tracey Thomas is still the Secretary and the Committee are all involved with the Sunday League with the majority of Clubs supporting the Competition at the Finals. The Competition has been raising funds for a long time whether it was Cricket or Football; all the money made went to the Cancer Research.

Clubs on entering the Competition as well as paying a fee to enter, have collecting tins for each match. At the Finals a Large Raffle is organised, Sponsors are obtained to assist in purchasing the Trophies.

It has to be one of the most profitable fund raising Cup Competition in the District.

George Dutton Challenge Charity Cup

George Dutton was President of the Leamington and District Referees Association, a Councillor on the Football Association, representing the Birmingham County Football Association, of which he was a member.

He was involved in the Leamington Saturday League before the War and on its resumption after the War. In January 1976 George Dutton met with an accident and taken to Hospital whilst he was in Hospital he did not recover from the accident and after a short illness he passed away in February, 1976

Andy Semple and Arnold Rouse decided to set up a Charity Cup Competition in memory of George Dutton. The Competition would be based on Junior League Champions from Saturday Leagues and Sunday Leagues. At the same time, we talked of distance and it was suggested we look at a radius of 18 miles from Leamington checking the Birmingham County Handbook. The distance covered fairly good quality Football Leagues on a Saturday and Sunday.

Tracey Thomas, Secretary of the Leamington and District Sunday League was also on the Birmingham County Football Association. Tracey advised us what to do, register the Competition invite Clubs to a meeting discuss Rules, and finally contact the County F.A. to have Rules sanctioned. We then started the Competition, whilst awaiting approval from the County FA. Before we actually began sending invitations to Leagues requesting their League Champions compete in the Competition we needed cash and if possible, a trophy. The Committee was formed and a small amount of money was contributed to get the Competition moving.

The Football Association and the Birmingham County Football Association, was written to and so were the Local Leagues and Referees Associations. The replies I received from the Large Associations were amazing. The stock answer was "sorry, we would be setting up a precedent" From the smaller Leagues we received donations which helped. We placed an advert in the local Newspapers and the 'Coventry Evening Telegraph.' Later on that week, I received a phone call from a Mr.Morgan, saying he had a Cup for me if I would go over to Coventry and look at it. We went to D.J.Morgan, Silversmiths and Engravers, Coventry, and were handed a magnificent Trophy. All it needed was engraving .as follows – **"George Dutton Challenge Cup."** When the engraving was completed, the Trophy was taken to the Referees Meeting and shown to the members. (see photograph).

The Committee comprised of the following members- Sid Sharp, Derek Silk, Bill Burnell, Gordon Hyam, Brian Hackleton, Andy Semple, Arnold Rouse, Secretary. Members from the Association were always available if we needed them. We wrote a letter thanking Mr.Morgan, also to the Coventry Evening Telegraph for their support.

We had approval from the County Football Association, they informed us the Finalist must play mid-week, this was because one Team would be from a Saturday League, and the other from a Sunday League. The Rules were very strict and had to be observed, it meant players could only play for either a Saturday Team or a Sunday Team, but not both, in this Competition.

Our inexperience soon showed up, we had to deal with a player, who played for the Saturday Team, and then went on Sunday and played in the Sunday Team, We did use a little common sense, instead of removing the Club from the Competition as per Rules because it was the very first offence, we ordered one of the matches to be re-played and banned the player from taking part. The team the player played for lost on Saturday, when he played for the Sunday Team they won, so the Committee instructed the Sunday match to be replayed. The decision was correct in the Committee's view, the information was sent to the two Clubs, and the match was arranged for an evening match. The defaulting Team lost the match.

We had teams from Birmingham, Nuneaton, Redditch, Banbury, Coventry, Daventry, Stratford, Solihull, Berkswell, and Kineton and Leamington .This made it into an interesting Competition. Once the draw had been made and Conference Dates fixed, the Clubs and League Secretaries received a copy, also we sent them the Rules and suggested Charities were also asked them to help raise funds. The Clubs were asked if they had any objections to collecting tins, the answer was usually "No."
Andy Semple, Sid Sharp and myself went to quite a few matches to raise funds, the Clubs generosity and the player's varied.

The first season went very well; the Final was arranged at the "Windmill" home of the Lockheed Leamington Football Club. After twelve months, we now had a Cup and Trophies for the Players. The Committee donated the Referee and Linesmen's Trophies. The two Finalists were Bartley Green from the Birmingham Metropolitan League and Westlea Wanderers from Leamington and District Sunday Football League. The Referee was Mr Peter Reeves, Football League Referee from Leicester

The Linesmen were Fred Tebbs and Derek Silk both from Leamington RA. With a local Team in the Final we expected a good crowd; unfortunately we were not very lucky with the weather. The game itself was an excellent contest between two evenly matched teams and Westlea just manage to outplay Bartley Green, by the odd goal. After the game, we put on a few sandwiches for the players. Our first Charity was "Leukaemia" and we presented them with nearly £200.

Since that first match in 1977, we have gradually increased our donations by changing the rules, reducing the distance and inviting Local Clubs from certain Leagues. Pinvin FC brought this about. They had won the Cup the second year by beating Southam FC at Stratford and went on to win again the next year by beating Bartley.Green FC at the Windmill ground in 1979 on a penalty in the last minute. Twelve months later Pinvin FC played "Bartley Green" at Racing Club Warwick and after a very hard game, Bartley Green won. Whilst both Teams were good sides, the distance they came and the support they brought to the Final made it very difficult to raise money for Charity the local support was very poor. We had little financial return from both Clubs.

The Competition that season was earmarked with trouble. In one game the Manager said the Pitch was not up to FA, Standards. I asked him what he meant and I received no answer. In the next round of the Competition this team was drawn away to a Coventry side and the weather during that period was very difficult, to get the game played with frosts and snow in December.

We did arrange the Fixture for the last Sunday in December. Both teams turned up to play and again the same team said the Pitch was in a poor state, we had a few words and the Chairman of the Club decided not to play, the Committee Chairman who was Mr Sidney Sharp asked the Club Secretary to write to the Competition Secretary giving him all the details, he also asked the other team to do the same,

A week later the Competition received a letter from the Birmingham County FA, asking for a report on the incident regarding the match why it wasn't played and the statements over the pitch. Also my observation, on the complaint, that had been sent in to the County Football Association.

A hearing was set for January in Birmingham and the Chairman and I went with a colleague from Coventry Representing the Home Club, at the meeting was the Chairman of the County, the Secretary, and members of the Disciplinary Committee, also the Secretary of Worcester County Football Association as an Observer.

The Club concerned put their case and we then went into the meeting room to put ours. When we had finished the Chairman asked us if we had any objections to the team coming into the room, to listen to what the Chairman had to say before the Committee made their decision. We did not object' after a fair and frank discussion we all trooped outside and had a good talk between ourselves.

After about half an hour we were all called back in to the room and the County found in favour of the Competition, with the Club paying all the costs. When it was all over the Committee decided to change the Competition Rules making it more local.

Once we had changed our rules slightly and obtained sponsors through "Warwick Squash Centre", "Wallwin Pumps Warwick" and eventually "Wade Engineering", the finances increased, although the standard of Football was not as good, the Teams that took part enjoyed the Competition.

The Competition has progressed and is still going strong. The Committee has changed over the years, we had Andy Semple Chairman, followed by Sid Sharp, Dave Aston and then Bill Burnell, Arnold Rouse, was Secretary until 1989, then John Austin took over till 2000. when Ray Morgan became Secretary. The support from members has dwindled, so the George Dutton Committee have returned the Competition back to the Association's Management Committee, where the Chairman and Secretary have made changes and still promoting the Competition. Whilst talking about the George Dutton Cup the first winners, Westlea Wanderers, had a misfortune when the Club Chairman, Maurice Billington, collapsed and died. To commemorate his name, the Club decided to set up a Charity Competition and they obtained an exact replica of the, 'George Dutton' Cup from D.J.Morgan, Coventry. The Cup is called the ***"Maurice Billington Charity Cup"*** It raises money for Charity through the Leamington Sunday Football League.

Nicolet Campbell / Andy Campbell Cup 1984

Andy Campbell was a Vice-President of the Leamington and District Referees Association, also Chairman of Nicolet Instruments. In 1984, Andy passed away after a short illness with cancer. A meting was held with the Managing Director of Nicolet Instruments concerning the setting up a Charity Football Cup Competition in memory of Andy Campbell.

The Company were in agreement with this and told me to arrange it, he also said they would sponsor the Cup. Talking to a few of the Club Secretaries from division three and four of the League it seems a Competition for them was needed.

The subject was broached to the League Secretary who raised no objection. The Committee, which was organising the George Dutton Competition, was in agreement to run the two Competitions and I was asked to write to the Birmngham County Football Association. We decided on a name and called it the, "Nicolet Campbell Cup". Having written to the County and sent the rules through to them, we also registered the Competition. I was informed that to use the Company's name, I would have to seek permission from the Football Association. When I wrote to the Football Association, they wanted to know what financial gain the Company would get from the Competition. I explained that Nicolet was an American Computer Company and the Warwick branch was a subsidiary, the financial gain would be negligble as the amount of money would go to Charity.

Approval was given by the Football Association and Nicolet purchased the Cup (see photo) and sponsored the Competition. Nearly 40 Clubs entered the first season, helping us to raise an excellent amount of money, we were using collecting tins as well, but some of the Clubs were very generous. The first Final was played in 1985 at Racing Club, Warwick and a reasonable Sunday afternoon crowd saw a very good match, considering the Clubs who entered were from the Lower Divisions of the Sunday League and most of them enjoyed the competitiveness of the Competition.

After a while, the Competition lost its sponsors, the new Managing Director was not Sports minded and withdrew his sponsorship. This meant we had to change the title, after a discussion we informed the County F.A. the Competition would be called the **"Andy Campbell Cup"**. The County accepted the change. We obtained fresh sponsors and the Competition carried on raising money for Charity.

The Cup unfortunately was damaged, we never found out how it happened, the surface was bent and it was twisted. It meant that we had to purchase a new Cup if we wanted the Competition to carry on. The Committee was in favour of continuing, so the Secretary John
Austin contacted Nicolet Instruments, told them what had happened, they told him to go ahead and purchase a new Cup up to a certain amount in value. The present Cup was bought and is being competed for at the present time.

The organising Committee is the same as the George Dutton, and the Committee has to seek Sponsors every year, at this moment in time the Competition is sponsored by Norman Stephens Unlimited. The money raised goes to the small charitable organisations in Warwick, Leamington and the surrounding District.

The Sean Horgan Cup,

This Cup was given to the League to set up an Invitation Competition through the League to raise funds.
The Cup was donated to the Leamington Celtic Football Club by the family of Sean Horgan, who presented it to the League. At one time the team selected to play for the opportunity of winning the Cup had to play Leamington Celtic FC.
When the League took over the Competition, Various teams whether they were Cup Winners or League Champions the Management invited them to play for the Cup then a date and ground would be arranged.
Sean Horgan was a very important member of Leamington Celtic FC also a very hard worker for the Leamington Irish Club (which is now defunct) He was also a Gentleman. .

The Maurice Billington Cup

Maurice Billington was the Chairman of Westlea Wanderers FC and he was quite proud of the Club especially when they were the first winner of the George Dutton Cup.

It was in the autumn when Maurice met with an accident and passed away. It was a sad blow to the Club. Eventually the players talked of setting up a Football Competition in Maurice's Memory.

This they did and a cup was purchased from Morgans in Coventry and the cup they purchased was a replica of the George Dutton Cup. This is played for every year in exactly the same way as the Sean Horgan Cup. The teams are selected by the Management Committee of the Leamington &District Sunday Football League and Teams are invited to enter, all the funds, raised go to Charity.

Maurice was another Gentleman, very keen on football and worked very hard for Westlea Wanderers Football Club and the players were all local lads and very good sportsmen.

Coventry Referees Benevolent Charity Cup

In various parts of the Association minutes you will come across the word Benevolent and the fact that the Association played in a few Finals and won the Competition outright a few times.

It also mentioned the word Benevolent Fund. The two are tied together and the story is as follows.

The Cup which is a nice Cup and has been around since the end of the War was donated to the Coventry Referees Association by a gentleman called Freddie Chapman, so the Coventry Referees and Nuneaton Referees would have something to play for when they played each other at Football. It has been led to believe that both Associations played each other at football as a friendly get together before the War, very much like Leamington did in the 1930s with Rugby Referees.

After a certain number of years, Coventry Referees decided to invite other Associations. Any money made at the Finals would be distributed amongst the Associations. To do this they had to register the Competition with the Birmingham County FA. From those early days the Competition was expanded to raise money for Charity, this was agreed by the Committee that was set up under Doug Paget, who was the first Secretary. The change was sent to the County Sanctions Committee who approved and the Charity the funds would be raised for was the Referees Benevolent Fund.

Thus the Competition was given the go-ahead, and nearly all the Associations in the Warwickshire and Birmingham area entered, all the matches were played on an evening between Mondays to Friday, this left the Saturday free for the referee's job of refereeing. In the early years quite a lot of fun was had between the Associations and good friendships were made and money was being raised at the same time with a raffle, whilst the players and supporters were enjoying a good Buffet.

When Sunday Football was allowed if a match was arranged for the Sunday, you had to apply to the County FA for permission, this was normally granted because all the Referees Association was registered with the County. We were also registered as referees on an individual basis, so to play Football we had to pay twice. When these matches took place very rarely did we have any trouble. One or two of the Associations were beginning to play experienced players in the team and they were causing a little bit of bother. We gradually built up a reasonable team when we had a number of sports teachers join the Association as well as an ex-professional player.

We finished up, with a good selection of referees who could play football and cricket. We were able to turn out a very good cricket team. Majority carried on refereeing and eventually reached the standard of senior football.

The first Secretary was Doug Paget, he was followed by Ken Anderton, and then came Kieron Barratt and finally the Secretary to day is John Starkey.

It is a Competition where only the Cup is played for, and no trophies are given to the players or officials, although one match when Coventry played Nuneaton the players and officials did receive a silver medallion, this was either the 21st or 25th year the Cup was being played for.

Ken Anderton was the Secretary.

The Benevolent Charity Fund

This Fund is administered by members of the Executive Council of the Referees Association and they are elected at each Conference

The Fund is available to all members who are fully paid members of their Association or Society and Affiliated to the National Referees Association.

If a member receives an injury or suffers a serious illness and is struggling to make ends meet especially if he has a young family the Benevolent Fund will help out, providing all the information and situation is given on the application Form

The Funds of the Charity are healthy and quite a few referees and their families have benefited.

At every Conference during the Mid-day break a Silver collection is taken which helps to swell the funds. A number of Associations or Societies raise funds by having raffles, we at Leamington organised Six-a-Side Competitions to raise funds which goes into the Benevolent Fund and over the years have donated a considerable amount.

That is the extent of Charity Cups & Competitions.

Cup & League Finals

At the end of every season Cup Finals and League Finals are being played, either to determine the winners of a League Cup or the winners of a Charity Competition. A selection of Officials are needed for the match to be played and a Referee and two Linesmen are selected. The Finals today have a 4th Official whose job it is to assist everyone who is involved with the match.

There are exceptions when certain 'Charity Cup Finals' are played during the season, these are arranged because the Teams competing are selected from the previous seasons League or Cup results. A Cup Final is another part of a Referees involvement, to receive an appointment to be the official at a Cup Final is a boost to the Referee.

The Linesmans title changed in the 1990s and they were called "Assistant Referees" for the purpose of this chapter they will be called 'Linesmen.'

To mention every Referee and Linesman (Assistant Referees) who has been involved with Cup Finals would be a difficult task, as no official record has been kept and reports in the Association minutes do not cover every Cup Competition.

If we start with the Football Association Challenge Cup we have had one member who was involved with the Final. In 1937 George Dutton received an appointment as one of the Linesman for the Final this was to be played at Wembley Stadium. The teams were Sunderland versus Preston North End. The result was a win for Sunderland by 3 goals to I(one).

In 1944 John Wildsmith was the Linesman in the Football League Cup between Aston Villa versus Blackpool played at Aston Villa on the 6th May 1944. This was a two legged affair and the return match would be played at Blackpool (The appointment letter makes interesting reading see artifacts on John Wildsmith)

Whilst we are still involved with the Football Association. We did have a female Referee in Mrs Christine Cairns who was a "Linesperson in the Womens Football Association Cup Final." This was played on May 15th 1977 at Dulwich Hamlet F. C. London between Southampton and Queens Park Rangers. Christine Cairns was the Associations first Lady Referee.

Moving from the Football Association to the Birmingham County Football Association. The 'Senior Cup' has always been considered the premier Cup to Referee. We have been fortunate with the selection of referees and linesman when the Finals are being played. George Dutton refereed the 'Senior Cup Final' in 1936 this was between Hednesford v Burton Albion in which Hednesford won by 3 goals to1(one).
John Sollis refereed the Senior Cup at Birmingham in 1967/8 between Kidderminster Harriers versus Nuneaton Borough the result was a win for Kidderminster 6 goals to 3 (three). Andy Semple also from Leamington was one of the linesmen in the match, this was a coupe for Leamington having two officials on the same match. This happened a few years earlier when Harry Owen was linesman to George Pankhurst. They both were involved with an Amateur International :- 'England versus Ireland' played on February 3rd 1951 at Birmingham.

We have senior referees on the Football League as a Linesman. They have received appointments abroad in a number of the Major Cup Competitions. It was an experience one imagined they enjoyed. The Referees who received these appointments were John Jays, Alec Walters, John Sollis,Lionel Fleet, George Pankhurst and Peter Watson.

Frank Wall received a Linesman Appointment in the Senior Cup, with Jack Taylor as the Referee the Final was at Dudley. We have had other members who have received Appointments either in the Semi-Final Stage or the Final. They were John Austin, Dennis Reynolds, and Brian Hackleton and Lionel Fleet. Brian has also been the 4th official when Birmingham & Walsall were involved.
A number of referees from Leamington have been involved with the Canpbell-Orr Shield which is a Competition for Saturday Leagues. John Sollis has had the Final and we have had other referees such as Lionel Fleet, John Austin and Duncan MacAulay involved with the competition. While we are still on the County Cup Finals. The Featherstone Cup, the Junior Cup and the Minor Cup are all Saturday Cup Competitions.

Following on from the previous page and starting from 1934 season we have had a Junior International being played at Birmingham. The match was between Birmingham Couny Football Association v Scotland Football Association
Jack Joyner refereed the semi-final of the Cinderella Charity Competition in 1937.
War time appointments were limited and with John Wildsmith and George Dutton on the Wartime Midland Football League. They would probably referee the matches while members like George Pankhurst and others would have been used as Linesman.

The period between 1952 to 1960 are void of minutes and this makes mentioning referees rather difficult although there were a number of matches from the Saturday League that would need referees and the County were beginning to distribute the Finals and Semi-finals around the County. The recording of any Cup Finals Appointments have not been as accurate as one would have wished. To put down on paper that a certain referee had a junior or senior cup appointment would not be fair unless it was accurately quoted. Over the years quite a few referees have been fortunate in receiving Cup Finals, either from the Local Leagues or the County Football Association.

The Saturday League 3rd Division K O Cup was played in 1955 at Warwick Towns Football Ground, this was done so that the teams would not have very far to travel, this also applied to the officials. It was ideal for me as the referee, because it only took me about 8 minutes to walk to the ground. The reason was the Suez Canal War with Egypt and petrol rationing was imminent.

The remainder of the Leamington Saturday League Cups are as follows:- The Birmingham City Shield, The Aston Villa Cup, The Junior Cup and the Presidents Cup.

The referees who would have been given matches in the early post War period would have been Charlie Jackson, Jack Joyner, Alex Walters, Henty Hall, Tom Story, Jack Wright, Peter Watson, Bert Millership, John Sollis and Arnold Rouse. If you move to the latter part of the 1950s the following referees would have had the experience to referee the Finals, members such as Frank Wall, Ted Warwick, Dennis Hodson, Barry Ebsworth, Bill Wall and Stan Green. In The 1970s with the Saturday League having problems the trophies were not played for.

On the resumption the League carried on untill 1977 when the Aston Villa Cup was played and Tom Machin was the last Referee to have the Final. The Aston Villa Cup was the plum appointment for many referees over the years, if you was a Class 2(two) referee and you was appointed to the Final. It was recognised that if you had a good game promotion to Class 1(one) was on the cards. The Final was always played at Henry Griffiths ground Tachbrook Road on Easter Monday morning.

When the Referee receives a letter from the League Secretary telling him he has been selected by the committee to Referee a Cup Final. It does tell the Referee that his marks from the Clubs or Competition have been good and consistant. It is usually the best Referee who gets the appointment, although it is not always the case. We do have referees who seem to click for Cup Finals quite often. and the Secretaries of the various competitions are fully aware of the situation, appointments are distributed accordingly. When the list is read out at the meeting the Referees who have been selected are usually congratulated by colleagues.

Patrick Gwynne during his career has been involved with Womens Football and has travelled the World Refereeing at Womens Football Tournaments. In places like Taiwan. He has written articles on his journeys and one is being placed in the section of short stories. We also had Christine Cook one of our female referees who was involved with Charity Cup Matches as a Linesman , she also refereed in open aged football, being the only Female Referee at the N E C Indoor Tournament where she acquitted herself very well. Locally Christine refereed at a Womens Football Competition on Newbold Comyn having the Final which she says was hard work.

Herewith a list of Cup matches with the referees from about 1963 to 1978

European Cup:- Dulcia vBenfica	John Jays	Linesman
FA Charity Cup:- Barnsley v Huddresfield	John Jays	Linesman
FA Charity Cup 5th rd	John Sollis	Linesman
Stratford League v West Midland Alliance	Dennis Hodson	Referee
B C F A Senior Cup	W(Bill) Wall	Linesman
B C F A Senior Cup	Roy Joyner	Linesman
FA Preliminary Cup	Dacid Clarke	Linesman
Aston Villa Cup Final.	Clive Darkes	Referee
3rd Division KO Cup Final	Joe Beard	Referee
Advertiser Cup Final	Lionel Fleet	Referee
FA Cup Everton vTranmere	Lionel Fleet	Linesman
BCFA Campbell –Orr Final B,ham Wks v Cov Wks	Lionel Fleet	Referee
BCFA Senior Cup	Sidney Sharp	Linesman

Junior International	Frank Wall	Referee
B,ham County FA v Irish FA	Alan Windsor	Linesman
Youth International	John Sollis	Linesman
FA Chanllenge Cup	Lionel Fleet	Referee
Fairs Cup Qtr /Final	John Sollis	Linesman
Youth Cup Semi/Final	Roger Palmer	Referee
BCFA Youth Inter League Cup	Harry Walton	Referee
Cancer Cup Final	Fred Tebbs	Referee
Coventry Evening Telegraph Cup Final	Fred Tebbs	Referee
BCFA Sunday Premier	Dennis Reynolds	Referee
Warwickshire Constabulary Final	Patrick Gwynne	Referee
George Dutton Cup Final	Fred Tebbs	Referee

The Above mentioned Finals or Semi-Finals are only a brief number, over the years we have had quite a few Referees who have been fortunate in receiving Cup Finals. There are Saturday Leagues in the area, and we also have the Charitable Cup Competitions. Majority of Clubs enter.
Herewith some of the major Cup Competitions that Referees can be selected to referee or act as an Assistant Referee. The Coventry Evening Telegraph Challenge Cup, The Foleshill Charity Cup, Bedworth Senior Nursing Cup, there are others and Stratford have similar Cup Competitions for the Saturday teams.

Once the season is over and all the competitions have been played the Leamington Saturday League used to organised a presentation evening for all the Clubs and Referees. The Sunday League eventually did the same. To present the Trophies and medals the Committee invited a well known player from one of the professional clubs. They were excellent evenings and everyone enjoyed the atmosphere, they gradually faded away, when a number of Clubs decided to set up their own presentation evening, which did not always turn out the best way
The County Football Association have a very strong list of Cup Finals and the Referees who receive County Appointments usually have had a good season and been recommended. The same applies to the Saturday and Sunday Leagues where a very good list of competitions should benefit the referee

In the Competitions below the Football League we have had members who have had an Amateur Cup game mostly from teams in the area that were not on a Semi-Professional League.
Harry Owen received F A International Line Appointments and he also ran the Line to George Pankhurst at Coventry (see the Artifacts).
Alan Windsor had a Line appointment in the County FA v Irish FA in 1967 and Sid Sharp was referee to a County Schools Senior Cup at Atherstone FC ground and a similar National Competition went to a member at Rugby Towns Football ground.

A number of Referees have received appointments for League and Charity Cups. Especially in Coventry members like Fred Tebbs, Bill Burnell and Peter Liddington one could carry on talking about the Senior Referees who have been mentioned in the various Chapters, we have had a number of referees from Leamington who have had appointments in the Quarter and Semi-Final stages of the County Cup Competitions. They could be either the Saturday or Sunday Cups.

Appointments from the 1980s & 1990s

Birmingham County Football Association
Junior Cup   Simon Rogers   Referee

Saturday Vase Preliminary   Alan Peachey   Referee

Sunday Vase 4th & 5th Rounds   Duncan MacAulay   Referee
                                                  David Leslie   Linesman
                                                  John Sharp   Referee
                                                  John Austin   Referee
                                                  Colin Parker   Linesman
                                                  David Hartshorn   Linesman
                                                  Berkley Bugg   Referee
Saturday County Vase Final   Andy Dalziel   Referee

Saturday Vase Semi –Final   G W(Bill) Burnell   Referee

County Senior Cup   Tom Prendergast   Linesman

Minor Challenge Cup Semi/Final   John Mander   Linesman

County Junior Cup 5th rd   Simon Rogers   Referee

Appointments from the 1995 & 2001 to 2004.

Birmingham County Football Association
County Vase Sunday   Brian Hackleton   Referee
                                                  John Austin   Referee Challenge
Cup Semi-Final   John Mander   Referee

Allden Memorial Cup Final   John Sharp   Linesman
                                                  Terry James   Linesman
Saturday Junior Cup Final   John Mander   Linesman

County Saturday Vase 4th round   Tom Prendergast   Referee
                                                  Peter Donague   Linesman
Stockton Cup Final   Peter Liddington Referee

Coventry Evening Telegraph Cup Final   Peter Liddington Referee

Midland Combination Cup Final   Michael Bingham   Referee

County Sunday Vase Final   Michael Bingham   Referee.
                                                  Packer Bahi   Linesman
                                                  Antonio Parasmo   Linesman
Womens Cup Final   Paul Anderson-Kirby Referee

•

- To cover matches over possibly 60 plus years with the names of the referees who would have received a Cup Final you would need a long list of referees and we know all the records are not available.

When Football restarted after the War it was played during the week and on a Saturday afternoon, eventually Sunday Football was allowed, this increased the local Cup and League Finals to be played for at the end of the season. The Leamington Saturday folded up through lack of support and the teams moved elsewhere, this was a dissapointment to the referees especially at the time a few members were on a Feeder League. It also reduced the number of Cup Finals that was available.

Majority of Referees eventually refereed in other areas on a Saturday as well as officiating on a Sunday so the scope for Cup Finals was broader. To cover all Cup Finals and League Cup or Championship matches would take time although there are plenty of matches where the Referee and Linesmen are needed, especially in area's like Stratford and Coventry even the The Midland Combination where our referees are giving good service. We also have the Hotel & Caterers Sports Association(Midlands) and the Mid-Warwickshire Boys / League for youth and boys football who have a number of Finals each year, they are good experience for the young Referee.

We have Schools Football and some of the school teams can be very competitive. Then we have the Ladies Football which is getting stronger. Every game is important to the Referee and his Linesmen even the 4th official has an important role to play and to those Referees who sent me a list of Cup Finals they have refereed, I hope you will understand why it would be a little difficult to mention everyone..

Chapter 12

Football Leagues

This section of the book will give a brief excursion into the Football & Junior Leagues that referees were involved with from the turn of the Century. A few were mentioned before the First World War and the majority between the 1914 and 1939 Wars. After the 1939 War we had new Leagues being formed and they benefited the amateur and the professional players..

Stratford Football League was the first League to be formed, other Leagues are mentioned in the minutes of the Association and Football was played on a Saturday only. It wasn't until the 1960's that Sunday Football was allowed and the Sunday Football League eventually became a very strong League which benefited the Leamington & District Referees.

Here are the names of the Saturday Leagues mentioned in the period between 1920 and 1939:

Henley &	**District**	**League**
Kineton &	**District**	**League**
Leamington &	**District**	**League**
Stratford &	**District**	**League**
Southam &	**District**	**League**
Warwick &	**District**	**League**

If we look at the Henley & District League, finding information about the League was difficult. The only mention of the League is in the minutes when referees appointments were made. We had a Referee assaulted and the player was charged, the Court Case was heard at Henley,

The same could be said about the Kineton & District League, Football matches are mentioned between two Villages and that is all.

The Southam & District Football League was active between 1920 and 1939. This was shown when they were involved with the Leamington & District Referees Association at an AGM in the early 1920s. The League could have been arranging matches at the turn of the century, when the Southam Charity Cup was being played for.

The Warwick &District League, started in the 1890's although no actual record can be found, although minutes from 1898 to 1904 were discovered in the County Library. Teams are mentioned in the Warwick and Warwickshire Advertiser. A fixture list was printed and quite a lot of information was found browsing through the Advertiser and the Courier in the period before the First World War until about 1926. Items of interest concerning local Football was well presented, after that date, it did not seem to be as well reported. The Leamington & District Saturday League, who at the beginning had the prefix Warwick in their title, this was eventually removed and the Warwick & District Football League carried on with the full title. If all the minutes could be found it may tell a different story.

Three photographs were shown to me concerning Warwick West End and Warwick Town football teams in the 1921 to 1924 perod when Warwick Town won the Birmingham Junior Cup. The Chairman in the photographs was my father Arthur H Rouse. With these photographs were two medallions of Warwick West End winning the Warwick & District Thursday League. Further research into the archives at the County Library may mention the League at the moment it hasn't been possible to find anything out about the League.

The Leagues mentioned above have been providing football for players local Derbies and football matches, between the villages and football teams from the town could easily have been played on a friendly basis.
The actual date some of the Leagues were formed is extremely difficult to find.
It suggests according to the Newspapers of the time, that they formed as Leagues after the
First World War, the Majority are mentioned in the Association minutes between 1931- 1939, and in earlier correspondence between the Leagues and the Referee Association

Warwick & District Football League

Everyone was under the impression that the League started in 1904, having found further information concerning the League from the County Library. A minute book dated from 1898 to 1904 was shown to me and it seems the League was in existence before that date, holding meetings at the Brittania Inn Emscote. It was also financially sound when they were able to purchase a Cup for £3-10s (three pounds ten shilling) and it was to be called the 'Champions Cup'

The Secretary mentioned in 1898 was Mr Tallis with the Chairman Mr Williams. The referees on the list came from Solihull, Aston Cantlow, Coventry, Stratford, Kenilworth, Knowle, Warwick and Leamington. The League consisted of 24 Teams In 1902 they had Two Divisions of eleven in each Division. The Teams came from Solihull, Cubbington, Leamington, Budbroke Stratford, Warwick, Kenilworth and Wilmcote, monthly meetings were held alternately between Warwick and Stratford. The management consisted of the Chairman, Secretary, President and three Vice-Presidents. One interesting point was that Leamington Celtic had a team in the League in 1902 and the Royal Warwickshire Regiment were Champions in 1904, medallions were being purchased for eleven players at a cost of 3/6 (three shillings and sixpence each). The League is mentioned again in 1926. We all thought Pepper Talbot who was Chairman of the Leamington Referees was the first Secretary. That wasn't the case, finding those minutes proved he wasn't. He retired from the referees in 1926 to carry on with the League. Other names mentioned who were involved with the League was a Mr Snell, Chairman and Mr W Hunt Secretary, George Dutton was the referees' Delegate to the League and appointments were made through the Referees' Association.

The following Teams formed the League which was very strong in 1927: Ashow, Alveston, Aylesford, Engineers Reserves, Five-Way Wanderers, Hatton & Hasely, Kenilworth St Nicholas, Leek Wootton, Lillington, Leamington Rangers, Saltisford Rovers, Tachbrook, Tiley Rovers, Warwick Town Reserves and finally Wellesbourne &Wroxall..
The League continued to give good service to the Clubs who were in the League. The referees were also looked after by the Committee. All the complaints were listened to in general it was a good League to referee on. Changes did happen when the Delegate from the referees became 'Secretary of the Leamington &District Saturday Football League' this caused a few problems to the referees and to the Association. It was eventually settled and was mentioned in the minutes, eventually like all other Leagues in the area they had to close down at the beginning of hostilities in September 1939 and never really recovered enough from the War to restart the League.
The League was very generous to the Charity Cup Competitions the Clubs who were invited to take part in. This was to raise money for the Hospital and the Cinderella Charity Cup.

According to Tom Story the Secretary of the Warwick & District Football League in the latter years was a Mr Walker who lived in Guy Street Warwick. Unfortunately the information was mentioned too late as Mr Walker had died, so the minutes or other information of the League was lost for good.

Henley & District Football League

This was a small League that only accommodated clubs within the vicinity of Henley so the football teams from the various villages could have a competition without travelling great distances. Very little is mentioned in the minutes, although one of the Association Referees was assaulted by a player. It was reported to the Police as well as the County FA. The case was heard at Henley Court

It seems the beginning of the 1939 War was responsible for the demise of Henley &District Football League.

Southam & District Football League

This was another small League mentioned in the 1931 to 39 Minutes also in the section called 'The Beginning' when a letter between the Leamington Referees Association and the Secretary of the Southam & District Football League was read out at the Annual General Meeting.

The Chairman mentioned was Mr W W Sturley and the Secretary was Mr Amour. It was a very strong League with teams from outside the Southam area making up the Second Division. Whether the League was operating at the beginning of the 20th Century it is not quite certain, although it has been said the League started at the same time as the Southam Charity Cup which was 1904. No one seems to know, looking through the Warwickshire & Warwick Gazette of the period up to 1914 not much information was found. Although later on the fixture list for 'Southam & District League' was mentioned herewith the teams: - **Division One** Napton v Ryton Star, Bishops Itchington v Long Itchington. **Division Two:** - Southam Vics v Stockton Albion, Bubbenhall v Napton Rangers, Marton Rangers v Ryton Star Res.

Other teams were mentioned, and Radford Utd was subject to a complaint lodged by Southam United FC, this was held at the Black Dog public house, the story will be mentioned later on. There was another case at the Leagues Annual General Meeting where quite a few Clubs were involved and the referees were mentioned this was in 1921.

It seems the League however strong it was, may have been unable to reform after the war, no mention made in the Minutes of the Association in 1948.

Kineton & District Football League

Another League that seemed to be very strong between 1914 and 1939, matches were being played between villages within a certain radius to Kineton. In all probability it was the only entertainment for the local people and travelling to each ground would not have been a difficult proposition. Yet teams from Warwick went out to Kineton to play Football.

Stratford-upon- Avon & District Football League

This was the earliest recorded Football League. When a meeting was called in April 1896, at the Unicorn Hotel to organise and promote a Junior Football League to play on a Saturday Afternoon. **Delegates from the various Clubs that was present, were, Bidford, Binton, Claverdon, Newbold –on-Stow, Stratford, Welford, Wilmcote, with Kineton and Aston Cantlow promising to join.**

When everyone had agreed to form the League a 'Title' was suggested, it was called the Stratford –upon-Avon District Football League and the entrance Fee was 5/-(five shillings).

The first Chairman was Mr Doonan and the Secretary was Mr T R Ellerker. Delegates from each Club were formed into a Management Committee, the Committee then proposed the Rules and Regulations; these were drawn up and sent to the (English League Secretary for conformation.)
The League continued to grow, and Leamington & District Referees Association was involved at the beginning, by providing the referees. Eventually a Referees Association was formed which was called the Stratford and District Referees Association under the guidance of George Dutton and others from Leamington this was in the latter part of the 1930s.

During the 1914-18 and the 1939-45 War years The League closed down. On it's reopening in 1946. The 'Title' was changed to the 'Stratford-upon-Avon & District Football Alliance' eventually becoming the 'Stratford-upon-Avon Alliance.' The Alliance celebrated their Centenary in 1996 at the Moat House Stratford with Sir Stanley Matthews as the Principal Guest and over 350 Club and other Football Representatives attending. During the speeches the Mayor of Stratford made comments about refereeing and other issues concerning the League and how proud he was to be involved with a Football League with so much History. All this information was credited to the Chairman at the time, his comments which were recorded in the Stratford Herald was that refereeing was a, "valuable training ground for politics, it showed the value of having a thick skin and believing you were always right."

The Alliance is still going strong with Dave Hayward as Secretary and Phil Cooper who was Chairman when the Alliance celebrated their Centenary. Both these Officials retired in 2005 and the new Secretary is Michael Loram. The Stratford Alliance has an impressive record in Junior Football reaching the Final of the Campbell-Orr Shield and losing to a very strong Birmingham Works Team.
An interesting article was printed in the Stratford Herald about the Centenary Year. It was written by Victoria Minett. The reporter called the Alliance a thriving Saturday Football League and goes on to say that 'Grassroots football is alive and kicking, like a beacon in the desert.' It glows as brightly as one of a dying breed. After writing an interesting article Victoria finishes with the following paragraph. "It is the Saturday and Sunday minor leagues which keep football imaginations fired, and keep football dreams alive-lose them, and we lose it all".
The information was given to me by Phil Cooper (Chairman)

Leamington & District Saturday Football League

We are fortunate to find that the Leamington League has recorded a brief History of the League since it was formed in 1909. It is in the form of a Brochure produced for the Golden Jubilee Dinner held at the Regent Hotel in 1959.

When the League was formed it was called the Leamington, Warwick & District Junior League this was a result of clubs playing friendly games, on a somewhat haphazard footing.
The first meeting was held in the Blenheim Coffee House Leamington Spa at a cost on One Shilling to hire the room.
The following were the leading Clubs in those days, Leamington St Johns, Warwick West End, Warwick All Saints, Southam United, Cubbington Albion, there were other teams not mentioned who were involved with the League
The first Chairman was Mr J Walker and the Secretary was Mr J W Hancox with a Mr Tasker as his assistant

Travelling in those days was by Horse Wagonettes making a long and tedious journey. The League continued to make steady progress, its success was in no small measure to the untiring efforts of a loyal band of helpers and referees, who officiated and helped the League. Most of the officers were all associated with the Referees Association many have now passed on to a higher life.

All activities ceased in 1914 and on the resumption in 1919 the League opened up with a new Chairman Mr J Hancox and the Secretary was Mr Lines. Many considered the twenty years from 1919 to 1939 were years of steady progress. Only four teams completed the double being League Champions and Junior Cup Winners between 1919 to 1923, they were Depot RWR, Warwick All Saints, and for two years running Cubbington Albion

Twelve Clubs constituted the League:- Avon Rovers, Banbury GWR, Bishops Itchington, Cubbington Albion, Depot RWR, Emscote Foundry, Fenny Compton, Harbury Albion, Kineton Albion, Leamington GWR, Southam United and Warwick St Pauls.

A Handbook was printed and new Clubs were joining, Leamington GWR, was still the only Leamington representative on the League. In April 1935 it was felt that new blood was needed both on the executive side and playing side and special meetings were called. In June 1935 Mr George Dutton was elected as Secretary taking over from Mr G E Bagulay. George Dutton improved the standard of the League by inviting other Clubs with reasonable facilities to join. This eventually made the League stronger.

Rules were drafted and submitted to the BCFA for approval. Mr F Cattell a previous Secretary was elected Chairman and Mr W W Sturley was elected Vice-Chairman.

In 1936 Mr E Scruby who acted as Assistant Secretary during the illness of the Secretary did a valuable job for the League.

Two Divisions were formed in 1936 and with the finances becoming sound. Goblets were purchased for the Division I and Division 2 Champions and runners up, and the Leamington Junior Cup.

In October a new Trophy was presented to the League by the Directors of Aston Villa Football Club. This Trophy was called the, 'Aston Villa Cup' .and played for by teams in Division Two The Final was always played on Easter Monday and played at Henry Griffiths ground, usually a good crowd watched the match which was a money spinner for the League. The first winners were the 'Kenilworth Baptist Football Club'.

At the outbreak of the War in 1939, the League had to close down, which was disappointing, because the League had 10 (ten) Teams in Division I (one) and 14 (fourteen) Teams in Division 2 (two). Quite a few clubs requested to be allowed to carry on playing as long as they could. The Chief Constable once he had Home Office approval allowed matches to take place providing, "All the spectators carried their respirators".

After the War in 1946 all Football activities were resumed the League formed two Divisions, this soon was increased to three by the 1949 season. Each Division had 14 teams; this was a credit to the Secretary and the Committee.

The introduction of the Birmingham City Shield, which was donated by the Directors of Birmingham City FC and W Camkin Esq. The League Chairman Mr Horace Webster made it known to the Clubs in the 3rd Division and later on another trophy was presented to the League. This was from the Coventry Evening Telegraph. With further applications to join the League Division 3(three) was eventually split into sections and called Division 3A and 3B. The first holder of the new trophy was Avon Rovers F C.

The Chairman Mr Horace Webster expressed his delight at the growth of the League and the high esteem it is being held through out the County. Mr Webster eventually left the District and a new Chairman who was elected was Mr George Pankhurst. The League was flourishing and in the 1953 season the League started to have a shortage of referees, complaints were made about referees opting for the allocation system organised by Coventry Referees. This was not true, the allocation system stabilised the movement of referees and it did not affect the League for the standard of football was still maintained.

In the 1953/54 season a new League was formed by George Dutton, who had been approached by clubs from the Division 1(one) to upgrade the standard of football. An approach was made to the Birmingham County FA and permission was given.(more about the League later on)

The Leamington League carried on although it had lost a few of the top Clubs the standard of play was as good as ever, and a gradual increase of referees helped the League. With the allocation system closing down the League more or less set up its own list of referees. It was shortly after, that George Dutton informed the Committee that he would be resigning from the League, to take up the Secretary's duties with the South Birmingham Football League.
The new Secretary of the Leamington Saturday Football League was Mr Frank Bambrook. At the same time George Dutton resigned from being Secretary of the South Warwickshire League he had started. George Pankhurst took over as Secretary and still retained his position as Chairman of the Leamington & District Saturday Football League.

During this period between 1954 and 1959, there was always going to be a change of fortunes, with Clubs folding up due to lack of finances, or players leaving and joining other Clubs in other Leagues. The League gradually suffered through the movement of players, with over fifty clubs in the early 1950s and by the time the 1959 season was approaching the League was down to thirty six clubs.

In 1959 the League were in the process of holding a, 'Golden Jubilee Dinner' which was finally held at the Regent Hotel on the 9th October 1959.
To organise the event a committee was set up to find a suitable Hotel. Also to assess how much money would be needed to entertain certain Dignitaries from the Football Association, the County Association plus representatives from the Professional Clubs. Various ideas were put forward to raise money and events concerning, Six- a- Side football competition with a League match against a top amateur team.

The estimated amount that would cover all the activities would be about £200 (pounds), fund raising was a must, and Clubs in the League were asked to take part.
The Chairman of the Committee was George Pankhurst, with Sid Adams as Secretary, and Harry Owen with Eddie Curtis as Treasurers and fund raisers. The Football Association had confirmed the date selected as clear of the Football Association Cup Fixtures.
The minutes as written suggested it would be a lavish affair with so many notables being invited that tickets for the event would be limited.

Arrangements for the Six-a-Side arranged at Southam and Leamington had been sanctioned by the Birmingham County FA at a special cost of 2/6 (two shillings and sixpence). The match against a selected team possibly Pegasus also received permission and it would be played on Saturday the 10th October 1959 at the Lockheed ground.

Problems had arisen when it was realised that £200 (pounds) would not cover the cost and further funds would be needed. Mr Curtis suggested we look for Sponsors to help produce the menu card and brochure. Harry Owen suggested a Football Match be held on 'Eagle Recreation Ground on Christmas Morning' between players from Leamington versus players from Warwick. The event took place and the committee was disappointed at the returns from the match which was not a financial success with only 16/6 (sixteen shillings and sixpence) taken on the gate.

To increase funds the committee members visited all the Clubs in the League and persuaded them to contribute cash to help the Committee reach the amount they needed. The amount had reached the figure of £130 (one hundred & thirty pounds). Funds were still needed said the Chairman.

Pegasus the Amateur Football Team eventually agreed to play a select team from the League and Dave Montgomery was appointed as Manager. He had already picked a certain number of players and the Match was arranged for October 10th the day after the Jubilee Dinner.

The total number of people attending the Jubilee Dinner which would include the Guests and Management Committee would be about 124.

Before all these events took place, there was an upset in the League Structure; at the Annual General Meeting in May 1959 the new Chairman elected was George Dutton, who defeated George Pankhurst for the position. George Pankhurst was elected Vice-Chairman. This was upsetting to George Pankhurst, who had been Chairman since 1951 and had been Chairman of the Committee to promote the Jubilee Dinner.

Funds were gradually building up towards the total amount the committee would need and all the guests had been invited and accepted. It had been a lot of hard work by the Committee, and the event proved very successful.

In the Football Match, Pegasus versus the Leamington Select, Leamington finally won by (four goals to three).

When the Treasurer presented the accounts to the League at the next meeting it showed a loss of £21(pounds). The total expenses reaching £339 (Three hundred and thirty nine pounds) the League finally settled the account and all the players who were selected received a Blazer Badge.

Finally the committee was wound up on December 9th 1959.

Whilst all the arrangements were being made for the dinner, the Clubs in the League carried on with the league programme and played in various cup and charity competitions.

When George Dutton resigned from being Secretary to the League in 1954, Frank Bambrook who took over as Secretary kept the League going forward although problems with Clubs resigning, it was still a very strong League. This was beneficial to the referees; it gave everyone the experience that was needed.

In the 1964 /65 period Frank Bambrook decided to retire from the League and the new Secretary who was elected was Ron Locke from Nuneaton. He brought a few changes with him and tried very hard to keep the clubs in the league interested. He also started a Youth League to be played on a Sunday Morning with about 9 (nine) teams. It seems that the Football Association and the County Association had agreed to allow Football to be played on a Sunday. The Lords Day Observance Society had finally decided to allow sport and other activities to take place on a Sunday as well.

For some unknown reason Ron Locke decided to resign from the League. He said he was not getting the support from the Management he deserved.

This did not mean the Saturday League would fold up, but there was strong pressure to start a Senior Sunday League.

The next Secretary to be elected was Tracey Thomas and at the Annual General Meeting on the 28th June 1967, the Sunday League was formed. (The Sunday League will be mentioned later on). With the changes and the move to Sunday Football the Saturday League still carried on and the Assistant Secretary of the League Guy Reeves took over and worked with Tracey Thomas. This time the League was involved with the 'Feeder and Contributory system' the Birmingham County Football Association was bringing into the area, it was a move to place referees who were Class I (one) on a pyramid system and to encourage Clubs and Leagues to improve the playing standard.

With certain Leagues made up to a 'Feeder League' and the Clubs who would form the Contributory Leagues would be partially Semi- Professional. This meant that the Feeder League would have to find matches for the referees in a certain age group as long as they were Class 1(one).These referees would have to complete about 20 matches a season so movement to the Contributory League would be the next step.

The Leamington Saturday League continued until it became impossible to fluctuate with the number of clubs left in the League. This was a problem and caused the Saturday section to become dormant in the early 1970s for two years. Every effort was made to persuade Clubs to join and in 1974 the Saturday section reformed with 10(ten) teams forming the League.

The Secretary Guy Reeve had a choice as far as the referee was concerned. He could arrange matches between the League and the Coventry Combination. This would allow the referee to obtain the number of matches he would require to maintain his marks in the Feeder League system. The alternative would be to organise a 'Supplementary Cup Competition'. This was not very successful. The Feeder League status was withdrawn from the League and it left the committee no other choice but to close the League down. All this happened in 1979 it was a sad day for all, after 70 years there would be no Saturday Football or League in Leamington.

With the Saturday League closing down, Clubs had gradually found vacancies in other Leagues or closed down completely and reforming as another team and joined the Sunday Section. When these things happen it is the referee who suffers, there is no system where he can just go and join another League he has to apply to be placed on a 'Feeder League'. Most Leagues will take the referees on board, but they will only choose the most experienced and with good references. It is a difficult time for the referee and some referees lost 12 to 18 months to establish themselves in the system again.
The Information on the Jubilee Dinner was given to me by Ken Eastbury and Tracey Thomas has loaned the actual minute book.

The Leamington & District Sunday Football League

With the Saturday Football League closing down it enabled the Sunday League to take over and provide Football in 'Leamington and the surrounding District.' It also enabled the referees to referee locally and gain experience. Since its formation in 1966/67 the League has gone from strength to strength.
At the beginning 17 (seventeen) teams made the Division 1 (one) with 9 (nine) teams forming the Youth Section.
The first League winners were North Leamington FC. In winning the League it must have been a pleasant feeling for Gerald Bunn the Secretary who was one of the prime movers to Sunday Football.

The standard of Football was considered to be a very high with players playing in senior football on a Saturday afternoon, and then playing for another club on a Sunday morning. Concern was expressed that these players would treat the Sunday game as a gentle workout. This was far from the truth as history showed the majority of games were played with plenty of tight finishes. We did get the occasional 10-I victory but that could have happened at any time. Every referee who was involved with the League often remarked that every club went out to win.

Writing about the League is not going to be easy even though a Brochure covering events since 1966 has been printed, when the committee celebrated the 'SILVER JUBILEE' in 1991.

This booklet gave many details of the League, from the beginning up to the Season 1990/91. The Roll of Honour gave the names of members who have held office from the beginning it also tells you that Tracey Thomas has been Secretary since 1966/67 and as we are now in the year 2005 he is still Secretary. This now covers 38 years service to the League. There are many others who have given over 35 year's service.

Congratulatory comments were written by the local Sports Editors Doug Hughes, Roger Draper and Niall Campbell complementing the League for its success. Success did come Leamington's way over the years, winning the County F.A Harrison Shield three times in four years and runners up once.

The League is still going strong with new Clubs applying to join every season. When a club decides to resign, the reason given by a majority is lack of finances, or players wanting to move on and retire from playing football.

Rule changes are an essential part of the League and the Football Association has implemented a standard code of Rules all Junior Leagues must abide by. This makes the rules a little difficult to apply especially when problems arise with players; the management committee have to have a good knowledge of the rules. They have to make decisions which are binding, subject to Clubs appealing to the County Football Association. They also have to have a sound working knowledge of the League. This is helped by the stability of the officers who have held positions of importance for 30 years or more.

The majority of the clubs who's Headquarters are in the Leamington and Warwick area play their matches on the local parks pitches, either at Warwick St Nicholas, or the Newbold Comyn Leamington and the teams from Kenilworth play at Castle Farm. Teams from the local Villages do have the facilities at hand; they are so good that most of the Finals of the League Cup and Charity Competitions are played on them.

Successful Clubs over the years have been teams like Long Itchington, Stockton, Southam, Westlea Wanderers. As well as continued League success they have been successful in County Competitions. Other clubs have followed suit, such as Hodcarriers and now we have Leamington Hibernian carrying the banner.

The teams from the lower divisions have also been successful in winning Cups and Trophies. The competitive nature of the teams has ensured excellent games have been played and well supported. All the clubs support the Charitable Cup Competitions the League is involved with and over the years thousand of pounds have been raised. No club is forced to enter but majority do and take the games seriously and play in good spirits.

Leamington & District Referees Association have been involved with the Sunday League since its inauguration. It is possible that more that 255 referees over the years have been coached and are still being coached so that they can officiate in the league. A few referees have been on the list since the beginning and quite a number have found refereeing on a Sunday morning different, but continued to support the League.

The League is still going strong and Clubs are always keen to be accepted, if vacancies exist the clubs that apply must meet the criteria set by the League. The Committee who interview them are quite strict. The majority of new clubs do not realise the amount of work that it entails in looking after a club and being successful in the league, unless they have had experience. It does not matter how much you tell them or advise them, they do run into problems. The continued service by the officers is good for the League it shows an enormous amount of confidence placed in them by all the clubs.

Hotel & Caterers Sports Association (Midlands) Football League

This Sports Association Football League was formed in 1971 when a match was played between Benfords and Lockheed Ladies. In 1972 season Patrick Gwynne was elected Secretary and has held that position to the present day which is 33 years. The aim was to provide Football for youngsters who had to work every day in the (Hotel and Catering Trades) and Sundays was the only partially free day they would have. Arrangements were made to play their matches on a Sunday afternoon. Patrick Gwynne has also represented the League as their representative to the Birmingham County Football Association for over 30 years and a few years ago was elected a Life Vice- President by the County FA.

The League is well organised and the referees from Leamington are well looked after.

Warwickshire Combination

The beginning of this League started in 1953, when teams in the Leamington Saturday League were looking for a better standard of Football. There were also teams from outside the district who were also looking for the same opportunities.

A request was made by George Dutton to the Birmingham County Football Association and to the Football Association to form a new League. Sanction was given by the County FA on January 21st 1953 and a meeting was held at the Avenue Hotel, Spencer Street, Leamington Spa.

The following Clubs were represented at the meeting they were :- Badsy Rangers, Banbury Spencer, Bedworth Town, Cheltenham Town, Cubbington Albion, Flavels, Lockheed, Saltisford Rovers and Warwick Town. Other Clubs had been invited and all facilities were being looked into.

The new League was called "The South Warwickshire Football League" the first Secretary elected was George Dutton, with the Acting Chairman George Pankhurst.

Rules and regulations were set out with copies going to the Clubs, they were asked to make recommendations to the League Secretary.

Finally all the Rules were settled with Fines, Entrance Fees, etc. the Executive Committee was elected. The number of members at Council or Executive Committee meetings to form a quorum was compiled, and these were submitted to the County Sanctions Committee for approval.

This meant that if approval is given, a new League has been set up by officers from the Leamington & District Referees Association. It was a wonderful opportunity for the referees in Leamington and for referees from other Associations. At the August Meeting George Dutton came and gave a talk about the new League to the members and suggested that every one apply to be placed on the list whether as linesmen or as referee. This every one did and some of the Senior Class2 (two) had games in the middle.

At the Annual General Meeting of the League the Election of Officers took place. This was to put the League on a firm footing, the Secretary and Chairman had only been in a position as Acting Chair and Secretary until the County Football Association had approved the rules and regulations.

The positions were soon confirmed when George Pankhurst became Chairman, and George Dutton became Secretary with an Executive Committee being elected. Mr Camkin was elected as President.

Mr Cringam. (Banbury Spencer FC) intimated to the Committee that his Managing Director Mr Allen would be pleased to present a Cup to the League. It would be called the 'Champions Cup' and at the next meeting it was presented to the Committee.

The President who was at the second meeting informed the Committee he would be responsible for the Advertising in the League Handbook

A list of referees had been drawn up this included those who had applied to be placed on the list and it would include linesmen as well.

New Clubs were still applying to join the League and were being looked at, the ground facilities of each Club was important. All the Clubs that had been elected did have their own ground and all facilities, they also were financially sound.

Mr Cringam suggested a meeting by the League with the Birmingham Combination. It seemed the Combination were on the point of closing down. It was an opportunity to increase the number of Clubs if they were interested in a merger, although it was said that a majority of clubs from the Combination were looking for Senior Football. (Equivalent to Conference Standard).

A special meeting was arranged on the 15th April 1953 when the Delegate from the South Warwickshire League met the Officers from the Birmingham Combination, with Mr E H Spiers as Chairman at the Meeting. Mr Spiers told meeting that the Combination were considering an amalgamation and asked what the South Warwickshire League could offer. The Delegates suggested a change of Title to suit all concerned, it would be called the "Birmingham and South Warwickshire Combination." The suggested title did not agree with the Birmingham Combination who remarked through their Chairman that the title should remain with the Birmingham Combination.

After various points were put forward concerning Finances, Rules and Cup Competitions when these items had been discussed, a break was taken. Afterwards the South Warwickshire League was told there would be no amalgamation, they had nothing to offer the Birmingham Combination, and the Combination was considering lying dormant for at least two years. The Birmingham Combination then withdrew from the meeting.

Clubs were still applying to the League, and Worcester City FC enquired whether it was the intention to stay as an Amateur or a Semi-Professional League. The President replied that the clubs had decided to make it an all Professional League. At the First Annual General Meeting all the Officers and Committee were re-elected.

When the Annual General Meeting closed the meeting resolved itself into a special meeting to accept the following Clubs into the League bringing the total of clubs up to 17. The teams are as follows:- Ansley Hall, Birch Coppice, Coventry City A, Nuneaton Borough, Rugby Town, Stratford Town, West Bromwich Albion and Worcester City.

Revision of Rules, an application was made to the Birmingham County FA to change the title to the 'Warwickshire Combination.' Clubs in the League were not allowed to enter more than one outside cup competition other than the Football Association or County Football Association Competitions.

Referees who had applied to the League for the 1954/55 Season and were Class1 (one) had to be under 40 years old and only 40 were selected. The League had received over 50 applicants for Linesman and they would be sorted out before they were accepted.

Handbooks were being produced clubs and officials were asked to pay for them. The Secretary explained in detail the entry of Birmingham City and Aston Villa into the League it automatically amended the membership Rule from 18 to 20, this then formed the Constitution of the League.

A change happened in 1954/55 season when the President congratulated George Dutton on his appointment as Secretary to the South Birmingham League. George Dutton informed the Committee that he would have to retire from being Secretary of the Combination. A special meeting was called to appoint a successor.
Three names were read out applying for the position; they were F Bambrook, H Ryder and R Southern. The President then asked if George Pankhurst if he was interested, as he would be a suitable candidate. George Pankhurst accepted the position and then resigned from being Chairman.

Mr Fred Chapman suggested to the President that he would like his name to go forward, he was allowed to do so, and the three people who had applied for the job were discarded. A little discord had arisen over the selection and Mr Chapman was critical at the method used and the way it was done, the two members were asked to leave the room. The President addressed the Executive Committee and assured the members he had been strict in dealing with the issue.
After a careful discussion it was proposed George Pankhurst become Secretary and the Vice-Chairman Mr Morrall become Chairman. This was carried.

A presentation of a wrist watch to George Dutton for his service to the Combination took place in 1955. With a new Secretary and Chairman the Combination gradually increased the number of Clubs to 23. This made the Combination form 2(two) Sections called Western and Eastern. The majority of the Clubs had moved either into the Semi-Professional and Professional standard for the playing staff.
In the Camkin Cup and the Subsidiary Cup the Committee put the teams into three groups of six teams and one group of five. With the top two in each group going through to play for the Camkin Cup while the other teams played for the Subsidiary Cup.
Eventually the Professional Clubs left the League this allowed other clubs to apply and the majority were accepted.

In 1967/68 season a bombshell was dropped on the Combination. This was due to changes in the "Feeder and Contributory" Leagues being changed around. It meant that the Combination would have to close down once the changes were in place. Football Clubs would be seeking Leagues with a higher standard of Football and a higher level of Referees and Linesmen.

The Referees and Linesmen on the League would suffer, and the Secretary George Pankhurst sent a letter to all the officials, informing them of the situation and thanking them for their contribution over the years whether it has been for a short period or one that has been associated with the Combination for a long time.
He also went on to say all officials would be looked after, but if anyone wished to seek a position on another League he would be allowed to do so.

South Birmingham & District Football League

This was the League that George Dutton was elected to as 'Secretary' it was a very big League with Clubs from Birmingham and the surrounding District. The Amalgamation of the District with the Birmingham Combination made it a very strong League. It also was very professional and the name change was obvious, it was changed to the **"West Midland Regional Football League"**.

Over the years the title has changed from the "**Beezer Homes League**" to the present one called the "**Dr Martens Football League.**" The Referees from the Leamington Association applied to the League and they had to be Class 1(one). If they were accepted they were placed on the List as a Referee provided they were experienced, otherwise they would be placed on the list as Linesman.

Another League the Leamington Referees have been involved in is the *"West Midland Alliance."* This again covered teams South of Birmingham and they were purely amateur. The Secretary in the 1965 period was Mr Ray Paul. This was a superb League to learn about refereeing and Mr Paul was a very good Secretary, and helped referees when he could, if you were prepared to travel to areas around Birmingham you would enjoy your refereeing. The League may have closed down now and the Clubs may have amalgamated with either the Combination or the Alliance.

The Leagues in which most of the Referee's Officiate today is the, "**Midland Combination**" they have written their own Book on the History of the Combination. The other League is the "**Midland Alliance.**"

We also have officials on the Senior Leagues up to the **Conference** as Assistant Referees and majority of referees from Leamington have been involved with the **Coventry Alliance & Surburban League.** It used to be called the **Coventry Works League, The Coventry Combination, The Coventry &District League** and the **Coventry &North Warwickshire League** who have now amalgamated and formed one League.

Junior and Boys Football

Leamington & Warwick Old Boys Combination

One small Combination was formed in 1926 and it seems the idea was to get football teams of old boys from the schools so the ages could be from 14 yeas old upwards.

In September 1926—six teams formed the Combination, they were Leamington National, Leamington Central, Kenilworth Central, Kenilworth Council Boys, Weston T School, and Emscote All Saints. This was reported in the Warwick & Warwickshire Advertiser, in October 1926. No other reports or information was found and it was presumed the Combination quietly folded. No mention was recorded in the newspaper, neither was any mention made in the Association minutes of that period.

Souvenir Progress Report of the:-
Leamington Youth Organisation Committees Football League
"Peeps into the Past"

In August 1935 the J.O.C League was revived after a period of about three years the prime mover was (Mr W Harland M.A). Director of Education with George Dutton and Mr Fox invited to form the Committee. In 1935 /36 there were 10 Teams entered in the Leagues, and they were Althorpe St., Clapham Terrace B C., Central School., Lillington Central., Milverton and Shrubland St., Radford., Trades Hall., Westgate (Warwick).and the 10th Scouts.

We had a mixture of boys and Junior (under 16 years old) since 1935 when the J O C was formed. The name eventually was changed to the Youth Organisation Committee Football League. The Secretary in those early days could have been the Rev D G Marshall who left the district in 1946.The next Secretary was Geoff Perks who in 1950 produced a Souvenir Book highlighting the progress of the Y O C. he remained as Secretary until the Y O C eventually closed down

The reports have suggested that it was a very strong League, producing a stream of excellent players who were nominated for honours. The Division for the under 16 players was larger then the Senior Division.

One person who gave a lot of support to the League and served as the Fixture Secretary was Mr J. B. Drinkwater. The Secretary in his report gave great credit to Mr Drinkwater for the time and service he gave to the League.

Referees were involved with the Y, O, C. and they were Mr Tom Caswell, Mr W (Bill) Crew, Mr John Curtis, Mr Albert J Gwynne, and Peter Watson. Other referees mentioned were Mr Tom Williams, Mr Jim Lloyd, Mr George Dutton, Mr William Digger and Mr Eddy Malin. There were probably more whose names have not been mentioned the photographs of the teams in the report show a few member referees when they were 15 or 16 years old.

The "Courier Cup" (Senior Division)

South Leamington gave one of their best displays to gain a convincing win of four goals to nil over Lockheed Juniors and thus prevented 'the juniors' from recording a 'hat-trick' of Cup and League doubles. The Mayor, W H Walls grove, presented the Cup to the winners.

Quite a few of the players received honours, players like George Burrows who played for England Youth against Scotland at (Cowdenbeath Dec 3rd 1949) and Germany at Villa Park, 23rd March 1950. He also played for the Warwickshire ABC XI against Birmingham Boys' Clubs, also Worcester and Shropshire and Lancashire and Cheshire.

Others, who were honoured and played against the Federation of Boys' Clubs, were John Cookes, John Knight, Malcolm Sedgeley, Cliff Austin and John Morgan.

When the Y, O, C. eventually closed down two new Boys Leagues were formed, one became the (Leamington Boys League the Secretary was Brian Knibb). The other became the (Kenilworth Boys League and the Secretary was David Pickering.)

The amalgamation between the two Leagues happened when both were struggling for Teams and a shortage of referees. They eventually joined forces and with a new title. The League was called. **"The Mid-Warwickshire Boys League"** and David Pickering was the Secretary.

The League is still going strong although the title has changed to the (**Mid Warwickshire Boys/Junior League**)

As well as the **"Mid Warwickshire"** we had the **"Central Warwickshire League"** and the **"Coventry Minor League"** where referees from Leamington gave good service.

Women's Football

Pat Gwynne was a founder member of the **"Warwickshire Ladies Football League"** and was elected Chairman. The following season it became the **"Midland Ladies Football League"**
In 1970 he became a founder member of the **"Women's Football Association"** and was elected Vice- Chairman. After one meeting when the Chairman resigned he became Acting Chairman for the remainder of the season. In 1971 he was elected Chairman and in 1972 returned as Vice-Chairman before resigning.
Pat Gwynne was invited back in later seasons to become the Disciplinary Chairman. This was for his knowledge on discipline which he had gained as a member of the Birmingham County FA.

The Ladies eventually made Pat the President of the Midland Region of the Women's Football Association in 1984.

The Ladies Football is getting quite strong in the area and we are always reading reports of local teams playing and winning when their opponents come from other parts of the County.
It is unfortunate that whilst the Football is getting stronger, we do not seem to be coaching any Females to become Referees.

Chapter 13

Delegation and Service

In the Service records every Referee who has held office or been a delegate to the Birmingham & Warwickshire Joint Referees County Committee are mentioned. We also have had members on the Birmingham County Football Association.

George Dutton, represented the Warwick & District League, the Leamington & District League, and finally the South Birmingham League.

George Pankhurst, representing the Warwickshire Combination and the Mid-Warwickshire Boys League.

Patrick Gwynne, represents the Hotel & Caterers Football Association.

The West Midland Regional League was represented by George Dutton whilst he was the Secretary of the League. He retired in 1961 from the League but continued his service to the County Football Association and eventually became a Councillor to the Football Association.

From the delegates to the County F A we move to the delegates who have represented the Association at all the Leagues in the area. The first mention of delegates was in 1921 when the referees of that period were involved with Football Leagues in a management capacity, as well as refereeing. If we start at 1921 and try to mention all the referees that have beeen nominated to the Leagues over the years, we should have a good selection of members who have served the Association well.

In 1921 to 1926 we had Pepper Talbot as Chairman of the Referees, he was invloved with the Warwick & District Football League.

We then had George Dutton in 1933 who was a Delegate to the Warwick League and the Stratford League at the same time.

In 1936 quite a few changes were made and the referees delegate was more or less refused attendance to the Leagues. The Secretary had to write to the League concerned for permission so the delegate could attend even then he would only be able to state his case. This caused a rumpus in the Association and it wasn't until the Association was reformed that delegates were invited to the meeting. Even then permission to speak on anything to do with the League was only allowed, or if you were asked a question by the Chairman.

The first delegate to the Leamington & District Saturday League in 1950 was George Pankhurst until he was made Chairman of the League, and Harry Owen took over.

Leamington & District Saturday League

At the Annual General Meetings the Association had a number of delegates nominated to represent the Association. We had Harry Owen, Alex Walters then Henry Hall as delegates, later on Jack Wright was elected. Peter Watson took over from Jack Wright when he became Treasurer and Arnold Rouse became involved until 1961.

Herewith a list of Delegates from 1962 for the Leamington &District Satruday League to 1974.
1962/63 Ted Warwick & Jack Joyner.
1963/64 David Clarke & Sidney Sharp.
1965/66 Sidney Sharp & John Heywood
1966/67 Sidney Sharp & Clive Darkes.

1968/70 Sidney Sharp & Dennis Reynolds.
1970/71 Pat Gwynne & Tony Engel
1972/74 Pat Gwynne & Victor Shepherd

The following delegates were elected to represent the Association on the Leamington Saturday & Sunday Leagues to 1978 when the Saturday League finally closed down.
1974/76 Pat Gwynne & Derek Evans
1976/78 Duncan Macaulay & Bob Colley

Leamington & District Sunday League

The members mentioned below were delegates to the Leamington Sunday League from 1979 to the present 2005.
1979/84 Duncan Macaulay,
1980/81 Bob Colley,
1985/86 Phil Robbins,
1989/90 Roger Palmer, & Paul Anderson-Kirby.
1983/90 Pat Gwynne,

Since the 1990 period Pat Gwynne has been the regular delegate to the Sunday League up to the present 2005. To assist him in reporting the activities of the League he has had members such as Paul Anderson –Kirby, Peter Boyle and Ray Morgan.

Stratford –upon-Avon Alliance

A number of members have been delegates to the Straford League which is now called the Sratford Alliance and they are Derek Lock, John Mander, Duncan Macaulay, Dave Pratley, Denis Reynolds and WilliamTimson. They all served from 1970 to 1981. No delegates are mentioned on the A G M minutes up to 1990.

Mid-Warwickshire Boys Football League

(This is now known as the:-)

Mid Warwickshire Boys/Junior Leagues

Delegates have been representing the Association on the Boys League since 1974 and they are as follows:- Mrs Cairns, John Cotton, Derek Evans, John Fell, Duncan Macaulay and Dave Pratley. There may have been other delegates, no names have been recorded.

Coventry & North Warwickshire League

This was a very strong League in the 1950 and when they set up their own list of Referees they overshadowed the other Leagues in the area. One League improved the League status by inviting other Clubs to join. With Clubs moving from one League to another the standard gradually went down. The League still had delegates from Leamington Referees Association appointed to the C & NW and they were:- Berkley Bugg, David Clarke, Paul Cox, Arnold Rouse, Andy Semple, Victor Shepherd and Alan Windsor. They served the League from 1967 through to 1990, with Berkley Bugg giving 10 years representing the referees.

In the 1990 the Coventry & North Warwickshire amalgamated with the Coventry & District League and they are now called the **"Coventry District & Warwickshire League."** The delegates in this section would be from the 1990 to 2005 period. Arnold Rouse became the Associations delegate from 1990 to 1998 when Dave Aston took over until he moved away from Leamington. Since then no one from the Association referees on the League so no delegate has been elected.

Coventry Works League

This League represented majority of the Factories and small Businesses who had football teams in the League. The competition was wery strong and good football was played. The referees who were refereeing in the League became delegates representing the Association.
The first mentioned was Victor Shepherd who did 4 years from 1967 to 1970, John Sharp who was a delegate from 1970/71.
The Works League eventually changed its title and included more teams from other Leagues.
The new title of the League is:

The Coventry Alliance Football League

The delegates from the Association on the Alliance since 1971 were as follows:-
Sidney Sharp 1971/72, Victor Shepherd 1972, John Mander and Andy Semple 1973/74.
Derek Evans 1974/76, Brian Hackleton 1976/77, Bill Burnell 1977 through to 1986.
Pat Wright 1978/79, John Austin 1979/80, Fred Tebbs 1980/81
Bill Burnell has been the longest serving delegate to the Alliance he now is a member of the Leagues Management Committee.

The Coventry & District Sunday League

Delegate have represented Leamington since the League was formed in 1967 and the first member was Dennis Reynolds 1967/68, we had delegated representing the Association right through to the mid eighties. The following were delegates up to 1978, David Palacio 1968/69, Mick Warner 1969/70, Bernard Cullen 1970/71, Mick Mullis 1971/72, Roger Palmer 1972/73 and Tom Story 1973 to 1978. No records could be found from 1978. It would mean that there were no Referees from Leamington refereeing on the League, mainly due to the acute shortage of referees in the area, although Tom Story went to the meetings serving the Committee when he was able to travel.

Association Services

ASSOCIATION SERVICE RECORDS

Pre-War Service

YEAR	CHAIRMAN	SECRETARY	TREASURER
1921-1926	H.P.Talbot	H.Elkington	H.Elkington.
1926-1927	G Dutton	J.Wildsmith	J Wi;dsmith
1927-1928	G Dutton	J Wildsmith	A Montgomery
1928-1931	G Dutton	J Wildsmith	A Montgomery
1931-1932	G Dutton	J Wildsmith	A Montgomery
1932-1933	W Enstone	J Wildsmith	A Montgomery
1933-1934	W Enstonc	R West	T Hawtin
1934-1935	J Wildsmith	R West	T Hawtin
1935-1936	J Wildsmith	R West	G Lewis
1936-1939	J Wildsmith	R Rowson	G Lewis

YEAR	V-CHAIRMAN	AUDITORS	MANAGEMENT
1931-1932	W Enstone	A Bagulay & R Frost	S Soden
1932-1933	R West	A Bagulay & R Frost	S Soden
1933-1934	W Goodyear	G Smith & J Lakin	G Dutton
1934-1935	S Soden	W Enifer & J Wildsmith	G Dutton
1935-1936	S Soden	W Enifer & J Wildsmith	G Dutton
1936-1937	S Soden	S Castle & F Poole	W Enstone
1937-1938	S Soden	S Castle & F Poole	C Jackson
1938-1939	S Soden	M Horley & J Bragg	C Jackson.

1937 BIRMINGHAM COUNTY REFEREES COMMITTEE

The First Chairman in 1937----- J WILDSMITH
Committee Members-----R WEST & R ROWSON.

SOCIAL& MANAGEMENT COMMITTEE

From 1948 to 1980

1948-1952	THE OFFICERS WERE THE ONLY COMMITTEE until the SOCIAL COMMITTEE was added iin 1951.
1952-1956	R Pemberton , A Rouse, A Walters, P Watson.
1956-1960	K Eaestbury, R Pemberton, A Rouse, A Walters, P Watson., J Wright, & F Wall (co-opted)
1960-1961	R Pemberton.. J Sollis, F Wall, W Wall.
1961-1962	E Durant, R Pemberton, J Sollis, F Wall, W Wall..
1962-1963	A D Clarke, E Durant, J Sollis, B Talbot, W Wall.
1963-1964	E Davies D Hodson, J Sollis, F Wall.
1964-1965	E Davies D Hodson, S Sharp, J Sollis, F Wall..
1965-1966	J Heywood, A Semple, J Sollis, A Windsor.
1966-1967	A D Clarke, A Semple, J Sollis, A Windser..
1967-1968	A D Clarke, A Semple, J Sollis, T Story..
1968-1969	A D Clarke, A Semple, J Sollis, F Tebbs..
1969-1970	A J Engel, J Sollis, F Tebbs, A Windsor..
1970-1971	A J Engel, G Pankhurst, J Sollis, F Tebbs.
1971-1972`	V Shepherd, J Sollis, T Story, F Tebbs, F Wall..
1972-1973	V Shepherd, V Slark, T Story, F Tebbs..
1973-1974	B Field, G Pankhurst, A Semple, V Slark..
1974-1975	B Bugg, B Hackleton, G Pankhurst, A Semple..
1975-1976	B Bugg, A D Clarke, B Hackleton, T Machin.
1976-1977	B Bugg, B Hackleton, G Hyam, D Macaulay..
1977-1978	J Austin, G Hyam, R Marshall, F Wall..
1978-1979	G Hyam,, T Machin, L Staite, D Tayler, W Timson, F Wall.
1979-1980	I Birch,G W Burnell, G Hyam, T Machin, D Tayler, W Timson.

SOCIAL & MANAGEMENT COMMITTEE

From 1980 to 2006

1980-1981	J Brockwell, G Hyam,, J Mander, D Packer, Dtayler W Timson.
1981-1982	J Brockwell, G Hyam, J Mander, D Macaulay, D Packer..
1982-1983	J Brockwell, D Macaulay, D Packer, D Pratley, D Reynolds
1983-1984	J Brockwell, D Macaulay, J Mander, D Pratley, D Reynolds.
1984-1985	A Dalziel, D Macaulay, D Packer, D Reynolds.
1985-1986	D Packer A Peachey, T Prendergast, D Reynolds, D Silk..
1986-1987	D Packer, A Peachey, T Prendergast, D Reynolds, D Silk.
1987-1988	B Hackleton, D Packer, R Palmer, T Prendergast S Rogers
1988-1989	B Hackleton, R Morgan, D Packer, R Palmer, T Prendergast
1989-1990	J Austin, P Cox, R Morgan, R Palmer, T Prendergast.
1990-1991	J Austin, P Cox, R Palmer, T Prendergast.
1991-1992	P Anderson- Kirby, J Austin, D Packer, R Palmer.
1992-1993	P Anderson- Kirby, J Austin,, D Packer, R Palmer.
1993-1994	P Anderson- Kirby, J Austin, S McCarthy,D Packer, R Palmer.
1994-1995	P Anderson- Kirby, J Austin, S McCarthy, R Morgan, R Palmer.
1995-1996	D Aston, J Austin, P Bahi, R Brown, P Kirkhope.
1996-1997	D Aston, J Austin, P Bahi, , B Hackleton, P Kirkhope
1997-1998	D Aston, P Bahi, P Boyle, PKirkhope, M Robbins.
1998-1999	P Boyle, A Khan, P Kirkhope, M Robbins, D Swithin.
1999-2000	P Boyle, P Kirkhpoe, M Robbins, D Swithin, R Morgan
2000-2001	P Boyle, K Hancocks, T Hood, S McCarthy, I Murphy.
2001-2002	P Boyle, I Murphy, G Shanley.
2002-2003	J Archbold, P Boucher, S McCarthy, G Shanley.
2003-2004	J Archbold, P Boucher, M Gittins, G Shanley.
2004-2005	J Archbold, P Boucher, M Gittins, G Shanley.
2005-2006	M Gittins, T Jamie, J Poulson, R Poulson, L Taylor..

CONFERENCE COMMITTEE 1976 (SOLIHULL)

From 1972 to 1976

Chairman	**Frank Wall**
Secretary	**David Clarke**
Treasurer	**Derek Silk**
Acommodation Secretary	**Arnold Rouse**
Assistant Treasurer	**Fred Tebbs.**
Committee	**W(Bill) Alderson**

**Brian (Bob) Field, Andy Semple, Brian Hackleton
Pat Wright.**

LADIES COMMITTEE   1976 Conference .

Chairperson	**Pam Clarke**
Secretary	**Moira Slark**
Committee:	**Christine Clarke, May Field, Pat Semple**
	Jennie Silk Andrea Slark and Helen Wright

,

ASSOCIATION REFEREES ASSESSORS

1969-1975	JACK JOYNER, RON PEMBERTON, ALAN WINDSOR.
1969-1989	SIDNEY SHARP.
1969-2004	ARNOLD ROUSE.
SINCE 1980	JOHN AUSTIN, HARRY BOARDMAN, BRIAN(BOB) FIELD,, PATRICK WRIGHT, JOHN MANDER, JOHN SHARP.

ASSOCIATION FOOTBALL LICENCED INSTRUCTORS

Since 1990   JOHN MANDER, JOHN SHARP and JOHN AUSTIN.

LEAMNGTON ASSOCIATIONS NEWSLETTER

EDITOR

1987-1995	RAY MORGAN, JOHN MANDER, BRIAN HACKLETON,
1987-1995	TOM PRENDERGAST,
1995-2004	ARNOLD ROUSE.

YEAR	BIRMINGHAM&WARWICKS JOINT COUNTY COMMITTEE	AUDITORS
1948-1952	G Pankhurst	A Walters & H Owen.
1852-1957	G Pankhurst & T Story	A Walters & H Owen
1957-1960	G Pankhurst & T Story	A W Rouse & E Warwick
1960-1961	G Pankhurst & T Story	D Hodson & E Warwick
1961-1963	D Hodson & T Story	D Hodson & E Warwick
1963-1964	D Hodson & T Story	D Hodson & S Sharp
1964-1965	D Hodson & T Story	D Hodson & E Warwick
1965-1966	A D Clarke & T Story	D Reynolds & E Warwick
1966-1967	A D Clarke & V Sheperd	P Murphy & D Reynolds
1967-1968	A D Clarke & A W Rouse	P Murphy & D Reynolds
1968-1969	A D Clarke & A W Rouse	P Murphy & D Reynolds
1969-1970	A D Clarke & T Story	A J Engel & P Murphy
1970-1976	A D Clarke & T Story	A J Engel & P Murphy
1976-1978	G Pankhurst& T Story	A J Engel & P Murphy
1978-1979	A D Clarke & T Machin	R Jones & D Reynolds
1979-1980	I Birch & T Machin	A D Clarke & A W Rouse
1980-1981	J Austin & T Machin	A D Clarke & A W Rouse
1981-1984	J Austin & D Packer	A D Clarke & A W Rouse
1984-1985	J Austin & D Packer	S Rogers & P Wright
1985-1988	J Austin & D Packer	S Rogers & P Wright
1988-1989	J Austin & D Packer	A Dalziel & P Wright
1989-1994	J Austin & B Hackleton	A Dalziel & P Wright
1994-1997	B Hackleton & R Morgan	A Dalziel & P Wright
1997-2002	D Aston & R Morgan	A Dalziel & P Wright
2002-2003	J Sharp & P Wright	A Dalziel & P Wright
2003-2004	J Sharp & P Wright	A Semple & P Wright
2004-2005	J Sharp & A N Other	A Semple & P Wright
2005-2006		

ASSOCIATION OFFICERS from 1939 to 1978

YEAR	CHAIRMAN	SECRETARY	TREASURER
1939-1948	J Wildsmith	G Lewis	G L ewis
1948-1950	G Dutton	G Pankhurst	G Pankhurst
1950-1952	T Story	G Pankhurst	G Pankhurst
1952-1954	T Story	G Pankhurst	G Pankhurst
1954-1955	G Pankhurst	K Cox	K C ox
1955-1956	G Pankhurst	W Blount	WBlount
1956-1957	G Pankhurst	W Blount	WBlount
1957-1958	G Pankhurst	P Watson	J Wright
1958-1959	G Pankhurst	P Watson	J Wright
1959-1960	G Pankhurst	P Watson	J Wright
1960-1961	T Story	J Jays	AWRouse
1061-1962	T Story	J Jays	AWRouse
1962-1963	T Story	J Jays	AWRouse
1963-1964	T Story	J Jays	AWRouse
1964-1965	T Story	ADClarke	AWRouse
1965-1966	T Story	ADClarke	AWRouse
1966-1967	T Story	AWRouse	AWRouse
1967-1968	F Wall	AWRouse	AWRouse
1968-1969	F Wall	AWRouse	D Lock
1969-1970	F Wall	AWRouse	D Lock
1970-1971	A Semple	AWRouse	D Silk
1971-1972	A Semple	AWRouse	D Silk
1972-1973	A Semple	A Semple (prov)	D Silk
1973-1974	A Semple	D Reynolds	D Silk
1974-1975	AWRouse	D Reynolds	D Silk
1975-1976	AWRouse	D Reynolds	D Silk
1976-1977	A Semple	D Reynolds	D Silk
1977-1978	A Semple	D Reynolds	D Silk
1978-1979	D Macaulay	J Austin	D Silk

COACHING & LICENSED INSTRUCTORS from 1948 to 2006

1948-1952 H OWEN & J JOYNER
1952 1959 H HALL & A WALTERS
1959-1961 J JAYS & E DURANT
1961-1967 F WALL
1967-1969 A SEMPLE & A WROUSE
1969-1975 A SEMPLE
1975-1977 A SEMPLE & A WROUSE
1977-1980 A WROUSE
1980-1994 J MANDER
1994-1997 J MANDER & J SHARP
1997-2006 J SHARP

ASSOCIATION OFFICERS from 1978 to 2006

YEAR	CHAIRMAN	SECRETARY	TREASURER
1979-1980	D Macaulay	J Austin	D Silk
1980-1981	D Macaulay	J Austin	D Silk
1981-1982	T Machin	J Austin	C Ackroyde
1982-1983	D Silk	J Austin	C Ackroyde
1983-1984	D Silk	J Austin	C Ackroyde
1984-1985	D Silk	J Austin	C Ackroyde
1095-1986	D Macaulay	J Austin	A Dalziel
1986-1987	D Macaulay	J Austin	A Dalziel
1987-1988	D Macaulay	J Austin	S Rogers
1988-1989	D Macaulay	J Austin	S Rogers
1989-1990	J Mander	B Hackleton	S Rogers
1990-1991	J Mander	B Hackleton	S Rogers
1991-1992	J Mander	B Hackleton	S Rogers
1992-1993	D Macaulay	B Hackleton	S Rogers
1993-1994	J Mander	B Hackleton	S Rogers
1994-1995	J Mander	B Hackleton	S Portch
1995-1996	J Mander	R Morgan	S Portch
1996-1997	J Mander	R Morgan	S Portch
1997-1998	D Aston	J Sharp	S Portch
1998-1999	D Aston	J Sharp	S Portch
1999-2000	D Aston	J Sharp	R Morgan
2000-2001	D Aston	J Sharp	R Morgan
2001-2002	J Sharp	D Macaulay	R Morgan
2003-2003	J Sharp	D Macaulay	R Morgan
2003-2004	J Sharp	D Macaulay	R Morgan
2004-2005	J Sharp	D Macaulay	R Morgan
2005-2006	J Sharp	D Macaulay	G Shanley

ASSISTANT SECRETARIES FROM 1982 to 200

P ROBBINS from 1982 to 1987
J SHARP from 1987 to 1989 and 1992 to 1995
D PACKER from 1989 to 1991
T PRENDERGAST from 1991 to 1992
D MACAULAY from 1995 to 2001
G SHANLEY from 2001 to 2003

VICE-CHAIRMAN from 1939 to 2006

P BOYLE	from 2001 to
W ALDERSON	from 1973 to 1976 2006
A D CLARKE.	from 1970 to1972
J GREEN	from 1977 to 1981
J JAYS	from 1964 to1965
N JONES	from 1982 to1985
J JOYNER	from 1950 to1952 and1961 to 1964
T MACHIN	from 1976 to1977
J MANDER	from 1981 to1982 ,1985 to 1989 and 1992 to 1993
D MACAULAY	from 1989 to 1992 and 1993 to 2001
A SEMPLE	from 1969 to 1970
S SHARP	from 1965 to 1969
S SODEN	from 1939 to1948
T STORY	from 1948 to 1950 and 1954 to 1960
F TEBBS	from1972 to 1973
A WALTERS	from 1960 to1961
J WRIGHT	from 1952 to 1954

ASSOCIATION MEETING ORGANISERS   from 1960 to1980

DAVID CLARKE, LIONEL FLEET, ARNOLD ROUSE
JOHN SOLLIS, FRED TEBBS and FRANK WALL.
The position was taken back into Management in 1979

Chapter 14

1981 To 1999
The Last Two Decades

This period of the 20th Century is more or less the last two decades before a move into the 21st Century takes place, when everything concerning Referees will be changed. Although at the time the officers did not realise the impact it would have on the members when it eventually happened. In fact quite a number of issues would affect everyone before the end of the Century came into force.

When the 1970 to 1980 decade was drawing to a close, the Association at that time was beginning to settle down. The Conference had been a success and the members who had been involved with the organising of it, had decided to retire and leave the Association. We were very fortunate that the younger members who had recently joined were willing to take on the job of organising the members and taking office.

We had members like John Austin who became Secretary in 1978 and continued doing a terrific job until 1989 when Brian Hackleton became Secretary until 1995. We also had John Mander who became the referee coaching Instructor in 1980, and completed 17 years as the coaching and instructing the members until 1997. There were a few changes mainly concerning the Chairmanship. Tom Machin who was elected in 1981 had to retire through a change of employment, this allowed Derek Silk who was the previous Treasurer to be elected as Chairman at the Annual General Meeting in 1982, and he served for three years (as per rule). The new Treasurer elected at the same time was Chris Ackroyde who held the office until 1985 when Andy Dalziel was Treasurer for two years until 1987

The officers concerned began to move the Association in a forward direction and the Secretary suggested what changes he would like. Introduction of an Assistant Secretary was one item, the other was an increase in the number of management members and eventually the meeting organisers position would be transferred back into the management committee.

At the Annual General Meeting in May 1981. The President Arnold Rouse was made a 'Life Member of the Leamington & District Referees Association' for the service he has given to the Association since 1952. The President in reply, thanked the members for the honour they have bestowed upon him.

Referees Assaults and Membership.

In 1979 concern was expressed about the number of assaults that was creeping into the game. As we move into the 1981 to the 1999 period we find that the Referee is being subjected to a barrage of abusive language, as well as verbal and physical assaults, from the spectators and players. The following reports and meetings tell you the serious problems that were facing the Referees. It continued until the end of the century.

The Secretary John Austin told the members at a meeting that serious action was being considered by other Associations. There was talk of withdrawing referees from the Leagues where the Clubs have players and spectators causing the problems by abusing the Referee and Club Linesmen. This had previously been discussed at a monthly meeting when the Chairman of another Association came and talked to the members about the problems and what they are recommending referees do

The general opinion from the Secretary of one of the Leagues was that referees would be breaking a code of contract with the League they officiate on, this was a debatable point The members were also informed by the Secretary that the Birmingham &Warwickshire Joint Referees County Committee have been asked to keep a close watch on the situation, and record any assaults of referees in the Birmingham area.

The Birmingham County Football Associations position was outlined and referees could be penalised by taking action. At the Management meeting it was moved that we accept the policy of the National Referees Association as dated 1982, this supersedes all other proposals and we look into our own local case further.

The Secretary is to distribute a copy of the Referees Association circular as soon as possible.

Herewith the Management discussion on the issue of Assaults

March 1982

Assaults

A further and involved discussion took place regarding this issue with every Management member putting forward an opinion. Jeff Brockwell told the members that the B C F A was informing referees, that if they did not accept fixtures because a team had been involved in an assault on a referee, they will then have their registration suspended. It was decided all the facts should be taken by our representatives to the next Birmingham &Warwickshire Joint Referees County Committee meeting and the point should be made that we were being "blackmailed" by both the local League and the County Football Association. While we are waiting for help and advice from that meeting in Birmingham the members should be informed of the National Referees Association policy. This would be discussed at the next Monthly meeting with a prompt start at 7.30 pm.

The Secretary was asked to write to the Secretary of the B &W J R C C asking for the issue of assaults to be included in their agenda.

The assaults saga is still continuing. It is a serious situation, nearly every week we hear of a referee being assaulted. The following item will help to clear the matter up:

The Chairman brought members up to date with the present situation, and then gave a report on the meeting with the "Birmingham and Warwickshire Joint Referees County Committee." This took place earlier in the week. It was understood that if the B C F A. suspended any referee, the National RA if asked, would take up the case of individual members. It was stated the County Football Association do not comply entirely with the National Referees Association's Policy. The 7(seven year) ban on players Assaulting Referees is not enforced. Again much discussion took place with League representatives, with the Chairman and Secretary making valid points in trying to clarify the situation. The Chairman concluded by asking members if they understood the overall position and it was generally agreed that individuals knew exactly where they stood.

Players Assaulting each other

We have a problem of another kind all relative to players and spectators causing assaults to happen and excessive use of abusive language. This was brought to the notice of the meeting by a member, who asked for the correct way to deal with players from the same team fighting each other. This was explained to the member as follows:

This issue was discussed at the Monthly meeting, when the members were talking about assaults. One member asked the following question. "What is the correct procedure when two players from the same team start Fighting?"

The advice given was as follows: if the two players are sent from the 'Field of Play' a report should be sent into the County Football Association or the Football Association depending which League the Club is affiliated to.

If one of the players decides to take action against the player who assaulted him, the police will want to interview the referee. If you were the Referee make sure you send your report into the County or the Football Association, within the required date and time. You should also take extra copies for yourself and to be polite inform the Secretary of the League about the incident in brief and concise terms.

If the police request your Misconduct Form, inform the County Disciplinary Secretary. If still in doubt have a word with your Association Chairman or a senior member who may have dealt with a similar situation.

Referees have been asked by the Leagues Secretaries to crackdown on players and supporters who are creating the problems, they are adamant it should be stamped out.

This is a problem for the Referee and it not a very easy proposition to face a drunken crowd of youths and tell them to stop drinking or even to ask them to behave.

An item from the Referees Magazine stating that the Liverpool Referees Association is refusing appointments until the matter of assaults on referees are discussed. In 1982 there were 119 assaults on Referees, with 34 in the Midland Division.

It was also noted in the area that Clubs who allow their players and spectators to use Abusive Language, should be very careful. It transpires that some Parish Councils and District Councils have already been informed of the abuse being used. It could mean to quite a few Clubs, that all the facilities including the football grounds would be taken from them.

Referee Shortage

It was stated that there was a serious shortage of referees in the area and most Leagues were looking towards the Referees Association to produce more referee for their Leagues. The Leagues were told that until they support the move to ban Clubs who are causing quite a few of the problems at the week-end with abusive language and assaulting referees, the shortage of referees will continue. The Secretary of the Association said we are short of referees in Leamington and we have had a few problems, but nothing like other areas and the local League is making every effort to keep it under control. Concern was being expressed from the Stratford Alliance over the same issue and a meeting is to be called with representatives from the various Leagues and Referees' Associations in the area to try and obtain uniformity. Referees have been criticised for not turning up to matches, the problem evidently is caused by Clubs not notifying the Referee of the change of ground, or even the kick-off time.

Shortage of referees, strong words by the Secretary and Chairman of the Sunday League concerning the shortage both said if it does not improve, the League would be reduced in size with a reduced number of Clubs in the League It was considered it was an issue that could be sorted out at the League management, the committee did meet and various ideas were suggested. Clubs were to ask the members of their playing staff if anyone would be interesting in taking up refereeing and to let the Secretary know so that a coaching course could be arranged. Other ideas were talked about and the Leamington & District Referees Association was to be asked to help in the refereeing issue.

The issue with abusive language and assaults was causing problems in the various Leagues as well as the Referees Association. It meant that although the problems at Leamington are not as serious as other Leagues the problem is causing a number of Referees to think about carrying on refereeing or not. The management committee decided to discuss the whole issue before any of the Leagues called a meeting.

Herewith extracts of one of the items discussed in Management

The abuse situation continued right up to 1986 when a Leamington Referee was assaulted, the player was found guilty of Assault and banned sine-die (for a minimum period of two years) and fined £50(fifty pounds) Another player who had assaulted a referee asked for a personal hearing. The referee failed to attend, so the hearing went ahead and the player was found to have no case to answer.

The Secretary was instructed to write to the B&W J R CC to request details concerning the case from the County Disciplinary Secretary.

Assaults & Referees

The issue of Assaults and Referees attending a personal hearing, this is to be taken up by the Delegate of the Midland Division after complaints about the way referees have been left in the same room as players who have been called before the County Disciplinary Committee for violent conduct. Where this occurs, a representative was supposed to be present in the assembly room prior to the meeting. It is however recommended that a fellow referee is asked to attend to support the Referee, to prevent problems.

National Referees Association minutes for November reported a statement from the Football Association Referees Committee concerning 'CAUTIONS'. They may only be administered for offences covered by LAW 12. It is not permissible to caution persons for 'bringing the game in disrepute.'

Another report on Assaults from the Conference, with the FA stating over 300 assaults covering a few months was a worrying trend. The Referees Association issued a category for assaults

As follows: - Category Assaults
A --- 112 days and £100 pounds fine
B--- SINE-DIE £200 POUNDS FINE no REVIEW for 5 years.
C -- SINE-DIE no REVIEW

Please note the fines and length of suspension was issued in 1987. They have probably been altered since that date.

Referees are reminded to send all reports to the County FA concerned and they must be 'Correct, Brief, and Concise'. Personal hearings are lost due to poor reports and referees changing their report. There were 339 assaults on referees in the County. 35 were Class C also there were 35 assaults on linesmen. The cause of assaults was to be investigated by the F A and the R A

It seems referees are stepping in between players and being assaulted, wagging fingers at players, standing too close to players when cautioning them. Going into the dressing rooms all these lead to assaults on referees.

Another referee assaulted in a local Sunday match needed hospital treatment. The assault is being dealt with by the County FA.

In another instance two players were sent from the field of play by the Referee. No report has been sent to the County FA neither to the League Secretary. The referee had retired from refereeing and turned out to Referee the match because they had no one to do it.

Concern is being expressed by the County Referees Committee and the issue is being taken up by the Sports Argus on assaults and misconduct by the Teams.

If we move to the 1990s we find out that the assaults are getting nastier and players are getting assaulted as well. In fact in one case the injured player decided to sue the other player for the injuries he caused and is asking for the referees report on the incident. So that he could send it to his solicitor. The referee in this case was told to contact the County Football Association and inform them of the player's request

A local referee had been assaulted and a full report was sent to the County Football Association. The County Officials request that in all cases of assaults the form must be marked 'ASSAULTS' on the top of the form, so that the County can deal with it quickly.

Assaults on referees were becoming a regular issue with members. Casting our minds back to the 1980s and before that date when a 'Referees Association' were so incensed with the weekly assaults on referees they were prepared to withdraw all Referees from the League concerned. It seems that as well as assaults we had to deal with abusive language. The majority of the players were copying the professionals. This created all sorts of problems especially for the junior referee.

Special Meeting

In November 1995 a special meeting was held by the Association. The Chairman was John Mander. The Chairman and Secretary of the following Leagues were in attendance. They were: - The Leamington & District Sunday League, Mid-Warwickshire Boys League, and the Hotel & Caterers Association League. Also present from the Leamington Referees Association was the 'Management Committee'.

The discussion was mainly about the Assaults on referees and the Chairman explained why he was concerned. We have had four referees assaulted; two of them seriously and there have been others. The Chairman said this meeting was the third one we have had to discuss assaults on referees and concern was expressed on the amount of abusive language used by spectators and players. In September we had a very good discussion with the Sunday League on abusive language discussing all the problems with the managers, players and club secretary's

The meeting took place on Monday 6th November 1995. The Chairman outlined the reason for the meeting and explained that his members were very concerned over the recent assaults. He reminded every one that we have a large number of young referees and their safety must be considered.

Each representative had their say. The Chairman of the Leamington Sunday League said the threat of a life ban would not deter some players from committing any offences, which would lead to assaults on referees.

On private grounds the home Club should control the situation, but on Council pitches it is very difficult to control, only the Birmingham County F A can deal with it properly.

The Secretary from the Boys League told the members we are all concerned about assaults and the only information we receive officially is after the player has been dealt with by the County Disciplinary Commission. Information we do get is usually second hand.

The Secretary of the Sunday League told the meeting that a few years ago the League had its own disciplinary code of conduct by clubs and players, but we were ordered to withdraw it by the County Football Association.

Various other points were put forward and the general consensus was that the Birmingham County Football Association should deal very firmly with assaults on referees. Also any other type of offence that would involve the Police and the Hospital. The players should be banned for life with a heavy fine of at least £200 (two hundred pounds).

After every one had spoken the Chairman thanked the League Representatives for attending and said what we need is a super deterrent against the players, with possibly a 10 year ban on playing again.

The Chairman told every one that we have had 90 minutes discussion. We shall report back to the Association for the members to talk and discuss the issue, he then closed the meeting.

Assaults

Assaults have again reared its ugly head, along with spectator problems. The Leamington and Coventry Referees Associations' were concerned about the amount of alcohol being consumed on the touchlines, during the Saturday afternoon and Sunday morning football matches. A referee had been assaulted in Coventry and the Association had threatened to withdraw the referee's service to the League concerned if it is not stamped out. Referees are requested to report Clubs who allow intoxicating drinks to the County Football Association. A similar issue is happening at Leamington and Clubs are being reported to the League.

Two items were placed in the Newsletter, both were concerning referees. The first one was a referee who was involved in an assault and his Society had written to other Societies for financial support. The letter stated that the Competition was not sanctioned by the County Football Association or the Football Association and no action had been taken against the player concerned. In view of the circumstances relating to the referee refereeing non- affiliated football, no legal assistance to the referee was forthcoming.

Members were requested to report back and stress the importance of checking with the County Football Association or the Football Association to see if a competition is affiliated.

In another case where a referee was assaulted by a player, the County FA concerned refused to suspend the player until the Court case had been dealt with.

The player was subsequently suspended for another reason. The Midland Division said it was worrying that a County FA can allow a player to carry on after an assault. The President of the Midland Division said he needed clear evidence regarding the full facts of the particular case if the Association is to take it any further. Advice had been given to the Division that a player notified of a charge of assault on a match official should not participate in any football activity from the date when they are notified of the charge.

Referees were still being assaulted and it doesn't seem to make any difference to the players or spectators, the general opinion is, until the 'Football Association or the County F A' make a definite decision on the amount of fines and suspensions given to the players or officials of the Club concerned. The perpetrators can then be penalised correctly. We must remember that a majority of players and clubs appreciate a referee at their game; it seems the culprits are in a minority, yet they make the most noise. Below is a case that happened on a local parks pitch.

The ugly head of assaults on referees struck again in the local parks, a referee was assaulted by a player and then stamped on in a vicious attack. Not only is it happening in this area it is also happening in Coventry, what can be done to stamp this problem out .It is not only football, but other sports as well are being affected

At the Monthly meeting during a discussion on the subject of assaults one of our colleagues produced an article printed in the 'Liverpool Echo' concerning referees who were abused during the season. It seems assaults have trebled in the 96/97 season and the writer of the article, is quoted as saying the new figures showing assaults on 'Amateur Soccer Referees' are rising dramatically.

The Football Association has sent out a message, 'Hands off the referee- or we will boot you out of football'. Culprits face bans of five years or possibly life, depending on the seriousness of the attack. Permission to produce the article in the Association Newsletter was given by the Echo Newspaper.

The article went on to say that 12 (twelve) referees were seriously assaulted during matches, one referee had his jaw broken, violent incidents between players are also on the increase, and some take out their frustration on referees.

A further 50 (fifty) referees and assistant referees were subject to verbal abuse, with fines up to £60 (sixty pounds) and suspensions, ranging up to 91 days.

A referee was seriously assaulted at a football match; the County concerned suspended the player for life. But it was dismayed when the local Magistrates Court had not imposed a custodial sentence.

Others received fines and suspensions for abusive language, verbal abuse and threatening behaviour. There doesn't seem to be any let up from assaults and it makes you wonder how referees go out each week to referee matches not knowing what is going to happen. Not all the players are the same, majority do respect the referee and go out of their way to help, but you will always get the player who will bait the referee. To him it is part of the game. It's up to the referee to deal with that type of player, a chat and a joke often does the trick and majority of players like being treated as adult people, you get more response if you do it that way.

Birmingham & Warwick Joint Referees County Committe

Concern was expressed over promotions with the County Football Association .It was hoped to arrange a meeting to discuss the issues. It seems that only 37% (thirty seven percent) of Class 3(three) and 41% (forty one percent) Class 2(two) would be eligible for promotion. The other percent have failed to send a list of matches in to the B C F A. for Promotion. If the marks for the referee are not handed in to the League Secretary he would not be able to complete the form and return it to the County Football Association in time. If they are not sent to the County FA by a certain date, the referee has no chance of being promoted and the marks have to be of a certain standard. We have been fortunate at Leamington as the Sunday League has always sent the form completed to the County FA, in good time.

The Chairman explained certain Leagues had failed to send in marks for referees nullifying any opportunity they may have had to receive promotion. We had written to the Secretary of the Birmingham and Warwickshire J R C.C asking that this matter be discussed further. The Secretary had replied stating the matter would be taken up with the County F.A.

The Delegate from the Coventry Alliance Football League spoke to members on the dangers of players who had suffered head injuries, and being allowed to carry on playing, after telling the referee they are okay. He reminded every one that all head injuries, head contact, collisions, even heading the ball, all the players should be sent to the Hospital for a check-up. It had happened in Coventry and the player was in Hospital. He asked the members to inform colleagues who were not at the meeting to be careful.

Birmingham County Ruling – Throw- in Law 15

The Secretary read a letter from the County confirming the awarding of a foul throw against a player taking a throw from the wrong position is now discontinued, confirming previous reports given to the meeting by the Secretary.

The problem with throw-ins has been 'on-going' for a couple of years, when the law appertaining to 'throw-ins' was altered in the 1982-83 Rule alterations.

After a previous discussion from the County Referees Committee, the procedure was explained to everyone and awarding a foul throw against players taking the throw from the wrong position had been revoked. In the meantime, referees had received their copies of the rule changes. The delegate stated that as far as the Football Association. Was concerned, the 1982/83 rule was revoked and that Leamington members should obey the Football Association Instruction until further notice.

Birmingham County Misconduct Forms

The Birmingham County F.A are very concerned about the disciplinary forms for misconduct, they are not being completed correctly. A number of referees have been called before the County Referees Committee to be shown the correct way to complete the form. Concern was expressed, although no Leamington Referee had been written to or asked to attend a meeting in Birmingham. The management committee had suggested a meeting would be set aside to discuss and demonstrate the correct method of completing the forms for misconduct, also when a player is dismissed from the field of play. It seems that the referees' concerned with the form filling are not members of any Association but are informing the County that they are. It is up to the County Football Association to stop referee making false declaration when they register.

Accident Insurance Scheme

The Secretary pointed out the Referees Association was considering abolishing the compulsory Insurance scheme because of spiralling costs (which would increase the affiliation fee next year). The compulsory scheme (it was intended) could be replaced by a voluntary scheme .An indication of the wishes of the members of local referees association, was sought in order to assess the members requirements. A vote was taken and it was unanimously decided that the Leamington Referees Association, wished to remain in the compulsory scheme. The Secretary is to write to the National Referees Association informing them of the decision.

The point raised at a previous meeting regarding Insurance cover. This had been answered by the National Referees Association; (Members were covered, by their previous year's membership.) They are also covered by the policy when they are out on a training exercise, whether they in a group or train on their own. Once the new season had started they were not covered until the current membership premium is received at the Referees Association Office. If anyone has problems contact the Secretary.

Refereeing Incidents and Advice to Juniors

Junior Referees were instructed to seek the advice from senior members or the Secretary concerning incidents that happen when refereeing junior or boy's football.
In one incident, a young player was sent from the field of play and the offence was not reported to the County Football Association. It meant the youngster who was either cautioned or sent-off was able to play in a Cup-Final; the referee in this case was very inexperienced. It eventually came to light the referee concerned had passed the examination, but had made no attempt to join the Referees Association, therefore he was open to abuse, because he would not be covered by insurance or have the support of the Association behind him.

One of the members said we always seem to minute these various items concerning the junior referee and any incident that happens, but we do not really act on the information we receive, it seem that once its in the minutes it is slightly forgotten.

The Chairman and the Secretary said that we do take these issues up and in most situations speak to the referee concerned, we cannot force them to join the Association. If the Leagues that the youngsters referee in, decided to make all their referees belong to a Referees Association, there would not be any problems. But the County FA would not allow it to happen, they would say it would be a closed shop and referees should have a choice.

Refereeing problems do arise when the young and newly passed referees go out and referee. We do not have enough members to set up the Mentor scheme to keep an eye on these youngsters every week. This is unfortunate and we can only ask them to join the Association. If they do not, it means they are not covered by any Insurance against assaults or loss of referees' kit.

Reports from the Management

The Trustees from the Conference fund had received a letter from the Secretary with a request that they consider winding up the fund and placing the money in the funds of the Association. The Secretary explained the reason why it should be done. We have various articles we would like to purchase to help the 'Association Coach' with his training programme for candidate referees also for use at Council meetings.

Problems over Cup & League Final Tickets, The Association did not receive an allocation from the County Football Association. Members felt we should have had two tickets. The Secretary tried to explain that we did not register a Football team with the County FA. A few of the members were under the impression that as we are an Association we should be entitled to two tickets, the Secretary to enquire.

It was pointed out that at one time, you were able to obtain a ticket if you applied as an individual referee registered with the County Association. It seems that the County have stopped that now. The only way you will get an allocation is to register as a Football Team and play in a League which might be a problem.

Notice was brought to the attention of the management that a referee not a member of the Association but officiating in local Leagues. He had sent a player from the field of play and cautioned three other players in the same match, without it is alleged submitting a report to the County Football Association. The matter is to be raised with the League and the County FA.

The management members were concerned about this case and as one of the senior member stated it seems that every four or five years. We have these referees who do not join the Association and tell lies to the County that they are members of so and so Association; The County does not check neither does the League, although as far as the County even the Football Association are concerned a referee does not have to belong to a Referees Association it is supposed to be a free choice and not a closed shop. Just try to referee with out registering with the County F A.

Another point the member put to the meeting was that a few Clubs who have had players booked etc have asked the referee after the game if he is going to send the report into the County FA. If the referee say's yes then they give him a poor mark on the team sheet.

This situation has been reported to the League concerned and the Clubs have been told to leave well alone.

April 1985

Extract from the Managements minutes

Leamington Referee Association was asked by the Midland Divisional to stage the 'Midland Quiz Competition' in Leamington.

The Management discussed the project and the Secretary who had received earlier knowledge of the quiz told the members he had started to make temporary arrangements. He informed the Committee of the bookings he had made, which was as follows. He had provisionally booked the Leamington Cricket Club for the quiz and to provide meals, also a private room for the judges to meet.

The date the Secretary had suggested was Sunday April 14th starting at about 2pm. The members asked about the cost of hiring the room and providing a cold Buffet Lunch. They were told it would not cost the Association a penny, because Pottertons were prepared to sponsor the whole event.

The Committee were impressed by the amount of work that had been done and remarked all it needs on the day is the members to attend and support the Association. We will need members to organise the raffle and tickets also to generally to help administer the function.

The quiz was a success and Leamington was congratulated by the Vice- President of the Midland Division for a pleasant day and well organised.

The Social Side to the Association

Whilst the events of Assaults and Language had been talked about and with the members involved in attempting to move on we are forgetting the social side of the Association. This is where the bonding of members occurs and the Association benefit from the exercise. The six a side football competition which has been organised by the Association since before the Conference was beginning to show a handsome profit for the benevolent fund; with an amount of money being raised from £100 pounds to £200 pounds each year. This was due to the competition being well organised by the Management Committee and the support they received from other Associations.

So successful has the six-a-side been that the committee have decided to make their own goal posts suitable for the competition and it was suggested that it be discussed thoroughly at the Management meeting.

The Benevolent Cup which is an eleven a side football competition was again successful and this was due to the committee. Since the latter part of the 1960s we have had some very good footballers who have all qualified as referees and still enjoyed a game of football. This was quite handy for the Association; we were winning matches and reaching the Semi-Final stage a few times, as well being in the Final. We have played against teams like Wolverhampton, Birmingham, Sutton Coldfield and Coventry to be in that position.

Six-a –Side Football May & June 1985

The Benevolent fund which profits from the Associations Six-a-Side would be a little short on the Donation to the Benevolent. We have given a considerable amount over the years it must be the first time we have had to use the money for something else.

The reason being is that the Association had finally decided to make or purchase our own goal posts for the Competition this was mentioned in the council business. The question was how are we going to make them and from what material. If they are made out of wood they could easily get damaged. People are never careful with equipment they borrow.

One of the members said he had been talking to a colleague from Pottertons who had told him he would be able to obtain steam piping to make the posts providing we let him have the measurements.

The question of cost was mentioned and it was obvious that we would have to pay for the piping even if it was at cost price. A general talk between the members took place and an estimate cost was worked out. The Chairman mentioned the Conference Committee and suggested we produce a plan for three sets. Submit this to the Trustees and enquire if they would help with the purchase of Piping and the Brackets or Teg's needed to build them together.

This was done and the Trustees of the fund agreed to give the committee £ 200 (pounds) towards the cost, the remainder could come from the amount we make on the Sports Day. It would mean the Benevolent Fund would not receive as much this year.

The Trustees were thanked for their offer and 3(three) complete sets were made in such a way that they could be transported around without any difficulty, the posts were then painted white and stored at Pottertons.

At the end of the Competition the Treasurer told the members we would be able to send the Benevolent £100(pounds).

Later on in that year the posts were lent our for a small fee, this did not work out very well and after a short while a modification was made to the goalposts by increasing the length about 3 feet. We decided not to lend them out again and it was suggested we try to find a much better storage place.

Referees Quiz Competition

The Association quiz team has had an excellent amount of success during the previous seasons but have never managed to go any further than a Semi-Final. They finally reached the Final of the Competition and will be playing Wolverhampton Referees in Birmingham. Date and venue to be arranged. To reach this position the team were successful against Rugby Referees, Solihull, and finally beating Birmingham by six points in the Semi-Final. The team consisted of Chris Ackroyde, John Austin, John Birch, Dale Packer, Roger Palmer, Simon Rogers, Arnold Rouse, and William (Bill) Timson, we always had one or two extra members like Paul Anderson –Kirby who spent time holding Quiz sessions at his house and others who became part of the team when needed.

The members who belong to the team enjoy the competition against other Associations and quite a lot of friendships are made especially if you officiate on the same Leagues. The Six-a-Side Football Competition is still being organised by the Association who have made it a successful event, with the fund raising going to the Benevolent Fund, the Football eleven have had reasonable success over the season and the members who make up the team seem to enjoy the games they play, this is one event where it is getting difficult to have eleven or twelve players available on a Sunday afternoon there is a possibility that these matches or the competition would close down.

1985

David Schofield (Vice-President)

As we reach the 1985 period we learn of the death of one of our Vice-Presidents and a very valued friend who had passed away, David was very involved with the Association when we organised the Conference and helped the Association as much as he could, He was also the Chairman of the Birmingham County Football Association and a Vice –President of Coventry

Referees Association. The Chairman and colleagues were represented at the Funeral service. At the next Council meeting the Chairman informed the members of the Associations sad loss and said he will be missed. The members were asked to stand for a minute silence.

1986

Jack Joyner &Charlie Jackson

The members at the meeting stood for a minutes silence for two members Jack Joyner and Charlie Jackson.   Jack Joyner passed away in July 1986. Jack was a prominent member of the Association, being a Life-member and Vice-President; he was also a delegate to the various Leagues as well as the Birmingham & Warwickshire Joint County Committee. He joined Leamington Referees Association in the 1936 and refereed all over the Midlands, Jack also helped to reform the Association in 1948.
He was a very good sportsman who took up refereeing as a way of keeping fit, he was always picked for the football team and was a very useful cricketer who could bowl and bat and was always taking wickets

Charlie Jackson

The same could be said about Charlie Jackson who passed away in October 1986. His refereeing career was similar to Jack Joyner he also played for Leamington Referees and was a member before the War joining in 1938. Both were good sportsmen, Charlie served on Management and was a delegate .to the various Leagues. When he retired through ill health he looked after the ground at Leek Wootton. Charlie was another who took up refereeing to keep fit and again was a very good cricketer.
These two gentlemen were always given the respect they deserved, you could talk to them if you had a problem and they would most probably give you the answer, their passing was the Associations loss
The Association was represented at both Funerals.

After reaching the half way in this set of minutes from the first period, we find the Association has moved along in an orderly fashion with the business well organised. Meetings reasonably attended and reports from the various delegates have kept the Association in the forefront, new members are regularly being coached and passing the County Examination. A completely new system was being introduced by the Football Association with the Head of Refereeing, Ken Ridden removing the word coaches and calling everyone 'Licensed Instructors' they have to take a very thorough Instructional course on the method of coaching referee candidates as laid out by the Football Association (read a separate section on Coaching and Licensed Instructors)

One or two changes had been made the Treasurer had resigned through pressure of work and Andy Dalziel had taken over from Chris Ackroyde, Derek Silk had completed his three year stint as Chairman. Duncan MacAulay was elected as Chairman until the AGM 1988, there were a few changes on the Management Committee and the Secretary was still John Austin who had Phil Robbins and John Sharp as his Assistant Secretaries.

Coaching & Seminars

John Mander was congratulated on passing the Referee Instructors Course at Lilleshall. He is now registered with the Football Association as a Licensed Instructor.

Law changes – very few referees have received copies of law changes for the new season. A question was asked by a member, "why can't we get all Law alterations before the season starts and why do we pay our subs, when we have to chase items from the County"

A reply was sent to the Secretary and the member commented that it was not good enough. Evidently the "Law Changes" had been lost in transit that is why they are late. It was suggested that the Training Officer should hold a discussion to ensure as far as possible, we have a uniform interpretation.

The Seminar organised for Class 2 and Class 3 Referees is to be on January 27th, 1987 at Racing Club, Warwick

Referees are reminded, failing to attend either the one at Warwick or Bilberry could put them in a position of not being considered for promotion.

Both venues should have a full-house.

A member enquired if it was possible to set up a "Discussion Session" for newly qualified referees, so that problems they may find could be sorted out. Also if senior member could be involved not to tell the young referees what to do, but to advise them. The Training Officer said he would take it on board and discuss it with the Management.

Another member said it was wrong for the County Football Association to be dictatorial in making it compulsory for Class 1 referees to attend at a cost of £27 (twenty seven pounds) each.

After a discussion on the subject members said we should object and send a proposal to the Birmingham County Football Association and the Birmingham & Warwickshire Joint Referees Committee on the following lines, "The Leamington & District Referees Association object to the B C F A having a dictatorial attitude in making it compulsory to attend Bilbury seminars for promotion. The voting on the issue was unanimous.

Law Amendments & Coaching

Law Changes- Footwear is now compulsory; a player's basic equipment now consists of shirt or jersey, shorts, stockings and footwear. Shorts must be worn over tracksuit trousers if they are worn. Shin pads to be made compulsory for next season,

Feeder and Contributory system was well organised and referees had themselves to blame if they failed to make the grade, assessing referees was becoming more professional and it was pleasing for an assessor to watch the keen and well informed referee climb the ladder to success.

The Coaching was becoming very successful and referee candidates were passing the Examination but not joining the Association. This is a subject that concerns everyone, and it is was very disturbing, especially when you find them refereeing in junior or boy's football, it seems that every other Association has this problem. Is there an answer, only if the Football Association make the referee join an Association or Society, as well as registering with the County FA.

Sporting events and quiz competitions on the Laws of the game, were well organised and the Association participated very well, the members had a lot of success but never won a trophy outright.

During this decade we have had talks from various speakers on a variety of subjects. Coaching and training young referees Seminars for Class 2 and Class 3 also Sports Injuries' were all covered and they made interesting subjects to listen to and they were well presented.

Seminars for Referees Assessors

This was held in September at the Birmingham County Football Association Headquarters under the guidance of John Baker from the Football Association. The Seminar was a one day session. It was the first time a number of Assessors had met John Baker. Without realising it we were going to hear a lot more about him and his method of motivating members, also changes in the way referees are classified through the County Football Associations.

In his talk to a packed audience John Baker covered every aspect of the need for assessors; new forms from the Football Association were to be studied. Everything appertaining to refereeing was discussed, items such as pre-match briefing, the use of club and official linesmen, ground conditions, league rules and cup competitions.

He also mentioned assessors should concentrate on the assessment forms and not get involved with players. When you consider a referee can make up to 500 decisions during a match, the assessor has to note the good decisions, his judgement and faults on the type of match he is refereeing. All assessors at the seminar watched a special match and gave an assessment on the referee who had applied for promotion. The assessments were discussed and the average marks were explained.

It was an excellent day and everyone found it interesting and informative. John Baker was thanked for his talk and guidance during the day

League & County Report

They have instructed clubs that they must provide club members to take the referees instructional course provided by the Referees Association Coach John Mander. This will cover the game if the official referee fails to arrive, or not available. They would have basic knowledge of the game to referee the match. County approval has been given and eventually it will be placed in the League Rules.Leamington & District Sunday Football League has been considering the shortage of referees for a number of seasons. Grave concern was expressed by the Birmingham & Warwickshire Joint Referees' County Committee on the reductions of suspensions and fines on players guilty of assaults. They were also concerned about Referees and Linesmen who were not turning up at personal hearings.

When they do, they alter the report they have sent to the County Football Association. Players were then being punished for a lesser offence. The Committee has written to all Association and Societies in the area asking members to seek advice if they have trouble when compiling their report to the Birmingham County FA. They must attend disciplinary courts where their report and attendance is vital. By attending you would be making the issue easier for future referees.

Birmingham County report

Coaching candidate referees was another problem the Associations or Societies were having with the County Football Association. The Birmingham & Warwickshire Committee were seeking a meeting with the County FA to find out why the cost of coaching candidates through the examination will cost £20(pounds).

If that is the case then possible candidates would not be able to afford to take up refereeing. On top of the £20 the candidate would have to spend another £20 or £30(pounds) to purchase referees equipment and possibly register with the Association. It was felt that they should approach the Football Association who issued the directive.   .

League Report

A report was given to the members about a meeting of Clubs from the Premier Division of the Leamington & District Sunday League. The meeting concerned a move to have a panel of referees officiating only on that division. The selection would mean the most experienced and senior referees would be selected a suggested increased fee would be on the cards. Further meetings were to be held and the Secretary said he would inform the Clubs of the Association views. The information was not very well received by the members, but they were prepared to wait for further information.

1988

A complaint was made about referees. The person concerned thought the referees were over zealous with the way they were booking players. The Secretary pointed out they were only doing their job.
Shortage of referees was another issue. One member considered the clubs attitude to the referee was to blame, and a number of players consider a referee a waste of time.

The Leamington and District Sunday League had promised to support the Association in contributing 50% (fifty percent) of the fee to coach candidate referees. The candidates, when passing the examination would be requested to officiate on the League

A letter had been sent to the Secretary regarding room charges for coaching venues. An allowance was recommended, but efforts were to be made to keep costs to a minimum.
Shortage of referees, a request by the Sunday League to see if the Association had any candidate referees being coached. It has been suggested that a trained person from each club should officiate if necessary.
The Sunday League to bear cost of training, further discussion to take place before it can be implemented. It may have to be discussed at County level.

1989

Sidney Sharp

Tributes were given to Mr.Sidney.Sharp, who passed away in Warwick Hospital. Sid was a very keen and tireless worker for the Association, as well as holding the position of Vice-Chairman and Management member, he was also a Vice- President from 1975 to 1989. He qualified as an Assessor and enjoyed going out to assess the young referees for promotion. He supported the George Dutton and Andy Campbell Charity Cup Competitions as well as donating the trophies for the referees at the finals. Sidney was a first class Sportsman a very good footballer, and thoroughly enjoyed his cricket, Sidney and I spent many a Saturday afternoon watching a referee and having a good chat at the same time, he was a credit to the Association
Tributes were also given to **Jim Griffiths, Wolverhampton, who was Chairman** of the Birmingham and Warwickshire Joint Referees County Committee. Members stood for a minute silence in memory of these two gentlemen.

Moving from the 1980 into 1990 and the final part of the Last Decade

As we leave the 1980s and move into the last decade of the 20th Century, the Association was well established, with a good management committee and officers. No one envisaged the problems that would occur during this period.

Changes would eventually affect the National Referees Association but this would not happen until the 21st Century.

Other events were happening with VAT on subscriptions being demanded by Custom & Excise. It was the National President who finally settled the issue with the Income Tax people. Once that was cleared. It allowed the National Referees Association, to have their own Headquarters in Coventry with a full time Secretary. All these things happened before we reached 1996. Assaults were still happening. The members were being well catered for with an array of speakers, members were being successful in quiz competitions. Meetings were reasonably attended. The Six-a-side Football competitions organised to raise money for the Referees Benevolent Fund was continuing in the same way it was in the 1980s and again successful financially

Six-a-Side

The Trophy for the Six-a-Side Competition which was presented to the Association in 1972 was beginning to look well used. The Management Committee decide to purchase another Trophy for the Competition the members agreed to the proposal. It was purchased and named after Sidney Sharp who had recently passed away. Sidney was a keen supporter of everything in the Association and was also a Vice- President and well involved with the Association's two Charity Cups. It was pleasing to a good majority of members that his name was mentioned. This meant the competition had two Trophies and the new one would be for the major competition, whilst the other would be used for a small supplementary competition.

Lost Minutes 1990 to 1996

It is sad to say again we find a Minute Book between 1990 and 1996 has been misplaced or lost and not one of the officers seemed particularly worried. One would expect the minutes for that period to be available along with interesting correspondence, unfortunately it has not happened. Therefore information or articles placed in this period will be as accurate as possible.

Changes were happening with the Feeder and Contributory Leagues becoming a Supply and Contributory League. Referees were being assessed more and Licensed Instructors were attending specialist courses, with Seminars to obtain a Coaching Certificate. We are very fortunate at Leamington in as much we have three members who have taken the course and all have passed, although they are in various grades at the moment. The standard of teaching should benefit the new candidate referees as well as the members at monthly meetings.

In the local scene the Quiz team reached the Semi-Final of the Competition. They were rewarded with the opportunity of representing the Midland Division in the National Quiz Competition next year, taking place at Mansfield.

In 1991 problems were arising on the 'Field of Play' with referees constantly being warned by the Football Association and the County Football Association about football pitches in poor condition. They say referees should inspect them properly, if they do not and a player gets injured, the referee could be held responsible, especially if it was proven that the pitch was the cause.

National Referees Association Minutes

An item from the National Referees Association minutes was concerning a referee from Northern Ireland. One of the players who was playing in the match received an injury from stones on the pitch and is suing this referee. The Referees Association is seeking legal advice and made legal representation available to the referee. The reason the article was placed in the minutes was to make sure all Associations inform their members to check all football pitches thoroughly before refereeing the game.

The Birmingham & Warwickshire Referees' Committee have received a letter regarding Referees' Liability for injuries caused by unsafe pitches. The letter has been forwarded to the Football Association.
Another problem concerning referees was highlighted, this one concerned a player having been injured or assaulted during a match, asking the referee who refereed the match for a copy of his report. The referee was told to contact his County Football Association and inform them of the request by the player concerned.

1992

The Association was quite pleased to arrange a special evening for George Pankhurst in reaching his 50 years service to the Referees Association. The evening was held at the Globe Hotel Warwick and over 70 guests attended all from the football and refereeing fraternity. The National Referees President Peter Willis presented the Silver Salver to George. After the speeches were over Peter Willis presented a Certificate to the President of Leamington Referees Association Arnold Rouse, in honour of being made a Life-Member of the Leamington Association in 1981.

V A T (on subscriptions)

VAT on subscriptions has been a problem since 1989 when H M Custom & Excise demanded that VAT was paid on a member's annual subscriptions to the National Referees Association. The President Peter Willis is involved with discussions and the following letter was sent to all Associations and Societies. The President has given permission for this to be reproduced:

To all Members of the Referees Association - 3rd January 1992

This is a personal letter from me as your President to all members of the Referees Association. It is the first occasion since you appointed me as your President at Newcastle in 1984 that I have felt the need to communicate with you in such a direct manner.

Since my appointment as your President I have always devoted myself fully to the objectives of our Association. There have been many happy occasions when I have been proud to be your representative, you have permitted me to share with you some very special moments and have accepted me into your families as a friend.
This is something which I shall treasure for the rest of my life. It has given me enough special memories far too numerous to list here, to ensure that I will never be a man alone.
Together we have faced many problems; all have been dealt with in a manner where I have never felt that I have had anything other than your full support. As a reminder, I will draw your attention to the major problem of assaults upon referees, a problem which still exists. The numbers are falling, mainly due I feel to the fact that the Football Association agreed with our presentation to them to have the standards of punishments increased to reflect the seriousness of the offence.

Then we had the awful problem of the Inland Revenue and their treatment to some of our members. This created a vast amount of work to many people, not least Mr Harry Dempsey Hon Auditor. Again it was solved to the benefit of all referees, members of our Association or not. There are many other situations where the cause has been just and has always been fought with full

commitment. The claim against members for compensation by injured players, imagine how you would feel if you received a court summons to defend such an action against you.

The purchase of office premises at Coventry was a major achievement. I will be forever grateful to all of the Members and other bodies who made the financing of this purchase possible.

In 1989 at Annual Conference at Southampton I had the responsibility of informing members attending the Annual Conference of the decision by H.M. Customs and Excise that Value Added Tax was being demanded on membership Annual Subscriptions. At that time we were in active negotiations with H.M. Customs and Excise trying to show that our Annual Subscriptions should not be subject to (VAT) Conference was informed that we would not be making a charge for (VAT.) on the grounds that it was felt the charge should not be made.

To collect the (VAT), at that time would be prejudicial to our case. I clearly remember stating to Conference that if we failed in our negotiations with HM Custom and Excise. I was certain that the members would then accept the amount due would have to be paid and I fully trusted my membership if this became the case.

Since Conference in Southampton in 1989 the question of (VAT) has been fully circulated to all members via Council Minutes, Divisional Minutes and the Football Referee. No member can honestly say the facts relating to (VAT) were not fully documented. The negotiations with H.M.Custom and Excise have continued since 1989 until we were informed (VAT).had to be paid from September 1989 to the present time.

This decision was given to us in July 1991, a decision against which an immediate appeal was lodged. In order that an appeal could be lodged the sum of £10,982 pounds had to be paid.

This was the total (VAT) due to the end of the 1990 financial year. This sum was paid out of Association Funds and an appeal lodged. To date a meeting has been held with H.M.Customs and Excise in London and Council will be making a decision at the Council Meeting on January 11th, as to whether or not any further appeal will be made.

It was also made clear to our Association that all 1991 fees would also be subject to (VAT) at the rate of 52 (pence). After long and careful thought Council were of the view that the fairest way to the majority of members of collecting (VAT) was to charge each member the sum of £1(one pound), any shortfall was to be met from Association Funds.

All Societies were then fully informed by letter of this decision, in early August 1991, but sadly, many other Societies and members entered into immediate correspondence via letters, Society Magazines, and other means, giving reasons why they should not or would not pay the £1(pound). It was clear to me there was a clear lack of trust by some members in my stewardship of our Association so far as relates to the question of (VAT).

During this same period of time there have been other important matters which have been aired in magazines, letters to the office and at the some Society Meetings. I refer to the question of Insurance for Members, under the Association Rules (rule 4) Membership is conditional upon the payment of the Personal Accident Insurance premium. Currently £2 (pound). Although there are new negotiated extra benefits in addition to the personal accident clause covering injuries sustained as a referee. Many members appear to think that for £2 (pound) they are insured for all eventualities.

The Annual Premium for this Insurance cover is paid to the Insurance Company in 3 instalments between August and October each year. In many cases a number of members do not pay their membership until much later than this. There has also been raised the question of Membership of our Association and many questions are being asked about 100% Society Membership. (Rule 4). Again this subject has been aired in magazines, letters, minutes etc. You may by now be asking why I have written so much about matters with which you are all fully familiar. I would like to take this opportunity to explain.

During my time as your President I have a first class working relationship with all members of Council, Executive Council, Members, Society Officers and all other elected Officers of the Association. There may well have been differences of opinions, it would be a funny old world if there had not been, but at all times, without exception, every decision taken has been in the belief that it was for the benefit of all members.

Peter Willis finishes his letter to all members by informing them that the time for nominations to all the positions on the National Council, Divisional Committee, alteration
To Rules, should all be in the Secretary's hand by certain dates in February and March. So all the changes can be distributed to Associations and Societies and finalised for the Conference which is held in June each year.
His final words in closing the letter are as follows: - If you are not satisfied with your elected officers, you have the right to change them.
If you are not satisfied with the Rules of the Association, you have the right to propose changes.
The Rules of the Association are the foundation on which I am charged with looking after your affairs, I do not have any right to alter them in any way, only the membership can do that.

In the meantime I will continue to serve you all to the best of my ability, without fear or favour, to ensure that our Association and Members have the full benefits of the objectives for which we all strive.

Yours Sincerely

Peter N Willis
National President.
Referees Association.

1992

Annual General Meeting

Change of Headquarters

At the Annual General Meeting in May the members considered that we were not really wanted at the Farmers Club which had been our Headquarters since September 1966. The owners of the Club were moving into the catering business and wished to turn the club into a restaurant. This meant the Association would have to move. The Chairman said that feelers had been put out and we should have some information before the next Council meeting in August. The possible venue would be the, 'Liberal Club' Leamington.
We eventually settled into the Liberal Club and the Association members were all registered as members, with our own pass key, the meeting room was upstairs and members soon felt at home. Although it wasn't as plush as the Farmers Club, the beer was okay and every one enjoyed a drink afterwards.

Management meetings were a problem on some occasions having to share the room with another organisation; occasionally it became a little difficult to hold the meeting. We were then moved downstairs into a room that had been used by the 'Ancient order of Buffaloes.' This was reasonable but some of the members were not quite happy at the way we were being moved around and the club was in the process of employing a new Steward. Thoughts were on another move.

Headquarters

The Association were not happy with the Liberal Club and the Chairman decided we should look for another change of a Headquarters. He said it will be a long time before we find a place like the Farmers Club. One of our committee members told us about St Patrick's Club. If we were interested he would arrange a meeting so we could go and have a look at the facilities. One or two members went and came back with approval of the Club. Later on that year we left the Liberal Club and moved to the St Patrick's, where we have been made very welcome.

Tom Storey

At the beginning of the year we had two of our older statesmen pass away-one through illness the other with a sudden heart attack.
Tom Story who had been a stalwart in the Association since 1948, holding the position of Chairman and Management Member, he was also a Delegate to the County Referees Committee and over the years has held office in the local Sunday Football League. He was made a Life Member of the Association in 1954 and received in 1976 the National Referees Meritorious Service Award for service to the Referees Association. He was also a holder of the Birmingham County FA 21 year Award and was a Vice President of Leamington Referees Association.

George Pankhurst

George Pankhurst was another stalwart of the Association who collapsed with a heart attack one Sunday afternoon watching a Football match on Television. George had held various Offices in the Association from Management to Secretary /Treasurer and then Chairman and he too was made a Life Member of the Association in 1956 and in 1976 he was awarded the National Referees Meritorious Service Award and he was a Vice-President of the Association. George like Tom Story held many positions with Football Leagues and he was the Secretary of the Warwickshire Combination, as well as Chairman of the Leamington Saturday League and President of the Sunday League. George was also a Member of the Birmingham County Football Association.

It was a loss to the Association although both Gentlemen were not so active in the Association they both showed a keen interest in everything that was going on. The Chairman asked the members to stand for a minute silence for Tom and George. Representation was made at both funerals.

Change of Rule (financial)

The members of the Management at Leamington were considering a change in the financial year, instead of finishing in March moving it to finish on December 31st.
The new season starting on January 1st, it was stated that between May and August very few referees pay their subscriptions

If we submit a change of Rule to the Conference in 1993, recommending the financial year finishes on December 31st each year and the new season starts on January 1st, this would be distributed to all Associations to find out what interest there would be. One Association agreed with us, and seconded our 'Proposal,' we were pleased about this.

The Proposal was put to the Conference by our delegate and it was unfortunately defeated, although a number of Societies were in favour. When the Management knew of the result they decided to go ahead with the change at Leamington..

Financial Change Annual General Meeting 1994

Moves were then made within our own Association to change the season's financial structure. All the members were informed of the changes and that the fact next year would only be of seven (7) month duration. This was to be placed on the Agenda for the 1994 Annual General Meeting. The changes were brought forward and the members at the Annual General Meeting voted for the financial year to start on January 1st and ending on December 31st. Members were asked to pay their Subscriptions early to coincide with the National Associations Insurance policy which starts on April 1st.

When the Agenda on 'Rule Alterations' came up the rules were altered and accepted. The President said that every member should have a set of rules including all the alterations a further rule was added. The member who proposed the new rule explained the reason to the members and why it was needed. This new rule would be Rule 18, it reads as follows;- "The Association reserve the right to refuse Membership or expel from membership any member guilty of conduct Prejudicial to the Association" the voting was unanimous.

At the meeting the Treasurer Simon Rogers told members that he would not be able to carry on as the treasurer. This was due to the changes in the Schools National Curriculum which would give him extra work. Simon is a Teacher and he felt that it would be unfair on the members to have a Treasurer, who could only attend occasionally, Simon will be missed but we wish him well in new position.

The finances had been well looked after whilst Simon was in charge and at the AGM, the members elected Steve Portch as the Treasurer and a change in the Management with Steve McCarthy being elected with Dale Packer standing down.

Annual General Meeting 1995

Brian Hackleton retired from being Secretary due to a change of employment and extra travelling as well as other problems. Brian was thanked by the committee for the work he has done. The new Secretary who was elected was Ray Morgan, there was no other change and the meeting went reasonably well until an amendment to the rules was put to the members. It caused a problem and an objection was raised. The objection to the amendment by a member was taken from a document concerning the 'National Referees Association Rules.' These rules are only applicable if members or the Association are not affiliated to the National Referees Association. The amendment was

withdrawn for a word change, although the issue only concerned members who were not or had not joined the Association

Social Events & Coaching

The Annual Six-a -Side Football Competition was running into trouble with the Sports ground that is normally used. The event which was a money spinner during the 1970's and the early part of the 80's was having its finances curtailed, the Committee of the Sports Club told the Referees Management Committee they would be requiring £40 (pounds) hiring fee and an Insurance cover would be eventually added to compensate for damage that may occur. The Association was seeking other venues.

The speakers we have had have actually made the meetings interesting, yet we are still having a gradual decline of members attending, no doubt one day we will find out the answer. Social events are well organised and a trip to Hall Green Greyhound Racing with a four course meal included was an excellent evening out. Sessions at the Ten Pin Bowling Arena were also enjoyable. A Buffet Dance with the Treasurer providing the Music with his Disco was a success. All these efforts were well supported and enjoyed yet if we try to organise a Dinner Dance we run into trouble.

When we decided to implement the Mentor system with the new referee candidates we did not have the manpower to work on an individual basis. Senior referees who were still refereeing were giving these young referees the experience they needed. They had the youngsters operating as 'Assistant Referees' on the Coventry Alliance and other Leagues they also had the opportunity to act as Assistant Referees on a 'Junior League' under floodlights giving them confidence.

It has been very difficult to cover each referee on a one to one basis, with the slow decline of membership at Leamington it will take a long time to implement the Mentor system but it may happen one day. The Retain and Retention is a programme that will have to wait until the Association has sufficient members to talk to the young referees, who have recently passed the Referees Examination. They have made no attempt to join the Association or to contact any of the members. Contact with the League Secretaries has been thought of to see if persuasion from them would give the new referees support to join the Association.

50 Years since the Association was reformed

This was the aim of the Committee that was set up to organise the event. Members visited various hotels seeking a reasonable venue. They finally finished at the Manor House Hotel Leamington where they negotiated a price for the meal and fixed a date for the event to take place. Although some doubts were expressed about the year, the Association was reformed in 1948. The committee decided to carry on with the March date in 1997, the hotel was booked and the menus were left till later on. The committee finally selected the guests for the event and they were invited..

A request was made to the Management Committee to see if the event could be subsidised by the Association. It was difficult to get an answer at first. The Treasurer was away on business, the Management suggested a temporary loan, which was acceptable to the Committee until the Treasurer was available. The figure that was finally agreed upon was £850 (eight hundred and fifty pounds) this allowed for the guests and a subsidy for members and wives or partners.
It was an excellent evening well organised, the only thing that marred it was lack of support from the members of the Association. Unfortunately one of the members had organised an event which had been arranged on the same evening as the Association held their dinner and quite a few of the members had made arrangements to attend that one.

Association Reports

Dennis Reynolds (Vice-President)

The first item on the Agenda was the passing of Dennis Reynolds, he passed away very suddenly and the President asked Members to stand for a moment to remember Dennis who was Secretary for a number of years. Dennis was also a Vice-President a position he cherished and he spent time on the Management Committee, he was a very busy person who gave great support to the Association in numerous ways, he will be missed. Representation was made at his funeral by the officers.

Ken Robertson

Ken Passed away very suddenly in hospital after suffering with cancer. Ken hadn't been in the Association very long but had made himself well liked by the members. He took time to help in the Charity Competitions and supported events that were organised. He enjoyed his refereeing and was keen to learn as much as he could, but Ken had spent a lot of his time supporting his son in local football. Taking up the whistle late in life, he was a decent referee and enjoyed the companionship with fellow referees

Ken was married and had an adult family. His funeral was represented by the Secretary and a colleague, the members stood for a minutes silence at the meeting.

Extra –Ordinary General Meeting

An extra ordinary general meeting was called to elect a new Chairman. The previous Chairman retiring due to business commitments. The members thanked John Mander for the year's service he had given. He was also thanked for his service as the 'Association Coach and Licensed Instructor'. The Secretary was asked to write to John thanking for his time and service.

The Vice-Chairman David Aston was nominated by Bill Burnell and seconded by Mick Lucey

This was accepted by all. Dave duly took over as the Chairman and carried on with the meeting. The Treasurer also resigned through pressure of work, he said his problem was travelling between America, Halifax and Leamington.

Six-a-Side 1998

A successful Six-a-Side was marred by players from one Society. The players showed an irresponsible attitude to the rules and teams from other Societies. Every issue was questioned with verbal dissent and one player was dismissed from the Competition. In his temper he kicked two footballs into the river, only one was recovered.

The players concerned were reported to the County Football Association and the society's attitude was reported to the Birmingham & Warwickshire Referees Committee. The Society would not be invited next year. It was suggested that we tighten up the rules of the Competition and make it difficult for players to spoil everyone's enjoyment.

Financially the event was a success and a reasonable amount will go to the referees Benevolent Fund with a donation going to the St Johns Ambulance Association.

One of the members who was at the Competition remarked on the incidents and said, how can they behave like that when we are supposed to be football referees and set an example.

The Six-a-Side for 1999 was discussed and the Management was not very happy with the Committee from Pottertons. The Secretary was asked to write to Pottertons with a suggested date for next year, and suggest that the £50 (pound) we paid up front be returned to the Association as there was no damage to the ground or equipment.

The reply we received from Pottertons only concerned the £50 (pounds) which they say was a deposit and non-returnable. The Management were very upset about this and letters were sent to the Committee at Pottertons. We never had a reply and we never had our £50(pounds) returned. Other venues were to be looked at for the 1999 Six-a- Side Competition. .

The Association applied to the Millennium Fund through the 'Sports for All' to see if it Leamington would be able to apply for new Equipment so that the Licensed Instructor would be able to coach candidates in a wider area. The information received back was to apply for a form complete it and return it to Birmingham.

This was done and the Association applied for an Overhead Projector, a movable and large Screen, a Television with a video attachment, and a Camera. The form was returned giving all the details and statement of the Accounts also a copy of the last Annual General Meeting and a CV from a reliable source (someone who could vet for us and knew what we were trying to achieve) fortunately a vicar who I had known for years supported our claim. We were successful so we went ahead and ordered the equipment, the money from the Fund arrived shortly afterwards. With a little hindsight we should have gone for a more elaborate system so the the Instructor would be able to coach and give lectures by using the equipment. At a later date the instructor John Sharp purchased the equipment he needed. From Association funds.

Cup Final Tickets Allocated for the 1998 F A Cup

Problems have arisen with the distribution of Tickets; some members felt aggrieved when the tickets were won by members who only attend the meeting to enter the draw. It was proposed that a method of fairer distribution be discussed or a new rule entered into the Association Rules.
At the Management the Chairman discussed a proposed rule for a fairer distribution of the Cup Final Tickets. The members discussed the alterations a few times before it became possible to place it before the next council meeting. An EGM would be called so that it would be operable for the 1999 Cup Final attendance at the meetings was the prime move in the new rule and members would be allocated points. It was also discussed and approved by the members at the council meeting.

The new Rule No 18 was put to the members at the EGM council meeting on October 26th 1998 and is as follows:-
Members wishing to apply for Football Association or League Cup Final Tickets must do so in writing to the Secretary on or before the AGM each year.
Depending on allocation, the tickets will be issued in pairs to the person whose name is drawn. They must use the tickets and abide by the Football Association and County Football Association regulations regarding the use of the tickets.
Tickets not used by the member whose name was drawn, must be returned to the person next in line.
Each fully paid up member will be entitled to one entry in the draw plus a further entry for each Council meeting attended during the preceding twelve months.
The proposal was discussed at the EGM and the voting was unanimous (16) for the proposal and with no abstentions.
The Rule is printed in the Association Rules

Restructuring of Class One (1) Referees

A motion was put to the Conference in 1978 and reproduced in 1998 and was supported by sufficient votes to ask Council to pursue, re-structuring the Classification of Class One or Grade One Referees after a period of 50 years since its inception.
This motion was put to both Conferences i.e. 1978 and 1998 by Harrow Society.
The dialogue that followed between the Council and the member who proposed the motion was as follows:
Such consideration will be no task to take lightly, but rest assured that a tremendous amount of thought will go into any suggestions that might eventually go to any governing body over referees.
The Football Association who, will listen and recommend when the time is ripe.
The Referees Association can recommend, but it cannot implement in matters like this one, and referees must remember this fact. It is cooperation that usually wins the day.

The Birmingham County Disciplinary Committee

The Birmingham &Warwickshire Joint Referees Committee held a meeting with the BCFA and the following items were discussed.

At personal hearings a separate entrance is required by referees, at the moment players and referees are in contact with each other. This is not very good for the referee, it was remarked that referees could easily be intimidated and threatened by a crowd of players in close proximity. One referee from Leamington complained about the lack of courtesy when arriving at the County Football Association.

He said his hearing was for 7 pm and not dealt with until 9.30 pm the same night. The officials who were there complained about the aggression from the players, although not all the players were involved. After the discussion at Management it was suggested that any referee who had to go to a personal hearing and wanted support would have to contact the Secretary and no junior referee would be allowed to travel alone. It was hoped that the County FA would find an answer to the problem. If they do not then you will find that referees will not be attending personal hearings and the players will get away without being punished

During the period between 1981 and 1999 the Association have had a variety of speakers, who have given the members different views and a majority were very interesting, some were humorous which the members enjoyed. In the past the speakers we have had, have just been mentioned in the minutes. It has always been difficult to give a report on the subject the Speaker has talked about. When the newsletter was being printed, giving a good report about the various speakers was made easier and all the members were able to benefit.

Speakers from 1990

Eric Jones

We did have Eric Jones from the FA Panel of Speakers, who give the Association a very interesting talk and his subject was Sex and the Referee. It was an exhausting night

Kieron Barratt

The Cup Final Referee was the speaker and as Kieron is a member of Coventry Referees he didn't have far to travel, his talk was really brilliant he told members how he started refereeing and the difference between refereeing in a Football Stadium and taking matches on the Memorial Park Coventry.

He also mentioned to members how he graduated through the feeder and contributory system and finally being placed on the Football League, the change was tremendous. The crowds were larger and more supportive to the teams that were playing, starting as a linesman soon made him feel at home and the support from the other colleague and referee helped him enormously once he had settled down a gradual move was made until he refereed on the league, possibly one match a month and progress was made and he eventually made the gradual move to refereeing the 'Cup Final.'

Crowd control by the use of Horses, Dogs, and Police Pressure were some of the items he talked about, fitness was another issue which eventually became a focal point for referees. After he refereed the Cup Final Kieron retired and is now involved with county matters.

We have had talks from various speakers during this period, Coaching and training, referees seminars for Class 2(two) and Class 3(three) Sports Injuries' they were all covered and they made interesting subjects to listen, also they were well presented.

Bobby Gould Coventry City Manager

Speakers have been beneficial to the Association giving the members interesting views on referees and football in general. Bobby Gould the Manager of Coventry City was one of the speakers who gave the members a very interesting talk on referee's and how he looked at the game the referee had and the type of mark he would have to give the particular referee. Whilst we respect the referee and appreciate what he does, it cannot be easy trying to control 22 players, as well as making sure the match is running smoothly. When we mark a referee it is left for a while so that we can assess him fairly and if an Assessor is at the ground, it makes our job a little harder, he went on to give the members a general talk on Managers job at a Club like Coventry where so many issues are in hand, he also talked about the players and their attitude to referees during a game or when the referee occasionally trained with them.

He emphasized the importance of being fit or obtaining the fitness required, the fitness difference between the players and a referee does depend on the amount of training that has been done, referees always seemed to build up stamina whilst that does apply to players they also build up the muscle strength so that kicking a ball and body movement are all in harmony.

Alan Seville

Another speaker was Alan Seville from Birmingham who is a Referee on the Football League, his talk was entirely different to the one from Bobby Gould,, Alan covered all the aspects of being a Referee on the League and talked to the members on the problems they could encounter if they reached that level, it could easily happen to any member who has the experience and is within the age group. Alan went on to talk about the Assessors who are at every match and send in reports on the game. They do come and talk to you, also you need a Mentor and I am fortunate enough to have a Birmingham colleague who has retired from refereeing and act's as my Mentor; he is very valuable to me.

This was another interesting talk by Alan and the members thoroughly enjoyed. After the meeting a few of the older members had a serious chat to Alan and told him we are trying to push our referees on to the senior leagues, it is not an easy job to do because the referees have to be motivated and concentrate on refereeing with preference for a Saturday   A general discussion on refereeing and football in general created a certain amount of interest between the members and Alan Seville, this put the seal on an excellent Evening

Ray Tennant Rugby League

Ray Tennant from Castleford who was a Rugby League Referee He was absolutely brilliant in covering every aspect of Rugby League and how they referee the games, and the respect they get from the players, we probably do not make the mistakes that football referees do, because we have a little more time to give a decision and it has to be right. He also gave the members a general talk on the way the referees are promoted and in a majority of cases it is the way you handle various games, you are then moved up the ladder, until you referee the top teams. If you make a mistake you go back down the ladder until the committee are quite happy about your refereeing. We have to remember there is a lot more physical contact in Rugby League, the players are fit and you have to be as fit as them. There is no way we would accept the stick you referees get from players every match. The members enjoyed his talk and showed their appreciation of his visit to Leamington.

Steve Allatt (F A speaker)

In the October we had an excellent speaker in Steve Allatt who put this Question to the members when he started his talk by asking them   'What makes a good Referee?'

His answer was basically what is required from referees looking for promotion. He continued talking about promotion and said the requirements for promotion are really what is required at all times from all referees. Everyone was able to benefit from what Steve has told us. Steve continued with the following: with-knowledge linked to personality and external factors. So what knowledge is needed? We need knowledge of: the Law, Competitions (competition rules), Use of the Whistle, Advantage, Position, Application of Discipline, Players, Patterns of play, and finally Commitment which is essential. In as much we must make ourselves available.

We must be physically fit, we must adhere to correspondence we must be punctual and with good appearance.

What external factors might affect our careers in refereeing? The following are Steve's views, Assessors, Travel, Club Officials, Appearance and Expectations

"Referees have to be AN authority and IN authority."

Also "As is our confidence, so is our capacity.

Membership

We are gradually moving into the latter part of the 20th Century and over the years we have seen a fluctuation of membership, at one point rising to 70 (seventy) plus membership and gradually dropping down to a low figure of 30 (thirty). Each year we build up the membership through coaching, with candidates taking the referees examination and passing. They attend the first meeting and receive the referees badge which they wear on their referees kit, when the older members talk to them they all say yes we will join and come to the meetings. It is usually the last time we see them, until they go out refereeing and causing problems by not applying the 'Laws of Association Football' properly

Gerald Ashby (Football League Referee)

In January we were privileged to have the Premiership Referee Gerald Ashby as the Speaker and in his opening remarks, he spoke of the number of years he has been refereeing and the fitness he achieved mostly through playing football. When he took up refereeing he said he

was determined to reach the Nationwide League. He told the members he did not realise how hard it would be and how hard it is to stay there. He went on to say, to get the best out of refereeing you must not shirk a duty, always stand up and be counted. Above all never blame anyone for a mistake but always look for the reason for it. He went on to talk about his illness, how it affected his breathing and the trouble he had to get back to full fitness.

In talking about the media response to refereeing decisions, Gerald said that Sky TV on a majority of grounds have at least 24 Cameras giving every possible view of an incident. He gave the members a talk on how to treat the Media also doubtful pitches in inclement weather. If you are not happy to play then don't, remember you are responsible for the safety of every player. After his talk the Chairman thanked Gerald for coming to Leamington to talk to the members and presented him with a gift from the Association.

Speaker Arthur Jones

At the May meeting Arthur Jones from the Football Association was the guest speaker. He was introduced to the members and his talk which lasted nearly two hours was very interesting. He covered every aspect of refereeing, from being newly qualified, with the problems they are most likely to encounter. A majority of Associations or Societies use the Mentor system this is to keep a check on the young member and to give him advice when he requires it. Once they get settled in they then seek assessments, so they can apply for promotion, it is advisable to keep the young referee on the move by varying the type of games he referees. When they move into a higher category the confidence shows through.

Arthur carried on with his talk about the referees who referee on the Football League. How they are assessed, the methods they used to get fit and keep fit and the lessons they learn by watching other referees, also talking about the problems they encounter. It was a very comprehensive talk on referees and the members at the meeting showed their appreciation. Arthur Jones was presented with engraved glassware and thanked for coming to Leamington.

Speakers for 1998/1999 were Alan Jones and Dermott Gallagher

Speakers for the latter end of 1998 were **Alan Jones Secretary of Birmingham City FC** and Dermott Gallagher. Both speakers gave the members two different views on Football. With Alan Jones we obtained knowledge on how a large Club like Birmingham City are organised with different people doing work within the Club. They all know their job and enjoy

Promoting the Club to the public, everyone from the person selling tea and sandwiches, to the Board of Directors are involved with the finances. Alan said "every avenue that involves people within the Club is part of my job." I keep records of every meeting and discussion that takes place. He also went on to say everyone from the Chairman down to the stewards worked for the benefit of the Club

It was a very enjoyable talk from Alan Jones, he was thanked for coming to Leamington and a gift of glassware was presented to him.

Dermott Gallagher Football Premier League Referee

Dermott was another speaker who gave the members an excellent talk. It wasn't the first time he had been to Leamington. The previous time was when the Premier League had just started. Dermott was one of the young fast moving referees who had been placed on the League. Dermott did not disappoint the members with has talk, we had a few youngsters who had only recently passed the referees exam; he included these youngsters in everything he was talking about. He told every one he had travelled over 400 miles that day and still had to travel back to his home in Oxford

After a few jokes the session with Dermott turned into a question and answer session which every one enjoyed, he also told us his other pastime was Cricket. He related a story concerning a Charity Cricket match he was involved in when he ran out a top class International for three runs; he said he was not very popular after that.

He told us a story about the 4th Official in a Local Cup Final who was doing the job for the first time. One of his jobs was to collect all the Footballs and put them in the net. He did that and stored them away. Before he started the game Dermott signalled to the official to let him have one of the balls, he said every time I signalled to him he just waved back, in the finish he had to go to him and tell that he wanted a ball to play with. Before he finished he told the members about refereeing on the Premier League and its requirements, the main factors being confidence, dedication, fitness, and a fair and honest application to the Laws of Association Football.. When Dermot had finished we asked him to present to the young Referees their Certificates. He was thanked for an excellent talk and presented with a gift of Crystal Goblets.

A Visit to Loughborough Referees Association

In the November of 1999 the Association had an invitation from Roger Smith Secretary of Loughborough Referees to attend their Monthly Meeting to listen to Peter Willis ho was the National Association's President. The invitation was accepted and a few of the Members went to listen to Peter Willis.

In 1986 Peter Willis came to a Council meeting with colleagues from Coventry to give the members of Leamington a talk as the President of the National Association. The evening was very successful. His talk covered a wide variety of events and included his career as a Referee. The talk he gave to the members and guests at Loughborough was very similar in context to the one at Leamington, so rather than having two similar stories they have been built into one.

Whilst this is not a part of events at Leamington, we have always had good relationships with other Associations and the opportunity to visit was always welcomed and this invitation was a special one for a special event.

The President of the National Referees Association had travelled down from Durham so any opportunity to listen to him talk, we knew would be interesting.

His talk started with the way he became a referee and how he was able to be prompt in replying to the Football League Secretaries in the area where he lived. Being a policeman and working on nights was a boon, the replies were always returned prompt and he said he was always available to do mid-week games. Peter eventually reached the Football League status and Refereed the FA Cup Final.

As President he talked about the meetings he has been having with the Football Association and the impact FIFA are having on referees how they are selected for International duty.

The selection starts in January and out of 30,000 referees only 9(nine) are selected from this Country. He did not say whether they were all members of the Referees Association.

Fitness is very important to referees on the Premier list and on FIFA if a referee fails the tests he is put back to the Conference to continue his refereeing. This gives the referee the opportunity to work their way back to the Premier via the National League. Fitness is very important, so is age. If you are mid 30 (thirties) and pass all tests and are selected it is a ticket to paradise.

The President continued with referees at the top end of the system. We use all sorts of short cuts with appointments, to get to the top you have to be noticed, be prompt in replying to correspondence, when you arrive at the ground be pleasant, make sure the Secretary sees you examining the nets and the Field of Play, work hard and always seek

Promotion. In general have a good knowledge of the 'Laws of Association Football'.

He talked about the 'Referees Kit' which should always be immaculate, dirty kit loses marks. He told members never apologise for sending someone from the field of play and finished his talk with a few amusing stories. He then informed the members that he has enjoyed being, 'President of the Referees Association' it is a hard job but enjoyable.

Peter then talked to them members about the problems within the Referees Association, especially the issue with the Income Tax (V A T) and the way it was solved.(his letter to all Associations is printed in this chapter 1992) Other issues were mentioned concerning the move to change the status of all referees, being considered at Football Association level. There were other issues briefly mentioned.

The evening was a success and as far as the members from Leamington were concerned it was also enjoyable. An excellent Buffet was laid on by Loughborough which every one enjoyed, they are very fortunate as an Association because all their meetings and speakers even the Buffet for the members and guests are covered by sponsors.

Whilst a list of important issues was taking the Association into the 21st[st]Century, and the Millennium, we have to look at the past Century and assess the improvements that have been made to referees and the game of Football. The game has improved and skilful players are parading their skills every Saturday and Sunday and millions of people through the Television could watch the best sportsmen perform, the youth of today are being coached and encouraged to practice and train to become better players, the opportunity for all is there to be taken.

By the same token we could say that about referees, encouragement is the main word and referees are being coached by qualified instructors. The age group is gradually coming down to accommodate the young vibrant referee, fitness and knowledge is very important to every referee. So its goodbye to the past and a lot of people say the, "Good old Days." In the past sport was the mainstay of the older generation, who went and watched the various sports, it was football, rugby, horse racing or greyhounds. If they had a radio they listened to the major sporting events that took place. When Television came into being, it became another world to the older generation who could watch horseracing, golf and other sports even if it was in black and white.

The end of 1999

This is the end of the 1981 to 1999 decades and really it is the end of the 20th Century, what will the 21st Century hold for every one?. We realise that there will be changes in football and refereeing all we can hope for is that things will get better. It really is the 'FUTURE' we have to look fo rward to and the way movement is being made it has to be the Referee who will benefit. The final Chapters will no doubt explain it all..

Chapter 15

Rules of the Association from 1928 to the present 2006

Association and Societies, have Rules to govern how the Association is controlled and to make sure the finances are sound and in good hands. They also set out the aims and objects of such an organisation, the Constitution, Election of Officers, Management
Committee meeting times and dates, and rules governing the general behaviour of members within the Association

In Leamington the first set of rules was printed in book form in 1928, and they will be printed below. No doubt we shall find that various rule alterations will have been added over the years.

Leamington &District Referees' Association

Rules

Adopted by General Meeting June 1928

Rules

1. That the name of the organisation shall be the Leamington & District Referees' Association
2. The aims and objects shall be the education, development, and training of men to qualify as Association Football Referees, the study of football law and its application with the view to common interpretation and acquiescence, for the guidance of officials, and for the efficient government of the game for the well being, protection, and advancement of its members, and to carry out any other policy which is incidental or conducive to the attainment of the aims and objects.
3. That the officers shall consist of President, Chairman, Vice-Chairman, Treasurer, two Auditors, Secretary, and one other member, the whole of whom shall retire annually, but who shall be eligible for re-election.
4. The subscription shall be 4/-(four shillings) per annum and this shall ,unless otherwise agreed, include Affiliation to the National Referees' Association
5. Qualification for membership- Referees who have been examined and registered with the Football Association shall be eligible, subject to the approval of the Association in full General Meeting; also past Referees under the same conditions. The Association reserves the right to determine the membership of any member deemed guilty of conduct likely to reflect discredit upon them, shall deal with any such member as they think fit.

6. General Meetings shall be held once a month, at such time and place as shall be prescribe by the members in full General Meeting, or in default, by the officers of the Association.

7. The officers may whenever they think fit and shall, on a requisition made in writing by eight or more members convene an Extraordinary General Meeting, such requisition stating the objects thereof.

8. Any business may be transacted at an ordinary General Meeting, excepting the consideration of the accounts, balance sheet, annual report of the election of officers

9. No business may be transacted unless a quorum of members is present at the commencement. Six shall form a quorum

10. In the case of equality votes, whether on a show of hands or on a poll, the Chairman of the meeting shall be entitled to a second or casting vote.

11. Members failing to forward an apology to the Secretary for non attendance at monthly meetings shall be fined 3d

12. The number of officers, and the nature of their office, shall be determined at the Annual Meeting September 20th

13. No member shall be entitled to vote at any meeting unless all money due from him to the Association has been paid. A time limit shall be fixed for payment, and this rule shall operate immediately following the expiry of such time limit

14. Any Referee receiving an appointment and being unable to accept it shall at once notify the Secretary, who can then appoint a substitute. In no case shall any referee be allowed to appoint another referee to take his match.

15. The members of the Association present at a general monthly meeting shall be at liberty to discuss any matter (subject to Rule 8) relating to the aims and objects of the Association, or arising out of the Annual Report, but notice of any special business must be given in writing seven clear days before the date of meeting.

16. Each member shall receive seven days notice of Annual Meeting, also a copy of statements of accounts.

With the Rules laid out in such form. There must have been a record of the events that took place, even the minutes of that particular time. Items concerning rule changes would have been recorded. Whether any Rule changes were made, between 1928 and the 1931 period it doesn't say yet in 1932 a rule change was made when the Subscription Rule 4 was reduced from 6/6(six shillings & sixpence) to 5/-(five shillings). Rule alterations in 1932 also gave the date in which members had to pay or be in default was changed from September to October. In 1934 Rule 4 was altered to read that Subscriptions shall be 4/-(four shillings) per annum.

In 1935 a new Rule book was printed and the various Rules; 6,10,12,13 were altered, the alterations concerned a change of Meeting night. Equality of Voting with the Chairman having a casting vote; any Officer in default with the Association will not be able to vote or hold office whilst they are in debt. Whether the Rule Books were distributed amongst the members we are not sure, it is more than likely they were.

There were no alterations until 1948 when the Association was reformed and a separate meeting was set up to discuss the Rules and possible alterations. On looking at the 1948 Rule book which was printed after the special meeting and comparing it
with the 1928 book, very little change was made, just a change of dates or words, Rule 5, 'Probationers was added,' the fine for non attendance at monthly meeting was increased from 3d to 6d (three pence to sixpence) and the Annual General meeting date was changed from September to May.

A general browse through the Annual General minutes up to 1950 showed no change at all, one item stood out when reading the Rules and that was Rule 3 where in 1928 it
Says after Secretary, 'one other member' in 1948 the same wording was used. We know it changed after 1952, because Social Members were elected and in 1955.

The elected Management members and the two Social elected members worked together as a team and they eventually   became Management members.
Between 1952 and 1960 records were lost, so we had to presume that no changes took place. Members that were in the Association cannot remember any rule changes. So we move on to the 1960's where minutes and records have been kept.

This period in the Association was interesting and the younger members spent some time looking at the rules seeking changes. A majority of the changes were through the rules and the way they were set up

At the Annual General Meeting in 1964, a complete new set of Rules was proposed and seconded by one of the younger members. Each motion was clearly laid out, and every one was thoroughly discussed, they were voted on and accepted, except an amendment to Rule 5(five). This was a case where the Chairman and Secretary were given plenary powers to act for the members in an emergency. It was proposed and seconded that the amendment be carried; the voting was in favour with three dissenters. The main item in the Rule changes was the addition of a Meetings Organiser. The members who had moved the previous rule additions were very quick to have the following proposition added to the Association Rules.

It made sense to have it implemented, providing it would be used, the new amendment was as follows:
The Officers of the Association to be elected, by a secret ballot, in writing if a ballot is necessary This was added to the Rule along with a new section of Rule 9, stating that the business be restricted to30 minutes unless a motion be carried to extend the time for matters of great importance, it follows with the statement, the remaining time shall be devoted to activities by the meeting Organiser. The following year 1965 another Rule alteration was proposed and seconded by the same members as previous years. This was an Amendment to Rule 5, concerning officers in default, an Extra- ordinary General Meeting to be held as soon as convenient after October 1st. If a ballot is required it shall be in writing and in secret.
After a brief spell from Rule alterations, the next one came in 1967 when the Treasurer with the support from the Management requested the Financial Year ended on the 31st March every year. This was carried and duly entered in the Rules.
Another change of Rule came in 1968 after the Annual General Meeting was adjourned because of a tied vote for the Chairmanship of the Association. The meeting was held on the 24th May 1968, and the adjourned Annual General meeting was held on June 14th 1968, both meetings were held at the Warwickshire Farmers Club. The Secretary told the members present the reasons why the Extra Meeting was being called, and introduced the President George Dutton to the members.

The President suggested that when the rule alterations are reached we should make sure all eventualities are covered. The members accepted the Presidents advice.
It was proposed and seconded that Rule 5 be as follows. "The Chairman and Vice-Chairman to hold office for a maximum of 3 years if elected at the A.G.M."; Rules 4 6 7 and 8 were subject to a word alteration. Rule 15 was altered to allow Management to

deal with any matter not covered by the Rules. All the rules were accepted and eventually a Rule book was produced for the members at a later date.

Subscriptions were responsible for the Rule changes in 1973. When a proposition was moved, to increase the Membership Fee to £1.30 (one pound thirty pence), this was to include affiliation to the National Referees Association.

A counter proposal was submitted and accepted as an amendment, this was to increase the Subscriptions to £3.00 (three pounds). The proposer and seconder gave the reasons why they were asking for a large increase. This was to cover expenditure and the fact that non-active members are being subsidised. When the voting had taken place the amendment was defeated and the original proposition was carried by a majority vote. We again had members abstain from voting, which is a disturbing factor.

At the next Annual General Meeting further Rule alterations were submitted, this concerned Rule3 nominations for Office and Management. It is being proposed we use ballot forms for all Officers including Management. These forms to be sent to Vice-Presidents, Life –Members and paid up members 14 days before the A.G.M. then returned to the Secretary sealed before the meeting. These forms would be distributed with all other documents and an S.A.E.

The whole Rule change could not be satisfactorily resolved, even after a long discussion. It was finally suggested we call an Extra Ordinary Meeting to take place before the August Council Meeting.

This Meeting took place as requested with 14 members attending. All the major points were put forward and after a lengthy discussion, the Chairman asked the members to vote, either in favour of the amendment or against. This was done buy a show of hands. Voting for the Rule alterations was defeated with only 3 (three) votes for the amendment, and 8(eight) against the amendment, with 3 (three) members abstaining
All other items from the Rule Alterations were voted on and accepted, this included Rule 8 and 12, which covered a quorum for Council meeting from 6 (six) members to 10 (ten) and at Annual General Meetings increasing the number of members from 8 (eight) to 12 (twelve). It was suggested the Association needed to print and distribute new Rule books to the members.

In 1977 an addition to Rule 5 was proposed concerning Management members who fail to attend three consecutive meetings without a written apology shall be deemed not to be a member of Management. Another change was Rule 6 to be deleted and re-written, this concerned "Subscriptions, Affiliations and Capitation Fees, Probationer Referees joining before 31st December and new Referees joining after December".
An amendment that Coaching Fees should cover membership of the Association was defeated. The original was amended to include a rider that subscriptions be paid before being coached. This was carried.
An additional Rule was added in 1983. The new Rule concerned Delegates representing the Association when attending meetings where travelling is involved, such as the Birmingham & Warwickshire J R C C. Expenses to be claimed

The Officers and Management members seemed to be very keen to have a change of rule each year. In 1983 a new Rule was added and now in 1984 we have changes which should strengthen the Association Rules. Words were being deleted and one rule was re-written. They are as follows.

Rule 2 (delete), "and Acquiescence for the guidance of officials and for the efficient government of the game".

Rule 4 (delete) next and add "ratification after approval".

Rule 6 (delete completely) add new Rule. "The Subscriptions for the following season shall be determined at the A.G.M. and shall include monies payable to the National Referees' Association. Referees joining the Association for the first time after January 1st shall subscribe 50% of the Annual Fee.

Subscriptions should be paid at the A.G.M or before the commencement of the following season. Junior & youth referees shall be as follows under 17 years old pay 25% of Subscription under 19years old 50% of Subscription. Other Rules were just a change of numbers.

We had a quiet spell between 1984 and 1989/90 when various Rules were changed. Rule 3 Management members were reduced from 5 to 3 (three). An amendment to increase was defeated.

Rule 4   Line 2 (two) which says five members present. This was reduced to three and one must be an Officer.

Rule 6 (delete) all juniors and youth members; The Annual Subscriptions, up to the age of 18 years old, shall pay 50% of the Annual Subscriptions.

In the 1990's we had three or four Rule alterations and new rules admitted which were essential to the well being of the Association.

The first on was in 1995 when we were at the Liberal Club holding the Annual General Meeting. It was a completely new Rule and called Rule 18, the wording is as Follows;"The Association shall reserve the right to refuse membership or expel from membership any member found guilty of conduct Prejudicial to the Association".

The next rule alteration came about in 1997, as a recommendation from the Midland Division. The Rule was an addition to Rule 11. It concerned any person or persons refused membership, giving them the right to appeal within a certain time. The issue to be heard by the Management Committee, an independent adviser may be invited to the Meeting. Quite a few of the members at that meeting were not happy with the intrusion considering throughout the whole issue we had always maintained we were correct in our dealings and within the framework of the Association rules.

In 1998 a new rule was added to the Association Rules and called Rule19, this time it concerned the Allocation of tickets to the various, "Football Association or League Cup Finals", so that everyone had a fair bite of the cherry, providing they were fully paid up members and had attended monthly meetings.

The latest one to be placed on record was concerning the finances of the Association. Through careful prudence by the Treasurers over the years the Association is financially sound although not rich and concern was expressed over the lack of support we are getting at Council Meetings whether we have speakers or not. A Rule was set up covering all the points of this issue. It was decided to bring into play Three Trustees who would be responsible for the finances and the distribution of funds that have accrued; to protect them from any situation where the Association could be dissolved. The Trustees were elected Two from the Vice- Presidents, and the current Treasurer.

The proposal of this Rule 20 was accepted by the members and the three proposed Trustees were written to and acceptance was given at the August meeting 2002. At the same time a new position was set up for a Membership Secretary. This was proposed and seconded and added to Rule 3(three).

That was the extent of rule changes and additions until the A.G.M. 2006.
At the beginning you had the Rules from 1928 to finish herewith the Rules for 2005 printed below.

Leamington &District Referees Association

Rules

Altered and Amended at the Annual General Meeting February 25th 2002

1. **The name of the organisation shall be the Leamington &District Referees Association.**

2. **The aims and objectives shall be the education, development and training of persons who qualify or wish to qualify as association football Referees. The study of football law and its application, with a view to common interpretation, for the well being, protection and advancement of its members and to carry out other policy which is incidental to its attainment of the aims and objectives.**

3. **The officers of the Association shall be a President, Vice-President, Chairman, Vice-Chairman, Secretary, Assistant Secretary, Treasurer, Membership Secretary, and 5(Five) Management Members. All are elected annually at the Annual General Meeting.**

4. **The Chairman, Vice-Chairman, Secretary and Treasurer will be ex-officio members of the Management Committee. The Committee will not act with less than three members present. In an emergency, the Chairman and/or Secretary have the power to act for the Association and report to the Management Committee for their ratification.**

5. **No member shall be entitled to vote at any Management or Monthly Meeting, or to represent the Association at any official function unless all money due from him to the Association has been paid. A member will be considered to be in default of this rule if subscriptions have not been paid by 31st March. Anyone not paying by that date will be deemed in default and providing due notice is given, may be liable to a further £1.00 (one-pound) administration charge, Should any officer be in default, he shall be replaced at an extra- ordinary general meeting to be called as soon as convenient after 1st April.**

6. The subscription for the following season shall be determined at the A.G.M. and shall include monies payable to the National Referees Association. Referees joining the Association for the first time after 1st October shall subscribe the monies payable to the National Referees Association, plus an administrative fee of £2.00(two- pounds). Subscriptions should be paid at the A.G.M. or before the commencement of the following season. Subscriptions payable for those under 18 years of age on 1st January shall be a sum equal to 70% of the Subscription.

7. The Honorary Treasurer shall prepare annually a detailed statement of accounts up to 31st December of that season; which shall be submitted to the Auditors. Each member will receive a copy of such accounts seven days prior to the A.G.M.

8. The A.G.M. shall take place during the month of February and each member shall receive at least seven days notice of such a meeting. No business shall be transacted unless a total of 12 members are present.

9. The A.G.M. shall be presided over by the President or in his absence a Vice-President. If neither is available, the members shall elect a Chairman who will have for the A.G.M. all the powers, duties and privileges attached to the office of Chairman in the conduct of such a meeting.

10. In the case of an equality of votes whether on the show of hands or on a poll, the Chairman of the A.G.M, management, or monthly meeting shall be entitled to a second or casting vote.

11. Qualification for Membership. Referees who have been examined, and registered with the Football Association. Probationers shall be eligible to the approval of the Association in a full general meeting, and past Referees under the same conditions. The Association reserves the right to determine the membership of any member. Deemed guilty of conduct likely to reflect discredit upon them, and shall deal with any such member as they think fit. Any persons refused membership will be informed of the reason why. The person will then be given the right to appeal within 28days of being notified of the refusal. Any appeal. will be heard by members of the management committee, who in turn may invite an independent observer

12. General Meetings shall be held once a month at such a time as shall be prescribed by the members at a full general meeting, or in default by the officers of the Association. No business shall be transacted unless a quorum of members is present at the commencement. Ten shall form a quorum. Business at the meeting shall be restricted to thirty minutes, unless a motion is carried at the meeting to extend the time for matters of great importance to the Association. The remaining time shall be devoted to activities arranged by the Management Committee

13. The officers may, whenever they think fit and shall on requisition made in writing by eight or more member. Convene an extra-ordinary general meeting, such a requisition stating the objectives thereof.

14. Notice of any proposed alteration of rules must be made in writing at the monthly meeting prior to the A.G.M.

15. Any Officer or Management member not attending three consecutive meeting will be automatically removed from the Committee. Subject to the discretion of the members.

16. Delegates to the Birmingham & Warwickshire J.C.C. and any other representative bodies shall be entitled to reimbursement of travelling expenses as the Management Committee deems fit

17. The Management Committee is empowered to deal with any matters or item that is not covered by the rules as they think fit

18. The Association shall reserve the right to refuse membership or expel from membership any member found guilty of conduct prejudicial to the Association.

19. Members wishing to apply for F.A or League Cup Final tickets must do so in writing to the Secretary on or before the A.G.M each year. Depending on allocation. The tickets will be issued in pairs and the member(s) whose name is drawn to receive tickets must use the tickets for him/herself and their immediate family or friends. As well as abiding by the Football Association and Birmingham County regulations regarding the use of Cup Final tickets.
Tickets that cannot be used by the member(s) whose name is drawn, must be returned immediately to the Secretary, who will in turn, issue
them to the member who was the next one to be drawn. Each fully paid up member of the Association will be entitled to one entry in the draw and a further entry for each Council Meeting attended during the preceding twelve months, Members will be allowed a maximum of two tickets. The draw will take place at the first Council Meeting after the ticket allocation has been confirmed. (EGM 26thOctober1998)

20 Dissolution

If at a Meeting of the Association(of which each member has been given at least seven days notice) a majority of the members attending the meeting vote in favour of dissolution of the Association, the Association shall be (automatically)dissolved forthwith.
In the event that the Association is dissolved, the funds of the Association will vest in 3(three) Trustees namely the persons who hold office as Vice-Presidents, and Treasurer at the time of the dissolution. The funds of the Association shall be transferred into the names of the Trustees immediately upon dissolution of the Association.

The Trustees will have the sole power to decide on the timing and distribution of these funds, including the power to distribute part only of the funds. Providing always that any such distribution will be for charitable purposes only.

The names of the Trustees are: A J Engel   Esq. Vice-President
P   Wright   Esq. Vice-President
R   Morgan Esq. Treasurer

Annual General Meeting February 2002

This is the extent of the Association Rules up to the year 2006.

Chapter 16

Football Referees
From 1921 to 2006

This Chapter covers the Referees from 1921 to 2006, from the time they joined the Association, the level of refereeing they attained and the benefits the Association received from them as members

It will be impossible to mention every referee who took the Referees Examination due to minutes being lost, minutes too abbreviated. It is possible for members who have been in the Association not to have had their names mentioned; this was due to lack of information given to the Secretary of that particular era.

The Referees mentioned in the first part would have been refereeing before the Association was formed, when appointments to matches were either from the local League or through an approach from the clubs. It was only when the Referees formed their Association that appointments were organised.

When the Leamington & District Referees Association was formed in 1921, a majority of the referees were officiating in local Football. The first Secretary said it was difficult to get all the referees together to form an Association. We considered that we would be in a better position to talk to the County Football Association and the Football Leagues in the area. Whilst we were never going to be a large Association, we should be able to communicate with everyone as a complete unit. We could also make sure that Fees and Expenses are spread evenly among the clubs and the referees get better treatment and make sure the local football matches were covered. It is my intention to cover the Referees who have officiated on the Football League either as a Referee or as a Linesman and from there to mention members who have not reached that standard, but have contributed so much to the Association and they are still officiating at a very high standard in Senior Football. Once that has been completed, it is intended to mention the referees who have joined the Association since 1948 and give a brief resume of the standard of refereeing they reached and the service they gave to the Association. This then will give a continuity of membership from 1921 to 2006. It has been my privilege to having known a large majority of the referees being mentioned.

We have been fortunate in having members who were officiating before 1939 and they continued through the war years. When the Association was reformed in 1948 these members continued to do so for a number of years which helped the Association.

George Dutton and John Wildsmith started refereeing in the 1920s and they both reached the Football League before the War and continued refereeing until 1949 when they both retired. The service these two members gave to the Association is well documented. They looked after the referees and kept the Association moving along and at the same time made sure they were fairly treated by the Leagues in the area.

We had two colleagues who also gave tremendous support especially to junior referees. They were members before the War and refereed during the hostilities and continued after the War until they retired, the members were Jack Joyner and Charlie Jackson.

At one time the retiring age for Referees and Linesman on the Football League was 47 years. In some cases where a referee was exceptionally fit he as allowed to carry on until he was 50 years old, the age was eventually reduced to 45 which I believe is the same now. Removing referees from the League list is not an easy option for the League Secretary. A majority of referees who seek and are keen to obtain promotion to Senior Leagues have to be in a certain age bracket. If they reach that age, they are usually informed the reason why they have been removed.

Quite a number of referees are happy to referee locally and pass on the experience they have gained to other referees and they are just as happy to act as Assistant Referees on Senior Leagues. This is a big help to any Football League Secretary when he knows he has experienced officials to call on.

In this chapter, the Referees who have officiated on the Football League will be mentioned with brief resume of their activities within the Association and their service to refereeing.

Following on from the 'Football League Referees.' we will be highlighting the referees who have reached a standard equivalent to the Semi-Professional Leagues and given great service to the Association.
From there on the referees who have been involved with the Association without actually holding a position will be mentioned by name. After that referees will be listed as and when they joined the Association.

Charlie Jackson and Tom Storey

George Pankhurst and Alex Walters

John Sollis and Lionel Fleet

John Wildsmith and George Dutton.

Football League Referees

George Dutton
John Wildsmith
George Pankhurst
John Jays
Geoff Perks
Alex Walters
Peter Watson
John Sollis
Lionel Fleet
Eddie Durant

George Dutton

George Dutton was born in Stoke in 1895, he then moved to Coventry to work as an Insurance Agent

He eventually moved to Warwick with Mrs Dutton before the War and lived in Emscote.

When his wife passed away after a short illness, he eventually married Mrs Miles in his latter years.

George Dutton started refereeing in Leamington in the 1920 period and refereed on the Local Football League and the Coventry & North Warwickshire League. He became Chairman of the Leamington Referees Association in 1926 holding that office until 1933, he then served on the Management Committee.

George was made a 'Life Member of Leamington & District Referees Association in 1936' and received an 'Inscribed Mantle Clock' from the members. He then became Secretary to the Leamington and District Saturday Football League.

In the late 1920s and early 1930's George was placed on the Football League as a Linesman, having refereed on the Birmingham Combination.

In 1929 he refereed an Amateur Cup Match between Malvern FC and Hallam FC. In 1936 he was appointed as a Referee on the Football League at the same time the Birmingham County FA

Gave George the Final of the Senior Challenge Cup. This was between Hednesford Town v Burton Town with Hednesford winning 3-1. He also received a Football Association Cup Appointment at Bath at the beginning of the 1936/37 season.

In 1937 George received an appointment as Linesman in the 1937 Football Association Cup Final, between Preston North End FC v Sunderland F C with Sunderland winning 3-1. He was

Chosen to Referee the League War Cup Final at Wembley in 1940. In 1942 The Football League decided to let the Football League Clubs gradually start playing again. George Dutton was appointed to arrange fixtures for the Professional Teams and the Referees and Linesmen in the area were placed on the list. In all probability he would have refereed one or two of the games.

Whilst he was working in Coventry he became involved with Coventry Referees and during the War coached and advised candidates to become referees, they were also examined in Coventry.

In 1946 he achieved National fame when he refereed at the Bolton Disaster, the match between Bolton Wanderers v Stoke City at Burnden Park on the 9th March 1946. It was the "Football Association Challenge Cup." When this episode occurred, the Referee George Dutton made headlines in all the National newspapers, even the local Courier printed the story. The following is what was printed: "Councillor George Dutton of Warwick has been prominently in the news this week. As the Referee of the Bolton Wanderers and Stoke City cup-tie he was called upon to make one of the hardest decisions of his career when the crash barriers collapsed and 33 people were killed at Burnden Park on Saturday.

It was the worst disaster in Football history. The crowd present numbered 65,000 and after stopping play because they had encroached on the pitch. Councillor Dutton decided to restart the game. At first his action evoked harsh criticism in Sunday newspapers. These were later modified.

"Since speaking to officials and police, I have changed my mind" said the Vicar and Rural Dean of Bolton (Canon Davidson). "It now seems that to play on was the best way of avoiding what might have been a nasty panic". Mr T H Hubard honorary treasurer of the FA said, "I am sure it was the wiser course to carry on. If the game had been stopped there might have been rioting and complete loss of control." An official enquiry into the incident has been ordered, and in these circumstances Councillor Dutton has properly refrained from commenting on his action."

He Refereed an International Match in 1947, as well as receiving Cup Appointments George refereed at many of the top, Football Stadiums. He was always talking about the Gunners and when you walk through the Gates you know you have reached the top. In one of his talks he said his journey always seemed to take him to Manchester and places North such as Newcastle.

He finally retired from the Football League in 1949/ 1950 season and continued giving his service to the Referees Association. He was made President of the Association in 1965 a position he enjoyed.

George was Chairman of the Warwickshire Combination and became Secretary on the formation of the West Midland Regional Football League retiring in 1961. He was also Secretary of the Hospital Charity Cup Competition raising money for the Warneford Hospital Leamington. He was also involved with the Football Association where he became the Chairman of the Amateur Cup Competition.

George was on the Birmingham County Football Association and eventually became the Chairman from 1955 until 1970. From there he became a Councillor to the Football Association until 1976. George passed away in Warwick Hospital after a short Illness on February 25th 1976

John Wildsmith

John Wildsmith was born on September 22nd 1900 and lived on the Radford Road, Leamington. In 1934 he Married Miss Molly Christine Dickins at Lillington Church and they had three daughters, June, Christine, and Margaret.

He went to Clapham Terrace School Leamington. When he was 12 years old, he saved the life of a young lad named Frost from drowning in the Canal. He received the Royal Humane Society Award.

Just before his 18th Birthday he applied to join the Royal Flying Service, as Cadet J E Wildsmith. He was demobilised on cessation of hostilities, before receiving any instructions in flying. His demob date was the 17th December 1918.

John Wildsmith worked in the Family business, of Wildsmith & Sons 40 Court Street Leamington. A Master Baker, specialising in pork pies, He expanded the outside catering side of the business, catering for many of the Civic Receptions held at the Town Hall.

He also catered for Field Marshall Montgomery and Anthony Eden (MP) when they were made Honorary Freeman of the Borough of Leamington and numerous functions at Warwick Castle.

In one of his spare moments he sold ice-creams and teas from a punt on the River Leam. In 1928 he attempted to save the life of a Mr Winyard from the river Mr Winyard was drowned. It was another brave attempt by John Wildsmith.

In the Sporting World John Wildsmith played as a goalkeeper and played for various teams in Leamington. Teams like Leamington All Saints FC, St Mary's FC, Flavels FC and finally Leamington Thursday FC. He was also considered as the best goalkeeper in Leamington and reports on one Cup-Final he played in the newspaper report was to that effect.

He became a referee in the early part of the 1920s. Joining Leamington & District Referees Association. In 1926 he became Secretary and held it until 1934.

In 1932-33 Season he was placed on the List of the, 'Midland Mid-Week Football League' as a Referee. He was placed as a Linesman on the Football League in 1930 and he is mentioned in the 1939-40, Football League Hand Book.

By this time he was well established on the Football League having reached the Standard required through refereeing on the 'Birmingham Combination' and on the local Leagues.

Plum appointments came the way of John Wildsmith, with War Cup qualifying matches. He was given a Linesman position in the 1939 League Championship Match between Birmingham and Leicester City he also had some very good games in the London area, with teams such as Arsenal, Tottenham, West Ham United. One game he refereed was between the Royal Engineers v Scottish Command, these matches were played in London. It seems that John Wildsmith retired from the Football League in 1949.

During the time he was involved with Leamington Referees Association he served on the Management Committee. He became Secretary in 1926 and finally Chairman until 1939. With George Lewis they looked after the Associations Accounts and handed them over to the Association Members at the 1948 Annual General Meeting when the Association was reformed.

In 1934 a gift was given to John Wildsmith by the Association. He chose a Bureau which his daughter still has in her possession and a small brass plaque placed on the Bureau was inscribed as follows :-

LEAMINGTON REFEREES ASSOCIATION
PRESENTED TO J E WILDSMITH - Hon Secretary 1926–1934

When the (Birmingham &Warwickshire Joint Referees County Committee) was formed in the 1930s, it was called the 'County Referees Committee' and John Wildsmith was the first Chairman. We had other members from the Association on the Committee as Delegates during that period.

In 1932 he attended the 20th Annual Conference Complimentary Luncheon held at the Grand Hotel Birmingham June 18th 1932 (Chairman; Mr E H Spiers)

His other Hobbies besides football and refereeing were boating on the River Leam and anything mechanical, especially motorcycles and cars. He also had a great love for the Leamington and Warwick Operatic Society and was a member of the Parish Church as a Sidesman, and Chorister.

During the war John Wildsmith was a Captain in the Home Guard No 5 Platoon 1/BN/WAR & E. Company

In the 1952 the Family moved to Weymouth and owned and ran the Jephson Guest House. Later on he obtained a licence to take out fishing trips in Weymouth, which he enjoyed doing. John Wildsmith passed away in 1981, when he was 80 years old.
 A few of the artefacts will be on display in a separate Chapter.

It is thanks to Mrs Margaret Chapman for the above information; it cannot be used elsewhere without her permission. For the amount of service he gave to Leamington Referees in my opinion he should have been made a "Life Member"

George Pankhurst

Born in Kenilworth in 1914, George Pankhurst married Muriel on the 21st September 1940 and they celebrated their Golden Wedding in 1990. George was a Kenilworth Lad but moved to Warwick after he was married, and lived in Hanworth Road.

George became a Referee in 1941 taking the Examination in Coventry under George Dutton. He started refereeing in the Leamington & District Football League until the League closed down in 1942. He refereed in the local Coventry area although it was difficult because most Leagues had closed down due to the war.

Stanley Rous from the Football Association decided to have sections of the Football League playing in Competitions. The 'Midland Section' of the Football League was set up under George Dutton, by this time George Pankhurst had been promoted to Class 2(two) and was promoted to Class 1(one) in 1946 and placed on the Birmingham Combination. He was also placed on the Football Combination. George was appointed to the supplementary list of Football League Referees in 1949 season and went on to referee on the full list of officials in 1951.
Success came to George, in the 1950's first having an Amateur International, England v Ireland at Birmingham when Harry Owen was one of his Linesmen. At Coventry he refereed Galata Saray in September 1950. He had an International Line Appointment Wales v Scotland at Ninian Park Cardiff in .October 1954.

George had plenty of Football League Matches during the years he was on the League. The one he said he enjoyed was Blackpool v Charlton in 1954 with Stanley Matthews playing. After the War the resumption of Football at all levels was being played all over the Country. The Leamington & District Football League was reformed with George Dutton as Secretary and George Pankhurst Chairman. His involvement with Leamington & District Referees started when the Association was reformed in 1948, at the Bedford Inn at Leamington. Taking on the position as Secretary/Treasurer until 1954, when he became Chairman until 1960.
He was a Delegate to the Birmingham County Referees Committee and also served on the Management of the Association

George assisted George Dutton in forming the South Warwickshire Football League. Taking over the Chairmanship of the League, whilst George Dutton was Secretary, this was 1953/54 season. In 1955 George Pankhurst became Secretary and eventually changed the name through its committee to the, 'Warwickshire Combination' which continued until the 1968 period.

By becoming Secretary/Treasurer to the South Warwickshire Football League, George was elected to the Birmingham County Football Association, giving them 36 years service and
Eventually becoming,"Chairman of the Coaching and Youth Committees" he was also involved in other activities with the County Football Association and was made a Life-Vice-President.

George was made a Vice- President of Leamington & District Referees Association in 1971 and President on the Leamington & District Sunday League until 1994. He was a President of the Boy's Football League for a few years.

With his service to the Leamington & District Referees Association, George was made a Life Member in 1956 and received a plaque from Eric Babington National Referees Association Secretary at a Buffet/ Dance in 1967.

In 1975 the National Referees Association awarded George his Meritorious Service Award, which was again presented by Eric Babington at a Dinner Dance in 1976, at the Manor Hotel

In 1992 George was presented with his 50 year award 1941 to 1991, by Peter Willis who was President of the National Referee's Association, at the 'Globe Hotel' Warwick.

George was a very busy man and he loved to watch football, it did not matter where the match was, he would go and enjoy watching other people play.

Other pastimes that George had were Cricket. He played for Warwick Cricket Club and became a very good umpire; also he was a Member of the Warwickshire County Cricket Club, often going to watch County games and when possible Test matches, held at Warwickshire. I believe that George was very keen on Bowls.

One of George's mottos was, happy we have met, happy have we been, happy may we part and happy meet again. George passed away whilst watching a Football Match on Television on a Sunday Afternoon in 1994.

John Jays

When John Jays moved to Leamington, he was employed by the Leamington Borough Council Highways Department as the Superintendent (Civil Engineer).

John was on the Football League as a Linesman and refereed on the Football Combination. He immediately was placed on the Warwickshire Combination as a Referee and he also officiated on the local Leamington League as well as other Leagues in the area.

John soon became involved with the Association and assisted Alex Walters in coaching candidates through the referees course, he also helped by giving talks to the members on his experiences in the Football League. He eventually became the Secretary in 1960 and demanded support from the Members; he also talked of changes in the way the Association business is done. He helped to keep the Association moving and was responsible in setting up coaching classes for candidate referees.

During his time at Leamington and whilst he was on the Football League John received quite a few overseas appointments for the Football Association

After being Secretary for four years he retired through ill health and moved away from Leamington. He also retired from the Football League at about the same time

Alex Walters

Alex was born in Warwick and served in the Army during the War, meeting his wife Henrietta, in Belgium

They had one Daughter Jacqueline who is a teacher.

Alex took up refereeing in 1949/50 season and joined the Association. He became the coach with Henry Hall and they coached quite a number of candidates using the Referees Chart until they were ready to sit the Examination which they took in Coventry.

His enthusiasm to encourage people to take up refereeing helped to build up the Association, Alex was a very good referee consequently he quickly received his promotion to Class One in

1953. He was appointed to referee on the Warwickshire Combination and was eventually placed on the Football Combination as a Linesman.

In 1956 he was promoted to Referee on the Football Combination and he was then offered a position as a Linesman on the Football League. Alex was still refereeing on the local Saturday Leagues when he had a free Saturday from the senior appointments.

One of Alex Walters Football League matches was at Nottingham when they played Manchester United, known as the, 'Busby Babe's.' It was the period before disaster overtook the Manchester United Football Club.

A complete reorganisation was taking place between the Southern League and the Football Combination. Referees and Linesmen were being moved about and Alex unfortunately was transferred to the Southern League. This meant that he would be classed as a newcomer to the League and placed at the bottom of the list, his chance of refereeing on the Football League was a forlorn hope. Whilst he was on the Combination and the type of games he was having, he considered that they had given him a good chance of being placed in the middle of the Football League. It was a disappointment.

Eventually Alex retired from the Football League and finished with refereeing completely.

During his time in the Association Alex held various positions. He was the Coach and a Management Member also a Vice-Chairman and supported all events the Association organised.

Peter Watson

Peter was born in Leamington in 1931

When he was nearly 18 years old he tried to join the Referees Association, the Secretary was not quite sure about the age limit so they made Peter an honorary member until he was 18.

In passing the examination in Coventry Peter soon made his mark in local football. He obtained his Class 2 (two) in 1951, and his Class 1 (one) in 1955. He officiated on the Warwickshire Combination the West Midland Regional League. Eventually obtained a place on the Football League as a Linesman in the 1958 season.

His involvement with the Association started when he was elected on to the Social Committee in 1952 and eventually served on the Management Committee. He became the Secretary in 1957 or 1958 until 1960. Peter who was a Teacher at Leamington Boys College was offered a position as Head of the Science Department at Kimbolton College near London. He accepted the position and retired from the Association to move to the school. He also retired from the Football League at the same time. This was a shock to the members of the Association we all liked Peter and the members were very disappointed, because every one expected Peter to reach International level as a Referee.

It would have been a great boost to the Association one other feature that Peter possessed was that he also qualified as a rugby union referee and regularly took charge of matches whilst he was at Leamington College. The latest information I have is that Peter still lives in the same area and has retired from teaching.

Geoff Perks

Geoff Perks was one of the members who joined the Association in 1948 when it was reformed.

He was registered as a referee in the London area, his family had moved up to Kenilworth during the War years. He did say his father was on the Football League before the war.

Having joined the Association, it did not take him long before he was on the Football League as a Linesman. And when the Warwickshire Combination was formed he was placed on the list of referees he was also on the Football Combination.

As far as the Association Geoff did not get involved with the organising side, although he supported everything we did. Geoff was Secretary of the "Lockheed Juniors Football Team" until he went to the AGM in 1946 he was appointed Secretary to the "Youth Organisation Committee Football League." refereeing them on most Saturdays when he did not have a Senior Appointment

Little is known of his service to the Football League. He never told the Association when he received any FA Appointments. He did work with the Football Association and this was tied up to 'Wembley Stadium.' He was a Steward at all Cup Finals, International Matches, Schoolboy Internationals and Representative Games. This information was told to me by Geoff when we were travelling to Wembley by train to see the Cup Final, Geoff obviously was going to work he then told me all about his job as a Steward.

Jeff Perks was married and had children, when he finished refereeing he moved on and we lost contact.

John Sollis

John was born in Kenilworth in 1938.

He was married to Miss Ann Lawrence in 1960.

They have two daughters Hazel Amanda and Karen Louise and Ann and John have three grandchildren name Claire, Philip and George.

John was a 15 year old youth when he took up refereeing. After being coached he took his Examination at the B T H Club in Coventry in March 1953 and started refereeing on the Leamington &District Saturday Football League. Eventually he was refereeing in Coventry and was placed on the list of the "Warwickshire Combination" as a Linesman. John eventually obtained his Class 2 (two) in the 1956-57 season and finally received his Class 1 (one) in 1960.

John had completed his National Service where he refereed whilst he was stationed in Carlisle and at Paderssornamo Munster Germany. The experience he gained served him well when he returned to referee in Leamington; he soon received his Class 1(one). John was placed on the West Midland Regional League as a Linesman and began Refereeing in the Warwickshire Combination. He soon made a name for himself in the refereeing world it was obvious to everyone that John was going to travel to the top. He did make the Linesman's List of the Football League and why he never made it as a Referee we do not know. As well as being a good referee John was a very pleasant young man and always supported the Association. He never held office but served on the Management Committee for a number of years and was prepared to help out at any event that was organised.

In 1972 the Chairman Frank Wall told the members that John Sollis told him he would be retiring from the Football League and the Association. We were a little nonplussed by the statement and could not understand the reason for his retiring from the Football League. We all considered John a very good referee. He was approached by one or two of the senior members to change his mind and stay in local refereeing. This was of no avail and we were sorry to lose him as a member, his loss as a referee was a blow.

To reach the Football League standard was a compliment to his determination to succeed, to do this he trained very hard and was always fit; he didn't smoke and accepted a majority of appointments when they were offered. He was a model referee for junior referees to emulate.

Lionel Fleet

Lionel came to Leamington from Cambridge to take up a position as Deputy Headmaster At Blackdown High School, in the autumn of 1966. He was married and had a family of two boys, and two girls. A further boy was born following his moving away from the area.In refereeing circles Lionel was "in the middle" of the Football Combination and whilst at Leamington he was placed on the Football League as a Linesman in 1967.

Lionel was a good ambassador for referees. He had a motto which he frequently expressed, thus: "Have Whistle-Will Travel!" When not officiating on his senior leagues, he rarely missed a weekend, often both Saturday and Sunday. As far as his junior matches were concerned he often helped on the local Leamington League, but much of his local refereeing was on the Stratford on Avon League. In addition he received a number of cup matches at both local and county level.

From the point of view of the local Association and its monthly meetings, Lionel was a regular member and gave a lot of impact to the meetings. He served on the Management Committee whilst at Leamington and he was the meetings organiser for two years. We had some excellent meetings with speakers from places like Cambridge and other areas.

Lionel did not stay with us long as he had the opportunity to move to Dereham in Norfolk as Headmaster at the Dereham Boy' Secondary School as it became a Comprehensive School.

He left Leamington in January 1970. He told us that he did not continue with his refereeing after 1972, mainly due to pressure of work. At the end of 1978 he left education and retired early and took up work in local government, becoming part time clerk at the market town of Watton in Norfolk.

Eddie Durant

Eddie Durant came from Lincoln in the latter part of the 1950s, He told us that he had retired from the Football League and finished with refereeing. The Company he worked for was moving to Leamington and it benefited him and his wife to move as well. He then decided to join the Leamington Referees Association. He became very helpful in teaching candidates through the referees course. Eddie was an asset to the Association but unfortunately his health was beginning to fail him, so his family decided to move down to the South Coast

Eddie and his wife were charming people to meet and the time he spent at Leamington was beneficial to the Association.

This next part will cover the referees who never made it to the Football League. Quite a few reached a very high standard of refereeing and they also worked hard for the Association. Whether it was as Chairman, Secretary or Treasurer their contribution was essential to the well being of the Association.

Charlie Jackson and Jack Joyner were members before the War and carried on refereeing when it was possible. After the War they both were involved with Coventry Referees until the Leamington Referees Association was reformed. They both rejoined and helped in any way they could to keep the Association moving forward. What is written about these gentlemen, is my experience in meeting both of them, and the way they helped members who had any sort of problem with refereeing. We cannot recall any referee in the Association who did not benefit from their advice.

Charles W Jackson

Born 15th June 1912
Died 23rd October   1986
Aged 72 years
Married to Christine Mary
Children: - Pauline and Peter.

Charles Jackson was a member of the Leamington &District Referee Association having passed his Referees Examination in the 1937/38 season. He was informed by the Birmingham County Football Association that he had passed and they would require a Postal Order valued 2/6(Two shillings and sixpence.) to register for the 1938 season

Charles, according to the Minutes of that period, was soon elected on to the Management Committee in which he served before and after the War. When Leamington closed down, he joined Coventry Referees. Charles was in the Army where he spent nearly Five years from 1940 to 1945 firstly in the Artillery in North Africa, he then transferred to the Military Police and became one of the Guards at the Yalta Conference looking after Winston Churchill, Franklyn Roosevelt and Joeseph Stalin. Quite a responsible job at that particular time Charles also continued his refereeing career, the experience he gained refereeing in the Forces stood him in good stead.

After the war Charles rejoined Leamington Referees and along with other refereeing colleagues helped to reform the Association.

Charles Jackson refereed on various Leagues, such as the Leamington & District Football League, the Coventry & North Warwickshire Football League, the Warwickshire Combination and finally the Birmingham Combination. He received plenty of Cup Appointments from the County Football Association as well as the Local League Cup Finals and Charity Cup Competitions. He had the Aston –Villa Cup Semi Final, also the Coventry Evening Telegraph Cup Final between Rugby Town Res versus Birmingham City 'A' on

Saturday 9th November 1957. His refereeing career spanned from 1938 until he was forced to retire through suffering severe sciatica in 1960.

Before Charles became a Referee he was the goalkeeper for Leek Wootton football team, he was also involved with the cricket team. During his time with the Association he took part in all the sporting activities and represented the Association at Football and arranged Cricket matches at Leek Wootton.

Having been privileged to have known Charles, we used to call him 'Charlie.' When Charlie was the referee, you were given good advice. He would run the line for you as he did for me on more than one occasion. This happened in the Warwick League of Friends Hospital Cup. The match ended in a draw and the replay was to be at Cubbington due to shift work Charlie was asked to take over from me to referee the match. Every one who knew Charlie always enjoyed his company and if you needed advice he would give it to you.

When Leek Wootton played at home in the Leamington Saturday Football League the ground was always well marked out and there was always a cup of tea before the game, as well as afterwards.

Charles Jackson was still involved in cricket for the Leek Wootton Team and he
served on the Parish Council when he was elected in 1952.

According to Mrs Jackson she still has his jacket and referees shirt also his RA Badge, and whistles.

Jack Joyner

Born 2nd March 1911
Died June 1986 aged 75 years old.
Married to Hilda May on the 30th May 1936

Jack had one son Roy Joyner who also became a Referee in the Leamington & District Referees Association.
Jack Joyner and his family lived in Haseley, and eventually moved to Cubbington to live.
He was employed at Benfords Engineering Company in Warwick involved in essential work.
He served in the Warwickshire Special Constabulary for a number of years, reaching the rank on Chief Inspector. He was also a Church Warden at St Mary's Church, Cubbington.

Jack Joyner was another referee who was a Member of the Leamington & District Referees Association before the war, joining in 1936. When the Association was reformed in 1948 Jack rejoined and was soon involved with the Management side of the Association and was in the group of referee's along with George Dutton, George Pankhurst, John Wildsmith, and Charlie Jackson who were responsible for the re-formation of the Association in 1948. He was a delegate to the Birmingham and Joint Referees Committee travelling to Birmingham. He was also Vice Chairman taking the Chair quite regularly. His service to the Association was rewarded in 1966 when the Members made him a "Life Member" of the Leamington & District Referees Association. A position he treasured and Jack along with others who were, 'Life Members' received a Plaque from Eric Babington (Secretary National Referees Association) at a Buffet Dance in 1967.

Jack Joyner was very good at football; he was often selected for the Association Football Team. Jack's other sporting abilities was that he played cricket for Hatton & Haseley, also the Eagle Engineering Company, often taking 100 plus wicket during a season, as a fast bowler.

When the war broke out in 1939 Jack along with others went and joined Coventry Referees and refereed on all the local Leagues as well as the Leamington & District Football League, and most of the referees at that time were on the Allocation System, refereeing on the Coventry Works, Coventry Combination, also the Coventry &North Warwickshire League. .

Jack also refereed on the Birmingham Combination. Jack had an Amateur Cup-tie between Moor Green and Romford at Moor Green in the 1950s; also he had a Semi- Final in the Warwick Cinderella Cup Competition, between Warwick Town v Leamington Victoria FC. Jack finally retired in the 1960's and became more involved with the Association. He was well thought of as a Referee and many considered he would have made the step to senior Football, if the war had not intervened.
Having met Jack Joyner one could not have wished to meet a nicer person, nothing was too much trouble. As with all the older colleagues he had time to give advice.
Jack passed away following a stroke in June 1986; he was 75 years old.
After those two gentlemen we move on to the members who also gave time and effort in making sure the Association was kept on the move.

Harold Elkington

Secretary from 1921 to 1926

When we spoke to Harold in 1972 he told us that the only refereeing he did was in the local Leamington &District Saturday League and the Warwick & District League. Occasionally he went to the Southam League and also refereed Cup matches. Travelling to some of the grounds was always difficult at times especially if you lived in Bishops Tachbrook

He also told us he was a jobbing gardener and was kept very busy and this caused him to eventually retire from refereeing.

At the monthly meeting of the Association in 1972 the members decided to make Harold Elkington a 'Life Member' and a 'Vice-President' for his effort in forming the Association in 1921 The information was sent to Harold who thanked the members and wished the Association good fortune. Harold passed away in 1974 after a short illness.

Arthur Montgomery

Treasurer from 1926 to 1933

Arthur was the Associations Treasurer in the late 1920s and retired in 1933 handing a healthy balance sheet over to a Mr Hawtin. After retiring from being Treasurer he carried on refereeing in the local Leagues such as the Leamington & District Saturday League and the Warwick &District League occasionally having matches in the Coventry & North Warwickshire League.

Arthur was employed at Henry Griffiths Leamington as a carpenter he was reported to be an excellent goalkeeper unfortunately there is no mention of which Club or Clubs he played for. His nephew David Montgomery told me that all the family were very good sportsmen.

In 1932/33 Season the Leamington Referees Association made a gift to Arthur for the service he had given to the Association unfortunately the minutes of that time do not say what it was he purchased, and the family do not know.

George A Lewis

A long serving member who joined the Association in the 1920s, and became Treasurer in the 1936 season and held the Office until the Association was reformed in 1948. He handed a reasonable Balance Sheet over to the new Treasurer. It was not a large amount of money but it helped the Association to start again with funds to use.

He was responsible in obtaining the Secretary for the Association in 1937, when nobody wanted the position and the previous Secretary continually declined.

George seemed quite happy to referee it seems on the local Leamington Saturday League and no other League has been mentioned.

Sidney Soden

Sidney was Chairman in 1937 he was also on the Management. It seems that Sidney joined the Association in the late 1920s and was a Class 1(one) referee who officiated on all the local Leagues and possibly the Coventry &North Warwickshire League.

He enjoyed organising the Football Matches between Rugby Referees and Leamington. He was instrumental with others to reform the Association, when it was completed he decided to retire from the Association and gave up refereeing.

Sidney Soden was married and had a grown up family. When we talked to him he gave us the impression he was in the Building Trade.

After a long illness Sidney Soden passed away in 1966

Richard (Dicky) West

Richard West joined Leamington Referees in 1931 and soon established himself as a good referee. Most of his refereeing was in the Leamington Saturday League although the referees were allocated to other Leagues in the area he did referee in the Henley League. He was quite content to referee locally Richard or Dicky as he was known was soon involved with the Management side of the Association becoming Vice-Chairman and in 1933 became its Secretary until 1936. He became a Delegate to the 'County Referees Committee' along with John Wildsmith and Robert Rowson.

He was the first Referee to be assaulted whilst refereeing. This happened at Claverdon and the eventual court case was heard at Henley- in – Arden.

The player was suspended and fined by the Court. The Football Association were involved with the case and a certain amount of money was available for the Association to use.
Richard was a very good sportsman and he evidently was a good footballer for he was always selected for the team and any representative matches that were organised.
He was a married man with a daughter and had his own business as a baker with a shop in Smith Street in Warwick. In 1938 Richard was promoted to the London Combination and enjoyed 12 months in that standard of Refereeing. After the War Richard did not continue as a referee, but became involved with the Leamington Saturday Football League and then the Warwickshire Combination.
Richard West passed away after a short illness in 1966.

Robert Rowson

Secretary from 1937 to 1939
It seems that Robert Rowson was in a unique position; he was brought into the Association by George Lewis. This concerned the problems at the Annual General Meeting in 1937 when the Association did not have a member who was prepared to become Secretary. Attempts were made to the previous Secretary to continue, but this was of no avail. So Robert Rowson was rushed through the Referees Examination and then introduced to the members, who accepted him as a member. **The Extra General Meeting** continued and Robert Rowson was elected as the Association Secretary. He continued in that position until the September of 1939.
After the War there is no mention of Robert re-joining the Association in fact no mention is made of him at all. He was a member of the County Referees Committee with John Wildsmith and Richard West.

Tom Story

Tom was one of the Stalwarts of the Leamington Referees Association. Whilst he was Chairman the meetings were always kept under control. He was a Vice Chairman a few times and Delegate to the County Referees Committee, travelling to Birmingham quite regularly.
Tom was married and had one son called Raymond.
Tom Story only refereed in the Local Saturday & Sunday Leagues, age was against him moving up the ladder, but he was quite happy and enjoyed his refereeing.

Tom was made a Life Member of the Association in 1955 and in 1976 he received his Meritorious Service Award from the National Referees Association at a Dinner. He also received his 21 years service award from the Birmingham County Football .Association.

A well respected man was Tom for his service to the Leamington & District Saturday League and the Leamington and Coventry Sunday Football Leagues where he held positions as Chairman and served on the Management of both Leagues.

Tom was made a Vice- President of the Association in 1974, after being taken ill he was sent to Hospital where he passed away in 1994.

Henry C Hall

Henry Hall was one of the quietest referees you would meet, even so he was a very good referee and he was able to impart his knowledge of the Laws of the Game through the Referees Chart as we knew it in 1952 to anyone who wanted to become a referee.

I first came into contact with Henry at a British Legion Dinner. He was with Tom Story they were both talking about referees, we had a talk and he promised to coach me to become a referee. This he did and registered me with the County F.A. We had to go to the B T H Sports and Social Club Coventry to take the Examination on a one to one basis. Henry was brilliant in coaching his candidates.

Henry was in the Warwickshire Regiment. Evidently he joined as a 15 year old Band boy and served all through the War. When he retired he stayed in Warwick.

His refereeing career was brought to a sad end in 1953 when he snapped both the tendons in his ankles whilst refereeing. After numerous operations he was unable to walk properly and had to use sticks to help him along. Henry only refereed in the local Leamington Saturday League and the odd Cup Game. He was always interested in the members and did an amount of work in organising events, eventually working with Alex Walters coaching members, and he became Assistant Secretary under George Pankhurst. Henry passed away in 1967.

Kenneth Cox

Ken became Secretary/ Treasurer in 1954 when the previous Secretary retired. Ken had just about completed his second years in office when his Company moved down to Portsmouth. His family had to relocate them selves in the area. Ken continued his refereeing and within a short time was made up to a Class 1(one) Referee. It seems that his promotion was given to him after he had completed a match that was a County appointment. The Committee Member from the Portsmouth area told Ken he would be hearing from the County F.A confirming his promotion and he would be placed on a Senior League.

When he was at Leamington he was on the Social Committee and helped to organise events for the Association. Tom Story kept the Association informed about Ken when he went to Portsmouth visiting friends. Eventually we lost touch with Ken Cox , we checked the Portsmouth Society to see if he still lived in the area and what League status did he reach, we never had any luck in finding out.

Reaching the end of the period between 1952 and 1960 we had had an accumulation of Secretary's two have been mentioned; the other two were Wilfred Blount who left after two years to take a position with the Arab Airlines. Wilf was ex-RAF. The other was Peter Watson who was mentioned in the Football League Referees. Jack Wright took on the position as Treasurer until 1960 The Association seemed to find a certain amount of stability when John Jays took over as Secretary. Tom Story became the Chairman in 1960, and Arnold Rouse becoming Treasurer.

We had the younger members who had joined us in the latter part of the 1950s become part of the Association and getting elected to the Management Committee at the Annual General Meeting.
The first name to mentioned is Frank Wall who joined the Association in 1955 his brother Bill was already a member

Frank Wall

Frank Joined the Association in the 1955/56 season, taking the Examination in Coventry after being coached by Alex Walters.
He Refereed in local football on the Leamington Saturday League the Coventry Works League, and the Midland intermediate League also the Midland Floodlight League.
Frank was on the Football Combination for 9 years, 3 years as a Referee; he was appointed as Linesman in the Combination Cup Semi-Final Leicester City v Plymouth Argyle and again was one of the Linesmen in the Final of the Combination Cup between Leicester City and Tottenham Hotspur. He had two County F.A. Cup appointments Featherstone Cup under 18 at Sutton Coldfield, the other was the Senior Cup at Dudley with Jack Taylor as the Referee.
Frank had numerous local and Charity Cup appointments.
He finally retired from the Football Combination in 1972 and refereed locally till 1978.
Frank served the Association very well, as Chairman, Meeting Organiser, RA Coach, and Management Member and finally became Chairman of the 1976 National Referees Association Conference. Frank along with David Clark was instrumental in the Conference coming to Leamington. He was also a Vice-President 1981 to 1984. He was employed at Ford Motor Company Leamington in the Accounts department. Frank had quite a few hobbies, but he did like growing roses and he set up his own business and was very successful for a number of years. He had two children a boy Graham and girl Lynda. His first wife Janet and he were divorced in 1978 and he eventually went down to live in Somerset with his second wife Pat in 1992.

Ken Eastbury

Ken joined the Association in1955 and soon became involved with the Management Committee playing and supporting the Association football team. His refereeing started with the Leamington Saturday League and eventually refereed on the Coventry Leagues to gain experience, he also became a linesman on the Warwickshire Combination. When Ken received his promotion he then refereed on the Warwickshire Combination and finished on the West Midland Regional League.
Although he enjoyed his refereeing Ken had other hobbies, one was small bore rifle shooting, competing in the Rugby League. The other hobby was singing and he was a founder member of the Royal Naval Association Choir which gave concerts around the Midlands

He was employed at Lockheed as an Inspector and when he did have some spare time he enjoyed gardening growing all sorts of vegetables and flowers. Whilst he was in the Association he gave quite a impact to the meetings and at one time he was very concerned with the County F A over promotion and the time it took them to inform referees, which in some cases delayed a member from being placed on a Senior League.
Ken is married and had two Sons he also has three Grandsons and one Great Grandson. Ken was born in Radford Semele Leamington.

David Clarke

David was born and educated locally and started his career as a Civil Engineer with Coventry City Council. He was a member of the local athletic club Leamington C&AC before his work took him in 1955 to Tunbridge Wells in Kent where he started his refereeing career. From there he moved to Sale in Cheshire where through experience on the Altringham league, the Wythenshawe league, the Mid- Cheshire league and the Cheshire League he gained promotion to Class1 (one).

Moving to Harlow new town Essex 1960, he gained further experience in the Harlow, Corinthian and Athenian Leagues until he mo ved again in December 1961 back to Leamington area. He joined the Leamington & District Referees Association that season.

He soon became an active member of the Association accepting appointments on the management committee and in 1964 he became the Secretary after John Jays retired. When due to pressure of work he had to retire as Secretary in 1966. David still became elected to the management committee.

He represented the Association on the Birmingham &Warwickshire Joint Referees County Committee he also helped to coach candidates with Frank Wall.

David was always pushing for the Association to organise the National Referees Conference. The chance came in 1971 when the National RA accepted Leamington RA's offer to stage the event. David became its Secretary (further articles about the Conference in a separate section).

His refereeing in the Leamington area covered the Saturday Leagues, the Warwickshire Combination, also the West Midland Regional League. David received several County Cup appointments as well receiving Appointments from the Football Association.

His professional life outside refereeing was as follows: David was a Director of a local Civil Engineering company Roadrive and Director of the regional Building Company Clarke Bros.

When he retired from business in 1989 he became involved with his wife Pam in charity work, and worked for Christian Outreach (now known as CORD), built schools in India, refugee camps in Africa, worked for "The Churches Ministry to the Jewish people in Jaffa,"

David is married to Pam and has two children a daughter Christine and a boy Trevor

David was made a Vice- President in 1979 and he became a Life- Member of the Association in 1991.

Jeff Brockwell

Born in London, but spent most of his formative life in Essex and was involved in teams, run by an ex professional (George Pooley- goalkeeper Orient). Played in a very successful junior team, where a number of individual players subsequently became well known professionals, including Jimmy Greaves and Lea Allen (Chelsea/Spurs)

In later life Jeff had a senior amateur soccer career (mainly with Briggs Sports- a branch of Ford Motor Company). Whilst playing with them he suffered a serious knee and leg injury at the age of 29 and he had to retire from active playing. Became a Referee and trained under the guidance of a Class 1 (one) referee Fred Popplewell in Southend Essex.. Remained involved for several years, until he moved, in 1976 to new employment in the West Midlands (Warwick)

He initially became an active referee, joining the Leamington & District Referees Association in 1977. He refereed in the Leamington & District Sunday League and the Coventry Leagues on a Saturday. During this period he started a junior boys team with a local soccer enthusiast, (starting at under 10s (tens) and latterly to an under 17(seventeen) league).

Jeff then became the Club Chairman and eventually served on the Committee of the Mid Warwickshire Boys Football League.

During this period, became involved with Coventry City FC, through an ex- playing colleague (Eddie Plumley-then Secretary of C C F C) he met Eddie Plumley whilst completing National Service and worked with him in training and developing local youth soccer in the area.

While Jeff was in the Referees Association he eventually became elected to the Management Committee which he served for a number of years. He was also very active on the George Dutton Charity Cup Competition. During the time Jeff was in Leamington he was a Director of a large Industrial business. He provided sponsorships and playing facilities (Company Sports Ground) to the local Football Leagues and the refereeing fraternity The Association were privileged to use the Sports ground for the Six-a-Side Football Competition that they organised.

The problems Jeff has had with his knee years ago, returned with a vengeance curtailed his refereeing activities until he could get replacement surgery, which, at that time was in its infancy. Although not refereeing, he remained involved in the Referees Association, being made a Vice-President in 1987 and has always maintained a provision of sponsorship and support, particularly for youth soccer, until retirement from Industry even though he has retired Jeff is still involved with the Industrial world, In his spare time he enjoys playing Golf.

Jeff is married to Beryl and has three children two Sons and a Daughter and six Grandchildren The eldest son still plays the occasional Football and at one stage was captain of 'Wycombe Wanderers' F C.

Sidney Sharp

Sidney Sharp came from London and settled in the Warwick area, he was employed at the Central Hospital as a nurse.

Sid was married to Jess who was also a Nursing Sister at the Hospital and had a son called John and two Granddaughters Clare and Amanda. John is also a Referee.

Sidney Sharp was a very good sportsman and had numerous trophies that he had won. He also had two hobbies which were Greyhound racing and Horse racing. When he became a referee he set out to enjoy the game and began refereeing on the Leamington Saturday League. He also refereed in the Coventry area and did a spell on the Warwickshire Combination as a Linesman.

He joined the Association and he soon began to get involved by getting elected to the Management. He also became a Vice- Chairman and in 1975 he became a Vice- President. When he had more or less retired from refereeing, he kept his involvement with the game by becoming a referee's assessor with County Football Associations approval. This Sid really enjoyed and like all assessors the referees he assessed gradually climbed the ladder. Sidney was also involved with the Charities Cup Competitions that the Association was involved with, and was very generous in that he sponsored the trophies for the Referees and Linesmen at the Finals of the George Dutton and Andy Campbell Cups.

Sid was taken ill in 1989 and spent some time in hospital where he eventually passed away.

John Sharp

John became a referee in 1963 after being coached by Frank Wall. He became a member of Leamington Referees Association, and refereed for a number of years in the Coventry &District Sunday League. After a short break, John returned to the "whistle" in 1984 with the Midland Combination, a league that he still officiates on today.

In 1988 he became Assistant Secretary to Brian Hackleton and after six years he eventually became the Association Secretary taking over from Ray Morgan. He was Secretary for four years and in 2002 John became Chairman, a position he hold now.

John, like his father is always supportive of the Association and everyone knows that he leads a very busy life. His other hobby, if you can call it that, is the Scout movement and John is District Commissioner for Leamington District.

John is married to Sue and has two daughters, Clare an officer in the R.A.F .and Amanda a schoolteacher, John works as a Driving Examiner, being the Manager of the Warwick Driving Test Centre.

John is a F.A. Assessor and qualified as a Licensed Instructor in 1998 and took over as the Associations Coaching Officer from John Mander in that year.

Derek Silk

Derek Silk came from Birmingham in 1967 and joined Leamington Referees Association.

He was married to Jennie with a son John and a daughter Karen.

He is an Accountant by Profession and in business in Coventry although he has now retired and only does Consultancy work. In his spare time he likes playing golf and also enjoys playing snooker.

Once he was established he soon became involved with the Association by taking on the Treasurers position from Derek Locke in 1970. He held that position until 1981. He then became Chairman and served for three years. This was a position that Derek thoroughly enjoyed, unfortunately the rules only allowed the position of Chairman to be held for three years at that time.

He was involved with the 1976 Conference as the Treasurer he then became Treasurer to the George Dutton and the Andy Campbell Charity Cups until 1998 when he finally retired.

All the time he was Treasurer the Accounts for the Association were kept in good order and the same when he became Treasurer of the Conference and the Charity Cups.

Derek was a quiet Referee officiating in the Coventry area as well as Leamington Saturday League.

Derek Silk was made a Vice-President in 1988.

John Silk

For a number of years Derek and his family had been involved looking after his son John who was a tetraplegic. It was unfortunate that John had met with a serious accident in1995 whilst on a holiday it left him unable to look after himself. On his return to England he was taken to Stoke Mandeville Hospital for specialist's treatment, whilst he was their Derek and his family were fighting to get the best and correct treatment for John and they were also involved in raising money for Spinal Research.

Before John was injured he had qualified as a referee and played for the Association at Football when asked to and was very interested in the Associations Quiz Competition on the 'Laws of Association Football.' His professional occupation before the accident was as a Chef at Ettington Park Hotel.

Andy Semple

Andy Semple became a member in 1961 and once he had settled down as a Referee he soon became involved in the Association business, eventually getting elected to the Management in 1964/5 season. From there he went into teaching referee candidates on the 'Referees Chart' with Arnold Rouse and finally completed 10 years 'Coaching' candidate referees. He held office as Chairman for 4 years and was involved with the Conference in 1976. Andy with his wife Pat was responsible for the Conference delegates, who were placed the various Hotels in Knowle.

His refereeing reached a very high standard in the Football Combination he also refereed in Leamington Saturday League and the Coventry Leagues,
Andy was always disappointed with the 'Feeder and Contributory System' it always seemed to be running into trouble. The Warwickshire Combination was a disappointment to Andy as well. In his opinion, it's always the Referees who are let down when Leagues fold up and systems do not work. Andy with Arnold Rouse set up the George Dutton Charity Cup, which is still going strong raising money for local Charities.
He retired from refereeing in 1978 and the Association at the same time. Quite a few members were concerned when he resigned from being Chairman and efforts were made to get him to reconsider but to no avail. He told me he was disappointed with refereeing and wanted to concentrate on his other hobbies. He was Chairman of the 'Sports Day Committee' at the Lockheed. He also enjoyed gardening and was learning to play golf.
His employment was at Automotive Products (Lockheed Leamington) working in the Borg & Beck Division he was a Foreman when he retired. With his wife Pat they decided to open a business in Leamington. It was called 'Andy Save' which sold 'Confectionary' items, as well as other food products, it was very popular with the people who wanted to make cakes and other confectionary items to be able to purchase the ingredients. Unfortunately the very severe flooding we had in 1997/1998 decimated his business, which meant he had to close down completely.
Andy Semple was made a Vice- President of the Association in 1990.

Edward (Ted) Warwick

Ted Warwick joined the Association in 1955 after taking the Examination in Coventry. He took up refereeing to help the Warwickshire Boys League through an approach from Geoff
Perks. After a while he began refereeing on the 'Leamington Saturday League.' Ted was never the ambitious sort but he did like to see fair play, and he enjoyed refereeing on the Saturday League. As a person he liked a level playing field and was not frightened to complain if he felt that an injustice had been done. He often complained about the selection of Cup Final Officials.
If you wanted someone to help you Ted would offer his services and he served the Association well by being a Delegate to the Leamington Saturday League. He never made any
attempt to join the Management Committee but attended Monthly meetings as often as he could.
Ted was an Artist and his Sketches and drawings were very good, he also had a very wicked sense of humour
Ted had been married and had a grown up family. He was employed at the Lockheed in the Borg & Beck section. He had retired from work and sadly Ted has now passed away through illness

Victor Shepherd

Vic joined the Association in 1963 and started his refereeing in the Leamington Saturday League gradually working his way through the various Leagues until he reached the Football Combination. Vic was a very competent referee and at one time it was hoped that he might make the Football League. Unfortunately for Vic a change to the qualifying age meant that he missed out by just one year which ruined his chance. The chances of moving into the Football League at that level were very hard and extremely difficult, with so many referees for a few places.

Vic was elected on to the Management of the Association and was also delegate to various Leagues in the area. He is pleased that he contributed to the success of all the Leagues he served and in particular his first League, the 'Works League' now the Alliance.

Vic has made a name in local football by being involved with the Mid Warwickshire Boys League as Chairman. He has also been involved with Southam United Football Club as Vice-Chairman and Chairman.

In 2001 he moved to his home town club of Leamington FC [The Brakes] as Deputy Chairman to Mick Brady, where he represented the Club as Vice-Chairman on the Management of the Midland Football Combination. He also assisted in helping with their Business Plan and the regional FA meetings to obtain Step Six in the new non League Pyramid System. In 2006 Vic stood down from the position as Deputy Chairman of the Football Club to spend more time Assessing referees and visiting Clubs to give a Grading on the Ground conditions.

Vic is married to Margaret with a grown up family.

Dennis Reynolds

Dennis Reynolds became involved with referees in November 1962 when he joined the Association. Nothing was heard about Dennis even though he was refereeing quite regularly in the Leamington Saturday and Sunday Leagues as well as Officiating in Coventry. Dennis also enjoyed refereeing in the Sunday Catering League where he gave splendid service to the League.

His real involvement with the Association came about when the Secretary of the Association resigned in 1972/3 season and he was talked into taking on the position of Secretary. This he carried out extremely well, it was a position he held for five years.

Dennis like a majority of Referees took up refereeing to put a little back into the game and an excellent way to keep fit. His other sport was Cricket which he enjoyed and played for a team along with his brothers.

Dennis was employed at Pottertons Warwick as a Manager in the Personnel Department

He was married to Eileen and had two sons. Both became referees although Paul the youngest did not join the Association, because he was going to University, the elder brother Colin joined the Association in 1975 and refereed for a few years until he moved away.

When Dennis retired from the Association he was made a Vice-President in 1990.

In his retirement he went to live in Kenilworth and became very keen on golf which he enjoyed

He collapsed and died in 1997 whilst enjoying a round of golf.

William Alderson

Bill Alderson was born in Sunderland and had a reputation of being a strong person; he was also a promising footballer. With the possibilities that Sunderland were about to sign him as a professional player, unfortunately an Accident at the Shipyard were he was an Apprentice caused him to lose the sight of one of his eyes. After a while he was cajoled into becoming a referee. Bill told me how he passed the colour chart with the examiner. He said he put the card to his injured eye and read off the colours with his good eye and when the examiner wasn't looking the card was placed to the same eye and read the colours to him again, the examiner then told me I had passed the referees exam.

Bill and his wife Doris eventually moved to Oxford, where he enjoyed his refereeing and was given a fair amount of respect by the players and clubs. His next move was to Leamington when he became employed by the Lockheed.

He joined the Association in September 1967, and made himself known to the members, he was a dour character with a strong sense of humour. Once everyone had met Bill they enjoyed his company his nonsensical approach to every thing was great and he called a spade a spade. He soon made a name as a very strong referee. He refereed in the local Sunday League as well as Leagues in Coventry.

Bill loved writing poetry and penning short stories of which he had printed. The book is called **"Bill the Hat"** and the book of Poems is called **"Poems from the Cliff Top"** they are interesting books and worth reading. Bill with his wife Doris organised dancing sessions on a regular basis, they both taught people the style of dancing they enjoyed and it was called 'Old time and Modern Sequence'

Bill was also a very keen gardener and grew all his own produce and they distributed the produce amongst their elderly neighbours and friends. When he eventually retired Bill had the opportunity to have an operation on his injured eye, which he had done, and he was over the moon when he found he could see out of it again.

Bill was made a Vice- President of the Association in 1996 and he was proud that the members of the Association had remembered him and this honour was appreciated by Bill.

He had a nick name and he was known as *'Bill the Hat'* for he always wore one when refereeing.

John Mander

John Mander joined the Association in 1969 after being coached by Andy Semple and he refereed in the Leamington & District Sunday Football League. John also refereed in Coventry on a Saturday afternoon and eventually he officiated on the Midland Combination. It wasn't until the 1979 period when John was approached to see if he would be interested in coaching candidates to become referees. Once he was introduced to the candidates he continued until they all took the exam. From that time John continued teaching candidates until 1998 thus completing 18 years as the Association's Coach. John was eventually involved with the Football Association and became the Referees Area Adviser. This gave him responsibility for the whole area including 'The Birmingham County FA', and 'Counties from Gloucestershire and Worcestershire' as well as others.

He has received from the Football Association his 10 year Certificate for being an Instructor and was made an Honorary Licensed Instructor when he retired in 1997.

John was married and had two children, a boy Martin and a daughter called Beverley. In his spare time John is very handy doing D.I.Y work. His other sporting hobby is cricket which he has enjoyed for years. He was Employed at Benfords and held various positions within the company finishing as the Training Manager.

He was also Chairman of the Association for 7 years and handled the business side through difficult periods extremely well. He supported the Association on social events and gave his full support to the Six–a-Side Football Competition that was organised for the Referees Benevolent Fund. Whilst he was a Licensed Instructor he also was an assessor and has continued Assessing young referees for promotion.

Anthony Engel

Anthony or Tony moved from Northampton with his wife Sally to settle in Warwick and joined the Association in 1969. He became a member of the Management Committee for two years and was also the Auditor for three years, he enjoyed refereeing and refereed on the Leamington Saturday League and the Sunday Football League, he also enjoyed refereeing in the Stratford League.

On the sporting field as well a being a referee he enjoyed playing Cricket and arranged a friendly between Leamington and a team called Gayton (Northamptonshire). The Association took a very strong team over to Gayton and it turned out to be an enjoyable day, as far as the cricket went we were beaten by a good team, the wicket at Gayton was a matted affair and the mat was laid whilst we watched. We did have a return match at Central Hospital Warwick that was also enjoyable and we still lost.

The Association was very fortunate to have Tony Engel as a member. He is a Barrister by profession and when we have had a problem he has helped the Association sort it out.

Here with is a list of his achievements:

Anthony was educated at Carmel College.

St Catharine's College, Cambridge. Part1 Tripos: - Economics. Part 2 Tripos: - Law.

BA (Hons.) 1965, MA (Hons.) 1967 Called to the Bar 1965.

Barrister 1966 to 1984 Involved with Criminal Law, Common Law and Personal Injuries, Planning, Family.

Head of Chambers (1981-1984) and sat as Judge in Crown and County Courts. Tony then became a Prosecutor till 1986, promoted to Senior Crown Prosecutor (in charge of three Lawyers). He was co-opted onto the National Association of Prosecuting Solicitors and elected the first President of the Prosecuting Barristers Association.

From 1986 to 1989 he was involved with Lloyds of London as Head of Investigations/Prosecuting Section and Secretary of the Investigations Committee (of the Council) employing nine Barristers, eight Investigators and three Secretaries.

Insurance Litigator 1989 1990, Prosecutor 1990 to 1996. Re-joined the Crown Prosecution Service Warwickshire as Senior Crown Prosecutor

Took early retirement in 1996 and from then he became a Barrister /Tutor. Tony returned to practise at the Bar and taught (part-time) on Vocational Course in London.

Other Examinations he has passed are: - Law Society Accounts, Lloyd.s Introductory Test.

Tony has had a Publication Printed called, "Aspects of Insurance Law."

His Hobbies now are: Social and Tennis. His son Tom is also a Referee and he has just finished University.

Gordon Hyam

Joined the Association in 1968 and gradually became involved with the Management in 1976 and gave a number of years very good service. Gordon also became very interested in the Charity Football Competition the Association were organising and joined the committee and helped to raise quite a lot of money for charitable causes. Gordon was self employed any job that the Association wanted doing, he was prepared to help.

He was involved with the 'Lillington Boys Club' and after the building was vandalised the George Dutton Charity was able to help the youngsters and they really appreciated what the charity had done, they supported the finals for a few years.

Gordon was quite happy to referee in local football with the Leamington Sunday League and he had no ambition to move into Senior Football.

Gordon was taken ill at home and finished up in Warwick Hospital where he eventually passed away in September 1994. He was married to Ann and had two sons Richard and Peter. Ann has also passed away as well.

Michael Lucey

Michael or Mick as every one knows has been a member since 1978, and has taken part in the social and sporting side of the Association by playing in the Benevolent Cup. He has also represented the Association in the Six-a Side either refereeing or playing. Mick has been very much involved with the Charity Cup competitions as a member of the Committee and has helped raised money for the George Dutton and the Andy Campbell Charity Cups. He has refereed on the Leamington & District Sunday League and on the Midland Combination where he still enjoys being the Assistant Referee. Mick is a Class One referee.

In 2003 Mick with others from the Association received his 21 years award from the Birmingham County Football Association; they were presented by John Starkey who was the County Representative.

Mick was also responsible for the Association move to St Patricks Club where we are always made welcome. He also represented the Association at the Referees Conference in 2001 and 2002 as a Scrutineer when it was a joint affair with Coventry Referees. In 2003 he was the Associations Delegate at Cheltenham Conference and prior to that he was very much involved with the Mentor scheme taking a young referee under his wing to give him advice and support.

Mick has always made himself available at monthly meeting and has always said he enjoys attending so he can relax and listen to the interesting speaker we have had. He told me that he has had plenty of Cup games over the years, and enjoyed every one. Mick finally said he would recommend the Referees Association to any newly qualified referee.

Mick is a family man married to Christine and has a grown up Daughter.

John Austin

John Austin joined the Association in 1976 and soon became involved with the Association. He was elected on to the Management Committee in 1977 and in 1978, he became the Associations Secretary a position he held until 1989 after completing 11(eleven years) this made him the longest serving Secretary in the Association history As well as his Association activities John became a County Assessor taking over as Area Assessment officer for South Warwickshire in 1992 a position he still holds. He is also a Contributory League assessor as well as being a Licensed Instructor of referees.

John refereed on the local Leamington & Stratford Leagues and also the Coventry Alliance. He moved on to the Midland Combination where he refereed for 20 years, during this time he also officiated on the West Midland Regional League.

When he moved to Alcester he became a member of the Stratford Referees Association ad at present is the Chairman and Coaching Officer.

Besides football John's other hobbies are cricket and golf. He is involved with the George Dutton and Andy Campbell Charity Cups holding the Secretary's position for 12 (twelve years).

He became very involved with the Leamington & District Sunday Football League and finally retiring from the League as Vice- Chairman in 2003. He was made a Vice-President of Leamington Referees Association in 1996 and a Vice-President of the Leamington Sunday League in 2004

John is still the Assessment Officer for the area and goes out quite regular to assess referees in Junior and Senior Football.

Alan Windsor

Alan Windsor became a referee by chance when he suffered an injury, which caused him to take up refereeing and he joined Leamington Referees in 1963. In the Association Alan soon made his mark and like all referees at that time we were all became friends.. He became the Manager to the Association Football Team which is what he enjoyed doing and we had quite a lot of success. Alan who was married to Trudy had two sons David and Martin.

 They both joined the Association and played in the football team and also refereed. Alan was not the sort of referee who pushed to get to the top but he enjoyed refereeing locally and he did become a Class 1(one) Referee. When he retired he spent time assessing referees and helping those who were pushing for promotion. He was on the Management for a few years and was always available to help if he was needed.
Besides Football Alan was a very good wicket keeper and played for the local village of Stockton. He also liked playing Bowls, travelling to Rugby to play. One other hobby he had was a surprise. Alan enjoyed Painting and at an Exhibition in Stockton he had quite a few of his paintings on display and they were very good.
Alan passed away very suddenly in August 1997.

Fred Tebbs

Fred Tebbs joined Leamington in August 1967 when he moved from Coventry after obtaining his Class 2(two). He soon settled in to the Association and made a name for himself as a strong, firm, and a well respected referee. On his arrival at Leamington he quickly obtained his Class 1(one) Fred was also played cricket and was a very good wicket keeper, and was captain of Warwick Town cricket club. He was very helpful with the Conference and he supported the Association when they were in Quiz Competitions. He also served on the Management and became the Meetings Organiser for two years.

In his time at Leamington he received a number of Cup Finals he also refereed in Coventry and received Cup Finals from the County FA. When he retired he was officiating on the Southern League

During the Conference years Fred was on the committee as the Assistant Treasurer to Derek Silk. It was an important job with the cost of living index continually rising; they had to keep expenses in check. "He was also involved with his wife Renate at the conference ensuring the smooth running and well being on the delegates that were staying at the Hotels in Dorridge and surrounding area"
Fred retired from the Southern League in 1983 he then continued with his career until he finally retired from work.

Brian Hackleton

Brian Hackleton was just sixteen when he took the Referees Examination and joined Leamington Referees in the September 1972. We all thought at last we have found another young lad, to see if we could get him to the Football League. This would have been brilliant; as we have had two youngsters- one was 16 and the other was 17, when they started refereeing both finished on the Football League. It was not going to be easy with Brian, his education was more important since he was attending to Leamington College.

When he had finished studying for his A Levels he took up employment with G E C Telecommunications in Coventry. Once he was established within the Company after some years of college study, the opportunities arose for him to travel and he was asked to work in Scotland. From there he went to Nigeria and Germany for lengthy periods. Due to work commitments there were few opportunities to referee whilst abroad, although he never lost his interest in football. Brian returned to Leamington and began to enjoy his refereeing once again

As a Class One referee he was soon promoted to the Feeder and Contributory League System. Brian reached the Southern League as an Assistant Referee and served at this level for twelve years, he also refereed on the Midland Combination during this time.

Over the years at different periods, Brian served on the Management Committee in various offices and completed six years as Secretary of the Association. In addition he was the Assistant Secretary of the Birmingham & Warwickshire Joint Referees County Committee for three years.

Along with other referees he has received his 21 years Certificate from the Birmingham County F A. During his refereeing, he has received a number of Cup Final appointments and was Assistant Referee in the Southern League Cup Final in 1999. Brian was also Assistant Referee to Trevor Parkes, Football League Referee, in the Birmingham Senior Cup Final in 2000.

Brian has been happily married to Tina since 1989. He is keen to learn to play golf, so that when he finishes refereeing he will have another way of keeping fit.

Chris Ackroyd

Chris came from Oxford to live in Leamington. He was a Class one referee and a member of Whitney Referees Association. Whilst at Oxford he refereed in Senior Football In his professional life he was a Civil Servant. Chris was a married man and his wife is a school teacher.

With his move to Leamington Chris soon became an important part of the Association joining the Management Committee and eventually became the Treasurer. Chris was also interested with the Quiz competitions that the Association became involved in and with the bevy of teachers we had in the Association they made an excellent squad.

They reached the quarter and semi-final quite a few times but never won the competition outright. In 1985 Chris retired from the Treasurers position to concentrate on his career and to enjoy his Golf. He was a Linesman on the West Midland Regional League and refereed the local Sunday League and Leagues in Coventry.

Simon Rogers

Simon Rogers was the Associations Treasurer from the 1989 to 1994 when, due to increasing work commitments as a Senior Teacher in a Leamington primary school, he found he was unable to attend meetings regularly and therefore retired from the post.

Whilst he was involved with the Association he was very keen on the Referees' Quiz Competitions and with other members competed against other Associations in the West Midland area.

Simon refereed initially in the Coventry Alliance and the Mid Warwickshire Boys League. Promotion led him to refereeing in the Midland Combination and the Leamington & District Sunday League whilst also running the line in the West Midlands League for 8 years. Since then Simon has refereed in the Stratford Alliance and then spent several seasons visiting all the 92 Football League grounds with his younger son.

More recently Simon has returned to the Midland Combination as an Assistant Referee and has continued refereeing in the Boys League most week-ends.

Simon is married with two sons, Tom and Oliver. Tom became a referee when he was 15 and is developing into a good referee. Both boys are continuing their education at university and Tom is continuing his refereeing whilst at Newcastle in the Northern League. He also referees when he comes home at week-end or during holidays.

W G (Bill) Burnell

Bill as everyone called him always made himself available to help when the Association needed jobs doing. He helped members of the Management Committee of the Association and then was elected to become a delegate to the Coventry Alliance. He is now a member of the Management Committee of the Alliance. During his early years Bill played in goal for AP Works, Southam United, Whitnash, Avon Manufacturing and Long Itchington FC. He had a brief spell at Leamington FC as a schoolboy Bill had a trial for Notts County FC.

Cricket was another of Bill's sporting achievements, playing for Southam, AP Leamington, Flavels and Stockton. When he played for Flavels in 1972 his greatest achievement was winning the best bowling averages in the C&NW Cricket League. He had trials for Warwickshire. Having watched Bill bowling for Stockton he was very fast and accurate.

Bill enjoyed working for Charity and when the George Dutton an Andy Campbell Cup Competitions started he was soon on the committee and helped raise money for good causes. He took over as Secretary for a short while and finally became Chairman.

Family problems caused Bill to step aside from his Charity work, although he is still a member and supports events that are arranged.

His refereeing career covered refereeing on the Leamington Sunday League and in Coventry in the Coventry Alliance. He was also on the Midland Combination and finished on the West Midland Regional League. He has had plenty of Cup Finals during his career.

Bill is married and has two sons who are sports minded.

He joined the Association in 1972 where he soon made his presence felt at the meeting.

Steve Portch

Steve Portch became the Treasurer from Simon Rogers in 1994 and served the Association for six years. Steve has a grown up family of two sons, both keen footballers and they were following Steve's love for the game. Steve has his own business in the Computer world. This was very handy when the Newsletter was being produced, Steve helped to produce it.

Having his own business was a problem at one time when the Association wanted an update on the accounts; he would most probably be abroad although the Accounts were always well prepared at Steve joined the Association in 1992 as a Class 3 referee and soon reached the Class1 status. After refereeing on a Sunday morning in the Leamington & District Sunday League he eventually went on the Midland Combination Refereeing and acted as an Assistant Referee.

With his business continually taking him out of the country Steve finally retired after six years from being the Treasurer and handed the reigns over to Ray Morgan at the A G M 2000.

David Aston

Dave Aston joined the Association in 1992 Dave soon became involved with the Association and was elected to the Management Committee. He enjoyed helping the committee make arrangements for the Anniversary Dinncr.. The committee was formed to celebrate the 50th year since the Association was reformed in 1948.

One of David's tasks was when he was Social Secretary was organising a night out for the members. Various items were suggested, such as skittles, ten pin bowling, greyhound racing with a four course meal as well, all these events were well supported and enjoyed.

With changes being made and when John Mander retired in 1997 Dave took over as Chairman and held the Office for five years retiring at the A G M in 2002.

David Aston has three Children, Peter, Victoria, and Jennifer. He also had his own business at one time, as a Heating Engineer. Dave eventually sold up in Coventry and moved down to Felixstowe where he lives now with Norma. Nothing was too much trouble for Dave to sort out. Dave is still a member of Leamington Referees Association and is well known in the sporting world having been wicket keeper for AP Leamington Cricket Team.

He was also a very good goalkeeper playing for Henley- in- Arden on a Saturday. In Sunday football he played Leamington Celtic FC as a goalkeeper and he also had played for Hockley Heath FC as well as other good Clubs. At one time he was invited to join Lockheed Leamington but turned the offer down, he thought the travelling long distances at the week-end would interfere with his job. He enjoyed playing in the Associations Six-a-Side Football Competitions and like all good players he was very competitive. Dave enjoyed his refereeing and had a reputation of being a hard but firm referee.

He was one of the few Referees who were not interested in gaining promotion to Senior Leagues, he was quite happy to referee at local level.

Even though he lives in Felexstowe he is still interested in the Association and occasionally travels to Leamington to meet a number of old friends.

Ray Morgan

Ray Morgan joined the Association in 1987. His first job was to help with producing the Newsletter and later on he became the Secretary taking over from Brian Hackleton, after three years as Secretary Ray decided to retire. Rays refereeing was in the Leamington & District Sunday Football League, and as an assistant referee on the Midland Football Combination, and was quite content with that standard having received plenty of Cup matches and two Cup Finals.

In 2000 Ray took over from Steve Portch and became the Associations Treasurer, this position suited Ray because he is an Accountant by profession. Ray is married to Jenny and they have one son Andrew and one grandson. Both Ray and Andrew were good at football.

Ray is now the Secretary of the Association Charity Cup Competitions, i.e. the George Dutton and the Andy Campbell Charity Cups. Ray and Jenny both support a charity namely 'Young at heart' which provides support and funds for the Heart Unit of Birmingham Children's Hospital. They also support other charities. Ray also enjoyed setting the quiz questions for the annual Christmas competition for the members.

He retired from Refereeing in 2004 with recurring back problems.

Duncan MacAulay

Duncan became a referee in the 1966 season and refereed in the Leamington & District Sunday Football League as well as the Coventry Alliance, for a time he officiated in the Stratford Alliance and did a spell on the Midland Combination. Duncan is still refereeing on a Saturday afternoon and Sunday morning, he must be one of the longest serving referees on the Sunday League.

Duncan enjoys his refereeing and thinks nothing of refereeing three or four matches a week-end he even officiates at Schools Football.

During his time in the Association Duncan has served on the Management Committee, been Vice-Chairman and Chairman of the Association. He also served as Assistant Secretary and since 2002 has been the Association's Secretary. Since 1977 he has when asked been the delegate to the National Referees Association Conferences

With the Mid- Warwickshire Boys Junior Football League Duncan is the President and has held various positions in the League, from Chairman and Referees Secretary to Committee member he is also the minute and referees secretary to the Leamington & District Sunday Football League.

Duncan is married to Tina and is the supplies officer for the National Referees Association at the Headquarters in Coventry.

Patrick Wright

Pat joined the Association in 1968 and took his first exam under the careful guidance of Andy Semple.

Due to his regular attendance in the choir of St Peters Church he never refereed in the Sunday morning of the Leamington & District Sunday League. Pat did referee on a Saturday afternoon in the Coventry Alliance and the Coventry & District Leagues and always gave the Mid-Warwickshire Boy's League his full support.

He received his Birmingham County FA Long Service Award along with other members of the Association in 2003

In 1976 Pat and Helen his wife worked hard for the Conference we held at Solihull and Helen was on the Ladies Committee

Pat has moved to live in Leicester and he has been allowed to carry on assessing in the Birmingham County F A region and help out on the Coventry Alliance on a Saturday afternoon. This pleased Pat because he would be able to visit the grounds where he enjoyed refereeing.

For two years Pat represented the Association at the Birmingham County Joint Referee Committee with Arnold Rouse as a companion travelling to Birmingham every other month.

Since 1984 Pat has been one of the Auditors for the Association and has done an excellent job.

He was also made a Vice- President in 2001.

Pat Gwynne

Pat is one of the longest serving referees we have in the Association, joining Leamington in 1961. Pat has always supported the Association at social functions that are organised and he is a regular member at Council meetings. As far as his refereeing career goes he has given good service to the Leamington Saturday and the Sunday Leagues and he has never had ambitions to climb the ladder to senior football. For a great number of years he has been Secretary to the 'Hotels & Caterers

Football Association' and has been the Delegate to the Leamington & District Sunday Football League for a number of years. Pat's other sporting hobby is boxing. Coming from a sporting family, it is an interest he always had, as well as football refereeing; he became a Boxing Referee or Judge and said he enjoyed doing it.

Over the years Pat has been involved with Women's Football and has travelled all over the World with the 'Women's Football Association' refereeing quite a few games.

In 1997 he was made a Vice-President and in 2002 he was made a Life Member of the Association and in 2004 he received his 50 year award from the Football Association.

Brian Field

Bob as we know him has been a member for a number of years and has always supported the Association. Bob and his wife May both became involved with the conference committee in fund raising and working with the committee. During the conference Bob and May were responsible for all the delegates who were booked in the "Flemings Hotel Olton". This was to make sure the delegates were transported from the hotel and to the conference meeting and then back to the hotel.

In his refereeing career Bob refereed on the Leamington Saturday League, the Mid-Warwickshire Boys League the old Coventry Works League which became the, Coventry Alliance, The Hotel & Caterers League and eventually went on the Midland Combination.

When he retired he became an Assessor doing local matches and also assessed on the Combination. This was a job he still enjoys doing.. Bob was made a Vice- President in 1990 and still attends monthly meetings.

Tom Dean

Tom Dean was an ex-professional footballer who came to Leamington and was involved with the RAF at Gaydon. He had a position as 'Clerk of the Works' with the RAF and had travelled around the World. He was playing for either Burnley or Bolton from the First Division of the Football League when he was only seventeen. He then went to University and when he had obtained his Degree, he then signed for Grimsby Town, and finally took up refereeing.

When he came to Leamington he was working at RAF Camp Gaydon. He enjoyed his football especially when he played for the Association. Tom was also a very good referee. We were pleased at Leamington when he was finally promoted to become a Class 1(one) referee from a Class 3 (three) which what he was when he joined the Association. We pushed the County for his promotion and it only took two years. He was the ideal person to have as a referee, well over six foot tall, well built and very fit, the teams whom he refereed were impressed with him and enjoyed the talks he had with them. He was a good ambassador for Leamington Referees and every one enjoyed his company.

He served on the Management and was instrumental in helping the Association with the 'Six-a-Side Cricket Competition' at Gaydon. This was for the 'Birmingham & Warwickshire Joint Referees County Committee.' The event was a success and the 'Six-a-Side' was won by Leamington.

After a short while Tom was moved to Germany with the RAF it was hoped he would be able to referee in Germany. We were sorry to see him leave Leamington, his employment was important to him. It was our loss.

Paker Bahi

Paker came to Leamington from Coventry where he was a member, when he joined Leamington Referees he soon became involved with the Association, He was elected to the Management Committee and after a few years resigned due to pressure of work, although he still retained his interest in the Charity Cups the Association organised,
Packer is married and one of his sons became a referee and played for the Association at football.
When he came to Leamington Paker was a Class 3(three) referee, through hard work he eventually became a Class 1(one) referee. Always helpful and cheerful when you meet him, especially at the monthly meetings.

Paul Anderson-Kirby

Paul Anderson-Kirby joined the Association in 1987 and refereed in the
Leamington & District Sunday Football League, and the Mid-Warwickshire Football League. He also refereed on Saturday afternoon in Coventry. The Ladies Football League was always short of Referees and Paul completed two years on the list, which he thoroughly enjoyed. It did not take Paul long to obtain his Class 1(one). As well as serving on the Management for four years he was very keen on the Association Quiz Competitions and was quite prepared to spend time building up a good squad of members for the Quiz Team, he also helped by being the Minute Secretary recording the minutes when needed. Paul also enjoyed raising money for charity and thought nothing of entering a very severe cross country run in Wales to raise funds. He wrote about the effort and the arduous run, it was printed in the Association Newsletter.
His employment and working hours made it difficult for Paul to attend the Monthly meetings Paul who was married and has a son and daughter

Peter Boyle

Peter Boyle is the Membership Secretary of the Association accepting the position in 2001. He has been a member of the Management and currently holds the Vice-Chairman's position. Always a willing worker he became involved with his son playing for Alveston FC finishing up as the Secretary of the Club. Peter was developing into a good referee until he injured his ankle which has curtailed his refereeing. Peter has been a referee or 10 years, joining the Association in 1996 he has a;ways shown an interest in the Association. As Membership Secretary he is appreciated for the way he collects the membership subscriptions for the Association.
Peter is married and has a son and daughter. His refereeing is basically the Leamington & District Sunday League.

Tom Prendergast

Tom Prendergast came to Leamington from Kings Norton in the 1980s. He was soon elected to the Management Committee and serving it well for about 5 years, he became involved with the newsletter taking over the job as Editor and finally handing it over in 1995. Tom was very supportive of the Association when his employment allowed him to do so.

Whilst he was in Leamington he obtained his Class 1(one) and gradually worked his way to Level 5. He officiated as an Assistant Referee on the Southern League having completed 14 years, and retired two years ago. Tom still referees on the Midland Combination.
In 2003 Tom along with other Referees from Leamington received from John Starkey the Birmingham County F A. 21 years Long Service Award.
Tom is married to Jackie and has two children Mark and Marie.

We have had a number of Referees who have always been willing to help the Association in any way they could. Not every one was interested in being elected to the Management but they were always willing to offer a service to the Association. Members like **Bill Timson** always busy as a teacher, **Andy Dalziel** who was the treasurer for two years till his employment caused him to retire. You also have **Peter Liddington** who helped out with the newsletter, setting it up so that it could be printed and the older members like **John Wyatt** and **Bill Wall** who gave plenty of support and information. We also have people like **Phil Robbins** who became assistant secretary for three years and helped the Association over a difficult patch. **Dale Packer** was another member who was always available to help and so was **Roy Brown** who was always helpful and along with **Peter Kirkhope** who organised the Football Team for the Six-a-Side and the Benevolent matches. Peter also served on the Management for a few years.

We always seem to get a selection of good referees and they either retire or move on. At one time we had a number of referees from **RAF Gaydon**. They were always getting good reports from the clubs they refereed and they were a good crowd of lads who supported everything we did like football, quiz competitions and social events. We also had Sports Masters like **Neil Justice, Paul Robinson**, and **Clive Darkes** also **John Griffiths**, who were excellent at cricket and football, they had all passed the referees examination. As time went by they moved away to other parts of the Country. Whether they carried on refereeing it is hard to say

Female Referees

The Association has been fortunate in that we have had a few females wanting to take up refereeing and actually going out every week-end, irrespective of the weather and they must be applauded. The majority who take the referees course do so for a number of reasons, but not to actually referee. We have had females who only wanted to know the 'Laws of Association Football' so that when they were watching the team they follow they would have some knowledge to talk about when incidents happen. A few just want to have the knowledge because their little boy wants to play football and the largest number that has been coached was sports mistresses needing a certificate to further their education. It was no problem for any of the Association Coaches (Licensed Instructors) to teach the candidates, it was hoped that we might have a spin off. We have had three females who passed the examination and became referees, and we have had candidates taking the course and passed the exam. They joined the Association but never actually took up refereeing. We also had two husband and wife teams who passed the referees examination and only the husband of one of them took up Refereeing although they both joined the Association. The other couple took the examination to further their knowledge of the game because they were both involved with the organising and control of football teams from the age of 10 up to senior football. One husband and wife team of referees who joined the Association from Coventry--both refereed in local football.
Here is a short resume of the four female referees who did venture out and refereed..

Mrs Christine Cairns

Christine Cairns took up refereeing to help out in boys football, when her sons were playing they never seemed to have a referee and the people who refereed the game were usually from the touchline. They had little knowledge of the laws governing football. By taking the exam Christine considered the games would be played in a fairer spirit.
Once Christine was settled her husband Ron who went everywhere with the boys and Christine also took up the whistle and refereed quite a number of matches.

Christine soon began to make a name for herself as a very fit and fair referee. Christine was being coached by Andy Semple and Arnold Rouse and went to the Sidney Stringer School to take the examination in Coventry, although according to Christine there were problems about allowing her to take the examination, Christine was told that the Football Association did not approve of female referees and she was told to get permission from the 'Women's Football Association' before she could take the examination.

This Christine did and passed the referees exam eventually joined Leamington Referees Association Christine started refereeing in the 'Mid Warwickshire Boys League' and soon had a hankering to referee in open aged football. This was not easy to do at the time there were so many obstructions and obstacles not only to Christine but in general to all female referees over the whole Country. It would be years before a female would be allowed to referee in open aged football. (That was the opinion in the 1976/1980 period. At the end of the 1980s and in the 21st Century a change has been made with female referees, they are allowed to referee in open age football, we have even had a female as the assistant referee on the Football League).

Even though these things happened Christine Cairns kept on refereeing in the Boys League and eventually had quite a number of line appointments in cup competitions which resulted in Christine being selected as a 'Lineswoman in the Final of the Ladies Football Association Challenge Cup Competition.' This was played at Dulwich Hamlet FC ground on Sunday 15th May 1977 between Southampton Ladies and Queens Park Rangers Ladies, one could say the only other person to represent the Association in a FA Cup Final was George Dutton in 1937. This was an honour for Christine Cairns and a boost for Leamington Referees.
The Association received a very good report about Christine from Fred Newbold, a Birmingham League Secretary who was watching the game at Pottertons Football Ground in Leamington, Mr Newbold at the time was living in Emscote. He considered that she was having a good game and he said he liked her style of refereeing

Christine eventually retired from refereeing and husband Ron did so at about the same time. One reason for the retirement was the boys had grown up and the daughters were getting very involved in sports so Mum and Dad decided to support them in their chosen sport. When they retired from the Association it was a loss, because both of them supported all the social events that were organised.

Mrs Christine Cooke

Christine Cooke who was another sports minded parent who decided to take up refereeing because when her one of her sons was playing there was no one to referee.
Christine was married to Dave and had three boys all sports mad, once she had made her mind up to become a referee Christine took the referees course under John Mander and passed the exam. Christine and Dave joined the Association in 1986/7 season. After purchasing the referees shirt, shorts, boots and stockings plus the Referees badge and a whistle, Christine began refereeing on the Mid-Warwickshire Boys League. Christine did have the opportunity to referee in open aged football and by all accounts thoroughly enjoyed the challenge.

She was also given quite a few appointments as Lineswomen in the George Dutton and the Andy Campbell Charity Cups where she proved very capable of holding her own.
Christine was invited to referee in an indoor Tournament at the N E C Birmingham and she was the only female referee there, she was also invited to officiate at a ladies football tournament on Newbold Common Leamington. Talking to Christine about football she said it was much harder than expected and in the 'Final' she was given. Christine said that she was nearly lynched, for giving a penalty; some of the ladies are really tough.

After sending a player from the Field of Play for fighting and having to go to a "Disciplinary Hearing" at the County Football Association, Christine decided to stop refereeing open age football. It was obvious the player did not like being sent off by a female referee in front of his mates.

Christine was the Senior Nursing Sister at Warwick Hospital. Christine and Dave supported the Association in the Social events that were arranged.

Mrs Jill Locke

Jill Locke who is married to Spencer and has two children who are now grown up, became interested in refereeing and with her husband Spencer both took the coaching course organised by Coventry Referees Association. They both passed the examination which was in the 1994/5 season and became referees. Jill started to referee in the Coventry & District Minor League and eventually they moved to live in Leamington and Jill and her husband joined Leamington Referees.

Jill Locke also refereed in the Mid-Warwickshire Boys League and still continued refereeing on the Coventry Minor League where she was well respected. With Mrs Locke refereeing we had another female who always gave of her best and refereed firmly and fairly.

We did not see them at every meeting it seemed that the awkward hours they worked made it difficult, eventually they both retired from Refereeing.

Miss Nicola Townsley

Nicola decided to take up refereeing to ease the shortage in boys football, having taken the referees course under John Mander, every effort was made to help Nicola ease her way into refereeing under 10 year old boys, whose only interest was to play football and they only stopped when the referee blew the whistle.

Nicola refereed a few games on local pitches and she received plenty of support from the clubs.

After about 12 months Nicola damaged her ankle whilst refereeing and finally decided to retire. The ankle was taking longer to heal than she thought it would and it seemed fragile and painful when she tried to run. Nicola was the last female member to join the Association.

We have had other female members who joined the Association but never did any refereeing. They were a *Mrs Angela May and Mrs Sayers-Day* They became members for a short while and took a great interest in the Social side of the Association. The two ladies supported and eventually made up the team numbers for the Association Quiz Competitions in which they did very well, they both left the Association in the mid 90's and are still involved with local football. Mrs May is the fixture Secretary and on the committee with Leamington Hibernian's Football Club. Mrs Sayers-Day is the Secretary of the Mid Warwickshire Boys/Junior League. The other married couple who took the examination but never became referees were **Mr Jim & Mrs Joy Barry** both are responsible for starting the Football Club called **"Leamington Hibernians FC."** They cater for youngsters from 10 years old up to 'Senior Football'.

Football Referees from 1900 to the present 2006

The following referees are the ones that were refereeing in the 1920 to 1926 era and their names were taken from the Warwick & Warwickshire Gazette or the Leamington Spa Courier.

The names mentioned in this paragraph are in alphabetic order and quite a number may have been officiating before the 1914-1918 War. Possibly with the Warwick & District Football League and the Leamington & District Saturday Football League which started in 1909. A number of them could have been officiating on the Coventry & North Warwickshire League, or the Birmingham Combination.

Herewith the names:Mr E R Bartlett,   Mr S Blackwell, Mr M Beckitt,Mr C Carrington,Mr H Cole, Mr G Dutton, Mr A Ellis, Mr H Elkington, Mr Eustace, Mr R Evans, Mr J Fennell, Mr Hartopp, Mr J Herse, Mr E Hubbard, Mr Humpries, Mr W Hunt, Mr C Jones, Mr R Jones, Mr Lines, Mr Ludford, Mr A Montgomery, Mr A C Morgan, Mr W Mills, Mr H Scandrett, Mr Saunders,
Mr R Smith, Mr P Talbot, Mr Tasker, Mr D Wittacker, Mr T Whitehouse Mr J Wildsmith, Mr G Wright, Mr Worrall.
.

Referees in the Warwick & District Intermediate League in September 1921.
Mr Antrobus, Mr Ballard, Mr A Carter, Mr Chimes, Mr Fulford, Mr H Mills, Mr B Tandy,   Mr G Salmon, Mr Ward.

Referees in the Southam League
Mr Brown, Mr Burnell, Mr Cambridge, Mr Greenfield, Mr Foulds, Mr Rawsome,
Mr Shelley, Mr W Sturley.

The majority of the Referees' were local but quite a few came from areas like Stratford, Kineton, Henley, Kenilworth and Solihull. They were officiating in Leamington and the surrounding Districts which included Coventry. We also had members on the Birmingham Combination and the Football League as Linesmen. All were members of the Referees Association and they are placed in book order from 1931 and not alphabetically

Some were members from 1921 up to 1929 this includes members who have held office:
Mr G Dutton, Mr J Wildsmith, Mr W Enstone, Mr W Goodyear, Mr A Lewis, Mr S Soden
Mr A Montgomery, Mr G Bagulay, Mr Thornton, Mr Hemmings, Mr Lines, Mr Harris
Mr Rogers, Mr R Hunt, Mr Hutchings, Mr Booth, Mr Heath, Mr Wilson, Mr Tandy, Mr Roberts, Mr Turvey and Mr Vincent.
Here are the members accepted into the Leamington Referees Association between 1931/1939:-

September— 1931   Mr Aubrey, Mr W King, Mr A Larkin,
November— 1931   Mr J Larkin, Mr E Smith, Mr R West
August ----- 1932   Mr W Enefer, Mr J Partridge
March------ 1933-   Mr H Bridges
September- 1933   Mr A King, Mr Poole
August------ 1934   Mr Hawtin, Mr M Mumford
September - 1934   Mr Roberts, Mr Webb.
January----- 1935   Mr Thomason, Mr Toney
July--------- 1935   Mr Ball
July--------- 1936   Mr R Frost, Mr J Joyner
September-- 1936   Mr Adams, Mr Grif, Mr Horley.
July---------- 1937   Mr Caie, Mr Holiday
November-- 1937   Mr R Rowson, Mr Townsend
September-- 1938   Mr C Jackson, Mr W Hunt
November-- 1938   Mr J Bragg, Mr S Castle, Mr R Mann, Mr W Logus.

From 1948 the following Referees were members, the first names mentioned were members before the 1939 War, and they became part of the Association when it was reformed. Mr G Dutton, Mr J Wildsmith, Mr S Soden, Mr A Lewis, Mr J Joyner, Mr C Jackson.

The following were at the first meeting in August 1948 Mr G Pankhurst (1941), Mr T Story, Mr J Wright, Mr G Perks, Mr S Barnett. Mr L Cecil, Mr H Owen, Mr E Shuttleworth, Mr J White, Mr B Lowe, Mr S Brown, Mr E Teale, Mr F Woodward, Mr L Neale,
Mr A Walters and Mr H Hall were in all probability refereeing whilst they were in the Army
These Members joined the Association in the years as follows:

November---1948	Mr Handy, Mr F Hunt, Mr McTavish, Master P Watson (probationer)
February---- 1949	Mr Ayton, Mr D Clark, Mr Moffet, Mr D Tayler
October----- 1949	Mr F Clarke, Mr D Tickner, Mr D Tyson
February---- 1950	Mr C Aldred, Mr W Aldred, Mr S Brown.
November---1950	Mr K Cox, Mr C Stratton, Mr J Wyatt
October------1951	Mr W Blount, Mr Elstone, Mr B Gwynne, Mr F Mortimer
	Mr Millerchip, Mr R Pemberton
August-------1952	Mr A W Rouse, Mr C Wiseman

The following list of referees are the members who joined the Association between 1953 and 1960. The minutes for that period have been lost, making it difficult to give an accurate list, a book has been found with the membership details from 1953 to 1956. The names printed below will be in alphabetic order, it will exclude Life-Member George Dutton..

Referees Registered as members from 1953 to 1959

Mr C Aldred and Mr W Aldred
Mr L Barnett, Mr L Barnwell, Mr W Blount, Mr T Brennan, Mr P Bloor
Mr E N Clarke, Sgt Collier, Mr K Cox, Mr T Corley, Mr P Culshaw   PC W Draper.
Mr K Eastbury, Mr M Ebsworth, Mr G Elstone, Mr E Enefer, Mr H Eyton.
Mr A Gaudson, Mr J Gilks, Mr S Green, Mr A (Bert) Gwynne, Mr M Guest.
Mr H Hall, Mr J Hiley & Mr R Hiley, Mr D Hodson
Mr C Jackson, Mr J Jays, Mr J Joyner, Flt-Sgt W L Kenish, Mr C Lawrence, Mr B Lowe,
Mr A Macmillan, Mr P Martin, Sgt Marshall, Mr McTavish, Mr H Millerchip, Mr F Mortimer.
Mr R Moreton, Mr H Owen.
Mr G Pankhurst, Mr R Pemberton, Mr G Perks.
Mr A W Rouse. Mr Ron Rouse.
Mr J Sollis, Mr T Story, Mr C Stratton.
Mr D Tyson, Mr D Tickner
Mr F Wall & Mr W Wall, Mr A Walters, Mr E Warwick, Mr P Watson, Mr J Wyatt,
Mr C Wiseman, Mr J Wright   Sgt Young..

It is possible the number of the referees mentioned would still be members in the 1960s a few names have been mentioned and further investigation will take place.

New Members Joining the Association from 1960 to 2006

Members who joined from 1960 to the present 2006 will be mentioned, and the names have been taken from the Council and Management minutes. If any one has been missed, minutes and correspondence that have been lost or destroyed is responsible.

1960	Mr C Arch, Mr Brown, A/C Burrell, Mr W Draper, Sgt Hislop
	Mr N Hughes, A/C Morrow, A/C Quinn, Mr R Rouse.
1961	Mr F Coombstock, Mr A P Gwynne, Mr A Semple Mr H Walton.
1961	Mr R Curwin, Mr H Hodgkinson, Mr A Schultz
1962	Mr A D Clarke, Mr P Cox, Mr D Reynolds, Mr J Sharp, Mr I Shipway.

1963   Sgt Collins, Mr E Davies, Mr A Hesp, Mr J Heywood, Mr R Joyner, Mr S Sharp,
        Mr V Shepherd, Mr A Windsor..
1964   Mr T J Davies, Mr R Locke, Mr N Maltby, Mr D Pope.
1965   Mr D Hay, Mr K Hawtin, Mr J Heywood, Mr P Martin, Mr L Ray, Mr M Wright.
1966   Mr M Beard, Mr N Bryson, Mr C Darkes, Mr T Dean, Mr B Field, Mr N Hughes.
        Mr N Justice, Mr D MacAulay Mr T Williams, Mr R Vernon
1967   Mr W Alderson, Mr B Allen, Mr M Bissimire, Mr B Cramp, Mr L Fleet,
        Mr D Horley, Mr T Marshall, Mr P Murphy, Mr D Palacio, Mr C Shepherd,
        Mr D Silk, Mr F Tebbs, Mr M Warner,
1968   Mr G Hawtin, Mr G Hyam, Mr D Lock, Mr G Reeve, Master P Rouse, Mr R
        Skelsey, Mr J Thomas, Mr D Tinney
1969   Rev H Baker, RAF Brenton, Mr C Daniels, Mr A J Engel Mr D Evans, Mr J
        Eyton Mr D Henson, Mr D Jones, Mr M Lloyd, Mr J Mander, Mr R Marshall,
        Mr M Mullis, Mr C Steadman, Mr P Trotman
1970   Mr R Fisk, Mr P Godfery, Mr M Hollyoake, Mr R Mitton, Mr K Payne   ,
1971   Mr M Allen, Mr K Blyth, Mr J Crowley, A/C Dodd, A/C Foster, Mr R Gibson,
        Mr G Moore, Mr A Norris, Mr N Nurdon, Mr J Pawalec, Mr R White.
1972   Mr H Boardman, Mr B Bugg, Mr W Burnell, Mr R Cheney, Mr R Dyer,
        Mr J Fell, Mr B Hackleton, Mr J H Moffat, Mr R Palmer.
1973   Mr W Clarkson, Mr D Curtlin, Mr M Hollyoacke, Mr S Launchbury, Mr D Lee,
        Mr D Pratley, Mr A Partington, Mr V Slark. Mr J Wayne.
1974   Master D Cheney, Mr R Davies, Mr D Hood, Mr T Machin, Mr H Mann, Mr B
        Omerod, Mr E Poland, Mr B Tustain.
1975   Mr M Burrell, Mr P Clarke, Mr Colley, Mr M & N Crump, Mr D Evans, Mr P
        Gardener, Mr J Green, Mr K Hunt, Mr M Lewis, Mr M Ryan, Mr D Shirley,. Mr
        M Warner.
1976   Mrs C Cairns, Mr J Austin, Mr M Beard, Mr Clapham, Mr D Compton, Mr J
        Cotton, Mr J Donaldson, Mr A Harwood, Mr N Jones, Mr J G Lucey, Mr G
        Reeve, Mr C Reynolds,
1977   Mr J Brockwell, Mr R Cairns, Mr T Machin, Mr P Wright.
1978.   Mr R Benton, Mr M Lucey, Mr D Packer, Mr W R and V Smith- Ward,
        Mr I Staite, Mr V Shepherd, Mr D Taylor, Mr W Timson, Mr M Wright..

1979	Mr I Birch, Mr J Hough, Mr B Meacock, Mr R Paylor. Mr R Waiyne.
1980	Mr T Aitken, Mr A Black, Mr D Bywater, Mr P Flemming Mr E Hall, Mr P Mc Donald, Mr C Parker, Mr P Robbins,
1982	Mr R Davies, Mr R Holt, Mr I King, Mr J Nash, Mr P Perkins, Mr K Reynolds, Mr S Rogers, Mr W Saunders, Mr G Smith, Mr M Southam. Mr R Tedstone
1983	Mr R Brown, Mr J Bull, Mr M Grout, Mr D Hartshorn, Mr P Haywood, Mr P Kirkhope, Mr I Macaulay, Mr C Parker, Mr T Prendergast.
1984	Mr N Armstrong, Mr C Brown, Mr R Burns, Mr A Higgins, Mr D Leslie
1985	Mrs C Cooke, Mr N Evans, Mr D Nash, Mr A Peachy Mr R Palmer, Mr M Willis, Mr D Whitlock,
1986	Mr S Bates, Mr K Cooper, Mr R Day, Mr K Mawby, Mrs A May, Mrs T Sayers-Day..
1986	Mr A Dalziel, Mr B Finch, Mr J Sauvage, Mr D Whitlock,
1987-	Mr P Anderson- Kirby, Mr P Cox, Mr D Hartshorn, Mr R Morgan, Mr(Martin) Ryan
1988	Mr S Falp, Mr A Mansell, Mr K Robinson Mr D Welch, Mr A Winnington
1990	Mr P Donogue, Mr R Liggins, Mr Michael Ryan, Mr M Ward,
1992	Mr D Aston, Mr M Bingham, Mr P La Barbera, Mr I Lowe, Mr S Portch.
1993	Mr S Adams, Mr P Brown, Mr T James, Mr P Liddington, Mr P Mansell, Mr S McCarthy, Mr G Shanley, Mr P Smith.
1994	Mr P Bahi, Mr D Tovey, Mr S & Mrs J Locke
1995	Mr P Emery, Mr P Eyken, Mr J Griffin, Mr T Partington(rejoined) Mr T Woodcock,
1996--	Mr J Archbold, Mr P Boyle Mr P Fulham, Mrs N Townsley.
1997-	Mr A Griffin, Mark Robbins and Andrew Kwan, (Juniors)
1998	Mr K Hancock, Mr A Parasumo, Mr D Swithin,
1999	Mr M Durrant, Mr A Grantham, Mr T Hood, Mr I Murphy, Amrick Sing Bhamr Mr E Scott, Master G Lee, Mr R Warman,

New Members from 2000 to 2006

2000----	Master M Gittins, Master T Rogers, Mr D King, Mr M Powell
2001---	Mr P Boucher, Messrs G & M Grineaux, Mr I Murphy, Master G Sykes.
2002---	Mr J Barnwell.
2003---	Mr A Bendal, Mr A Perks, Mr R Poulson, Mr P Shilton,
2004---	Mr C Woodhead, Mr E Van Vliet
2005---	Mr P Alcock, Mr L Fogarty, Mr T Hardcastle, Mr A Hughes, Mr J Marsden, Mr K O'Rielly, Mr R Partridge, Mr L Taylor, Mr M Warnsman..
2006---	Mr R Edmond, Mr K Edwards, Mr M Edwards, Mr R Faries, Mr T Jamie, Mr J Poulson, Mr R Poulson, Mr R Smith, Mr J Mollart-Solity, Mr K Tranter, Mr C Walkland.

The list of Referees that are members has been extended to 2006 to allow for the Conference to be added. With the referee's future in the 21st Century, it is up to the referees to make the most of it and reap the benefits. Everything is being done for the future and they must grasp every opportunity.

Chapter 17

The Future
2000 to 2004

As we move into the Millennium leaving the 20th Century behind, changes already talked about and discussed in committee meetings would gradually be put into action providing acceptance at Conferences is given, it will also mean a new change for the Leamington and District Referees Association. It has to be for the future of referees and all the changes will be for their benefit, this section is only highlighting the movement forward. The main items will be the reclassification of Referees, the Child Protection System, FAMOA and the final piece will be the new and modified Referees Association of England.

The Referees Association has been in existence since 1908 when it was called the 'Union of Referees' although the first mention of any Referees Society was in 1893 when it was formed in London. It is now being put under scrutiny. Divisions and their Executive Committee Members would be gradually put to one side, other moves to modernise were being talked about and concern was expressed about the involvement the members would have

A complete change was made to the Classification of Referees removing the Class 1-2&3 categories. Instead referees would be graded from 10(ten) to 1(one) the Football Association are moving this forward under John Baker who is Head of Refereeing.

Both the Football Association and the Referees Association have published its "Child Protection Policy" which gives the legal framework. The procedures apply to anyone involved in football whether paid or voluntary, everyone who is involved in any sport involving children or youth will be subject to the scrutiny and eventually vetted as to their suitability.

Whilst theNational Referees Association are involved with restructuring and other issues that will benefit the Referee the Association have been concerned about the every day business. The Officers have tried to set a list of speakers also considering discussion groups as well. The Licensed Instructor has been very busy coaching candidate referees and encouraging them to join the Association. As well as the normal business the Association were committed to Conferences for the next two years with Coventry Referees this meant that it would be extra work for those elected to go on the committee. they also had to do a little bit of fund raising which seemed very successful.The Conferences were in 2001 and 2002 both held at Coventry.

The first report were made at the Conferences on the Management Consultancy Team and they were printed briefly in the Association monthly newsletter. The notices of motion were voted on and accepted which meant that the way forward was on the move. Leamington were also busy in raising funds for the Natiional Associaiton as well as Leamington and certain members surpassed them selves by selling a large number of books raising an amount of money.

It was in 2001 when Pat Gwynne was made a Life Member of the Association a position that Pat appreciated and told members he felt very proud to have been elected.

One of the speakers that had been invited to Leamington would be John Baker having listened to him at an Assessors meeting in Birmingham a few years ago, I knew we would be for an interesting time and the Secretary had also heard him talk and explain his new system for referees.

John Bakers talk is explained later and it is for the benefit of Referees. To understand it you will have to read it and it will explain to you the reasoning behind the Pyramid System. This has been talked about for a number of years mainly by Club Secretaries. They found out when appointing referees to games, all they had in the County Handbook was the fact that the referee was a, 'for example Class2(two) referee' there was no way the Club Secretary could tell if he was experienced enough to referee the game. With the new system the referee wil be Classified and at a certain Level. Before we have John Baker John Barnwell Chief Executive League Managers Association will be talking to the members in the October

Public Liability in Law

Referees have been warned by the County Football Associations and by the Referees Association to be more diligent when examining football pitches. It covers the "Field of Play" and the surrounding areas. The reason behind the statements is that players can sue the referee if they are injured during the game due to the condition of the pitch. A referee is expected to prove that the pitch was in good condition.

A case has gone to the Law where the player is suing the referee for negligence, allowing the game to be played on a stony pitch. Football grounds provided by the local Council where the public can wander at will, are the ones that should be examined. Although all pitches whether private or council should be thoroughly examined. If you as the referee do have problems with a football pitch make a note of what you have found. Whether the pitch was private or Council, log the date and the name of both teams, state whether it was a league match or a Cup Competition. You will then have a record of events.

John Barnwell: Chief Executive League Managers Association October 2000

In welcoming John Barnwell to the meeting, the President said that we are privileged to have a busy man at our meeting and I am sure we will enjoy listening to his talk.
In his opening remarks he said he was pleased we had invited him to talk to us and he reminded the members that the League Managers had been in Leamington a long time under the guidance of John Campkin.

His talk was very interesting and he said that his Association covered 92 clubs in the Premier and Nationwide Leagues as well as the Conference, they also have about 40 Associate Members who had retired from the game, in continuing with his talk he covered a very wide range of topics. John went on to talk about his first excursion into Football when he joined Bishops Auckland at 14 years and six months, they provided a Taxi to the ground and a Taxi back home, even paying for time I lost at work, when I was still at school.

At 16 I was transferred to Arsenal and they were nine years of enjoyable football playing with some of the great names of the day: Jack Kelsey a Welsh International and in my opinion one of the best in the country. Tommy Docherty was another. My first contract was for £11 (eleven pounds) the general contract was for £17 pounds in the winter and £15 pounds in the summer. My contract gradually increased to £17 pounds, everything went hay wire when Tommy Trinder paid Johnny Haynes the first £100 pounds a week.

John gave a brief resume of his Managerial career at Wolves and when he had to sell a good player to get Andy Grey, who did a good job for the Club. Howard Wilkinson did a terrific job at the Football Association and he put together 10 years work in 3 years. John gave his opinion on the selection of a new Manager for England 2000, he said it should be an Englishman.

Finally John Barnwell gave his opinion on Referees, he doesn't think referees are fit enough and they should be doing exercises such as Balance and Inbalance with right and left legs and feet. There is a whole range of exercises that the players do, and the referees do not.
In thanking John for his talk the members showed their appreciation; he was presented with a presentation box of Six Goblets.

John Baker: Referees and the Football Association

When Ken Ridden retired from the Football Association and John Baker became 'The Head of Refereeing' no one really realised the impact he would have on referees. Having heard John Baker speak at Birmingham at an Assessors Seminar we knew, whatever he said would make sense and the subject would be highlighted. The "Classification of Referees" was to be altered to a pyramid system and other issues would be brought into play to improve the status of referees.

At our April meeting we had John as the main speaker and he told the members, he had just completed 12 months being in charge as Head of Refereeing and it was becoming a challenge.

The moves and alterations he was making should give the referees an opportunity to be proud to be a referee. In his talk at the beginning he goes on to say that we are about 4,000 referees short to cover all football matches that is 20% of the total games played on a week-end.

Permission has been given by John Baker to produce the following articles on the changes made to Referees.

We have to attract referees to us, we are trying and the video and camera display at Stoneleigh was beneficial. It showed teaching and coaching clips, we also had experienced referees talking to possible candidates. New candidates will receive a folder from the FA with 4 books, covering the Laws of the Game, the Assistant Referee, how to complete Misconduct forms, and a guide on refereeing.

Regulations for the Registration and Control of Referees

From the season 2002 referees will be informed from their County FA that there will be 10 different bands, originally there were only nine, but the tenth was added to cover the declared non-active referees. These include Assessors, Instructors etc. The method of describing the status of referees has been modified to take into account promotion through classification and further promotion through the pyramid of Leagues, Some Senior members will be pleased to note that 1x and 2x classifications will disappear.

Herewith is the List from the top.

International: 1
Referees on the National list of Referees, who are in the year of classification; currently on the FIFA list of Referees.

Level 1:
 Referees selected by the FA to serve on the National list of Referees and who meet the requirements of the promotion criteria for this level.

Level 2:
Referees selected by the FA to serve on the Panel list of Referees and who meet the requirements of the promotion criteria for this level

Level 3:
Referees, other than those on the Panel list of Referees, selected to officiate on a Contributory League and who meet the requirements of the promotion criteria for this level.

Level 4:
Referees selected to officiate on a Supply League and who meet the requirements of the promotion criteria for this level.

Level 5:
Senior County Referees. This classification includes referees who have served at a higher level#

Level 6:
County Referees

Level 7:
Junior Referees not in level 8 or below

Level 8:
Youth Referees, Referees who qualify but have not yet reached the age of 16. On reaching that age, the referee will immediately move to Level 7

Level 9:
Trainee Referees – Referees who have participated in the two tier training programme and who need to register in order to be covered by public liability insurance. On qualifying the referee will immediately move to level 8 or 7as appropriate.

Level 10:
Declared non-active Referees ## this can include Assessors, Instructors, etc

 # Where a Referee has achieved a level higher than level 5 and is not retained at the higher level, the Referee is to be classified as a Level 5 Referee, with the option of further promotion in the normal way or until a status of non-active is declared by the individual.

A referee registering in one of the active categories is declaring himself/herself available for appointments

The above are just one of the improvements and developments being made by the Football Association with the Head of Refereeing John Baker.
The regulations also describe the requirements for promotion between levels.

Promotion to Level 6 and level 5 classifications shall be based on a referee's practical performance on the field of play. This will be determined by the marks and assessments given by the Assessor on a minimum of three games and club reports from the competitions officiated in as a referee. For promotion to Level 4(four) and above referees will be required to successfully complete a fitness test and a written examination as determined by the FA, on initial selection to a higher level.
Referees may be required to attend an interview to ascertain their suitability by the Football Association.

The current support and developments of match officials is supported in County Football Associations by area training teams. The teams were expanded this season to include a representative from each County FA Referees Committee, a fitness co-ordinator and a National List Match Official. There are nineteen teams working under the supervision and guidance of an Area Advisor, the amount of work they do has increased considerably with initiatives taken over recruitment and retention.
In recognition of the increased activities and responsibilities the FA has approved the funding of full-time "Regional Managers" The regional managers will each look after two training area training teams and support four or five County Football Associations,

A Two-tier Training Scheme for Referees.

The major features of the scheme

- ***Part one***: A four week course for all candidates to acquire knowledge and understanding of the Laws of the Game.
- A multi choice paper with a requirement to score 80% to move on to part two.
- Further attempts can be made to secure 80%
- The qualification attained in Part One is valid for two years
- If the qualification expires the multiple-choice paper will need to be successfully completed again.
- ***Part Two:*** A five week course which concentrates on referee skills.
- The referee will register at Level (9)
- A mentor will be allocated to the referee to supervise
- A code of conduct will be negotiated with leagues.
- Trainees will be encouraged to join the insurance scheme offered by the RA
- At the end of the course the trainee will take the written and oral examination.

Other improvements will be gradually brought into the Referees Association this will eventually benefit the referee in the future. In November 2001, various members of the Executive Committee went to the Football Association and met with John Baker Head of Refereeing and discussed a launching by the FA of the new 'Football Association Match Officials Association' (FAMOA)

A letter was received by the Association from the General Secretary of the National Referees Association, attached to the letter is the objectives and aims of FAMOA. This will eventually be issued to all FIFA Level One to Level Six referees with a tunic Badge in the next few weeks. Level Seven and Eight will receive only the letter, but after they have completed ten games they will be entitled to a tunic badge. The badge is intended for active referees, hence the intended distribution, and is not intended for wear on a blazer. The wearing of the badge is not mandatory and any registered referee can elect not to become a member of FAMOA There is also the aim of the FA to introduce plastic FAMOA membership cards.

John Baker stated quite clearly it is not the intention of FAMOA to interfere with any of the good work the Association does for all referees. There are specific instances where The Referees Association is mentioned in the FAMOA objectives. It is expected that FAMOA will provide an equality of opportunity for all referees, whether they are desirous for advancement or are simply "hobby referees" Part of the FA's Statement of Vision is, of course, to provide a suitable qualified referee to every sanctioned game under the FA's jurisdiction. The setting up of the Regional Manager's organisation and the introduction of FAMOA will help towards meeting this stated objective.

With the advent of the FAMOA, the future of referees' from 2004 looks extremely bright. They have the Football Association behind them and when they decide to become a referee, it costs about £10 which is the amount set by the FA.They are then coached by Licensed Instructors and taken through a 10 week Syllabus set by the County Football Association who then arranges a date when the Candidates can be Examined.

When this is done in most cases they all pass the examination and this makes them members of FAMOA and from the FA they receive and enormous amount of information. They are not told to join the Referees Association. It is left to the Association to approach them and get them to register, especially to have them covered with a personal insurance the referees provide. When they find out the cost, the majority decide not to join; they consider that FAMOA is sufficient.

Everything that can be done for the new referee is being done; they can gain points by being a member of a Referees Association. They can gain points by attending meetings, they get points for refereeing a certain number of matches and all these points can be transferred in the purchase of referees kit and equipment.

The young referee candidate does have to attend certain development days that are being held around the country. All referees are expected to book a place and attend the venue which was selected. They receive a magazine from the FA as well as a newsletter giving all the information they require.

Moving from FAMOA we move into a very sensitive area which could affect referees and anyone who is involved with Juniors in football or other sports. Everything that has been printed in this section should be read very carefully. Every Referee has to go through the questioning and answering sessions also they mat have to pay for the privilege of receiving a clearance Certificate from the Criminal Records Bureau (CRB)

In writing about the system it is hoped it makes it clear of the responsibilities we have to the youth and children of to-day. Herewith a section from the Referees Association. Although this is about Child Protection it is still part of the Future of the Referees Association.. We also have the change of Referees classification and information from the Consultancy Team will enlighten every one as to the Future.

Child Protection

Other very important issues are being placed in front of the young referee and one important item is the Child Protection programme for everyone who has contact with children, it also means the young referee of school age would be protected. The Football Association issued an update document in February 2001 called "ensuring safety in football." Various updates have been produced and the final one concerns every person involved with sport, who has to be approved. It is essential the information is placed in this chapter, it is part of the future of the Referees Association and the young referees who eventually take the referees examination will know it is for their benefit. With the following section on Child Protection following the chapter on FAMOA we shall finish up with the modernised Referees Association of England who have moved forward in such a way to benefit all referees. It is up to the members of Leamington & District Referees Association to accept the opportunity.

The Referees Association towards the end of 1999 sent a letter to all Associations and Societies on the Child protection Policy, telling them Referees Association recognises its responsibility to safeguard the welfare of all children by protecting them from physical, sexual and emotional harm or neglect. It is essential these children who are attracted to and participating in football do so in a quality, safe and enjoyable environment.

The Referees' Association in striving to attain this will give its full co-operation to the National Football Associations. The County Football Associations and those organisations affiliated through the County Associations which provide the opportunity to work with children up to the age of eighteen.

The key principles which underpin this Child Protection Policy are:-
The child's welfare is paramount. All children have a right to be protected from abuse regardless of their age, all suspicions and allegations of abuse will be taken seriously and dealt with swiftly.

Upon receipt by the Association of a notification in which a member has been charged with an offence and the member is the subject of an investigation by the police, or social service, or any other information which cause the Association reasonably to believe a member may pose a risk, then the Association shall have the power to suspend the member from all activities for such period or terms and conditions as it deems fit.

In reaching its determination, whether a suspension should be made, it considers whether a child is at risk, or of a serious nature, or whether a suspension is necessary

The period of suspension referred to above shall not be capable of lasting beyond the date upon which any charge under the Rules of the National Football Associations or any offence is decided or brought to an end

For the purpose of appropriate actions to take, all County RA's / Societies shall act through its Council. The Referees Association expects every member to meet fully his / her responsibility as regards Child Protection Policy.

After the Annual General Meeting in February, Pat Gwynne mentioned the Handbook produced by the Football Association and every one should get one from the County Football Association. He went on to say that the referees should spend time at a meeting to discuss the implications of the **'Child Protection Policy Statement.'**

In the Association we have a number of referees who officiate on boys, youth and ladies football, either on a Saturday or a Sunday and we have junior referees' who officiate in open age football.

The handbook gives a wide range of information on child abuse, the contents includes the introduction to the FA Child Protection Policy Statement, the objectives, the legal and Procedural Framework and finally the appendices.

We have mentioned some of the points from the Child Protection Policy Statements and these procedures apply to anyone in football, whether in a paid or voluntary capacity for example; volunteers, club officials, referees, helpers on club tours, football coaches and medical staff. It also covers the Football Association's responsibility to safeguard the welfare of all children.

The Objectives

In May 2000 the Football Association launched its Child Protection Policy. The policy sets out the following objectives.

The FA Premier League, the Football League and other Leagues must include in their rules the FA Policy statement concerning Child Protection. All bodies which provide the opportunity to work with children and young people up to the age of eighteen and are affiliated to the FA as Charter Standard Organisations, or affiliated through there County Associations, must include Child Protection, to provide on going development and opportunities in all organisations.

The Objectives also give the Legal and Procedural Framework.

It also says,"Non-action is not an option in Child Protection."

Appendices One

The Football Association Regulation

This gives two instances concerning Child Protection, any act or statement which harms a child or children or poses a risk shall constitute behaviour which is improper and brings the game into disrepute.

In these regulations the expression "Offence" shall mean any one or more of the offences contained in Schedule 1 to the Children and young Persons Act 1933 and any other criminal offence which causes the Association to believe the person accused of the offence poses, or may pose a risk of harm to a child or children.

Appendices Two;- What is Child Abuse

There are five forms of abuse; they are Physical Abuse, Neglect, Emotional Blackmail, Sexual Abuse and Bullying.

It gives the following:- Once the Club has Anti-Bullying Policy. It must ensure that everyone within the club clearly understands bullying will not be tolerated and what the implications are if bullying continues.

The Licensed Instructors in the Association attended a meeting with the Area Adviser and the contents of the Child Protection Procedures and Practices were discussed. It has been said that all referee candidates will eventually be coached with the Child Protection procedures and practices included in the course.

The advice given to all referees is to be extremely careful when refereeing boys, junior, or ladies football. We are in a changing world where everyone has to take care and one silly word or movement can create a problem.

In 2001 the FA produced a 3-hour Workshop- ensuring safety in Football.
It consisted of the following Contents
- FA Education and Child Protection Team
- Child Protection and Football
- Children—Ensuring Safety in Football
- Workshop Update
- Accessing the Workshop
- Workshop Costings
- Young Disabled Footballers and Vulnerable Adults
- Quality Delivery
- FA Charter Standard for Clubs
- FA./ NSPCC Helpline
- ChildLine
- Questionaire

The contents from above were circulated to various organisations involved in Training, Coaching, Referees, Development Officers, FA Protection Officers, FA Charter for Clubs.

Further developments will have taken place and most referees will have to pay for clearance when they have to complete the CRB checks. The FA states the following to safeguard children and vulnerable adults in football. The highly respected Child protection and best practice learning programme has already been undertaken by many referees.

The introduction of Criminal Records Bureau (CRB) checks across football is also underway, we wanted to make sure all referees, assessors, tutors, and mentors in England know what needs to be done.

The Football Association have issued a Child Protection and C.R.B. checks for referees and the deadline has been extended for referees, There are talks of a fee being paid to obtain your certificate.

Restructuring of the National Referees Association

The major issue involving the National Referees Association was the move by Erewash Valley Society in 1999 submitting at Conference a Notice of Motion for the Association to consider a major restructuring of the Referees Association and its Annual Conference any recommendation for restructuring to be presented to Conference 2001.

The notice of Motion was carried by a majority of three to one (3 to1)

Once the issue of restructuring was discussed the National Council advertised for volunteers to become part of the Management Consultancy Team so they could conduct a detailed examination of the Association's present structure with the Financial and Administrative procedures and to report with its findings and recommendations to the Council on the future of the Referees' Association.

The National Council made a selection of five to make up the Management Consultancy Team and those selected have accepted.

The five people who make up the team are involved in sport and four are members of the Referees Association. The Team leader drew up a programme of activity and the National Council feel the Membership is 100% behind the team, in the work and responsibility that lie ahead for them in the execution of their task. The team consists of retired professional business men who will bring all their expertise to the job in hand.

The Consultancy Team in their first initial statement, place on record how conscious they are of the importance and complexity of the task ahead. They consider the members want a fundamental and thorough re-examination of the whole of The Referees Association. The Team Leader.goes on to say that we come without preconceived solutions, in any case, our job is not to tell members what to do, evidence will be gathered using various means with interviews, documentation visits and questionnaires, we hope it will lead to a clarification of the fundamental question: What is the NRA about and for? What should it be about and for in the future?

The Team go on to say they aim to keep the consultancy process as transparent as possible. There may have to be some confidentiality in some of our workings, but there will be no secrecy. We are scheduled to present an interim/progress report to Conference 2000 and expect by then to be seeking guidance before drafting the final report to Council in September 2000.

Members will have to be aware said the Leader that while National Council and others will be consulted and will offer their encouragement, the final report with all the corrections of point of fact will be the consultancy Team's Report. This will be presented to Conference by National Council together with any Rule changes.

More importantly all the decisions about the future of the Referees' Association will be made by the members through their delegates to Conference.

In the February 2000 Newsletter the members received a Questionnaire from the Consultancy Team. With four items to consider and answer, this has to be returned to the Head Office in Coventry by the end of February. It asks members to complete the form and return it to the Association Secretary who will complete the Master Questionnaire on behalf of Leamington Referees. It will be returned to the General Secretary and then forwarded to the Management Consultancy Team.

Issues for consideration by the 'Think Tank' are as follows:.

(1) Vision of the Referees Association
      (a) At present the RA has neither a 'vision statement' nor a 'mission' statement, and so cannot easily say what it is about and where it is going, Could you suggest what a possible vision and mission might be.

(2) Membership of the Referees Association
(3) The Changing Football Environment
(4) The relationship with your County Football Association.

The future is yours and it's up to the members to complete the form and return it as requested.

The Consultancy Team was soon at work gathering information by interviewing and having discussions with individuals and small groups from the President to the rank and file members
The aim is to get a cross section of opinion, so we can finalise and distribute 'the questionnaire' we hope to devise a method that will give the most representative range of views and still be manageable.

Questionnaires out to roughly 16,000 members is out of the question, To seek more information the MCT sent out 350 'corporate' responses consisting of 93 questions and if we get a 100% return they said they would be reasonably happy.

The members at Leamington discussed and completed the questionnaire at the monthly meeting and returned it completed to the Head Office and one or two members sent in suggestions of their own. The Team were quite pleased with the response.

The contents of the report from the MCT, ***Restructuring the Referees, Association,***

Every member of the Referees, Association should have received a copy, together with an outline of the report and list of Recommendations.

The MCT have said when we started we promised 'transparency' and we have tried to keep every one informed. It is most important that every member should be aware of our findings and take part in the discussion of our recommendations for the future.

The Booklet contains 54 pages of text and 40 Recommendations, and the MCT consider that some signposting might well be helpful for members to get sense of the report and how implementation of the changes might be phased.

- Recommendations 1-3----- Vision, Mission, and Objectives
- Recommendations 8-24---- changes in the present structure and proposals for a new structure

To understand the meaning of the recommendations 8 to 24 you may possibly need to know the structure of the Referees Association this has been described in Chapter 10(ten). What it will mean eventually is that the Executive Council and the Divisions will disappear and the Referees Association will be run by a new body of Referees. This will be explained later on The third ,fourth and fifth recommendations covers the Administration Images and the functioning of the RA.those recommendations will be discussed more when the new organisation takes over .

Recommendations 1to3 are fundamental. The MCT believe the RA needs to know where its going and needs to make it clear to itself and others, it goes on to say that the recommendations would not need to be presented to Conference in the form of 'change of rule.'

That deals with two of the Recommendations and at the heart of the MCT report it deals directly to Restructuring. From the analysis of the masses of evidence we received and described in the report, it is clear the members want a more professional, more responsive, more pro-active, more visible, more credible Association. The MCT stresses in the report there are limitations to what can be expected of any voluntary organisation, it also believes the RA at present falls short of what is possible and without change will inevitably decline.

When the Divisions were discontinued it led to a reconsideration of the RA's relationship with members from Northern Ireland, Wales, and Overseas. The view that membership of the RA should be restricted to those registered or formerly registered with member bodies of the English FA, at the same time, possible new relationships with colleagues in Northern Ireland, Wales and Overseas should be explored.

The MCT recommend that the present Council be re placed by a smaller Board of Management with executive committees rather than sub-committees and clearly the Association should have a Chief Executive—a clearly defined post to replace the rather ambiguous role of President. They also recommend an age limit of 65 years for those seeking election/re-election to the Board and its Executive committees.

With the proposals so fundamental to the structure, the role of the present Council is not easy they must now debate the Recommendations and make their proposals to Conference 2001 as required by the Erewash Valley Notice of Motion.

If Council and subsequently Conference, accepted the restructuring proposals, either exactly as they are or with modifications, it would be necessary to have a transitional procedure because the changes could not happen overnight. We said in the Report- it was outside our remit to recommend an Implementation Team to see it through. All of the restructuring would imply changes to a number of the existing rules and would entail serious and careful re-drafting.

To display all the recommendations in full, from the Consultancy Team and the response from the Executive Council of the Referees Association would be asking readers to be thoroughly knowledgable of the workings of the Referees Association.

The main purpose of this Chapter is to follow on from the 20th Century and show that the future of Referees is gradually taking place. The M C T(Consultancy Team) have nearly completed their work and have submitted to the National Referees Association their findings, the National Referees Association will give their reply and the whole issue will be discussed at the Conference 2001

Both recommendations one made by the M C T and the responses from the Council have been printed in the Referees Association Magazine and the Council go on to say, it is in accord with the thinking behind the recommendation, it cannot agree the simple abolishment of the Divisional Executives as recommended. They also say there could be areas or regions where there is no direct links between the grassroots membership and the top body.

This section brings to the end the amount of work by the Management Consultancy Team. It will depend now at the Conference 2001 where a Society will put forward a Notice of Motion to set up an Implementation team to take forward the recommendations.

It was resolved by a 7,000+Majority that an Implementation Team of 9(nine) should be elected, to examine in detail the Consultancy report dated September 2000

The Implementation Team consisting of nine RA members elected in the Autumn were soon involved with the recommendations the (M C T) have made.

The authorship of the report; The Team (M C T)can reassure members that the resport is the Team's own in every sense. They go on to say they have quite properly been influenced by many members, but the conclusions they have drawn are their own. They hope that the efforts they have made will prove of real value for the future of the R A referees, refereeing, and Football.

As Winston Churchill once famously said:

"This is not the end it is not even the beginning of the end. But it is, perhaps, the end of the beginning."

The Rules of the Referees Association have been in existence since 1908 and was then called the Association Football Referees' Union (1908) The Objects consisted of only (10) items the current set of Rules are called, The Referees' Association and cover (13) items of their objectives

The R A has clearly been successful as an organisation, and it has managed to retain its overall members in the face of numerous difficulties, it continues to have many dedicated members, who exemplify the R A's motto 'Service before Self'. Above all it has a proven record of supporting referees and of providing numerous practical benefits.Herewith the Rules of the Referees Association from 1908 to the present, however, the state objects/objectives of the R A have hardly changed over its 92 years of existence.

Association Football Referees' Union (1908) That the Objects of the Union be:-	The Referees' Association (current) The objectives of the Association shall be:-
a. To improve the status of Referees	(a) To improve the status of referee.
b. To improve, as far as possible, the standard of Refereeing.	(b) To improve the standard of refereeing.
c. To promote a closer relationship between Referees and Associations and Clubs.	(c) To promote a closer relationship between referees and Football Associations and kindred bodies
d. To assist all Associations in promoting the best interests of the game.	(d) To assist all such associations in promoting the best interests of the game.
e. To assist all existing Referees' Associations in their educational and general work.	(e) To assist all such associations in promoting their educational and general work.
f. To watch and promote the interests of the Referees in general.	(f) To establish referees' Associations, Branches or Societies in districts where none exist.
g. To protect the members from injustice.	(g) To watch over and promote the interests of referees in general.
h. To assist or take action by or on behalf of any Referee unfairly or unjustly treated.	(h) To protect the members from injustice or unfair treatment.
i. To make such representations to the governing bodies as may be thought necessary for the good of the game and the benefit of Referees	(i) To assist or take action (legal or otherwise) for and on behalf of any member unfairly or unjustly treated.
j. The provision of a Benevolent Fund to aid Referees or their dependents in case of need, sickness, or death.	(j) To make such representations to the governing bodies as may be thought necessary for the good of the game and the benefit of referees and refereeing. .
	(k) To maintain a Benevolent Fund to aid members or past members or their dependents in case of need.
	(l) To assist in maintaining a steady supply of suitable candidates to take the referees' examination.
	(m) To provide social activities, as desirable, and to retain in membership those who have retired from active refereeing, that their experience may benefit the newcomer.

The Implementation Team since its election at Conference in 2001 has been inundated with e-mails and phone calls to the team members, with draft reports and documents passing between the committee and sub- committees have been created to look at specific areas which included the seven regional divisions, as well as the structure of the RA within England, Northern Ireland and Wales. The move towards a new managing body such as the nine –member board as recommended by the Management Consultancy Team, there were other issues that the Team would be looking at and they have the Authority to examine any of the Association's records and to interview and Council members, employees and will take into account the views of any member who makes representations to them.

There are (7) terms of reference proposed by the IT team and agreed by the Council, and they are briefly as follows:

(a)   To pay close regard to the recommendations on the MCT Report issued in September 2000.

(a)   To consult any persons including members of Council and the former MC Team with Council's permission.

(b)   To submit Proposed Rule changes/ or Notice of Motion for any preliminary changes in the organisation by February 2002, for presentation to Conference 2002.

(c)   Notices of Motion for any reorganisation Management for Conference 2002

(d)   To identify which of its proposals will and. which will not necessitate any increase in members. To submit proposed new Rules for the RA and subscriptions.

(e)   To complete its functions on a budget submitted and agreed to by Council, including the reasonable travel costs of the team members.

(f)   To publish bulletins on its work and findings periodically in the Football Referee and on the RA Website.

They also have a Timetable for findings and recommendations, the Chairman of the Administration and Policy Committee will act as a link between the IT team and the Council
The IT team are answerable to all RA members at Conference 2003.

To have the Implementation Team take over from the Consultancy Team is a move In the right direction and everything that follows from here is the start of the new Referees Association the first item to follow will be the the structure from the old R A and the Proposed new structure.
The Conference in 2003 will decide what happens, if other Conferences are anything to go by the IT team should not have any worries.
The problem remains who will be Elected Representatives   to the 'Board of Management'
The Election will take place in November 2003 but before we list the candidates you will be shown the (7) terms of reference proposed by the IT team. It is essential that the headings are highlighted and the information they possess is for every referee's benefit

The final Structure of the RA at present and the Proposed New Structure

From: **Societies, Branches, Associations and Clubs**
To: **County Referees' Associations**
To: **Divisional Executive Committees there are 8(eight)**
To: **Overseas and Service Divisions.**
To: **National Council comprising of Administration & Policy**   **Sub- Committee**
                                        Conference   **Sub- Committee**
                                          Finance   **Sub- Committee**
                                          Instructional & Publication   **Sub- Committee**

Proposed New Structure
From: **Societies, Branches, Associations and Clubs**
To: **County Referees' Associations**
To: **Other Associations**
To: **Board of Management comprising of :**

Corporate Affairs Executive Committee
Internal Affairs Executive Committee
Training & Development Executive Committee

No 1 Establish the Referees Association of England (RAE) with a streamline' structure
It is proposed to eliminate the Divisional Structure following the Consultants recommendations..
What we have now is from the local (ABSs)- County RAs- Divisions- (Overseas&Service) to RA Council.

What is proposed is local (ABSs) - County RAs- Board of Management

After the changes, there would be direct communications between the Board and County RAs. Also a liaison meeting would occasionally be arranged between the Board and groups of County RA representatives.
It is expected that Wales and Northern Ireland will want to establish their own National Referees Associations there are clear benefit to having separate 'national' RAs in each of the three countries

- To develop stronger relationships between the RAs and the FAs, concentrating on national issues
- To remove current confusion whereby the English FA meets with the RA, which is a multi-national body

No 2 Elected Board of Management for the (RAE).
A Board of nine members would be elected to run the RAE. There would be three executive committees that could include co-opted specialists.
Initially they would serve for a minimum of three years, they would then retire in planned sequence with annual elections. They could offer themselves for re-election for a further two years.
A system of favouring a spread of board representation from different regions of England would be introduced. At least one member would preferentially be chosen from each of three major regions. These regions are listed below:

East Midlands & North comprises the FA regions covering the Football Counties of;
Cumberland, Cheshire, Derbyshire, Durham, East Riding, Isle of Man, Lancashire, Leicestershire&Rutland, Lincolnshire, Liverpool, Manchester, North Riding, Northamptonshire, Nottinghamshire, Northumberland, Sheffield & Hallamshire, Westmorland, West Riding.

Mercia & West comprises the FA regions covering the Football Counties of;
Birmingham, Berks &Bucks, Cornwall, Devon, Dorset & the Channel Islands, Gloucestershire, Hampshire, Herefordshire, Oxfordshire, Staffordshire, Shropshire, Somerset, Warwickshire, Worcestershire, Wilshire.

Anglia & South East comprises the FA regions covering the Football Counties of:
The AFA, Army/Navy/RAF, Bedfordshire, Cambridgeshire, Essex, Hertfordshire, Huntingdonshire, Kent, London, Middlesex, Norfolk, Suffolk, Surrey, Sussex
When you look at the map it is split into three sections

No 3 Covers the special case for the armed forces and those living on offshore islands..
The Three service FA's come under the jurisdiction of the FA and are, in effect, each a County FA, the same is true of the Isle of Man and the Channel Islands.
All members in these categories will become members 0f the RA(E) and their respective 'Football Counties' will be part of one of the 'electoral regions.'

No 4 Other provisions for the RA(E)
In the published Rules there are full details covering a wide range of procedural matters such as:
- General meetings
- An emergency committee
- Board committees
- The transitional arrangements for handing over authority
- Voting arrangements
- Suspensions and appeals.

No 5 New Arrangements for members in Wales, Northern Ireland and overseas within the RA.
The IT received strong representations from members in Wales, Northern Island and on behalf of those overseas. They decided to find a way to preserve the benefits of RA membership they currently enjoy.
They are prepared to pursue their specific national interests separately, they want to retain their access to the RA's common interest benefits:
- Insurance scheme
- Supplies
- Magazine
- Meetings and Conferences
- Technical and Legal Advice
- Head Office Administration
- The Benevolent Fund

[Note that the Insurance and Benevolent are not available to overseas associate members].

The IT proposes that the Referees' Association should continue as a multinational organisation and be reconstituted with specific roles:
- Operation of Head Office as a central administration service for the three National RAs
- The provision of the member benefits as now, insurance, supplies, magazine and advice

The 'RA' thus becomes a central commercial and administrative organisation solely to provide member services.

It will have no jurisdiction over the internal affairs of the National RAs.

No 6. Constitution of the Referees' Association

The three National RAs will be the 'members' of the RA not the individual NRA members themselves.
A Board of 7 appointees will run the RA. The respective National RAs will make those appointments:
- 5 members from England
- one member from Wales
- one member from Northern Ireland,

[This ratio reflects rather than replicates the relative numerical strengths of the three national RAs]

No 7. Key Benefits of Restructuring the Referees Association

By reconstituting the RA itself and forming three separate National RAs, there will be a number of very significant benefits that the Management Consultants pointed to.
- The spirit and best traditions of the RA will flourish in a modernised environment.
- The valued benefits enjoyed by members at home and overseas are preserved-supplies, insurance, magazines etc.
- The National RAs will be free to extend their partnerships liaising and negotiating with the respective Football Associations.
- A smaller Board of Management of the RAE will be more cost –effective and operate more decisively
- A fresh approach will be brought to the central administration of the RA.
- With a layer of admin removed, the new RAE will develop into a more forward- looking and streamlined organisation with better communications.
- There is a minimum cost saving of over £17,000 p.a. which can be ploughed back into improving services at no cost to members.

Every ABS and County RAs have received the full text of the proposed Rule Changes and Notices of Motion, they will in all probability be discussed at the next Conference 2003.
They have produced at least six interim reports of the progress they have made and each report has shown that the IT team are well ahead in the restructuring of the Association and have every intention to produce two sets of Rules, one for a restructured Referees Association, controlled by a Board of seven and to become a trading and administrative body retaining the assets of the Association and answerable to a separate National Associations for England, Wales and Northern Ireland. In the opinion of the IT, three separate National Referees' Associations will be better placed to forge closer links with their respective Football Associations for the benefit of their members.

A new National Referees' Association of England (RAE) will be the parent body for members in England. It will have an elected Board of Management of nine members of the Association, five of whom will serve on the Board of the RA. It is envisaged that Wales and Northern Ireland will constitute themselves in parallel national bodies. The County RAs will continue their current functions and also assume a new liaison role between the board of the RAE and the local ABSs.

Arrangements have been included so that after the election of the Board of the RAE in November 2003, there will be a phased hand over of responsibility from the Council of the Association to the Boards of the RA and the RAE during the year 2003/2004.

The Team is required to identify which of its proposals will and which will not necessitate any increase in members' subscriptions. In their opinion the proposals will not cause any increase in subscriptions, they say in fact, there should be substantial cost savings. Meeting expenses incurred by the Association should be reduced by some £17,000 p.a. by reason of the replacement Council and Divisional Executive Committees by the proposed Board.

In the sixth interim report the IT team have said the greatest concern voiced by members has been that of financing the changes. Fears have been expressed that we shall be moving towards an even more expensive operation. This report has been put together to dispel members' worries.
Over the past three years the Association has managed to accumulate a surplus of some £40k. Under current circumstances, a £10k surplus should be achievable each year before any exceptional expenditure.

During the current year the surplus has been necessarily and wisely invested in the increased security at Head Office, that was in August and Council have provided the IT team with a detailed breakdown. With a small table the IT show the RA Expenditure for the financial year 2001/2002 was reduced to give a proposed saving ot £17,000 to achieve this the IT removed the Presidents expenses disbanded Council, E C and Div Mtgs. The IT also set up a Budget for the R A.

The IT go on to talk about a remuneration for any Chief Executive would have to include an incentive package of a basic salary plus a bonus based on a percentage of any additional income generated through sponsorship. It is also our view expenses should be reimbursed at the lowest level possible. Societies will be expected to pay for their Delegate if they send one to Conference; they believe this should be true for County RAs paying their Delegates expenses.

To clarify the position on individuals' subscriptions, the proposal is the members pay £7.00 to the RAE, of that amount £6.00 would be sent on to the RA, they feel a need for the RA to pay each of the three National RAs a sum of money as seed-corn funding (assets set aside for the generation of future profits). Conceivably, this might possibly extend to the County RAs too. The National RAs will be able to set their own subscription level based on covering their own operational costs.

Thus, Individual members will pay no more than is currently the case. Their money will merely be distributed in a different proportion.
The sixth interim report was printed in the April 2003 issue of the Football Referee and the next step should be the 85th Annual Conference at Cheltenham in June 2003 where Item 15: Proposed Alterations of Rules &Notice of Motion, where the Kingston Referees' Society, on behalf of the IT team, propose the Rules of the Referees' Association be withdrawn and they be substituted by two new sets of amended rules namely:
- Rules of the Referees' Association and
- Rules of the Referees' Association of England.

The Society then gives the Reasons,
Terms of Reference of the IT to pay close regard to the Management Consultancy Team recommendations.
These proposals represent progress, the IT have declined to proceed on –one barring over 65 from senior office and the other is limiting the Association to 'English' referees.
After the Election in November 2003, there will be a phased handover of responsibility from the Council of the Association to the Boards of the RA and the RAE during the year 2003/2004.

Kingston Referees Society, on behalf of the Implementation Team has submitted to the 85th Annual Conference Item 15: Which is the: **Proposed Alteration of Rules & Notices of Motion.** The Society in commending these proposals to members, the team pays tribute to current and past members of Council for their selfless efforts over so many years and trusts they will wish to continue to serve in senior office in their respective National Referees' Associations.

The Proposed Alterations to Rules and Notices of Motions were proposed and seconded and after a lengthy discussion from the members and a response from the Council who spoke of much good sense in the proposals, but plenty of fine tuning was needed. The two members who proposed and seconded the Proposition put forward an excellent case for the change, modernising The Referees' Association and for the new Board to have direct links with the members, the Board would have the power to replace any of its Members at any time, this power is currently not available. They also talked about the savings that would be made with the changes. The two members who proposed and seconded presented an excellent case and to get the full implications the Proposals and Notices of Motions should be read by everyone.
The Voting went in favour of the Kingston Referees Proposals, by 8,081 for and 3,377 against.
All the other Proposals and Notice of Motions went the same way with a majority of at least seven to one.
At the Conference in 2003 quite a few members were concerned at the abruptness of change that happened, it was the end of 95 years service to Referees although members have complained that the Executive were not forward thinking enough, financial restraints made it rather difficult and one must remember the Association was always run on a shoestring with a part time Secretary and having to rent Office Accommodation.

The voting in November 2003 for a position on the Board of Management of the Referees' Association of England, resulted in 19 candidates seeking support from the members the voting forms gave the names of the nineteen candidates with a brief CV there was a mixture amongst the candidates, some had held office with the various Divisions and a few candidates who had never been on such Committees. At the Associations monthly meeting each candidate was discussed and the members voted for the final selection. The results were sent to the Head Office

The counting took place on November 15th 2003 and the nine members who were elected were as follows, with number (one) receiving the highest number of votes.

1	Bart O'Toole	Anglia & South East
2	Richard Blackman	Anglia & South East
3	Leonard Randall	Anglia & South East
4	John Harden	East Midlands & North
5	Nigel Genner	Mercia & West
6	Alan Poulain	Anglia & South East
7	Ray Mallery	Anglia & South East
8	John Starkey	Mercia & West
9	Sid Harrison	Anglia & South East

The representation of the Board Members reflects that the possibility of Anglia & South East would be the main players in the new Referees' Association of England

Once the Board was elected, in January 2004 meetings were held and the various Committees' were selected, by a unanimous choice Bart O'Toole was made Chairman of the Board. The seven members were invited to attend the meetings of the Council and its Committees so a phased handing over can be facilitated, this will be done until the Conference 2004 in Cardiff. The President John Bunn who would only serve 12 months as President, in his Christmas message he hoped that the Members and the Board will work closely to ensure a smooth transition from the old to the new is effected, always bearing in mind that our service is to our members and their needs.

The Board of both new Associations wish to clarify the plans for the future of Conferences and AGMs of the Associations after 2004.

The rules of the (new) RA require its AGM to take place in April, to be attended by the 7 members of the Board, five from England and one each from NI and W

- Approve the RA annual report, annual accounts and auditors' report ready for circulation to the National Associations in England, Northern Ireland and Wales.
- Receive the annual report and accounts of the trustees of the benevolent fund.
- Debate rule changes and notice of motion.

The rules of the new RAE require its AGM to take place in England one day during June or July. All members of the RAE will be invited to attend. It will serve mainly to:

- Approve the RAE annual report, annual accounts and auditors' report.
- Receive similar reports from the (new) RA and its benevolent fund.
- Confer RAE awards.
- Debate rule changes and notice of motion.

The annual Conference weekend will be organised for the foreseeable future by the RA, not the RAE. It will remain as it always has been an event for all current members of the Association in England, Northern Ireland and Wales.

The M C T and the IT both give their recommendations for future Conferences. They both say that the RA Board not the RAE Board would assume responsibility for organising the Annual Conference for the foreseeable future. They also said that the rule changes and motions should not be a debate for centre stage; it should be an occasion for training, workshops and a social gathering for members in England, Northern Ireland and Wales, as well as overseas members.

At the Conference 2003 a rule change was proposed as a separate rule, it was not a specific recommendation in the MC Report. And the reason being it envisaged a distinguished, well known, present, or former referee serving as a ceremonial, figurehead, President would promote the Association effectively within the game in England.

The rule reads as follows, "at its last meeting before the AGM every third year, or at other times where necessary, appoint a suitable member of the Association to serve as Honorary President for three years commencing immediately after the AGM."

In March 2004 the Board of Referees' Association of England are delighted to announce that leading former FIFA and Premiership Referee David Elleray has accepted our nomination as Honorary President of the Association for three years with effect from Conference 2004. The RAE go on to say they are pleased that a person of David's immense experience as a referee at the highest levels and with an outstanding reputation as an ambassador for refereeing and for football is to take on this position.

David Elleray will become the first Honorary President of the RAE at the Conference 2004 in Cardiff.

At the last meeting of the Referees Association which was held in Coventry on Saturday 17th April 2004 the Chairman John Bunn welcomed the members of Council and the members of the RA Board and he remarked that he would make further reference to the fact it was the last meeting at the end of Any Other Business.

In AOB of this meeting the RA Chairman Bart O'Toole thanked President, John Bunn, and Council members for allowing himself and Board members to shadow Council since their appointment. This had been of great value to himself and his colleagues in terms of the knowledge gained relating to the workings of Council and the Association. He hoped the transitional period would continue to be a smooth one and he and his colleagues would continue the excellent work carried out by present and former Council members over many years

In closing the final Council meeting John Bunn said we still had responsibility for the control and workings (excluding financial) of our Association until midnight on Saturday 19th June 2004. John Bunn goes on to thank all Council members for the friendship and fellowship we had enjoyed, we have had the occasional contretemps, but by and large there had been a tremendous camaraderie. We may not see so much of each other unless we meet at future conferences he hoped so as it would be such a shame to sever all connections.

Thanks were expressed to the General Secretary for the excellent way in which he had been a very necessary link between Council and the Board and for looking after the affairs of both and seeing that all that needed to be done in both camps had been done. This had assisted greatly in the transitional requirements and helped and supported John Bunn in his year as President.

In conclusion, the President John Bunn was grateful for all that we and our predecessors on Council offered in the service of The Referees' Association, enjoying many happy hours together along the way. He hoped the members of the Board would take with them the very best wishes of Council as they continued in Service. He trusted that our Association would go from strength to strength in their very capable hands.

The end of the Referees Association as thousands who were members, would be played out at the Conference 2004 in Cardiff, the President who had only held office for 12 months would have to hand his President's Badge over and the new Referees' Association of England would take over under the guidance of Bart O'Toole who was made the Chairman and the Board of Management which consisted of only 9(nine) elected members

Their choice of President is David Ellerary, who the Board consider an important asset to the Referees Association of England. His appointment is for 3 years.

With the restructuring of the Association the forward move will be with the 'Board of Management.' The Conference in 2005 will be very important to them. If it is a success it will be for the benefit of all referees.

Association Business

In 2003 an event took place at the Monthly Meeting of the Leamington & District Sunday Football League when four members of the League received their 50 year Awards from the Vice- Chairman of the Birmingham County Football Association on behalf of the Football Association

The Four members although involved with the League they are also involved with the Leamington & District Referees Association three were referees and the fourth one is a Vice- President of the Association; they are as follows :-

Pat Gwynne: His award is for playing football, taking up refereeing in the 1960's and organising the Hotel & Caterers Sports Association of which he is the Secretary. He also is involved with the Ladies Football Association as a Vice- President. He is a member of the B C F A and has completed 34 years he is also a Vice- President to the B C F A.

David Morris: Has played for Cubbington Albion as a youth and has been involved with the Administrative side of the Club holding practically every position, he also became a Referee and refereed in the Local League

Arnold Rouse: He became a referee in 1952 and refereed locally and in senior football. He has held every position of importance in the Referees Association finishing as President. He has also served on the Sunday League Management, as Vice- Chairman, Chairman and President.

Tracey Thomas: Has been involved with the Sunday League as General Secretary since 1966, before he was Secretary of Lockheed Leamington FC, and on the Committee of the Warwickshire Combination nd is a member of the B C F A completing 35 years. He is also a long standing Vice- President of the Leamington Referees Association

The four recipients received their awards from Jim Horrocks Vice- Chairman B C F A; this was in the form of a medallion with a Lapel Badge and a letter from the Chairman of the Football Association. It was an enjoyable evening with Club members and referees including old friends making it a night to remember.

Arnold Rouse being presented with his life membership award by the President John Bunn

Arnold Rouse admiring his silver salver awarded for 50 years service.

The Football Association 50 year Award

50 Year Awards Presented By Jim Horrocks
Vice Chairman Birmingham County FA

Members relaxing after a Meeting.

The new RA and RA of (England)
2004 to 2005

Before we move into the new period of change with the RA/RA(E) taking over after the Conference in 2004. The Leamington & District Referees Association still has its normal business to attend to. The Licensed Instructor at an earlier meeting was very concerned about the young candidate referees, who had not shown any inclination to join the Association. The newsletter was about to close down, no one seemed interested in taking it on, this meant that information to members would be limited.

The changes which were made at the end of the 20th Century are well established and the referees who have become members of FAMOA are receiving the benefit from the Football Association. If they take the referees course it cost a certain amount of money and one or two items are mandatory, the course fee is one and registration to the BCFA is another. The following such as joining the Referees Association, purchasing a whistle and the red & yellow cards are voluntary. The statement was a dissapointment as most members considered joining the Referees Association should also been mandatory. It is at the beginning of their career they need the Association behind then, even though we cannot have them watched every match, they can be guided through the minefield.

The Chairman has also informed everyone that we now have a two tier system of coaching, this has been implemented into the Instructors training. One covers just a general knowledge of the "Laws of Association Football" covering 4(four) weeks lectures with a multi –choice examination at end. The other is a full course for candidates to become a Referee. The Instructor at Leamington prefered the candidates to do the 10(ten) weeks course. He also tells the members so they can get the full benefit we should provide 'Mentors' for the new candidates, unfortunately we do not possess enough available referees..

After refereeing 10(ten) games you can claim your course fee back. You also get your fee returned from games which are supported by your Mentor, you are also entitled a fee from refereeing Football Matches whether it is Sunday/Saturday League or even Schoolboy games.

At the Annual General Meeting of the Association in February 2004 when all the business had been completed the President closed the meeting and allowed the Chairman to take over and welcomed the President of the National Referees Association Mr John Bunn amd Mrs Bunn to Leamington

The Chairman John Sharp explained to the members why The National President is at Leamington and told them it was to present to Arnold Rouse his Silver Salver for 50 years service to the Referees Association and also to present him with an Award to show that at Cheltenham Conference 2003 Arnold was made a Life member of the National Referees Association. The President then told the members, guests and friends who were at the meeting what a member has to do to be made a Life Member, he said that Arnold had acheived that position and he has also completed over 50 years in the Association. Photographs were taken and a excellant Buffet had been laid on by the Association..

The Take Over

At the end of the previous chapter which concerned the future of the Referees Association and referees in general. The Chairman of the RA(E) Bart o'Toole received the 'Chain of Office' from the President of the National Referees Association John Bunn Esq.

With the new Chairman of the RA(E) taking over the Referees Association at the Conference in Cardiff 2004. It meant the Referees Association as we knew it, with all its Divisions was being quietly put to rest after 96 years of service to Referees and Associated Bodies

To involve the new Board of Management with the way the Referees' Association had been operating the Chairman along with other members were invited to attend meetings the Executive Council held. For this intrusion the Chairman thanked the National Referees Executive Council for the help and advice that had been given. This allowed them to familiarise themselves with the way the workings of the executive council were carried out. It didn't mean the Board of Management would follow the same pattern, with all the work that was done by the Implementation Team it suggested streamlining and modernisation will be to the fore.

The first meeting after the Conference 2004, the Honorary President David Elleray in an open discussion on the way forward, likening his role of President to that of a constitutional monarch with a few defined powers of duties, but a right to warn, a right to advise or encourage and a right to be consulted. He went on to say we have a major opportunity to play a key role in the future of refereeing through our education and support for grass roots refereeing.. Here are a few items discussed by the Board and the Preisdent.

- Relationship with outside bodies including FAMOA
- Summer Conference for Young Referees
- Promotion and Development of the RA(E)
- Free RAE First Year Membership
- The R A Website
- Conference2005.

Once the take over was completed the elected officers had various jobs to do. The Chairman of the Referees Association was Mr Len Randall. The Chairman of the RA(E) was Mr Bart O'Toole who's position is for twelve months only so in January 2005 a new Chairman would be elected.

Since the Board of Management was elected, the Committees from the RA and the RA(E) have been busy holding meetings to discuss the changes taking place. All new Committees take time to blend together and reading the minutes of both organisations they have done extremely well. A wide variety of items were discussed, such as Membership, Subscriptions, Certificates, Child Protection, Conference 2006 and Rule Alterations. The Notice of Motions and Rule ammendments are to be placed at the Annual General Meeting of the RA(E). It was pleasing to note the RA(E) had finally a representative on the Football Associations Referees Committee and the priviledge has gone to the General Secretary Arthur Smith

The new Chairman elected In 2005 to represent the RA(E) was Alan Poulain who took over from Bart O'Toole. In the News Digest 2004/5 a brief resume about Alan Poulain is written and it seems he will bring a wealth of business experience to the position. A lot will depend on his approach to the first full year, in which the new RA(E) and the RA will be implementing their method of moving the Associations in a forward direction, which will blend all level's of the Association together.
The News Digest also covers the Insurance and the increase in payment, Subscriptions and Membership figures were also discussed and concern was expressed with the gradual decline in members not joining the Association.

The Conference was the starting point for the new Board of Management. The Conference would be a three day affair with the Annual General Meeting held on a Friday and on Saturday the whole organisation would be geared to having workshops, given by Referees from the Premier League and other speakers from the Football Association.

The Conference at Southport 2005 was according to the Delegates a success and the changes were most noticable, with the RA(E) holding their AGM on the Friday afternoon. The Friday evening function was held and the Long and Meritorious Service Awards were presented to the members by the new Honorary President David Ellerary. This allowed the Conference on the Saturday morning to complete the business of registering your attendance, with the Chairman of the RA welcoming every one to the Conference. Once that was done they could continue with the Programme. With the main speakers setting the day in motion, it allowed the Workshops to open up and start functioning. The programme laid out with speakers like John Baker, Ken Ridden Steve Bennetts and Mike Riley augured well for the benefit of the Referees who were in attendance.

Finishing this section of the Leamington & District Referees Associations business we now move to the reason this Chapter was written, quite a fair amount of information has been printed about the change and the report from the delegate was proof enough, the future was looking good.
To understand all the issues involved with restructuring of the Referees Association in this Chapter the full report has been printed in the 'Football Referee' on a monthly basis. What I have written is only a brief resume

Whilst we do commiserate with the previous organisation who served the members exceptionally well, we must congratulate the new and more professional organisation on the way they are moving forward. Everything has changed completely in less than a Decade. Referees are organised in a more professional way. Coaching by qualified 'Licnsed Instructors' has made the referee more confident when refereeing a match. All the information from FAMOA and the Football Association has improved the referees attitude seeking promotion. All the changes are for the Referee it is up to him to grasp the opportunity and continue to move forward.

Instead of saying this is the end of the story, we can move on for another twelve months and finish writing about the History of Leamington Referees Association by mentioning the members who were working at the Conference 2006 at the Hilton Hotel. Warwick.

THE ADDENDUM 2006

This additional section will be more or less the finish of the Book. At the beginning we talked about the Association and how the first Secretary was found, and Leamington Referees was mentioned. By talking about the new RA's and mentioning the Conference 2006 we should finish with Leamington Referees again, which is absolutely brilliant. It means the Book has covered 85 (eighty five) years of past history and worked its way into the future.

Also in the addendum will be the second Annual General Meeting of the RA and the RA(E) it will show you how progress has been made with the new RA of England. The Conference was set for three days and having it transfered to Warwick would benefit the Association. Before we talk about the Conference the Association have had their Annual General Meeting and a new Treasurer was elected replacing Ray Morgan who was thanked for his service since the 2,000/2001 season. The new Treasurer would be Gerry Shanley. There were also changes on the management committee and one or two of the younger members were elected which gives the management a youthful look. With the Conference at the Hilton Hotel Warwick it meant that Leamngton Referees would be involved.
They would be used as Scrutineers at the Annual General Meeting to record the number of votes taken, they would also to be available to do other jobs if needed.

Herewith the names of the members who were at the Conference:- Peter Boyle, Brian Field, Thomas Jamie, Duncan MacAulay, Jeremy Poulson, Richard Poulson, John Sharp and Luke Young.

With the Conference at the Hilton it was an opportunity for members of the Association to attend the Conference to find out how the RA and the RA of (E) function. Bearing in mind it would be only the second Conference since they took over in 2004, even so the members who were elected to the, 'Board of Management' are all experienced people and they are doing their utmost to promote the RA of England to everyone.

Herewith a brief resume of the Conference 2006 as Dave Aston and myself recall how the various issues were discussed and voted on. With the A G M taking pace on the Friday afternoon at 2.30pm.

Dave and I were welcomed along with other members of the R A and RA(E) as we entered the Conference room by the elected President David Elleray. When everyone had settled down. The Chairman Alan Poulain opened the meeting by welcoming the delegates to the second Annual General Meeting of the RA(E).

Standing orders were approved, and the first Media were granted permission to record the proceedings on tape. The next item was the approval of the scrutineers needed to examine and collect the votes when they were needed. He went on to talk about the relationship with the Football Association and he said that a high level of co-operation with the 'Head of Refereeing' was in place to develop further working relations with RA(E)

Disappointment had been felt at the low sales of the magazine, 'Refereeing Today'. Sales figures of just over 2,000 from a membership of 12,500 was creating difficulties.

The membership, as in most ABSs had declined and must be tackled vigorously with the ultimate aim of 100% membership.

The Chairman spoke of higher aims of communications, the revised design of the new necktie and the value to ABS of the comprehensive Manual of Guidance. In concluding his remarks the Chairman said he had been able to see many different ways in which R A societies did their work..The Board wanted to help all members.

Talks of a Strategic Plan had been considered not yet ready for issue to ABS, the aim was to produce a model document for local adaption or rejection. Another important issue was brought to the notice of the delegates and that is the FA-imposed charges for training purposes. According to a delegate it must be challenged and its rescindment requested. The Chairman said the Board was in serious dialogue with the FA on this matter.

Annual Accounts

Richard Blackman (Chairman of the Finance and General Purpose Committee) introduced the accounts and delegates soon mentioned the rebate figures and said if the members want a fine organisation it could not be achieved with a deficit every year, adding that an annual subscription of £15 would be more realistic than the increase proposed by the board. The delegates were told that the money the RA(E) received from the £7 pounds the RA receive is £1(one pound) and if the amount is increased to £9 the RA(E) would receive £2 (pounds,) quite a reasonable discussion took place on the accounts and a general change of attitude was mentioned.

Chairman's Comments

The Chairman spoke of the nation-wide publicity to help the Association. The Honorary President, David Elleray, had been invited by SkyTV earlier in the day and the twenty-minute interview would be screened hourly during the remainder of the day. There would be more coverage on the next day, when the Conference with its World Cup theme would be featured on Television.
Conference 2007 would be held on the week-end of the 8th-9th June, at the Hilton Hotel Warwick..

The Delegates were registering for the Conference at 09:30 am and the RA Chairman Richard Blackman opened the meeting. The morning session is a selection of Workshops which have been arranged for the younger and active members so they would benefit from the talk the speakers gave. It was noticable that there were more youngsters and female referees at the meeting than you would normally meet at a Conference. The speakers would now have to live up to their reputations, which should not be a problem, when you see the quality that have been invited by the Board of Management.

The first speaker was Mike Riley: Premier League Referee who was scheduled to talk about (Preparing for the World Cup Finals) This was a very interesting talk from Mike Riley he covered everything that a Referee is require to do at the World Cup, the Referees who have been selected are reputed to be the best in the World and fitness should not be a problem although he said that a fitness instructor and a dietician were on board. The Referees would also have to use the Red and Yellow Cards possibly more if FIFA tighten up on the Laws of the game..
Other speakers scheduled to speak were David Elleray: on (Assessment & selection at World Cup Finals). Mark Warren: (Lining at the World Cup Finals)
The session from the three speakers lasted from 10am until 12:15pm for Lunch.
The issues talked about were very interesting and the delegates and the young referees would have learned from the talks.
Lunch was served in the Restuarant and there was plenty of food and a variety to choose from, by the time every one had eaten, it was time to go back to the Conference Hall where a large screen was ready for the Match:- England v Paraguay.
When the match had finished about 4:15pm. we listened to Sian Massey give a talk on Female Referees and what she is hoping to achieve, at the moment she is classed as a Level 4(four) referee, and she hopes to reach Level 3(three) which is a high rating for a girl so young. Still it was an enjoyable talk. After Sian we had Neale Barry: talking on (Law changes for Season 2006/2007) the talk more or less took everyone to the end of the Conference at 5:30 pm, when Richard Blackman closed the meeting

The last piece of the jig-saw was the Gala Dinner in the large Conference room where a splended three- course meal with coffee was arranged.
To set the seal on an excellent Conference the President David Elleray presented awards to the new Life Members of the RA(E) and presentations were made by the President to those who officiated in England's most prestigous matches in Season 2005/6 It was the end of the Conference.

It also is the end of the 'History of Leamington & District Referees Association' and after 85 years it is the correct end. We started with Leamington Referees forming an, 'Association in 1921' and we finish with the members of Leamington Referees involved with the Conference in 2006. It is not quite the finish at the moment even though members were doing a duty at the Conference , We had one member from Leamington and that was **Duncan MacAulay** who on the Friday evening received from the **President David Ellery** his medallion to say he had been awarded the, " **Long and Meritorious Service Award"** for service to the Referees Association over 20(years) Duncan has been a member since 1966 and has held a various number of Offices since 1978 and is at present the Secretary.

FINISH

A Brief Autobiography of Arnold William Rouse

President of Leamington & District Referees Associaton 1976

When I started to compile the History of the Association, I never realised the amount of work it would entail in putting dates and names together. Quite a few interesting facts have emerged from the exercise. The beginning was to check on the information which had been given to me, this meant browsing through reams of Micro-Film at the Library. Gradually information was received from past and present members. The minutes of the Association were in a reasonable condition although two or three sections were missing. It helped when the members were still available to give me the information needed. While presenting it in a reasonable form I have tried to mention as many Referees of the Association as possible in the various Chapters.

Herewith a brief resume of my life to the present day, which includes the service to the Referees Association.

I was born in Warwick on the 2nd July 1924.
Married to Sheila Bartlett in May 1950
We have two sons Paul and Peter, four Grandchildren three boys, Simon, Matthew and Christopher and a Grandaughter Samanatha
We also have one Great Grandaughter 'Emma'
My Education was at Warwick All Saints Church School, leaving when I was 14 years old. From there I went to Evening Classes till I reached the age of 17, studying design, mathmatics and drawing,

Employed at Constant Speed Airscrews Warwick and the Lockheed Hydraulic Brake Company until I was called up into the Fleet Air Arm 1943. Went to Manchester to do my basic training. From there I had to report to the R A F Camp at Hednesford to train as a Mechanic on Aircraft Engines. After passing the examination I went sent to Eglington Northern Ireland after a few months I was with a large contingent of Fleet Air Arm Sailors we were sent abroad to the, "South Asia Command until 1946".where like others, I was demobbed.
After being demobbed I became employed at Fords (Leamington) went to evening classes at Thornbank and then to Coventry Polytechnic College for three years studying Engineering
In 1950 was employed at Hearsall Pattern & Engineering Company and in 1954 went to Armstrong Whitworth Aircraft Company. In 1965 started work at Automotive Products and retired in 1985 due to health problems.

Played local Football until 1951 became a referee in 1952, was coached by Henry Hall and joined the Leamington Referees Association in 1952. Started refereeing on the Leamington Saturday League as a Class 3(three), obtained my Class 2(two) in 1953 and then received my Class 1(one) in 1959 refereed on the Coventry Allocation System the Coventry & North Warwicks and all the other Leagues in Coventry, The West Midland Alliance, The Warwickshire Combination as a Linesman and then officiated on the West Midland Regional League. Also I refereed one season in the Leamington & District Sunday Football League.
My service to the Referees Association since 1952 has been recorded in the article on Presidents of the Association.
My Social life and Hobbies are as follows: Gardening specialising on Chrysanthemums and Carnations, working with Wood, making toys and furniture and jewellery boxes.

For a completely relaxing hobby, I enjoy Fishing and have done so since I was 10 years old. I had to learn to swim before I was allowed to go on my own.

Watching youngsters play Football is somthing I also enjoy. It doesn't matter what age they are, they always seem to put a terrific amount of effort into their game. I have watched both my sons play Football or Rugby and my grandsons playing Football. The youngest one is playing for a team at the moment.

Raising money for Charity and belonging to Charitable organisations. The Warwick Court Leet is another organisation I belong to and have been a member for 25 years. I was involved with Warwick Carnival producing the Programme and Sponsorships. For 14 years from 1980 to 1994

Being President of Leamington Referees Association and the Leamington Sunday Football League are positions that I have been proud to have acheived and have enjoyed every minute
My motto has been "**Service before Self**" and it still is.

Arnold W Rouse 2006

Appendixes

Short Stories

To complete this Book I have decided to print a few short Stories about the game of Football.
A few have been written by the members and have been placed in the Association Newsletter, or they may have been taken from the local and National newspapers. Permission has been given by the Editor of the Courier Press to use any article taken from the Coutier or the Warwick & Warwickshire Advertiser also permission has been given to print articles from the National Newspapers
The first one is called the:

Advent of Football

The Summer has gone and brief respite from football is over once more. Henceforward the prospects and performance of the various clubs wil be eagerly discussed by thousands of enthusiasts, who today, 'Hail the Advent of Football.' It will be a long time until the brief season in which no football is played comes again and many will be reluctant that Summer should pass so soon..Crickt is not yet finished and Tennis still holds sway, while the weather is unsuitable for any winter games.

Yet to-day the first match of the season takes place and football will have a larger following, as ever, for there are many who would welcome it all the year around. The decision of the Football Association to say the season should begin in August and not end until May has been much criticised, for it means football begins before any Cricket Championship is finished and ends when the weather is absurd for the playing of the game.

The Summer period is short enough as it stood, without a week at both ends being taken by football. Nine Months of strenuous footballing in league and cup matches is a great strain, even for the most robust of players and sooner the Authortities realise that the season is at present too long, better footballing will be seen. If players begin to lose their skill in a hard season, people will not pay for admission to the matches, for those who watch play, do so in the hope of seeing some really good play.

No Club can exist with out followers and consequently the players must be kept fit so they can give of their best. To play more than formally is rather an unusual way of reducing the strain.
Exponents of the more gruelling Rugby code are aware of the necessity for keeping the season in bounds. No Rugby Club's matches start before September and the fixtures are finished before the Association season ends. The rotaries of the handling code are wiser than their brother sportsmen who play soccer, even if they do run the risk of being called 'oysters'

Then, is there really a "close season" for football?. The organisers of Flower Shows and similar Village functions arrange, "Six-a-Side" matches and competitions to help swell the coffers. The reduction in the number of players forming the teams does not alter the fact, that it is properly organised football, although the money gained by such a competition may often be for a worthy cause. Any player taking part in any such matches is liable to be suspended by the Football Association. So far no action has been taken in the matter and from this it would seem the authorities would be in favour of football all the Year round.

Shakespeare said :- "How many things bt season'd are
                    To their right praise and true perfection.
How else can the "true perfection" of football be reached except by playing the game in Season

The Referee Decided not to Continue

This article was taken from the Warwick & Warwickshire Gazette dated 14th February 1923.
A meeting in connection of the "Horse & Jockey Cup" took place at the Horse & Jockey Southam on Tuesday evening. Mr A J Hedges presiding.

The meeting was called to consider a protest lodged by the "Old Boys F C" re their match with Ladbroke F C, on Saturday last, which the latter won.
It was explained that full time was not played. Messrs, Fitchett, Worrall and Williams for the Old Boys, alleged an argument took place between their goalkeeper and the Referee. Which resulted in the referee leaving the field and refusing to officiate. Eventually the referee was persuaded to resume his duties, by a spectator, but he failed to allow for the time wasted with his arguement with the goalkeeper. This was about 7 minutes.

The Ladbroke representative said the referee was 'inefficient.' After considerable discussion the Committee decided the match must be replayed on or before March 3rd and the "Old Boys" goalkeeper be suspended, for the replay. It was also decided not to re-appoint the referee. .
The Chairman said, because the competition is not affiliated and consequently the Committees decision are final, but they have no power to enforce the punishment given. The case referred to the above clearly shows the necessity of being affiliated to an Association which is able to control football, for the benefit of sport, referees and players alike.

Herewith an interesting story from the: **"Warwick & Warwickshire Advertiser and Leamington Gazette"** permission to print has been given.

Saturday January 7th 1922
Leamington Town FC v Bournville FC

The fixture was a League match and a large crowd was peresent, play commenced sensationally when Rowlatt, after a beautiful solo effort, opened the Homesters' account after one minutes play. His shot was a beautiful one which gave Willmott no chance.
Thorne added a second goal. Rowlatt initiated a good movement, when he was checked, he passed to Thorne, whose oblique shot glinted into the net off the bar.
Wright was the next player to essay a movement, but his centre was cleared. The visitors then became the aggressors, but Horley saved the situation. After the resumption Perry opened the visitors account and Pountney and Wright added further goals for the Town.

A regrettable incident marred the play in the second half. Pountney and one of the visiting players indulged in a free fight. But after the Referee had spoken to the players and issued a warning to both Teams the game continued.
Result:- Leamington Town FC 4—Bournville FC 1.
Printed as written, no mention of which League.

Did the Fox know the "Laws of Association Football

On this particular Saturday afternoon in 1957. I was refereeing a football match out at Exhall Coventry. It was the third round of the Boyd Carpenter Cup Competition. Between two teams from the Works League.

The ground was situated on the edge of Exhall and the country lane from Covenry went through two wooded areas, the field of play was well marked out with changing facilities available. When you came out of the changing room and turned right to go towards the pitch, you had a wooded area going away from the ground, most of the spectators went and stood along the hedgerow.

Having started the game which turned out to be well contested and enjoyable, no fouls, no appeals, but plenty of football and at half- time the score was 0-0. A cup of tea was offered to me along with a quarter of an orange which was accepted.

After a reasonable break a little bit more the five minutes, the game resumed and goals were being scored. While this was happening we could hear the sound of the Hunting horn, talking to the Captain of the home team. I asked him if it ever came this way, he said not very often it usually goes the other way towards Tile Hill.

After that assurance we carried on playing, but the horns sounded louder and it seemed to be getting nearer. A throw-in was given on the touchline by the hedge and one of the supporters shouted hear comes the Fox. At this point you could hear the hounds as well as the hunting horn being blown. What happened next you would never believe, the Fox came through the hedge in-between a few supporters and stopped on the touch line. It then turned right and ran along the line until he came to the corner flag post.

The Fox then turned left and raced across to the next field, then went through the hedge at the bottom and across the road into the wooded area the other side. In the meantime the hounds came yelping through with their tails wagging and went straight onto the pitch. It was fortunate that I had stopped the game when the Fox appeared. The huntsmen came through the hedge where there were gaps and the horn was sounded, the hounds raced off towards the sound and went through the hedge where the Fox had gone.

Quite a number of the riders shouted that they were sorry about what happened, although most of the players didn't seemed worried neither did the supporters, every one seemed pleased the Fox had reasonably got away.

The talking point at the end of the game was about the Fox and some one asked if it had been taught not to go on a Football pitch, because it seemed to know where it was going.

We finished the match and the visitors won by the odd goal in five, talking to the home team players they were asked if they knew where the Hunt came from, the Secretary was asked and he was not quite sure. After filling in the team sheet and making a few comments, the Secretary came and paid me the usual 12/6 (twelve shillings & sixpence) the extra was because it was a Cup match. Every one said cheerio. I enjoyed the match and it was a pleasure to find two teams that really enjoyed the game

Herewith more articles from the **Warwickshire & Warwick Advertiser and the Leamington Gazette**. Taken from the Paper in August and September 1927
Permission has been given to use by the LeamingtonCourier.

Southam & District Football Le ague

At the monthly meeting of the League, the Secretary read copies of correspondence he had sent to Radford and the Leamington & District League arising out of the fining of Radford at the last League meeting of £1(one pound) for failing to resign from the Southam &District Football League, in the specific time. He said he has not received a reply.

The Chairman Mr W Sturley said he understood that Radford had already played matches in the Leamingtom League and he suggested that the whole episode be reported to the County Football Association. It was decided unanimously it should be done.

The Secretary stated that since the last League meeting he had received applications from Leamington St Marks, also Fenny Compton for membership into the League. The applications had been accepted. The meeting approved the actions of the Sub-Committee.

Here is another story concerning a football team from **Kineton** reported in **Warwickshire & Warwick Advertiser and Leamington Gazzette**

Kineton Albion Rovers Censored

Kineton Albion Football Club was fined 10/6 (ten shillings & sixpence) and severly censured by the Leamington Area Disciplinry Committee of the Birmingham County Football Association.

The Referee of the match between the Albion Rovers and Coten End Old Boys, which took place at Kineton on Boxing Day Decenber 26th 1928. Stated in his report that at the conclusion of the match C J Robotham and R Mander of Albion Rovers both struck at him while H J Young same club, assumed a threatening attitude. It was also stated that the Kineton supporters threw mud sticks and stones at him and threatened to throw him in the pond at the bottom of the field.

Robotham and Mander were each suspended for three months and fined 5/-(five shillings). But owing to the fact that at the time of the incident, Young had apologised and he was dealt with more leniently. The Commission suspended him for six weeks and fined him 5/-(five shillings).

The Club was warned that should there be another occurence of such behaviour by the supporters the ground could be closed.

At the same Commission F Appleby Hatton &Hasely was fine 2/6(two & sixpence) and suspended for 14 days, for striking an opponent in the match against Wroxall. Another player was alleged to have used bad Language in the same match. A W Skeen, Hatton & Hasely who did not appear was suspended until he did so.

Birmingham County Football Association

Disciplinary Commission

The Commission was held at Henley –in –Arden on Friday 20th December 1929. The disciplinary Commission appointed by the Birmingham County Football Association, comprising of Norman Smith and R A Eden enquired into the reports of two Henley League matches. The first one arose out of a match at Rowington on November 16th when Hatton & Hasely were the visiters. R Woollaston (Rowington) was suspended for 14 days, for using bad Language to the referee. E Bullevant (Hockley Heath) was suspended for a similar period and also removed from the captaincy of the Club for the rest of the season for ungentlemanly conduct after being cautioned. Hockley Heath were fined 10/-(ten shilling) and cautioned as to the future conduct of the members, for refusing to carry out the referees Instructions and thus causing the match to be abandoned. W Sewill (Hockley Heath) Linesman was suspended for acting, as linesman for the rest of the season.

The second case concerned an incident which occured during a match at Tanworth –in Arden on December 14th 1929 when W Cross(Tanworth Old Boys) and B Coughton were ordered from the field of play for striking. The referee stated that Cross tripped Coughton who then struck Cross, where upon the latter retaliated. The two were suspended for seven days and fined 2/6 (two& sixpence) each

The Referee

In Spanish he's the arbitro and he's arbitrary by definition. An a bominable tyrant who runs his dictatorship without opposition, a pompous executioner who exercises his absolute power with an operactic flourish. Whistle between his lips; he blows the wind of inexorable fate either to allow a goal or to disallow one.

Card in hand, he raises the colours of doom, yellow to punish the sinner and oblige him to repent, and red to force him into exile.

The Assistant Referee, who assists but does not rule, look on from the side. Only the referee steps onto the playing field and he's absolutely right to cross himself when he first appears before the roaring crowd.

His job is to make himself hated. The only universal sentiment in soccer: everybody hates him. He always gets catcalls, never applause.

No one runs more. The only one obliged to run the entire game without pause, this interloper who pants in the ears of every player breaks his back galloping like a horse. In return for his pains, the crowd howls for his head.

From beginning to the end he sweats oceans, forced to chase the white ball that skips along back and forth between the feet of every one else. Of course he'd love to play, but never has he been offered the privilege. When the ball hits him by accident, the entire stadium curses his mother. But even so, just to be there in that sacred green space where the ball floats and glides, he's willing to suffer insults, catcalls, stones, and damnation.

Sometimes, though rarely, his judgement coincides with the inclinations of the fans, but not even then does he emerge unscathed. The losers owe their loss to him and the winners triunph in spite of him Scapegoat for every error, cause of every misfortune, the fans would have to invent if he didn't already exist. The more they hate him, the more they need him.

For over a century the referee dressed in mourning. For whom? For himself. Now he wears bright colours to mask his feelings'.

World Womens Football Tournament

This is an article written by Pat Gwynne who was very fortunate in being invited to take part in the World Womens Football tournament held in Taiwan 1978.

NA HOKUE 1   NA WAHINE 3

On my arrival in Taiwan in 1978 for the tournament I realised that I was the first foreign Referee to arrive. I was then taken away from the English group to a Hotel on the other side of Taipei. The reason for the move, as I was informed that Referees are not allowed to stay with their teams. I was then assigned to the polynesian squad, who are in fact a side from Hawaii.

Each country taking part, are only allowed one team in the tournament, but because the USA are already represented by a team from Texas the Hawaiian side are therefore called Polynesia.
As we Referees do, we invariably made friends as I did with the polynesians, in fact I was their flag bearer on one of the Parades prior to the tournament. This was alright by me as the Hawaiian state flag bears our own Union Jack in one of the corners.

1992 and whilst oh holiday in Hawaii I received a telephone call on a Friday night at 10pm. Jan Allen had passed on my name and would I like to do one or two matches on the Sunday morning. With temperatures in the nineties, I opted for just one match and my directions are quite simply as follows; Pitch 1, that's the pitch nearest the Ocean at Kanaplis Park. Wakiki Beach at 11am.
At the time of the phone call I had been rather looking forward to attending the Honolulu Cricket Club Party on the Sunday, but the phone call changes all that. Much as I would have liked to attend the cricket club party. I had declined to referee on a tournament in 1981 in preference to going away and seeing the England Cricket team and on a previous visit to the Island had declined to Referee as I had no kit with me.

This time, though, I knew that if asked it would seem discourteous to decline, so had gone prepared. I was informed that rules were in accordance with FIFA but that 3 substitutes were allowed and these could go on and off as they wished. The match was an Oahu Womens 2nd Division League game. On arrival at the pitch, Jan Allen was already refereeing a match herself which had kicked off at 9am. With her match over, Jan informed me of who my teams were but there was no Linesmen available for me. However, she would run one line and persuaded the coach of one of the teams (himself a Referee) to run the other one.

Prior to the kick-off, I am handed two large rings, one from each side with an identity tag. Complete with a photo of every player taking part in the game. When I enquired what are these for, I am told in case I have caution or send off any of the players and they then can be identified. Fortunately it does not come to anything like that. In fact throughout the entire match only one decision is questioned and even then it was just the player telling me that it was impossible for her to have got out of the way and the other player hadrun into her. On three occasions play did stop when one player or another came of worst from shoulder to shoulder encounters and it was thought I might award free kicks, which I did not and the game carried on. What I did find enjoyable was the introduction of the subs because in the heat it gave me a chance to have a rest and the subs were coming on and going off at quite regular intervals for tactical purposes.

The second half is in progress when I give an offside decision and looked over at the Linesperson who it so happens is the one who replced Jan Allen. Jan left me to go and referee another match. The Linesperson had signalled the offside and she had her flag raised. Shortly afterwwoards when the ball appears to be going out for a throw –in, it is stopped by a player and the new Linesperson expertly signals to the player that it is still in play. Quite a good Linesman, this one, I thought. Eventually the game is over. I enquire of the substitute Linesperson and asked her where she had got the play-on signal from, she told me that she used to be a Referee and I would imagine she was pretty good too.

Now I am presented with the match result sheet and I have to state who scored the goals. How would I know? I did not know any of the players. As it happens though , the other Linesman had made a note of it. The match result sheet also wanted to know how the players behaved and were there any crowd problems. Glad to report, it was excellent on both counts. My match fee was $20 Dollars. Did I want it? They could write a cheque out for me if I wanted it. As it was I did not want it, they could donate it to the (Hurricane Relief Fund). Two weeks before going out there a hurricane had devastated the next Island. Players from both sides came over to congratulate me and one player even said I was welcome to Referee all their matches, because I gave obstruction which their Referee did not.

That took my mind back to the previous week when watching a match, I had noticed that such incidents did not seem to get punished. I watched a little of the next match and noticed that when a goal is scored the referee did take the number of the goalscorer. Despite the heat I had enjoyed the experience of this game and afterwards enquired of another refereeing friend what the names of the teams meant. It was explained that, 'Na Hokue' means the Stars and 'Na Wahine'is the Women. Looking back, had it not been for the events of 1978 and making friends with the Polynesians. It is doubtful that I would have been refereeing that fixture on Sundaay 4th October. My appoint ment previous to that had been at Wilmcote and the one that followed Wakiki was at Wellecbourne.

What struck me most was the attitude of players towards the game itself. To them the most important thing was the playing of the game. With the result of the match of secondary importance and there was no recrimination towards anyone when a goal was conceded. It was just one of those things that happen.
Even the team coaches did not lay the blame for defeat on any particular individuals, but at the end of the game all aspects of it were analysed. Another nice thing was the way the two teams lined up at the end of each match, basketball style and went along the opposition line slapping hands. Payment of Referees was not left to the home club, this was settled by the League Treasurer.
Before returning to England I did discover that Jan Allen had taken the Referees exam here in England through the RAF when her husband hadbeen stationed at Lakenheath with the US Air Force. However, in those days this country did not recognise Womens Football of Women Referees and she subsequently had to regester with the Womens FA.

In conclusion I would like to thank Jan ,Mark, and Alexis Kane for helping me to have this appointment and hopefully maybe one day I will be back to take another match.
It was also a pleasant experience to sit with the playesr of Mark Kane's Team after there matches and listen to the team talk. Which was followed by a picnic meals.
One final point is that I was made very welcome by all the Hawaiiian Referees I came into contact with.

Patrick Gwynne

Ban on Womens Football

The question of women football player's was among the matter discussed on Monday by the Football Association Committee and the following resolution was passed unanimously. "Complaints having been made as to football played by women, the Council feel impelled to express their strong opinion that the game of football is quite unsuitable for females and ought not to be encouraged.

Complaints have also been made as to the condition under which some of these matches have been arranged and played and the appropriation of receipts to other than Charitable objects. The Council are further of opinion that an excessive proportion of the receipts are absorbed in expenses and inadequate percentage devoted to charitable objects?

For these reasons the Council request Clubs belonging to the Association refuse to use their grounds for such matches.

This article was printed in the Warwickshire Advertiser & Leamington Gazette on December 10th 1921

A Marathon Football Match
Birmingham CountyJunior Football Cup

The report of this unusual match was taken from the Warwick. Warwickshire Advertiser & Leamington Gazette January 8th 1921 with other matches recorded in February. Permission has been given to all "Short Stories".printed in this book

In the Junior Cup Competition a match between Collycroft (Coventry) and Leamington Town FC seven hours of Football was played under trying conditions before a result was reached.

The first tie was played at Collycroft and a 1-1 draw was the result, the match was played in a gale. The next match was at Leamingtonand the game was abandoned due to bad light. The 3rd replay which was played at Collycroft was also abandoned with the score at 2-2.

The ground at Collycroft was in a wretched state and partly under water. The players mentioned for scoring Leamingtons goals was Rowlatt and Evans, who had much better exchanges and would have won quite easily on a good day. On each occasion Collycroft ground has been almost unfit to play on.

As the game was abandoned at the 4th attempt of both teams, the match will be at the Windmill ground. This will be the 5th attempt to play the match and the report goes on to say that after nearly seven housr of football under trying conditions Leamington Town finally beat Collycroft in the Birmingham Junior Cup.

The Town were at full strength and a large crowd of supporters were at the game. The ground was somewhat heavy, but the visitors at once showed they were a determined side. Their forwards combined well and after about 20 minutes Gilbert scored a good goal from a goal mouth scrimmage, with the Town goalkeeper Alcock out of his goal. Rowlatt scored the equaliser with a pass from Gumley and before half –time Jones put the home team ahead from a free kick.

The visitors goal keeper Tyler played one of the best games we have seen at the Windmill ground.this season. Okey playing at inside left was not having a very good game, yet he scored the third goal for Leamington with Key making it 4-1 to the Town.

In the next round they were scheduled to meet Leamington St Johns and on the 29th January 1921 the Town beat St Johns 2-0

The Town went on to play Rushall Olympics in the Semi-Final and won 2-0 to play in the Final of the Birmingham County Junior Cup against Lower Gornal Athletic in Birmingham on the 9th April 1921. They won the match, but the score is not known. The previous year the Town lost to Leamington St Johns 3-1

Royal Engineers (All England) F. C.

Journey's End

This is a short story about the Engineers Football team which was printed in the programme of the match against the Scottish Command by Harold Palmer.

To-Day's game is proberly the last scene in a soccer drama that started on the Fulham ground just a year ago. Action in the rest of this soccer play has taken part in the London area.

The story is woven round the rather presumptuous challenge of one army unit, the Royal Engineers, to all and sundry service teams regardless of the star studded nature of their eleven.

Even if the Engineers arrange any further fixtures, they are unlikely to so strong a team as they field to-day, for many of their players will soon be demobilised

The Royal Artillery Depot Woolwich where a whole eleven of experienced Club professionals had collected, were the Engineers' first opponents last February. The skill of such players as Winter, Chelsea's Welsh International back, and Steele, Stoke City and England centre forward, contributed to the R.E.'s rather crushing defeat.

A few weeks later they tried again. Against the R.A. Depot won but only just. Team spirit was developing in the R.E. team. The players were beginning to revel in this giant-killing act.

The Only Regular.

The R.E. team was picked from the London District. This reason they have extended their choice to the whole of England, with a natural strengthening of their team. Now only one player remains of the eleven who started to blaze the trail last February, it was Sapper Powell-Bossons, the left back.

Powell- Bossons was at one time a Golders Green player and last season he was on Arsenal's books. Still an amateur, he is now playing for West Ham reserves. There are few players more whole hearted in their effort. Bossons has not missed one of the Engineers' games and it can be truly said that he has never let them down.

This season the Engineers embarked on an even more ambitious programme. After warming up against the Irish Guards whom they beat 7-1, they again tried their luck with the R. A. Depot.

Another heavy defeat did not deter them and the proceeded to put up a good show against London District, who had all the R.A.Depot players available to them. There followed a convincing win over the R.A.F's Technical Training Command. A rather unlucky defeat by a talented Eastern Command team.

The Same Spirit

Newcomers to the R.E. team, who soon developed the same team spirit as their predecessors, gave it solidity and not a little inspiration. The solid effect has been provided by Shinwell of Sheffield United and Thyne, Darlington's Scottish International centre –half. The inspiration has been in attack, where Harrison and Pye have shown their football skill.

These two make an ideal pair in the inside forward position. Both show some drive, but Pye, in particular, does the fetching and carrying and Harrison keeps well up, always ready for a quick break through. There is some doubt about Pye playing to day, because he is one of England's reserves for the match against Belgium at Wembley on Saturday. He will not be asked to play to-day if there is a possibility of him being needed on Saturday.

Scottish Command have a strong team. I doubt whether it is any inferior to their team that recently met England in the Army International at Tottenham. Juliussen is a dashing centre –forward, who before the war was a Huddersfield player. Black is a clever player, likely to make chances for him. McNeil is a young centre- half discovery who may one of these days get a chance in a full Scotland team

It would be a great finish to the R.E. adventure if they could beat these Scots. Fact that they will try hard is one assurance of a good keen game.

That is the end of Harold Palmers story about the Engineers and it is noticed all the Officials come from the Midlands. Unfortunalty the result of the match is not known and neither is the issue of whether the Engineers carried on playing. With the de-mobilisation on the move in 1946 the War would be over.

The Referee is Human

In England, Referees come from all walks of life in all shapes and sizes young and old fit and semi-fit, they all want to be a referee. Becoming a Referee is like becoming a Policeman a Nurse or a volunteer worker in a Charity organisation, it's more than a job it is what we call here in England "a vocation" in other words, most of us have a special urge to become a Referee

We don't do it for the money (because it does not pay very well!) and we do not look at it as a career, if you ask a Referee. "Why do you referee?" They will reply with some vague half –truth saying they love the game after being a player. But in truth, it is a 'power thing.' It is the ultimate test of a person's ability to funtion in the most difficult of places.
It was once said, " The pen is mightier than the sword," in the Refereeing world, " The whistle is mightier than the word." To be able to use a small piece of musical plastic to control 22 potential murderers, is something even a storywriter could not have invented.

To do this, you must exhibit the same characteristics on the field of play, as you do in your ordinary life. Honesty, fairness, knowledgeable, passionate and most of all - a sense of enjoyment in providing a calming influence which enables members of the human race to get some enjoyment and relief out of a world that at times can be cruel.

Refereeing also enables you to adopt a huge family of colleagues who are one of the closet knitted communities in the world. It is here, outside of the game itself, your everyday life can be enhanced by joining a Referee's Society, by socialising with colleagues, attending semminars and training and a million other things that you never did before.

But the greatest gift it gives, is a trusted calmness, this can be used in many day-to-day situations in life.

The gift of listening to people, and reacting only when you have to.

This article was taken out of the Football Referees Magazine..

The Brotherhood

Aston Villa and International Footballer "Billy" Walker was given a splendid reception when he visited Warwick Brotherhood on Sunday afternoon April 30th 1928, he was accompanied by Mr Bemwell, who kept goal for the Aston Villa Club several years ago.

They were welcomed to Warwick by the Mayor (Councillor A Tandy) who presided and in his opening remarks said; "It is my pleasant duty this afternoon to welcome a number of visitors as well as our popular speaker, Mr "Billy" Walker. Perhaps many of you do not know that we also have with us on this platform, Mr Bemwell, who used to keep goal. We therefore have with us a gentleman who tried to keep them out and a gentleman who tried to put them in."

"I have always noticed when Mr Walker is taking part in a game," continued the Mayor "that he always plays the game in the very best spirits. He is, in fact, a link in a long chain of men who have lived to bring the game to such a high state of efficiency and spirit on which it is played. It is a game in which we can take great lessons from. Perhaps there is no game in the world which taxes a man's temper more than football. In any game, however a man who loses his temper has lost the game."

Mr Walker said he had to confess he was no speaker and added, "I can assure you I would much sooner be using my feet than my tongue. However, I hope you will bear with me if I am lost for words. I can only say I feel much happier and much more at home facing a thousand people at a cup final than speaking here. But after all, footballers and public speakers have one great resemblance. Both classes of men must be earnest and enthusiastic before they became successful.

"I admire all our English pastimes" continued Mr Walker. "They were given to us in the first place for recreational purposes and recreation is the keynote of good health. All our games are much too good to be fooled with. If we take up a certain game we must take it up earnestly and enthusiastically."

"Of course, my game is football and it would be very wrong of me to individualise, but I can say cricket, in my case, runs football very close and it would not take me long to be a golfer. If anything is worth doing -be it work or sport- it is worth doing well. But to excel at a certain thing enthusiasm and constant practice is necessary. There is a growing opinion that games have become to commercialised. Personally, I do not think they have, for as I said before, if a thing is worth doing it is worth doing well.

Frankly speaking there are too many fanatics connected with sport. The red-hot club fanatic and the fanatic who has no time for games himself---both these are injurious to sport. I refer, of course, to the supporter who can never understand why his team should lose, or why a visiting team should have a win. The 'happy medium' supporte is the best." During the last twenty years the character of our English players has changed considerably. In olden days men were carried away in their enthusiasm. Modern footballers are more methodical. I would be the last to suggest that modern football is better than in past years, but I suggest modern players are prepared better for the game. No man who smokes a lot and who feeds on bread and cheese before the game, can enter into the game in a fit state.

Modern football is very fast and there is no place for the weakling today. It is a game of brains and brawn. In olden days it was a game of brawn only. The outlook for football is very bright. It is also bright for the youth who perseveres. Enthusiasm, perseverance and sportsmanship are essentials in all walks of life. In conclusion, Mr Walker emphasised the necessity of team work in all forms of sport and work and referred to the splendid way in which English sportsmen are received in other countries.

The Mayor next called upon Mr Bemwell, who laughingly said he certainly could not agree with all Mr Walker had said, but he agreed entirely that team work was most essential. During the afternoon Mr Charles Haxter gave two songs. "Nearer, my God to Thee" and "Abide with Me."
This ended the talk by Mr "Billy"Walker
The article was printed in the Warwickshire Advertiser & Leamington Gazette on Saturday May 5th 1928.

Here are two incidents that occurred whilst I was playing and refereeing. The first one was when I was injured with a damaged ankle, at the time I was able to move reasonably well but could not kick a ball:

A Jolly Good Burn up

On one Saturday afternoon in the1950's I was scheduled to referee a difficult match between a Village team and a team from Leamington, both teams were good sides but played the game hard.
We changed in the local Pub and then walked to the ground which was situated by the Railway track and the main road from Leamington.
The game itself was enjoyable and only one player was booked for handling the Ball after being spoken too. During the match a crowd of supporters from the visiting team arrived to support their Club and they congregated around the pitch and near the home clubs goal posts. At this point the home team were attacking and I had to blow for a corner, but before it could be taken, a shout was heard, Ref! the Goal posts are on fire, on turning around I noticed they were and so was the grass which was spreading towards the hedge.
With the players we ran to the other end of the pitch and started to stamp out the burning grass. The trainer had a bucket of water which we used to put out the fire around the goal posts, the only damage was the paint being burnt. With all the grass and the area behind the goalposts clear of burning grass I started making enquiries by talking to the visitors(who were a little bit merry) and it transpired the one of the visitors had lit his cigarette and flicked the match away, before he realised what he had done the grass which was dry soon caught fire, he said he tried to stop it spreading but the grass away from the pitch was longer and the flames soon spread.
Every one realised it was an accident and the person was asked to be a little bit more careful when lighting up. I didn't report the issue to the League, for I considered we had sorted it out. The match resulted in a 3-2 win for the home team.

A Snow Storm with no Thanks

In my first season(1952) as a Referee the match I was appointed on the last Saturday in September was at Norton Lindsay who were playing local neighbours Barford FC, This again was another nice little game with two teams who were only interested in playing football and both teams had a few excellant players who made the game interesting. At half time the game was a nil-nil draw and both teams were enjoying the game and talking to each other, the only remarks said to me was,(its blowing up cold Ref)
When I started the second half you could feel the difference and the supporters dwindled away to the Club room and watched through the windows. The game itself was still enjoyable and Norton went ahead with a good goal from the centre forward within a few more minutes they scored again from a corner, still the game was enjoyable and Barford eventually scored making it 2-1 to Norton.

With about 15(fifteen) minutes to go the Snow started to fall and as the time neared the 90 minutes a skirmish occoured in the Norton penalty area ,which resulted in me giving Barford a penalty. By this time the Snow was really beginning to settle and playing football would difficult. Barford were prepared to take the penalty and I gave the signal which resulted in Barfod scoring. The score was now two all and the snow was falling very fast. The players asked me how long to go and are you going to abandon the match. I yelled back we have only a few minutes left, so i carried on for a couple of minutes and actually the game was becoming a farce so I blew for time and every one made for the Club room. When I checked my watch I had blown for full time with about 5 minutes left, but no one seemed to worry.

After giving myself a good rub down with a towel (we had no showers in those days). I put my clothes on and looked at the weather, It was still snowing and I remarked to the players that I had to cycle home. The Barford lads said you won't be the only one. After I had filled in the team sheet and received my 7/6(seven shillings & sixpence) collected by bicycle and set of for home. It really was snowing and very difficult to cycle, in fact walking seemed the easier option.

On the way home and before I reached the road Junction with Claverdon and Warwick all the telephone lines were down. On reaching home and parking my bike, I went down to the Telephone box and rang the Telephone company and spoke to the girl who answered my call. I told her the lines were down on the Norton Road. She told me to put the phone down as it was not my business. That was all the thanks I was given.

A Game of Two Referees

This article has been printed in the Association Newsletter in February 1999 and was written by **David McKie from the Guardian Newspaper**. permission was received from the Guardian to use at that time. Because it will be reproduced in book form additional permission has had to be given.. This has been granted to me ("the Licensee") on the 16th March 2006 Licence number ref (R227Y3) It is thanks to: Penny Jones Permission Executive, Syndication, Guardian Newspapers Limited.

The supreme body of European football, UEFA, is planning trial games using two referees, though UEFA spokesman admitted last week, that the details of how this would work had yet to be sorted out. Technical problems remain: what would happen, for instance, if the two referees disagreed? The same idea was tried in the thirties, but was not a success.

Part of that, though, may have been due to an infamous, though now largely forgotten, game at Histon, near Cambridge, in the season of 1930-31, which ended with two referees squaring up to each other and both teams leaving the pitch. a side representing the celebrated Cambridge University secret society, the Apostles, was pitched against Chivers Jam Works X1. The mathematician/ philosopher G H Hardy had unwisely asked Bertrand Russell to referee.

When the teams reached the ground, the captains agreed that, since Russell was nearing 60, he might not be able to keep up with the game and a second referee should be picked from the crowd to share his duties. Unhappily their choice fell on Ludwig Wittgenstein, newly returned from Cambridge after years of exile. Though Russell had been Wittgenstein mentor, they were now on uneasy terms, partly because of deep philosophical disagreements over the nature on mathematics and partly because Wittgenstein had described Russell's new book, The Conquest.of Happiness, as "unbearsble".

The Apostles were having a wretched season, attibuted to the retirement because of chronic ill-health of their veteran goalkeeper, Lytton Strachey. Though an erratic performer, he was often astrangly effective, with many a goalbound shot getting trapped in his huge red beard.

This was an ageing side, whose two central defenders, the captain, John Maynard Keynes, and the novelist E M Foster, had and aggregate age of 98. To make things worse, the Apostles' left back, Guy Burgess, who'd had rather too much to drink, fell madly in love straight from the kick – off with the blond Chvers' wingman he was allotted to mark. "So lissom! Such grace! Such litheness! Adorable" he would sigh, as the delicious youth tripped nimbly past him.

Up front, their principal striker, Anthony Blunt, kept contorting himself, whenever given a goalscoring pass, into a posture based on some figure in a painting by Poussin, before playing the ball so that chance after chance went begging. After only 12 minutes, Apostles were down to 10 men, as their inside right Arthur Koestler- a last minute replacement for Kim Philby, who had failed to turn up-limped off the pitch, claiming a groin strain.

Before long the Chivers team was scoring at will. Even the normally imperturbable Keynes went to pieces, miising header after easy header, "Only connect," his centre back pertner Forster kept roaring at him, but somehow he couldn't. The incident which caused the subsequent scandal occurred soon after half –time. The Chivers centre- forward hit a 25yard screamer which struck the underside of the crossbar and rocketed back into play. Russell, who was panting along in the other half of the pitch, was clearly unsighted, and referred the decision to Wittgenstein.

The problem which arose was one that Russell should have foreseen, as he would later write in his auto-biography, in the context of the wartime experiences of that strange Austrian genius, Wittgenstein, was 'the kind of man who would never have noted such small matters as bursting shells when he was thinking about logic'. The poor man was clearly quite unaware of what had occurred. Pestered by both sides to make a decision he simply replied, "Where of one cannot speak, thereof must be silent."

At this point the brilliant young mathematician Alan Turing who'd been running the line, raced on to the pitch. With the aid of a theodolite, borrowed from a surveyor who happened to be on the crowd, he produced an irrefutable mathematical proof that the ball could not have crossed the Apostles' goal line. This verdict incensed the jam-makers captain, who argued that theodolites ans such like religious gear had no place on a football ground. Claiming a moral victory, his team was 14 goals up at this time, led his troops off the pitch. The subsequent inquiry by the Cambridgeshire FA banned the Apostles for the rest of the season and the team never played again.

The following Thurday, the Histon and District Chronicle, now defunct, suggested in a powerful editorial comment that the dire lessons learned from this match would serve the Apostles well in the long run, "though of course," it added, "in the long run, we are all dead." Keynes noted this down in his pocket book for subsequent use, observing to Mrs Keynes as he did so that perhaps after all, the aftrnoon had not been entirely wasted.

The article was sent to me by an Association member David Swithin and it with thanks to the Guardian for giving permission to use again.
It was obviously a match with two referees that didn't work out, although it is a subject that has been talked about quite often.

Fate Deprived Jim Finney of Two Prestigious Finals

Some say he was the greatest English referee of all time and who could argue? If fate –both good and bad-hadn't played its part, Jim Finney would have taken charge of two of the most prestigious footballing occasions ever- the 1966 World Cup Final and the 1971 European Cup.

Currently 'enjoying' France'98 at his home in Three Elms Road, Hereford, Jim believes the standard of refereeing leaves a little to be desired. He has been especially suprised at how much shirt pulling is going on. "I think it started off extremely well, with referees being allowed to use and let the games flow," he said.

Red card fever
'But since we've had this stupid directive telling them they must use more red cards, I thimk they are all afraid and the standard has deteriorated. Red cards are being flashed for no apparent reason,' For Jim, now 73, the World Cup will always hold a special place, in particular the 1966 finals in England which marked the pinnacle of a career taking in hundreds of league matches, numerous international ties ans an F A Cup Final in 1962.

"I particularly remember the finals from a refereeing point of view, because it was the first time the card system was used in matches," he explained. "In fact the Argentinian Rattin was the first player ever to be red-carded in a World Cup match," he added. During the tournament, Jim took control of a hot-tempered quarter –final between Germany and Uruguay at Hillsborough, a game he remembers vividly but not for the quality of the football on show.

Latin unrest
During the match he sent off two Uruguayans, including the captain Troche, a decision that did not go down to well with the rest of the South American team. "Needless to say Uruguay lost the game and as we were coming off the pitch the players did the usual 'run the guantlet' where they form a tunnel to run down," said Jim.

"As I walked along, protected by my two linesman, one of the Uruguayans kicked me up the backside. I was outraged, so I grabbed him by the neck, pushed him into the main tunnel and said"I'll kill you for that. I would have done as well if I hadn't been pullled away by my linesman," he added. The offending player, Cortes, was banned from International football for a year- the longest suspension the professional game had seen at the time.

It is common knowledge that had England not made the final, Jim wuld have had the honour of officiating the match. "In many quarters I was regarded as the number one referee and it would have been quite an honour to take charge of such an occasion at Wembley. But at the end of the day it was a victory for the nation and my personal prestige, quite rightly, took a back seat," he explained.
While Jim may have been regarded as the top official in his day, theres is no doubt in his mind who the greatest player was –Pele.

Pele was best
Indeed he had the honour of refereeing a match between Scotland and Brazil just before the 1966 finals, in which the great man stood head and shoulders above the rest. During the game, Jim remembers an altercation between Pele and the late Billy Bremmer which resulted in an argument where the Brazilian proved he was just as much a wizard with words as he was with a football.

Leamington & District Referees Association

Jim saw the 1966 final, with his wife Betty, from seats positioned just in front of the Royal Box, not an ideal spot to witness 'that goal' which sparked a 30 –year controversy. "My old friend Godfrey Deinst was the referee involved, but to be honest if the linesman confirmed it went over the line, that's the end of the story. In all the years since it happened I have never been convinced the ball crossed the line, but you can't complain about the linesmsn as he was perfectly positioned as he was perfectly positioned to make the decision," he added.

Five years later, in April 1971, Jim was driving to preston with Betty and their three children when a car pulled out of a junction in Dorrington causing a crash that would end his glittering career. Initially Jim was more concerned about his wife who had been thrown through the windscreen and required 120 stitches to he face when she arrived at the hospital, but Jim soon realised that he was not in a good way. Superficially, he had seemed tohave escaped the incident with barely a scratch, but as he developed pains in his stomach and shoulders doctors became more concerned..

"When the surgeon had finished his examination he told me I would be dead in 45 minutes unless something was done immediately and I was rushed into surgery," he explains "It turned out that when the car's steering shaft rammied into my stomach it caused terrible internal injuries which doctors honestly believed I wouldn't recover from," he added.

Wembley Final
In a sad twist of fate, that morning Jim had received a letter, to say he had been selected to referee the 1971 European Cup Final
From being one of the most active referees in the game, Jim was forced to quit and spent the next 12 months sat at home looking at his back garden from the same chair in his conservatory. Nowadays Jim continues to follow his beloved Hereford United, but with increasing sadness and disappointment at the state ofaffairs at the Edger Sreet club. He also with Betty and their three children travels down to Cardiff once a week to help out behind the scenes at Ninian Park,

The day the Austrians made Jim their 'Public Enemy' number one

In May 1963 Jim Finney took charge of a 'friendly' International at Hampton Park when minor dissension 'snowballed into wholesale skulduggery' and the Hereford referee ended up as public enemy number one in Austria.
A crowd of 94,596 had gathered to witness what should have been a pleasent encounter between Scotland and Austria, but as the home team romped into a comfortable first half lead their opponents decided to play dirty. According to Jim the trouble began when their star player Nemee complained about a'perfectly legitimate' Scotland goal which he believed should have been ruled oofside. He ran across to the centre circle when I was about to restart the game and spat at me. Then, he did it again, he explained.

Jim promptly sent Nemee off, but the Austrain manager Decker was having none of it and refused to let Nemee leave the pitch, untill other officials became involved. During the half–time interval Austria complained that the referee had spoilt the game by sending off their best player who apparently couldn't help spitting due to a rare medical condition.
"I've always wondered why, if this was the case and with five acres of football pitch all around us, he had to spit at me." said Jim.

The Austrains came out for the second-half with seemingly little intention of playing football. As the tackles increased more player were booked for bringing the game into disrepute. The crunch moment came when Austrain forward Hof brought down Dennis Law with a tackle Jim describes as one of the worst he has ever witnessed. Hof was dispatched for an early bath and once again there was uproar from the Austrain bench.

The match was promptly suspended as Jim picked up the ball and walked off the pitch, cheered all the way by the Scottish fans. Austria, meanwhile, have never forgiven a referee they claim 'lost his head' and Jim says if he ever goes to vienna, even for a holiday, he will probably get lynched.

Taken from the Hereford Times, first printed June 1998
Printed in the Association newletter August 1998.
Permission has been given to reproduce in 1998 and again in 2006

Refereeing Has Some Right Cards

When the Referee's note book comes out and his hand reaches for his pocket. Ted Ring watches what happens next.

The story goes that some years ago, when yellow and red cards were introduced, a Referee in a lesser–known F.I.F.A. Nation contacted his FA after his first game, asking them to send him some more yellow cards. He had literally given a card to each offender.

Well, Referees have come a long way down the road to correct practice with cards since then. Or have they? Make your own mind up after considering just a few of the teccchniques adopted by Referees when they use their cards.

Meet the **NOSTRIL-SWEEP**. He thinks he is a chimney–sweep dressed in another kind of black overall. Seeing the nostril like a fire place, he quickly decides that the opening needs attacking immediately. Out of deference to his match-day duties he uses a card instead of a brush, but it is only just in time that he decides to hold back. The card stops fractionally short of a nasal penetration!

Then there's **THE SEMAPHORE BANDIT.** He can't forget that he spends some of his match-day's as an Assistant Referee, but only once he has the man-in-the-middle duties to perform he acts like a one armed officer on an aircraft-carrier. His card is definitely going to be seen by everyone in the ground as well as any approaching jet-pilot. The only trouble is that the offending player is too close to really appreciate this flag-brandisher's histrionics.

Hello, here comes **TELETUBBY!** Almost creeping slowly out of the ground comes his card, just like that teletubby-phone emerging from the rabbit infested meadow. "Time for Teletubby byes-byes," he seems to be saying apologetically, as he reluctantly shows red to that both-boots-in the-stomach tackler. Let's hope that like our infants who watch their TV favourites, this Referee will one day act like a mature adult.

Now, what about **THE FLASHER?** Substituting his shirt pocket for a dirty raincoat, he flashes the card so fast that the person facing him gets a fleeting glimpse but can't be really sure about what was flashed at him. Perhaps our flasher thinks he will get away without being seen by his local 'policeman,' today carrying out assessing duties on the touchline.

Have you ever met **THE DELAYED-ACTION MAN?.** He takes so long to take out and show the yellow card that his victim has already, some forty or fifty yards away, worked out that his caution admin-fee will cost him 'a pint and a pizza' next week-end. Rumour has it that Delayed –Action Man has forgotten whether he keeps his yellow card in his breast –pocket and his red in his back one, or the other way round.

There's also **MEMORY MAN**. Actually, thats a sarcastic name, as he invariably forgets to show the cards anyway. Or maybe he just forgets his cards!

SPRINT-AND-THRUST MAN sees the offence, knows what he's going to do and does it. as the local 100-meetres champion, he is out of his blocks, well ahead of everyone else, and the card is half-a-metre in front of the culprit's nose before the latter has time to spread his 'Who? Me?' arms out wide in false appeal.

More often than not you will see THE APOLOGIST, No, not the one who apologies for what he is doing. You might need to check in the Oxford Dictionary or in Collins for his name's meaning. Let's just say that he can argue the case via his actions for doing his card showing technique in the recommended manner. Never the showman, always the perfect practitioner, he just knows his job and does it and if he's on T V, he does it so well that even the commentator doesn't notice him

So how far down the right road have our card-lovers really come? All the way, or do they still suggest that the local cardiologist will never be short of work?

Artifacts – Conference 76

The first prize in the Conference Raffle organised by the Birmingham & Warwickshire Joint Referees' Committee was a BLMC Mini, won by Mr. P. Clarke with ticket No. 89861.

Mr. Clarke is seen here collecting his prize before taking it back home to Worcestershire, where, quite by coincidence, he happens to live in the same area as the National President, Mr. Ken Burns.

In the photograph (by courtesy of Maurice Mead of Leamington Spa) are, from left to right: Ken Anderton, Vice-Chairman of the B. & W.J.R.C. and Chairman of the organising committee for the raffle; Tony Launchbury, Chief Salesman of Pitkin Motors Ltd.; W. Eastwood, Chairman of B. & W.J.R.C.; Mr. P. Clarke, the new owner of the Mini; and David Clarke, Secretary of the Leamington R.A. Conference Committee.

The organising committee wishes to thank everyone who took part in the raffle in any way at all, and points out that those Associations who assisted benefitted in donations to the tune of some £3,000 in all. Particular thanks are expressed to Ken Anderton, whose hard work played a major part in the venture which has resulted in a substantial boost for the Conference Fund.

Ladies Conference Committee
Jennie Silk, Pam Clarke, Moira Slark, Helen Wright,
Pat Semple, Ann Hyam, May Field

Conference Committee
Bob Field, Andy Semple, Vince Slark, Fred Tebbs, Bill Alderson
Derek Silk, David Clarke, Frank Wall, Arnold Rouse.

Ken Baker Football League Referee, refereeing the Conference
Six-a-Side at Harbury for Conference Funds

Alan Robinson Football League Referee with EricAdams presenting
Trophy's to the winners of the Penalty Competition

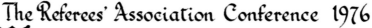

The Referees' Association Conference 1976

ROYAL LEAMINGTON SPA

CHAIRMAN
F. Wall, Esq.

SECRETARY
A.D. Clarke, Esq.
11, Constance Drive,
Harbury,
Leamington Spa.
Phone Harbury
612311

ACCOMODATION SECRETARY
A.W. Rouse, Esq.
130, Stratford Road,
Warwick.

Phone Warwick 43041.

TREASURER
D. Silk, Esq.
17, Grange Avenue,
Kenilworth,
Warwickshire,
Phone Kenilworth
56104

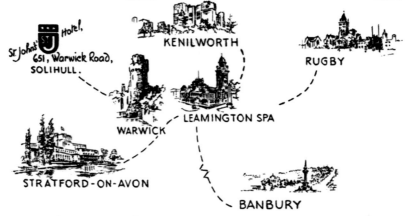

St John's Hotel,
651, Warwick Road,
SOLIHULL.

KENILWORTH

RUGBY

WARWICK

LEAMINGTON SPA

STRATFORD-ON-AVON

BANBURY

58th Annual Conference of the Referees' Association   11th, 12th & 13th June 1976.

The Leamington and District R.A. have pleasure on behalf of the Midland Division in inviting you to attend the 58th Annual Conference of the Referees' Association which will be held in the Conference Hall of the Saint John's Hotel, Solihull.

As hosts we have endeavoured to provide suitable entertainment for Delegates and their Ladies on Friday & Saturday evenings, also at the St. John's Hotel.

Arrangements have been made for a Ladies Luncheon followed by an organised outing for those Ladies who are interested

Every attempt is being made to hold the booking fee to a minimum and fund raising is proceeding vigorously to achieve this objective.

Booking forms will be available in December, 1975.

We are sure you will enjoy your visit to "The Heart of England" and very much look forward to meeting you.

Yours sincerely

F. Wall
Chairman.

Secretary's Report

When Leamington and District R.A. first asked for permission to stage Conference, we knew the task was not an easy one and on costings made before commiting ourselves it was anticipated that £3,000 would be needed. In the ensuing period many disasters and misfortunes have occurred which the Conference Committee have accepted and overcome in a remarkably cheerful and efficient manner. To list a few of these difficulties will give an idea of the work of the Committee.

The Spa Centre was booked for Conference and Social functions but when it opened in 1972 it proved to have several failings for functions of the size of an R.A. Conference. In particular, catering could not cope with the numbers.

The Automotive Products Ballroom was then booked for Conference, together with The Chesford Lion Ballroom for the Social functions. Then at the end of May 1975 The Chesford cancelled the booking, causing major replanning with the subsequent booking of the St. John's, Solihull for all events.

The accommodation for all delegates had by May 1975 been reserved through all large hostels and guest houses in the area, but these had to be cancelled and new reservations made in the Solihull area—not an easy task when it is realised that bookings for the new National Exhibition Centre nearby were being made!

Add to this the effects of inflation to our budget, which has resulted in costs escalating to over £6,000, and one can realise why money-raising featured high in our priorities. Every event run by the Committee has made money, from the Whist Drives that made profits in the tens of pounds to the Sponsored Walks which raised hundreds of pounds for Charity Organisations and ourselves in equal proportions.

Mention must also be made of the Car Raffle organised by the Birmingham and Warwickshire Joint Referees' Committee, which resulted in a substantial donation to our funds and thousands of pounds returned to local R.As. as a donation to their funds.

One event, the annual Six-a-Side football competition for Referees Association teams, instigated by the Committee, has proved a great social success, bringing together for the day hundreds of Referees and friends from all over the Midlands. Football League Officials from a wide area helped out with this and with the Under-13s Penalty Competition run concurrently. The photograph shows the winner and runner-up of the Under 13s being presented with their trophies in the 1974 Competition.

Our activities over the last four years have been supported by many organisations and individuals. We offer our thanks to them and all who have helped us, especially:

1. Sir Jack Scamp.
2. R. A. Harwood, Esq.
3. W. Johnston Wilson, Esq.
4. Birmingham/County F.A.
5. Coventry R.A.
6. Shirley R.A.
7. Aston Villa F.C.
8. Coventry City F.C.
9. A. P. Leamington F.C.
10. Leamington and District Football Leagues.
11. Coventry Sunday Football Leagues.
12. Warwick District Council.
13. Harbury Parish Council.
14. Cartwright Sports, Leamington Spa.
15. Thorburn Bros., Ltd., Leamington Spa.
16. Avia Ltd.
17. Admiral Sportswear.
18. Mike Ingle, Bromsgrove Sports.
19. St. John's Hotel Ltd., Solihull.
20. Automotive Products Ltd.
21. Rackhams Ltd.
22. Roadrive Ltd.

We apologise to any contributors who have inadvertently been omitted from the above list.

A. D. CLARKE.

Standing, from left: Andy Semple, Arnold Rouse, Pat Wright, Fred Tebbs, Bill Alderson, Brian Hackleton
Seated, from left: Bob Field, Vince Slark, Frank Wall, David Clarke, Derek Silk

Standing, from left: May Field, Pat Semple, Helen Wright
Seated, from left: Christine Clarke, Jenny Silk, Moira Slark, Pam Clarke, Andrea Slark

LEAMINGTON REFEREES' ASSOCIATION CONFERENCE COMMITTEE
FOR
THE REFEREES' ASSOCIATION CONFERENCE 1976

Chairman:	Secretary:	Treasurer:
F. WALL, Esq.	A. D. CLARKE, Esq.	D. SILK, Esq.
MILL LANE	11, CONSTANCE DRIVE	17, GRANGE AVENUE
HARBURY	HARBURY	KENILWORTH
NR. LEAMINGTON SPA	NR. LEAMINGTON SPA	WARWICKSHIRE
'Phone: Harbury 569	'Phone: Harbury 311	'Phone: Kenilworth 56104

The Solihull Conference of 1976 turned out to be one of the best Referees Association Conferences that has ever been held.

The letters reproduced in this booklet are a visible expression of the gratitude of delegates and guests for the hospitality afforded to them on the weekend of June 11th, 12th and 13th, 1976.

Many telephone calls and verbal expressions of gratitude have been received in addition to these and they are all a very satisfying testimonial to the four years of hard work and planning put in by all those involved in the organisation.

It is hoped that as you look through this booklet it will bring back pleasant memories of a job well done, of the many new and lasting friendships made and of the co-operation and friendliness of members of the Referees Association.

13th November, 1976

National Referees Executive Committee and Midland Division Officers with 1976 Conference Secretary David Clarke.

Artifacts: – Pre-War

ALBION NEWS   April 27th, 1946

WEST BROMWICH ALBION
Colours : White Shirts and Black Knickers

Right				Left
	MILLARD (2)	SANDERS	KINSELL (3)	
WITCOMB (4)		TRANTER (5)		RYAN (6)
ELLIOTT (7)	CLARKE (8)	BANKS (9)	BARLOW (10)	HODGETTS (11)
WOOD (11)	MACAULAY (10)	SMALL (9)	HULL (8)	WOODGATE (7)
	CORBETT (6)	WALKER (R.) (5)		FENTON (4)
	CATER (3)		BICKNELL (2)	
Left		MEDHURST		Right

WEST HAM UNITED
Colours : Claret and Blue

Referee : Mr. G. TEDDS (Nottingham)
Linesmen : Messrs. J. E. WILDSMITH (Blue) and F. J. CHAPMAN (Red).

Linesman Mr J E Wildsmith (Leamngton)

33, St. Mary's Crescent,
Leamington Spa.
19 . X . 38.

Dear Mr. Rowson,
I am sorry but as I have to preside at a General Meeting of the N.U.T. at the Pump Rooms tonight at 7 p.m. I shall be unable to be present at the meeting tonight. As regards the Audit my presence is not at all necessary as you have the figures, receipts & bank book. As regards that 3/- I cannot myself remember or find a note of it, but if Mr. West is certain that this Association did eventually receive it and it was handed on to me I am quite willing for it to be ~~handed on~~ added on to the Balance as cash in hand which will make it straight I think. In any case I would like to assure the Committee that it must have been an oversight in some way.

Excuse scribble but I am extremely busy. Hoping you have a good meeting,
Yours sincerely,
George H. Lewis

Leamington Referees Association

Treasurer :
G. A. LEWIS,
23 St. Mary's Crescent,
Leamington.

President :
G. ORME TILEY, Esq.
Kineton,
Warwick.

Chairman :
J. E. WILDSMITH
42 Court Street,
Leamington.

Secretary :
R. W. ROWSON,
188 Rugby Road,
Leamington.

Headquarters : GUARDS INN, High Street, Leamington

STAMP   A/C   —   SEASON   1937 – 8 ..

DEC. 1937   (Including 2 Parcels Envelopes)   2 · 11½

JAN. 1938   1 · 1

FEB.   "   2 ·

MARCH   "   1 · 8

APRIL   "   1 · 2½

MAY 14th "...   1 · 7½

10 · 6½

Received
15/9/38

R. W. Rowson ·

SECRETARY'S EXPENSES .

No 7943

REPAIR DEPT. & GARAGES—22 GUY STREET

THE MOTOR TRADE ASSOCIATION

HEAD OFFICE & SHOWROOM—
21 THE PARADE.
LEAMINGTON SPA.

May 15th 1938

Mr Rowson

IN ACCOUNT WITH

HART-DAVIES & HAGGARD. LTD.

MOTOR AGENTS AND ENGINEERS.
ACCESSORY SPECIALISTS.

TELEPHONE - 464 LEAMINGTON.
(PRIVATE BRANCH EXCHANGE)

To	Hire of car ½ day		12	6
	2½ Gals Petrol		3	7
			16	1

HART DAVIES & HAGGARD LTD
RECEIVED
16 MAY 1938
WITH THANKS
21, THE PARADE,
LEAMINGTON.

Leamington & District Referees Association

Annual Statement of Accounts 1938-39

Income:- From :-	£	s	d	Expenditure:- To :-	£	s	d
Cash Balance Bank £3-1-5				Jackson Test. (2nd Payment)		10	6
1937-38. in Hand £2-4-7	5	6	0.	15 Subs. National @ 1/-		15	0.
Mr. Brme-Tiloy (Cheque)	2	2	0.	15 - Birmingham C.A. @ 1d	1	3.	
Warwick & District F.L.	1	1	0	Advert. in Magazine.		2	9.
14 Subs. @ 2/6d		15	0.	Xmas Social.		17	6.
9 Subs. @ 1/- to Soden Test.	9	0.		Soden Testemonial	1	0	0.
Bank Interest.			6.	Printing (Maisey & Son.)		10	9.
				Spiers Testimonial		5	0.
				Secretary (Postage Etc.)		17	4
				Balance Bank £5-3-11 in Hand 9-6d	5	13	5
Total £	10	13	6	Total = £	10	13	6

Bank Reconciliation to 31 December 1947.

	£	s	d
Cash in Bank (as per pass book) at 31 Dec. 1938 =	5	3	11.
Bank Interest for 1939 - 1947 Inclusive.		6	9
Cash in Bank (as per pass book) at 31 Dec. 1947 = £	5	10	8	P.T.O.

Presented by:- George A. Lewis. Audited by:-

Profit on Working of 1938-39 Season = 4-5d

Total Balance at time of present meeting (ie. sometime in 1948) = £ 6-0-2d

Signed:- George A. Lewis
Hon. Treas.

J.E. Dragg,
S.H. Soden 12. 7. 49.

FOUNDED 1875.

TELEPHONE CENtral 3427

BIRMINGHAM COUNTY FOOTBALL ASSOCIATION.

SECRETARY:
E. A. EDEN.

UNITAS HOUSE,
24, LIVERY STREET,
BIRMINGHAM, 3.

Dear Sir,

     We have pleasure to advise you that
you were successful in passing the Referees'
Examination held on the 6th instant, and we shall
be glad to receive at your earliest convenience a
postal order for 2/6d. to complete your
registration for Season 1938-39.

Yours faithfully,

Mr C Jackson passing County FA Referees Exam 38

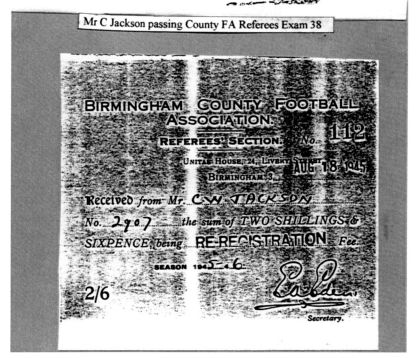

BIRMINGHAM COUNTY FOOTBALL ASSOCIATION.

REFEREES' SECTION. No. 112

UNITAS HOUSE, 24, LIVERY STREET
BIRMINGHAM, 3.

AUG 18 1945

Received from Mr. C.W. JACKSON

No. 2907 the sum of TWO SHILLINGS &
SIXPENCE, being RE-REGISTRATION Fee.

SEASON 1945-6

2/6

Secretary.

6 Mulberry St.
Stratford-on-Avon
31. July 1939.

Mr. R. W. Rowson

Dear Sir

Please find
enclosed 2/6. P.O. my
Subscription for joining
the Referees Association.
I shall be pleased to
meet you at the meetings
which I hope to be
able to attend, thanking
you for good wishes etc
I Remain
Yours Sincerely
W. J. Hawk

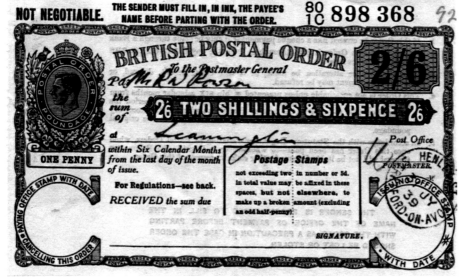

345

Warwick Engineers were very disappointed last week, when they met and were defeated by Leamington All Saints', for they had fully 90 per cent. of the exchanges. There was no score in the first half, and in the second the Warwickians were more often than not within the penalty area of their opponents, but could only score once. During the second half the Saints made two breakaway, and scored from both. To the end of the game the Engineers' forwards rained innumerable shots on Wildsmith, who succeeded in keeping the ball from the net. The Engineers attribute their defeat in no small measure to this player, who played a wonderful game throughout. Simmonds, the Warwick centre-forward, took a penalty kick in the latter stages, but placed it wide of the post.

Leamington Town Football Team 1904

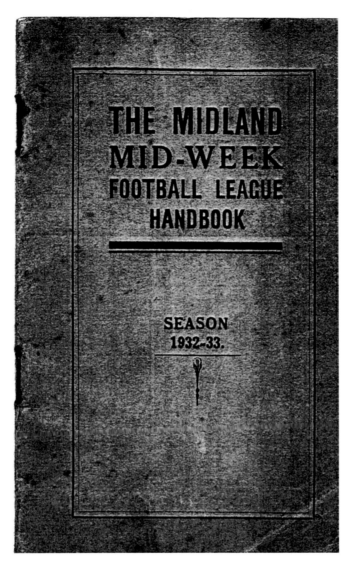

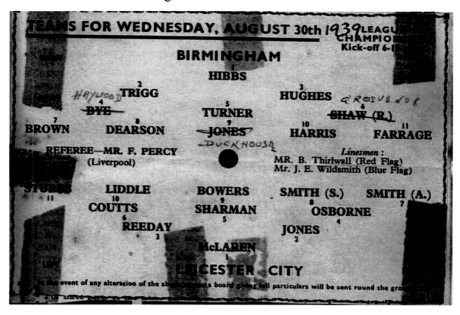

TEAMS FOR WEDNESDAY, AUGUST 30th 1939 **LEAGUE CHAMPION** Kick-off 6-1

BIRMINGHAM

1 HIBBS

2 TRIGG *HAYWOOD*   3 HUGHES *GROSVENOR*

4 ~~DYE~~   5 TURNER   6 ~~SHAW (R.)~~

7 BROWN   8 DEARSON   9 ~~JONES~~ *DUCKHOUSE*   10 HARRIS   11 FARRAGE

REFEREE—MR. F. PERCY (Liverpool)

Linesmen :
MR. B. Thirlwall (Red Flag)
Mr. J. E. Wildsmith (Blue Flag)

STUBBS 11   LIDDLE 10   BOWERS 9   SMITH (S.)   SMITH (A.) 7

COUTTS 6   SHARMAN 5   OSBORNE 8   4

REEDAY 3   JONES 2

McLAREN 1

LEICESTER CITY

In the event of any alteration of the above a board giving full particulars will be sent round the ground

---

THE FOOTBALL LEAGUE

102 Fishergate,

Preston.

24th April 1944

The Football League War Cup. Final Ties.

Dear Sir,

The Draw and Officials for the Final Ties of the above Competition are as follows:-

April 29th Blackpool v Aston Villa
     Referee: J.H.Parker, 128 Bedford Street, Crewe.
     Linesmen: D.Schofield, 104 Hadfield Street, Oldham.
           C.P.Womersley, 27 Beechfield Road, Davenport,
                           Cheshire.

May 6. Aston Villa v Blackpool
     Referee: J.H.Parker, 128 Bedford Street, Crewe
     Linesmen: E.R.MacLachlan, 78 Pine Tree Avenue, Humberstone,
                                Leicester.
           J.E.Wildsmith, 40 Court Street, Leamington Spa.

Kick-off in both matches 3 p.m.
NOTICE 1. Regulation 7 reads "In the event of a draw after the second
         match, extra time of 10 minutes each way must be played. If
         the result is still a draw the match must be played to a
         finish, the first goal scored determining the winner and
         terminating the Match".

NOTICE 2. Match Officials must acknowledge receipt of appointments
         immediately to the League and the Home Club.

                   F.Howarth,
                   Secretary.

Lillington Football Club 1910
The Clergyman on the right is the
Rev R B Roberts Vicar/ Curate Lillington Church
Assume Team is from the Church

• • •

Mr. John Wildsmith, who has been elected captain of the Leamington Thursday F.C. is one of the best goalkeepers in Leamington and district. Apart from actual participation in the sport, he takes

a keen interest in administrative affairs. He is a local referee, and as hon. secretary of the Leamington Referees' Association has done much to place that organisation on a sound footing.

• • •

• • •

Warwick Engineers were very disappointed last week, when they met and were defeated by Leamington All Saints', for they had fully 90 per cent. of the exchanges. There was no score in the first half, and in the second the Warwickians were more often than not within the penalty area of their opponents, but could only score once. During the second half the Saints made two breakaways, and scored from both. To the end of the game the Engineers' forwards rained innumerable shots on Wildsmith, who succeeded in keeping the ball from the net. The Engineers attribute their defeat in no small measure to this player, who played a wonderful game throughout. Simmonds, the Warwick centre-forward, took a penalty kick in the latter stages, but placed it wide of the post.

* * *

THE WEEK'S FOOTBALL.

TOWN'S DISASTROUS DEFEAT.

AT THE HANDS OF FLAVELS.

"Wanted. Five forwards able to score goals!"—Such was the proposed wording of an advertisement by a Town supporter on Saturday, after the Warwickians had failed so blatently to their nearest rivals, Flavels. One of the Leamington players stated prior to the match that the works side had no hopes of winning, but only desired to give the Town a good game. They did play a good game—far too good for the weak finishing home team. It was only feeble forward play that lost the Town the match, for their tackling and defensive play was streets ahead of that of Flavels. In face of the score, 6—2, this may appear ridiculous, but it was so, for almost every one of the Leamington goals were scored from breakaways. Wildsmith, in the visitors' goal, played a large part in the defeat of the Warwickians, and it would not be too much to hazard that if a weaker man had been in that position Flavels would have lost at least one of the points. Last year Wildsmith saved nine out of ten penalties taken against him.

* *

During the first twenty minutes the play of the Town was magnificent. The ball was swung about with exhilarating freedom, and Flavels' defenders were continually out of their depth. In the first minute the home forwards hotly assailed the Leamington goal, and splendid work between Askew and West resulted

Leamington Referees with Clarrie Bourton as the Referee
Wearing a Blazer standing by the Goalkeeper. 1937

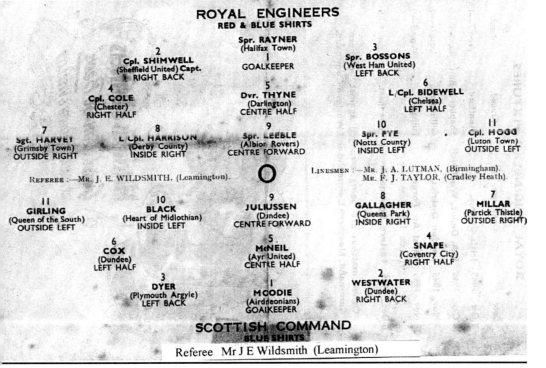

ROYAL ENGINEERS
RED & BLUE SHIRTS

Spr. RAYNER
(Halifax Town)
1
GOALKEEPER

2
Cpl. SHIMWELL
(Sheffield United) Capt.
RIGHT BACK

3
Spr. BOSSONS
(West Ham United)
LEFT BACK

4
Cpl. COLE
(Chester)
RIGHT HALF

5
Dvr. THYNE
(Darlington)
CENTRE HALF

6
L/Cpl. BIDEWELL
(Chelsea)
LEFT HALF

7
Sgt. HARVEY
(Grimsby Town)
OUTSIDE RIGHT

8
L/Cpl. HARRISON
(Derby County)
INSIDE RIGHT

9
Spr. KEEBLE
(Albion Rovers)
CENTRE FORWARD

10
Spr. FYE
(Notts County)
INSIDE LEFT

11
Cpl. HOGG
(Luton Town)
OUTSIDE LEFT

REFEREE :— MR. J. E. WILDSMITH. (Leamington).   O   LINESMEN :— MR. J. A. LUTMAN, (Birmingham).
MR. F. J. TAYLOR, (Cradley Heath).

11
GIRLING
(Queen of the South)
OUTSIDE LEFT

10
BLACK
(Heart of Midlothian)
INSIDE LEFT

9
JULIUSSEN
(Dundee)
CENTRE FORWARD

8
GALLAGHER
(Queens Park)
INSIDE RIGHT

7
MILLAR
(Partick Thistle)
OUTSIDE RIGHT)

6
COX
(Dundee)
LEFT HALF

5
McNEIL
(Ayr United)
CENTRE HALF

4
SNAPE
(Coventry City)
RIGHT HALF

3
DYER
(Plymouth Argyle)
LEFT BACK

1
McODIE
(Airdrieonians)
GOALKEEPER

2
WESTWATER
(Dundee)
RIGHT BACK

SCOTTISH COMMAND
BLUE SHIRTS

Referee Mr J E Wildsmith (Leamington)

RUGBY TOWN RES. Black & White Shirts, Black Shorts

A. BARNWELL

R. BACHE
2

A. HARGRAVE
3

R. WRIGHT
4

J. LLEWELLYN
5

J. JOHNSTON
6

J. WRIGHT
8

D. BERRIDGE
8

B. KELLY
10

E. HUGHES
7

J. KELLY
11

BIRD A.
11

HUGHES W.
7

HIGGIN R.
10

PICKARD E.
8

GROGAN A.
9

PENZER E.
6

WALLINGTON
5

LOUW
4

JONES A.
3

O'TOOLE B.
2

MORRIS P.

BIRMINGHAM CITY Blue Shirts, White Shorts

SATURDAY, 9th NOV., 1957 Kick-off 2.45 p.m. | Referee G. JACKSON (LEEK WOOTTON)

BIRMINGHAM COUNTY FOOTBALL ASSOCIATION

TELEPHONE:
CENTRAL 3427.

UNITAS HOUSE.
24, LIVERY STREET,
BIRMINGHAM. 3.

SECRETARY:
E. A. EDEN.

C.

25 APR 1956

REFEREES SECTION

Dear Sir,

I have to inform you, that subject to your having completed your registration, the Referees' Committee has been pleased to promote you from Class 111 to Class 11 for Season 1956-57.

If you have not already remitted your Annual Subscription, please do so at once as failure to register will render the promotion void.

Yours faithfully,

Mr. J.C. Sollis (5548)

BIRMINGHAM COUNTY FOOTBALL ASSOCIATION

TELEPHONE:
CENTRAL 3427.

24, LIVERY STREET,
BIRMINGHAM. 3.

SECRETARY:
W. A. COLLINS.

25th April, 1960.

REFEREES SECTION

Dear Sir,

I have to inform you that the Referees' Committee has been pleased to promote you from Class 11 to Class 1 for Season 1960-61.

This promotion will not become effective until you have registered for the coming Season, failure to register will render the promotion void.

When remitting your Annual Subscription please send 12/6d. which is the amount payable by Class 1 Referees.

Yours faithfully,

Mr. J.C. Sollis,
(No.5548)

Promotion to J Sollis 1956 and 1961

LEAM. & DISTRICT REFEREES ASSC.

STATEMENT OF ACCOUNTS 1948-49.

INCOME		EXPENDITURE	
Subscription Mr. Orme-Tiley	£3. 3. 0.	Rule Books	£1. 10. 6.
" Members (20) at 6/6d	£6. 10. 0.	Notice of Meeting Cards	13. 6.
News Letter	1. 0.	Acknowledgement Cards	15. 4.
Fines as per Rule	2. 0.	Subscriptions National R.A. (13)	19. 6.
Acknowledgement Cards	15. 9.	" County R.A. (13)	6. 6.
		News Letter	1. 0.
		Postage	£1. 2. 11.
			£5. 9. 3.
	£10. 11. 9.	Cash in Hand	£5. 2. 6.
Cash in Bank as per Pass Book 31.12.47.	£5. 10. 8.		£10. 11. 9.
Total Balance to Date 21.5.49	£16. 2. 9.		

NF. 392
660

- DUPLICATE for retention as record -

(Mandate for operation on the Accounts of informally constituted bodies [Clubs, Societies, etc.].)

* Committee of Management or as the case may be.

† Name of Club or Society.

At a Meeting of the *_____

of the† LEAMINGTON & DISTRICT REFEREES' ASSOCIATION

duly convened and held at _Willoughby Arms, Augusta Place, Leamington Sp._

on the _15th_ day of _May_ 1957 at which Meeting

‡ Quote Number.

there were present‡ _14_ Members thereof.

It was Resolved—

That NATIONAL PROVINCIAL BANK LIMITED be, and they are hereby, authorised to pay all Cheques drawn upon any account or accounts for the time being kept with the said Bank, in the name of the

§ Full Name of Club or Society.

§ _____ LEAMINGTON & DISTRICT REFEREES' ASSOCIATION _____

when signed by the Chairman and the Secretary, both for the time being

whether such account or accounts are overdrawn by the payment thereof or are in credit or otherwise, and that all documents requiring endorsement may be endorsed

by EITHER of these officers

and that all receipts for the delivery of securities, papers or property may be signed

by BOTH these officers

That the said Bank be furnished with a list of the names of the signing Officers from time to time and that the said Bank be from time to time informed in writing of any changes which may take place in them.

That these Resolutions be communicated to the said Bank and remain in force until revoked or varied by notice in writing given to the said Bank by the Chairman or the Secretary purporting to act on behalf of the Club or Society and the said Bank shall be entitled to act on such notice whether the said Resolutions or any of them shall have been duly rescinded or not.

(Signed) _Geo. Pankhurst_   (Signed) _T. R. Storey_

Secretary.   Chairman

NAMES IN FULL.	SPECIMENS OF SIGNATURES.
THOMAS ROBERT STOREY - Chairman (of 72, Guy Str., Warwick)	
GEORGE PANKHURST - (Treasurer and Secretary) (of 105, Hanworth Road, Warwick)	_Geo. Pankhurst_

NOTE:—A copy of the Rules of the Society or Club should be obtained and held at the Branch, and this Form should be altered, if necessary, to comply with the said Rules.

W. & S. Ltd.

Officers Signatures for Bank Information

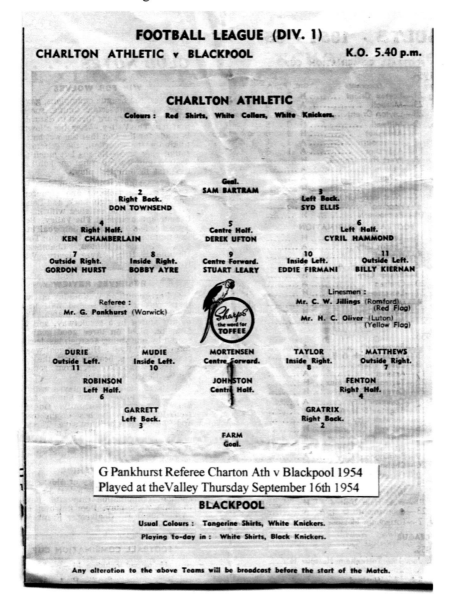

FOOTBALL LEAGUE (DIV. 1)

CHARLTON ATHLETIC v BLACKPOOL   K.O. 5.40 p.m.

CHARLTON ATHLETIC

Colours : Red Shirts, White Collars, White Knickers.

Goal.
SAM BARTRAM

2
Right Back.
DON TOWNSEND

3
Left Back.
SYD ELLIS

4
Right Half.
KEN CHAMBERLAIN

5
Centre Half.
DEREK UFTON

6
Left Half.
CYRIL HAMMOND

7
Outside Right.
GORDON HURST

8
Inside Right.
BOBBY AYRE

9
Centre Forward.
STUART LEARY

10
Inside Left.
EDDIE FIRMANI

11
Outside Left.
BILLY KIERNAN

Referee :
Mr. G. Pankhurst (Warwick)

Linesmen :
Mr. C. W. Jillings (Romford)
(Red Flag)
Mr. H. C. Oliver (Luton)
(Yellow Flag)

Sharps the word for TOFFEE

DURIE
Outside Left.
11

MUDIE
Inside Left.
10

MORTENSEN
Centre Forward.

TAYLOR
Inside Right.
8

MATTHEWS
Outside Right.
7

ROBINSON
Left Half.
6

JOHNSTON
Centre Half.

FENTON
Right Half.
4

GARRETT
Left Back.
3

GRATRIX
Right Back.
2

FARM
Goal.

G Pankhurst Referee Charton Ath v Blackpool 1954
Played at the Valley Thursday September 16th 1954

BLACKPOOL

Usual Colours : Tangerine Shirts, White Knickers.
Playing to-day in : White Shirts, Black Knickers.

Any alteration to the above Teams will be broadcast before the start of the Match.

TEAMS for to-day's Match, Monday, 18th September, 1950

Kick-off 6 p.m.

GALATA SARAY (Red and Yellow Shirts and White Knickers)

Right   Seren   Left

Ozkaya
2

Sezer   B. Eken   Tokac
4   5   6

Tuncaltan   Kilic   R. Eken   Ozar   Varol
7   8   9   10   11

Erdogdu
3

Linesmen :

A. Owen
(Yellow Flag)

Referee :
G. Pankhurst
(Warwick)

F. P. Clarke
(Red Flag)

Lockhart   Chisholm   Roberts   Allen   Warner
11   10   9   8   7

Simpson   McDonnell   Barratt
6   5   4

Mason R.   Timmins
3   2

Left   Wood   Right

COVENTRY CITY (Blue and White Shirts and White Knickers)

G Pankhurst Referee Galata Saray v Coventry 1950
Played at Coventry Monday September 18th 1950

NAMES AND POSITIONS OF PLAYERS
(Any alteration in teams will be announced over Loudspeakers).

WALES (Red)

RIGHT   **KELSEY** (Arsenal)   LEFT

2 BARNES, *Captain*   **3 SHERWOOD**
(Arsenal)   (Cardiff City)

4 PAUL   **5 CHARLES**   **6 BOWEN**
(Manchester City)   (Leeds United)   (Arsenal)

7 REED   **8 TAPSCOTT**   **9 FORD**   **10 ALLCHURCH**   **11 CLARKE**
(Ipswich Town)   (Arsenal)   (Cardiff City)   (Swansea Town)   (Manchester City)

Referee :
Mr. W. LING
(Stapleford, Cambs.)

Linesmen·
Mr. G. PANKHURST (Warwick)
Red Flag
Mr. T. JEPSON (Mansfield)
Yellow Flag

11 RING   **10 FERNIE**   **9 BUCKLEY**   **8 YORSTON**   **7 WADDELL**
(Clyde)   (Celtic)   (Aberdeen)   (Aberdeen)   (Rangers)

6 COWIE   **5 DAVIDSON**   **4 DOCHERTY**
(Dundee)   (Partick)   (Preston North End)

3 CUNNINGHAM   **2 YOUNG** (*Captain*)
(Preston North End)   (Rangers)

LEFT   **FRASER**   RIGHT
(Sunderland)

SCOTLAND (Blue)

G Pankhurst Linesman Wales v Scotland
International at Ninian Park Cardiff
Saturday 16th October 1954

FOREWORD by The Rt. Hon. SIR ANTHONY EDEN, K.G., M.C.,
President of the Leamington and District Football League.

FYFIELD MANOR,
PEWSEY,
WILTSHIRE
PEWSEY 3138

August 17th, 1959.

Dear Mr. Curtis,

I would like to send this letter to congratulate the Leamington and District Football League upon their Jubilee Dinner. I have been happy to be their President over a number of years and I want to take this opportunity to pay my tribute to the splendid football they have provided for Leamington and district. They have given health to some and enjoyment to many.

I hope that for many years to come they will continue to flourish as they most certainly deserve to do.

With every good wish to you, to the players and to all concerned with the League's excellent record.

Yours sincerely,

Anthony Eden

Edward Curtis, Esq.,
"Emsdene",
Wellesbourne,
Warwicks.

THE FOOTBALL ASSOCIATION

REFEREES' CHART

AND PLAYERS GUIDE TO
THE LAWS OF THE GAME

AUTHORISED BY THE INTERNATIONAL FOOTBALL ASSOCIATION BOARD

REGISTERED COPYRIGHT

BIRMINGHAM COUNTY FOOTBALL ASSOCIATION

TELEPHONE:
CENtral 3427.

UNITAS HOUSE,
24, LIVERY STREET,
BIRMINGHAM, 3.

REFEREES SECTION.

Dear Sir,

An Examination of Referee Candidates will be held at the **B.T.H. Social Club, Holyhead Road, Coventry**

on **Thursday 19th March 1953** at **7-30** p.m.

Will you please make it convenient to attend.

Yours faithfully,

E. A. EDEN, *Secretary.*

To comply with Football Association regulations all Candidates must produce their Birth Certificates when attending for examination.

R.2. 1M. 9/52.

This is the type of Notification members received when taking the Referees Examination in Coventry

Leamington &District Saturday League Cups and
Trophies Presentation Evening
Junior Cup   winners   Banbury Spencer FC
President Cup winners   Kenilworth Albion FC
Aston –Villa Cup winners   Whitnash FC
Division 2 Champions Harbury Albion FC
Birmingham City Shield winners 251 Coy RPC
Knock Out Cup winners Section A 251 Coy RPC
winners Section B Radford St Nicholas Res FC
Champions 3rd Division
winners Section A 251 Coy RPC
winners Section B Radford St Nicholas FC

Some of the distinguished football personalities who attended the Leamington and District Football League Golden Jubilee dinner on Friday night. L. to r.: Mr. G. Pankhurst (vice-chairman), Mr. S. Adams, The Mayor (Counc. T. Saunders), Mr. W. Dare (Birmingham City F.C. director), Mr. G. Dutton (chairman), Mr. F. Normansell (Aston Villa F.C. director), Mr. E. Curtis (treasurer), Mr. W. Collins, Mr. E. A. Eden (vice-president of the F.A.), and Counc. E. H. Fryer (vice-president of the league).

Leamington & District Referees Association Football Team 1956/7
Back row - Hughie Eyton, Alex Walters, Ron Pemberton, George Pankhurst
Frank Wall, Roy Batchelor, Fred Mortimer, John Wyatt, Brian Hiley, Ken Eastbury
John Sollis, Jack Wright, Steve Barnett, Bert Gwynne, Wilf Blount
The team played Stratford Referees on Warwick Towns Football Ground.

BIRMINGHAM COUNTY FOOTBALL ASSOCIATION.

REFEREES' SECTION. No. 788

UNITAS HOUSE, 24, LIVERY STREET,

BIRMINGHAM, 3, **AUG 18 1945**

Received from Mr. *C.W. JACKSON*

No. 2907. the sum of FIVE SHILLINGS,

Registration Fee in Class 3

SEASON

5/-

Secretary.

Leamington League referees

The following referees have be
placed on the Leamington a
District League list for 1956-7
F. R. Banner, L. W. Barnett, S. |
Barriball, L. Benger, A. W. Billing
Dennis E. Clarke, E. Clark
A. W. Cork, L. Davenpo
W. J. L. Draper, K. Eastbury, H.
Ebsworth, C. J. Eley, H. Eyte
S. C. Flick, J. K. Hobley, C. V
Jackson, W. Jones, B. Martin, F.
Mortimore, R. A. Pemberton, D.
Paget, N. P. Paget, A. W. Rous
J. C. Sollis, F. W. Stevens, L. V
Stiles, T. R. Story, Frank Wall, W
Wall, A. Walters, R. G. Warnl
W. R. Woodward and J. V. Wya
A few more referees are requir

Leamington Referee Charles Jackson

Banbury Spencer Football Club

SPENCER HOUSE,
BRITANNIA ROAD, BANBURY.
TELEPHONE:- Office 2265

GROUND ENTRANCE:-
FROM BANBURY G.W.R. STATION
APPROACH.

12th August, 1953.

Dear Sir,

As we are having the pleasure of your controlling
our game against Bedworth in 1st Round Birmingham
Senior Cup, please note date August 25th (Tuesday), Kick Off 6-45 p.m.

Hoping you will have a very successful Season.

Yours truly,

J.A. Cringan.

Lockheed Juniors, Div. 1 Champions '47-8, '48-9, '49-50.

Back row (left to right) : Mr. F. Yeomans (team manager), D. Cleaver,* R. Bethel, D. Grimwood, D. Hodson, C. Lewis, D. Gray,* Mr. S. R. Jackson ; front row : R. Jones, W. Draper,* D. Onions, A. Horley, D. Moore.

Photo by Leamington ' Morning News ' Ltd.

Players with * following their name were members of the 1949-50 team. Others reached the age limit before commencement of last season.

Leamington Boys' Club, 1948-49.
Winners of the Warwickshire Boys' Clubs' Trophy and Finalists of the ' Courier ' Cup.

Back row (left to right) : Mr. K. Dodkin (leader-secretary), Cookes, Mr. G. Perks (secretary, Y.O.C. League), Millar, Morgan, Rowlatt, Knight, Mr. T. Williams (chairman of the Boys' Club), Clarke Shipway ; front row : Barton, Austin, Hunt, Brison, Burrows.

Photo by Leamington ' Morning News ' Ltd.

7

Artifacts: - 1961 – 1980

LEAMINGTON REFEREES ASSOCIATION

FOR ONE DAY REFRESHER COURSE
on Sunday June 28th, 1970

PRESENTED BY

10.00 a.m.	Assemble
10.00 - 10.45	Introductory lecture - Course leader
10.45 - 11.15	Group discussion
11.15 - 11.30	Group summaries
11.30 - 11.45	Coffee break
11.45 - 12.30	Lecture. Referee personality
12.30 - 1.00	F.I.F.A. film "Referee - Linesman A Team"
1.00 - 2.00	Lunch
2.00 - 2.30	F.I.F.A. film "Law 12"
2.30 - 3.00	Group discussion
3.00 - 3.15	Group summaries
3.15 - 4.00	E. Babington
4.00 - 4.30	Group discussion and summary
4.30 - 4.45	Tea
4.45 - 5.30	Lecture Course leader
5.30	Course summary

COURSE LEADER C.S. ALLATT

GROUP LEADERS M. PRICE, E. ADAMS

Refresher Course June 1970.
Organised by Andy Semple and Arnold Rouse.

Management Committee, Artiste from the Leamington
Courier Press. 1967

BIRMINGHAM COUNTY FOOTBALL ASSOCIATION

TELEPHONE:
CENTRAL 3427

24 LIVERY STREET
BIRMINGHAM 3

SECRETARY:
R. E. EDEN

REE/JB

19th April 1966

REFEREES' SECTION

Dear Sir,

I have to inform you that the Referees' Committee has been pleased to promote you from Class II to Class I for season 1966/67.

This promotion will not become effective until you have registered for the coming season, failure to register will render the promotion void.

When remitting your Annual Subscription please send 12/6d which is the amount payable by Class I referees.

Yours faithfully,

Secretary.

P.S. If you have already paid Class II fee please forward a further 2/6d.

Promotion to Andy Semple 1966-67

7910 A.G.SEMPLE

BIRMINGHAM COUNTY FOOTBALL ASSOCIATION

PRESIDENT
THE RIGHT WORSHIPFUL THE LORD MAYOR OF BIRMINGHAM.

TELEPHONE:
021-236-2427.

SECRETARY:
R. E. EDEN

REE/RG

24, LIVERY STREET.
BIRMINGHAM, 3.

10th. February, 1967.

       Senior Challenge Cup Final(First Leg.)Kidderminster Harriers v.Nuneaton Borough on the ground of Kidderminster Harriers F.C.'Aggborough',Hoo Road,Kidderminster on Saturday 18th.March,1967. Kick-off 3-0 p.m.

       The following officials have been appointed:-

       Referee. 5548   J.G.Sollis.

       Linesmen. 4882 W.Hedgley.
               7910 A.G.Semple.

       When confirming the appointments,will you please indicate whether you wish to receive the fee or an award.

Secretary.

Notification of Final to John Sollis Andy Semple and Bill Hedgley ; teams   Kidderminster V Nuneaton

THREE REFEREES ON THE BALL FOR 83 YEARS

REFEREEING a football match is not always an enviable job.

But that has never bothered three Warwick men who have more than 83 years' experience of refereeing between them.

Their ability of keeping two opposing factions apart was recognised at the golden jubilee celebration dinner of the Leamington and District Referees' Association.

Mr Tom Story, of 72 Guy Street, and Mr George Pankhurst, of 105, Hanworth Road, were presented with the meritorious service award of the National Referees' Association.

Chairman

The award is the highest distinction the association can give to members who have completed more than 20 years' active refereeing.

Mr Story has been a member of the Leamington Referees' Association for 28 years and was its chairman for 11 years. For 21 years, he has been the association's delegate to the Birmingham and Warwickshire Referees' committee.

His colleague, Mr Pankhurst, has also held various offices in the association and began his refereeing career 35 years ago by serving on the management committee of the Coventry R.A. for six.

The awards were presented by Mr Eric Babington, secretary of the National Referees' Association and also chairman of the Birmingham County F.A. Referees Committee.

It was a double night of celebration for Mr Story. Together with Mr Arnold Rouse, chairman of the Leamington R.A., of 130, Stratford Road, they were presented with a long service award for their work with the Birmingham County R.A.

All levels

The jubilee dinner was to celebrate 50 years of the Leamington association, whose members are F.A. referees at all levels of the game.

It was founded in 1920, but was suspended during the Second World War years and re-formed again in 1946.

8.10.65

LEAMINGTON LEAGUE

CELTIC PLAYERS STAGE PROTEST —BUT LOSE

Five Leamington Celtic players walked off the field in protest during their 4-0 defeat at the hands of big local rivals North Leamington at the Eagle Recreation Ground on Saturday.

Their protest, against referee Mr. A. Clarke's handling of the game, was made after the scoring of the final goal.

But the furious five returned to complete the match when the referee—who is secretary of the Local Referees' Association—decided against abandoning the fixture with Celtic's remaining six quite prepared to continue.

Two names were taken and a report of the affair is to be sent to the Birmingham County F.A.

North's gamble in fielding a side including five Irish players certainly paid off with their new-found fighting spirit quite equal to Celtic's approach play.

Billy Mitchell and Tony Walker shared the goals to enable North to record their first win against Celtic for three years.

Leamington & District Sunday Football League
Official Handbook 1966-67
Contains;- Secretaries' Addresses, Rules etc price 2/6

Arnold Rouse Displaying the George Dutton Cup
to Members at the Farmers Club 1976

BIRMINGHAM COUNTY FOOTBALL ASSOCIATION

PRESIDENT
THE RIGHT WORSHIPFUL THE LORD MAYOR OF BIRMINGHAM.

TELEPHONE:
CENtral 1427.   REE/JR
SECRETARY:
R. E. EDEN

24, LIVERY STREET.
BIRMINGHAM, 3.
22nd April 1965

<u>INTER LEAGUE COMPETITION (CAMPBELL ORR SHIELD)</u>

<u>FINAL TIE</u>

Birmingham & District Works A.F.A. versus 4

Birmingham & District Youth & Old Boys A.F.A. 0

    referee: 5548 J.C.Sollis

    linesmen: 7577 J.W.Shaw

               5151 H.Hughes

To be played on the ground of Moor Green F.C.
The Moorlands, Sherwood Road, Hall Green,
Birmingham 28, on Monday 3rd May 1965,
Kick-off 6-45 p.m. (Extra time to be played if necessary)

Referee and Linesmen to confirm to the Association
and Competitions (BY POSTCARD) as soon as possible.

Please indicate, when replying, whether you wish
to have the fee or the Award.

DONE 23-4-65

SECRETARY

                Secretary.

Addmission ticket enclosed.

Leamington Association Life- Membership Awards being presented by
Eric Babington (Hon General Secretary to theReferees Association to
Tom Story, Jack Joyner, George Pankhurst with George Dutton Life
Member 1936 Association President, and David Clarke Secretary
Leamington RA

v Brandon and Wolston; Button
v Avon Rovers.
Olliver Cup Final: Long Itch-
ington v Stretton Athletic (to-
night, Southam United 6 p.m.).
CANCER CUP FINAL
Sunday: Bishops Itchington v
South Leamington (Windmill
Ground 3 p.m.).
LEAMINGTON SUNDAY
LEAGUE
Division One: Leamington St.
Mary's v Hockley Heath;
Crown Athletic v Avonside
United; Leek Wootton v Chad-
wick End.
Division Two: Whitnash Youth
v Hockley Heath Reserves;
Whittle Wanderers v Leaming-
ton Postal.
Division Three: Avon Manu-
facturing v Radford United;
Rail Wanderers v Thwaites.
Division Four A: Barston v
Chrysler Staff; Midland Red v
Offchurch.
Division Four B: Turriff v
Whitnash Youth Reserves; B
and B Trailers v Harbury
Albion Reserves.
WEDNESDAY—Division One:
St. Dominic's v Hockley Heath;
Westlea Wanderers v Avonside
United.
Division Four A: Chrysler
Staff v Brandon and Wolston.
MONDAY — Open Cup: Hock-
ley Heath v Marton Rovers;
Leek Wootton v Whittle Wan-
derers.
Division One: Leamington
Southend v Westlea Wanderers.
NAPTON BOYS' LEAGUE
Sunday: Bubbenhall v Kine-
ton; Southam v Napton; Bishops
Itchington v Stockton; Priors
Marston v Fenny Compton; By-
field v Harbury; Woodford
Halse v Long Itchington.
KENILWORTH BOYS'
LEAGUE
Saturday: Ajax v Burton
Green "A" (Kenilworth Rangers
F.C. 3 p.m.).

But in making the save from Lewin, Edmundson knocked himself out against the post. The recovery is about to start with referee Mr. Andy Semple joining in.

C/4/127

Champions

Leamington Southend are champions of the Coventry and District League Division One.

Andy Semple treating an Injured Player
Fixture List for Local Football

LOCAL REF'S HONOUR

Not for 35 years has a member of Leamington Referees' Association been chosen to officiate at a Birmingham County F.A. Senior Challenge Cup final.

The honour this year has been accorded to John Sollis, of 122, Warwick Road, Kenilworth, a member of the Leamington Association. He will have as one of his linesmen a former Kenilworth resident — Andy Semple, who before marriage lived in Guy Road. His home is now at Cubbington.

Mr. Sollis will be in charge of the first-leg of the final. It is between Kidderminster Harriers and Nuneaton Borough, and will be staged at Kidderminster's ground. The match is scheduled for March 18.

That two officials from the Leamington Association have been appointed to the match creates a record as it is the first occasion a couple of officials at the final have hailed from the same organisation.

Local Ref. Enhances Association

"The prestige of the Leamington and District Association has been further enhanced with the news that member John Sollis has been promoted to the Football League Linesmen's List, and on behalf of all members we offer sincere congratulations."

That comment, by Mr. J. C. Jays, secretary of Leamington and District Referees' Association is of interest to Kenilworth, for the John Sollis he mentions is a local resident—and he lives in Warwick Road.

Mr. Jay's remarks are included in a pre-season message to members of the Association. Among his advice is: "Remember your obligations; pay particular attention to all correspondence, honour your appointments, be neat and efficient in appearance, know the laws and be fair and impartial in their application."

Referees preparing for action

With the opening of the new football season members of Leamington and District Referees' Association will go into action on August 24.

In a pre-season message to members, Mr. J. C. Jays, hon. secretary of the association, says: "Remember your obligations ; pay particular attention to all correspondence, honour your appointments, be neat and efficient in appearance, know the laws and be fair and impartial in their application."

Mr. Jay's message adds : "The prestige of the Leamington and District Association has been further enhanced with the news, that member John Sollis has been promoted to the Football League Linesmen's List, and on behalf of all members we offer sincere congratulations.

"We can now boast from our comparatively small membership, two Football League officials, one Football Combination and several West Midland League officials. This is something of which we may be justifiably proud, and proves beyond doubt that the way to the top is, indeed, open to all."

Meet the local REFEREES - 3

OCTOBER ?? 1965.

Class One referee John Clive Sollis, of 122 Warwick Road, Kenilworth, started refereeing at the age of 15 with the Leamington and District League and the Coventry and N.W. League.

Today, after 12½ years' service, he is a member of the management committee of the Leamington Referees' Association and a Football League linesman, at the age of 27.

Before becoming an official, Mr. Sollis played for Kenilworth Secondary Modern School 1st XI and the Pick of Mid-Warwickshire Schools' team.

He also played for the Kenilworth St. Nicholas' Boys' Club team which won the Lockheed Cup in the 1951/52 season.

Nowadays, Mr. Sollis plays for the local referees and keeps fit by training twice a week at Lockheed Sports and Social Club's ground.

He has worked at Lockheed, where is an equipment fitter, since he left school. Married in 1960 to a local girl, Ann Lawrence, he has a 1½-year-old daughter Hazel Amanda.

Today, John Sollis referees with the West Midland Regional League and the Warwickshire Football Combination. In his spare time, he is leader at Kenilworth St. John's Church Boys' Club.

Looking back on his active career, Mr. Sollis singles out his appointment to referee the Cambell Orr Shield final at Moor Green, Birmingham, last season, as his best and most honourable match.

John Sollis, well-known young Kenilworth referee has been appointed to referee the final of the Leamington and District League's Aston Villa Cup, which is the internal trophy for second division clubs. The match is between Recreation Rovers (Stratford) and Bishops Itchington, and will be played at Henry Griffiths Ground, Tachbrook Road, Leamington, at 10.45 a.m. on Easter Monday. John, who commenced refereeing at about his sixteenth birthday, has officiated on the Leamington League list for about seven years, except when stationed in Germany on National Service. On his return he again went on the Leamington League list, and has continued to show considerable promise.

L ocal Referees at Leamington

ASTON VILLA FOOTBALL CLUB LIMITED

Telephone :
021 - 327 6604

Villa Park, Birmingham B6 6HE

ASTON VILLA v ......O.X.F.O.R.D...U.T.D. 16 OCT 1972

I am writing to confirm your appointment as .LINESMAN......

in the S.J.F. CUP... League, kick-off ...7.30.pm..

Yours faithfully,

Secretary.

POST CARD

THE ADDRESS TO BE WRITTEN ON THIS SIDE

Dear Mr Temple

By arrangement with the Comb can you do this game fee £1.50 plus travel

Regards

Appointment at Aston Villa v Oxford United
October 1972 as a Linesman in the S J F Cup

374

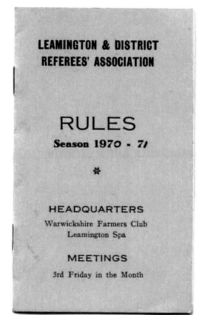

1973-74 Monthly Speakers for the year, organised by
the Meeting Organiser Arnold Rouse

A Company of Instructors at the end of their Instructional Course at Rednall 1965
Andy Semple the Asociation Coach is sitting crosslegged in front row with Alan
Richardson from Coventry sitting next to him. The group consisted of Football League
Referees and Linesmen as well as people like Ken Aston, Pat Partridge, Jack Taylor, and
Ken Ridden the future Head of Refereeing for the Football Association

Andy Semple receiving his Trophy

LEAMINGTON SPA COURIER

Ref falls foul of the men. . .

. . .but it's top scores for Women's Lib

Mrs Christine Cairns in a referees pose when the photograph was taken
After she had passed the Referees Examination and became a football referee

SOUTHAMPTON

v.

QUEENS PARK RANGERS

DULWICH HAMLET F.C.
DOG KENNEL HILL, DULWICH, LONDON, S.E.22

SUNDAY, 15th MAY, 1977

3.00 p.m. Kick-off
Officials for the Pony WFA Cup Final
Referee Mr J E Bent
Lineswomen
Christine Cairns: Red Flag   Carol Aylett: Yellow Flag

22 — 4893

Artifacts: - 1981 – 2000

The Nicolet Cambell Cup being shown to League and Club Officials at the
League Monthly Meeting Racing Club Warwick by Arnold Rouse

Arnold Rouse being presented with his Long & Meritorious Award for service
to Referees by Eric Adams Vice-President of the Misland Division

Arnold Rouse displaying his award to the Members

A group from the George Dutton Cup Committee with Mr Yurwich
From the Central Hospital

SPORTSHORTS

The Dutton Cup?

Leamington referee's Association is to promote a challenge cup in memory of their late president George Dutton.

Birmingham FA have already given their blessing and the competition will be run on a cup-winners cup basis between local league champions. All local soccer leagues are being approached in the area to give their backing to the tournament.

Arnold Rouse is the new president of the Leamington Football Referee's Association.

After his election at the Association's AGM at the weekend, Mr Rouse, who follows in the footsteps of the late George Dutton, said: "I don't intend to be a president in name only but an active one."

Mr Rouse joined the Leamington RA in 1951 and has held most posts in the Association during that time. He is currently busy as ac-commodation secretary for the National RA Conference which is to be held in Solihull next week.

FINALS

THE Nicolet Campbell Cup final between Avaon Sports and Kenilworth Rangers Reserves, will be played at Racing Club Warwick on Sunday, May 4, kick-off 3 pm.

The game is to be sponsored by Nicolet Instruments Ltd of Warwick and Leamington, and all proceeds go to Myton Hospice.

The George Dutton Cup final is at Southam United on Friday, May 16, when Black Horse meet Welston, kick-off 4.30. Proceeds this year are for the Crossroads Care Attendants Scheme, and Welwin Pumps are the competition sponsors.

DUTTON HONOUR

LEAMINGTON and District Referees Association are planning to stage a new cup competition, in memory of the late George Dutton.

Mr Dutton started his refereeing days in Leamington and eventually became a Football League referee. County FA chairman and councillor to the FA.

Now the Leamington RA are hoping to stage a competition for the winners of leagues, within an 18-mile radius of the town - Stratford, Coventry, Nuneaton and Rugby.

A meeting is to be held next month for interested leagues to discuss the rules of the competition, and the Leamington RA are also looking for donations to provide a trophy.

SOCCER OFFICIAL HONOURED

SOCCER clubs in the Leamington area are being asked to contribute towards a challenge cup in honour of the late Mr George Dutton, one of Warwickshire's leading football administrators. Mr Dutton, who died in February, was a former League referee and president of Leamington and District Referees' Association, one of many offices he held in the football world. The memorial cup was announced by his successor, Mr Arnold Rouse, who was elected president at the association's annual meeting. The trophy will be competed for on a cup winners cup, inter-league basis. Mr Rouse, of 130, Stratford Road, Warwick, was formerly chairman and has been a member of the association since 1953.

● Chairman of the Friends of Hertford Hill Hospital, Mrs Maureen Yurwick, receiving a cheque for £350. Making the presentation is Mr Sid Sharp, chairman of the George Dutton Charity Competition, one of the area's leading charity football cup competitions.

● **HINTON RACING** — who became the first holders of the handsome Nicolet Campbell Cup when they beat Green Man 4-1 in Sunday's final at the Windmill Ground.

They took a 12th-minute lead when Norman Leet headed home a Dhesi free kick. Ten minutes later good work by Mark Davison resulted in Dave Draper volleying in number two.

With wind and rain beating into their faces, Raing had to face Green Man pressure as well, and Griffin pulled a goal back from 30 yards.

Hinton got well on top in the second half, and Steve Davison had little to do in goal. The result was secured when Mark Davison netted the third after Kevin Couchman had caused Man problems in defence. Anthony Aitken swept the fourth after more hard work by Mark Davison.

The competition has been sponsored by Nicolet Instruments Ltd, and the trophy was presented to the winners by Mrs Jackie Campbell.

● In the picture are, back row left to right — Cliff Woodward (trainer), Dave Draper, Anthony Aitken, Darren Hunt, Steve Davison, Stuart Floyd, Norman Leet, Danny Lane, Graham Rose and Pete Cousins landlord of the Black Horse who is sponsoring Racing next season. Front — Pete Martin (manager), Costa Maroudis, Jaime Connell, Cary O'Neil, Darren Bradley, Kevin Couchman, Mark Davison and Harjinder Dhesi.

● In Friday's George Dutton cup final at Southam United, a goal five minutes from the end of extra time gave Kenilworth Rangers a 1-0 victory over VS Rugby Reserves.

Members and League Officials with Arnold and Sheila Rouse on the occasion of receiving his LMSA from Eric Adams Vice- President

Soccer

● PROMINENT sporting visitor to the Spa on Friday was Peter Willis, national president of the Referees Association.

Former Football League and FIFA official, Mr. Willis who is from Durham, regaled over 60 Leamington RA members and their guests with anecdote, advice, tips and recollections, which a long association in the game has generated.

He ended his career at Wembley in control of the 1985 F.A. Cup final in which Norman Whiteside's extra time goal decided the game in Manchester United's favour against Everton. And Mr. Willis only touched indirectly last Friday, on the instance during the game which will etch his and Kevin Moran's names permanently in the soccer history book. The United Midfield player became the first man to be sent off in an F.A. Cup final.

Pictured from the left are — Arnold Rouse (Leamington RA president), Peter Willis, John Austin and Duncan MacAulay, Branch secretary and chairman respectively. The meeting took place at Warwickshire Farmers Club, the Leamington RA headquarters.

Today's main soccer coverage is on pages 82 and 83.

● THE Nicolet Campbell Cup, and George Dutton Cup competitions again generated great generosity amongst local footballers last season, and the money was handed over at Warwick Squash Centre last week.

The Centre sponsored the Dutton competition, and manager Mike Smith presented a cheque for £460 to Maureen Tegerdine, area co-ordinator of the Crossroads Care Scheme.

The Nicolet Campbell Cup realised £1,125 for the coronary care unit of Warwick Hospital, and Graham Fraser, managing director of sponsors Nicolet Instruments, hands his cheque to Sister Kath Tipping. Also pictured are Staff Nurse Maxine Collins and Night Sister Chris Cook, together with organising committee members, and Leamington Referees Association officers. 7130/9

MANAGING director of Nicolet Instruments Ltd, Mr Alan Lord, of Warwick, presents a cheque for £620 to Myton Hospice administrator Mr Brian Caley. The money was raised by a charity football competition, which the firm sponsors. The Nicolet-Campbell Cup, named after the firm and its former boss, the late Mr Andy Campbell, is for teams in divisions two, three, four and five of the Leamington Sunday League.

It was won last season by Avana FC and so far 30 clubs have entered for the coming season.

At the presentation were from left Mrs Jackie Campbell, Mr Derek Silk, Mrs Sue Lord, Mr Gordon Hyam, Mrs Jenny Silk, Mr Arnold Rouse, Mrs Ann Hyam, Mr Sid Sharp and Mrs Sheila Rouse.

Charity Money being handed over to the Heart Foundation. And the Crossroads Care scheme by Dr Graham Fraser Nicolet Instruments and Mike Smith from the Warwick Squash Club

A Glittering array of Trophys from Leamington Hibernians being displayed at Racing Club Warwick, A mixture of Charity Cup Finals and League Championship Awards

Patrick Gwynne with colleagues at the 1979 World Womens Invitation Tournament. The tournament was in Taiwan. The Referees came from the following Countries:

A celebration

of the first 25 years of the

Leamington & District
Sunday Football League

(Sponsored in the Silver Jubilee Season by
N T Howard Associates)

Patrick Gwynne walking out beneath the banner of the World Womens Invitation
Tournament in Taiwan 1981. The referee is from Thailand.

The Andy Cambell Cup being presented to the Winning Team
by Arnold Rouse with Support from Dave Aston Chairman

George Pankhurst: 50 Years

78 year old George Pankhurst was presented with a silver salver by President Peter Willis to mark his 50 years membership of The RA. George passed the referees' exam in August 1941 in Coventry and joined their RA. In 1947 he helped reform Leamington RA; he became their secretary/treasurer and then Chairman 1954-60. Since 1957 he has been a Life Member. In 1976 he received The RA's MSA.

George officiated for 12 years on The Football League, with 6 years as a referee. He is a Life Member of the AFL R&I, Midlands section.

George Pankhurst is here seen with Peter Willis and members of Leamington RA; l. to rt: Arnold Rouse (President), Pat Gwynne, Brian Hackelton (Secretary), Dale Packer, John Austin, John Mander (Chairman), Peter Willis and Duncan Macaulay (Vice-Chairman)

Anniversary Dinners to Celebrate 50 Years since it was reformed
Guests from Left to right:- David Aston Chairman Leamington RA.
Tracey Thomas Vice-President, Arnold Rouse President, Arthur Smith General
Secretary National RA, Roger Wood Chairman B.C.F.A, Duncan MacAulay
Vice- Chairman, Ray Morgan Secretary, Ken Burns Immediate Past President
Peter Kirkhope Management Committee.

Sidney Sharp &Arnold Rouse at Edmonscote
watching a Cup Final and Assessing the Referee

Artifacts: - 2000 Onwards

Members receiving their Birmingham County awards from John Starkey.
From Left to Right : Dale Packer, Pat Wright, Brian Hackleton,
Tom Prendergast, Michael Lucey and John Starkey.

Cheltenham Conference 2003
Peter Willis congratulates Arnold on receiving his life membership of the
National Association

Duncan Macaulay receiving his
Long & Meritorious Service Award
from John Starkey of the Referee Association
In October 2006

ABBREVATIONS

AFARS	AMATEUR FOOTBALL ASSOCIATION REFEREES SOCIETY
ASSOC	ASSOCIATION
A N	ASSOCIATION NEWSLETTER
A S B's	ASSOCIATION, SOCIETIES, BRANCHES
ASST REF	ASSISTANT REFEREE
B C F A	BIRMINGHAM COUNTY FOOTBALL ASSOCIATION
B & W J R C C	B' HAM & WARKS JOINT REFEREE'S COUNTY COMMITTEE
C F A	COUNTY FOOTBALL ASSOCIATIONS
C. L	CLUB LINESMAN
C & F L	CONTRIBUTORY & FEEDER LEAGUE'S
C R B	CRIMINAL RECORDS BUREAU
E C	EXECUTIVE COUNCIL or COMMITTEE
F A	FOOTBALL ASSOCIATION
F A MOA ASSOCIATION	FOOTBALL ASSOCIATION MATCH OFFICIAL
F L	FOOTBALL LEAGUE
HON. SEC	HON. SECRETARY.
I T	IMPLEMENTATION TEAM
L & D R A	LEAMINGTON & DISTRICT REFEREES' ASSOCIATION
L O A F	LAWS OF ASSOCIATION FOOTBALL
L & M S A	LONG & MERITORIOUS SERVICE AWARD
L M	LIFE MEMBERSHIP
M C	MANAGEMENT COMMITTEE
M C T	MANAGEMENT CONSULTANCY TEAM
M D	MIDLAND DIVISION
M D R	MIDLAND DIVISION REPRESENTATIVES
M C M	MONTHLY COUNCIL MEETINGS

N E C	**NATIONAL EXHIBITION CENTRE**
N W F L	**NATIONWIDE FOOTBALL LEAGUE**
N R A	**NATIONAL REFEREES ASSOCIATION**
PREM	**PREMIERSHIP**
R A	**REFEREE'S ASSOCIATION**
R A E	**REFEREE'S ASSOCIATION of ENGLAND**

INDEX

Leamington & District Referees Association